# Cambridge Semitic Languages and Cultures

## General Editor: Geoffrey Khan

This is the first Open Access book series in the field; it combines the high peer-review and editorial standards with the fair Open Access model offered by OBP. The series includes philological and linguistic studies of Semitic languages, editions of Semitic texts, and studies of Semitic cultures. Titles cover all periods, traditions and methodological approaches to the field. The editorial board comprises Geoffrey Khan, Aaron Hornkohl, Esther-Miriam Wagner, Anne Burberry, and Benjamin Kantor.

You can access the full series catalogue here:
https://www.openbookpublishers.com/series/2632-6914

If you would like to join our community and interact with authors of the books, sign up to be contacted about events relating to the series and receive publication updates and news here:
https://forms.gle/RWymsw3hdsUjZTXv5

# READING

# Reading

## Performance and Materiality in Hebrew and Aramaic Traditions

*Edited by*
*Hector M. Patmore, Hindy Najman, Stefan Schorch, Jeroen Verrijssen, Hanneke van der Schoor*

https://www.openbookpublishers.com

©2025 Hector M. Patmore, Hindy Najman, Stefan Schorch, Jeroen Verrijssen and Hanneke van der Schoor (eds). Copyright of individual chapters is maintained by the chapter's authors.

This work is licensed under an Attribution-NonCommercial 4.0 International (CC BY-NC 4.0). This license allows you to share, copy, distribute, and transmit the text; to adapt the text for non-commercial purposes of the text providing attribution is made to the authors (but not in any way that suggests that they endorse you or your use of the work). Attribution should include the following information:

Hector M. Patmore, Hindy Najman, Stefan Schorch, Jeroen Verrijssen and Hanneke van der Schoor (eds), *Reading: Performance and Materiality in Hebrew and Aramaic Traditions*. Cambridge, UK: Open Book Publishers, 2025, https://doi.org/10.11647/OBP.0464

Further details about CC BY-NC licenses are available at
http://creativecommons.org/licenses/by-nc/4.0/

All external links were active at the time of publication unless otherwise stated and have been archived via the Internet Archive Wayback Machine at
https://archive.org/web

Any digital material and resources associated with this volume will be available at
https://doi.org/10.11647/OBP.0457#resources

Semitic Languages and Cultures 36

ISSN (print): 2632-6906
ISSN (digital): 2632-6914

ISBN Paperback: 978-1-80511-548-9
ISBN Hardback: 978-1-80511-549-6
ISBN Digital (PDF): 978-1-80511-550-2

DOI: 10.11647/OBP.0464

Cover image: The Bodleian Libraries, University of Oxford, MS. Heb. b. 17/5b, CC BY-NC 4.0
Cover design: Jeevanjot Kaur Nagpal

The fonts used in this volume are Charis SIL, Scheherazade New, SBL Hebrew and SBL Greek.

# CONTENTS

Acknowledgements ............................................................. ix

List of Contributors ........................................................... xi

Introduction ...................................................................... 1

*Geoffrey Khan*

    Adaption and Creativity in the Tiberian Reading
    Tradition of the Hebrew Bible ..................................... 15

*Harald Samuel*

    The Double Nature of the Text of the Hebrew Bible ... 43

*Frédérique Michèle Rey, Sophie Robert-Hayek, and
Davide D'Amico*

    Layout and Meaning: Stichography in Hebrew
    Manuscripts; The Case of Psalm 83 in Mas 1e and
    the Hebrew Manuscripts of Ben Sira .......................... 73

*Martin Tscheu*

    The *Vorlage* of LXX Ezekiel: Orthographic Features,
    Phonetic Circumstances, and Reading Practice .......... 103

*Hindy Najman*

    Reading and Articulation in Ancient Jewish Texts .... 133

*Noam Mizrahi*

Reading the Fifth Song of the Sabbath Sacrifice against the Loss of Its Performative Tradition........... 155

*Amrei Koch*

'Teaching the Sinners': A Motif and Its Application in 4Q372 1 ................................................................. 183

*Dorota Molin*

Praise as Exorcism and Exorcism as Praise: Writing for Supernatural Audiences in the Hymns of the Maskil and Late-antique Jewish 'Magic'..................... 213

*Hector M. Patmore*

Philology and the Evolution of the Palestinian Targum.................................................................... 253

*Willem Smelik*

The Rabbinic Use for Translation............................. 291

*Shlomi Efrati*

To Read or Not to Read: Practicing (Non-)Reading Targum in Medieval Europe....................................... 347

*Jeroen Verrijssen*

On the Shores of the Red Sea: A Medieval Reconstruction of Palestinian Targum?..................... 385

*Gavin McDowell*

   Pseudo-Jonathan as a European Targum: Clues
   from *Pirqe de-Rabbi Eliezer* ........................................... 405

*Robert Harris*

   From פשטיה דקרא to פשוטו של מקרא: The Origins of
   Peshat Commentary in Eleventh and Twelfth
   Century Rabbinic Exegesis ........................................... 441

Index of Texts ............................................................. 467

General Index ............................................................ 477

# ACKNOWLEDGEMENTS

We wish to take this opportunity to express our thanks to the following people and organisations who have made this volume possible.

The colloquium that gave rise to this volume was jointly funded by the project 'TEXTEVOLVE: A New Approach to the Evolution of Texts Based on the Manuscripts of the Targums', which received funding from the European Research Council (ERC) under the European Union's Horizon 2020 research and innovation programme (grant agreement No. 818702), and the Oriel Centre for the Study of the Bible.

We are grateful to a number of colleagues who contributed to the planning and delivery of the colloquium. Shlomi Efrati, Rebekah Van Sant, and Elizabeth Stell made an enormous contribution to the administrative and logistical preparations from the colloquium. Additional support was provided during the colloquium by Cale Waress, Matilda Chapman, Joseph Harrison, Christine Rosa de Freitas, John Thuppayath, Pia Regensburger, Rahel Lamberth, Ruthanne Brooks, Hakseo Kim, Sarah Wisialowski, Annie Calderbank, Adi Weiner, Oliver Geffen, and Max Benster.

Arjen Bakker, Judith H. Newman, David G. K. Taylor, and Annie Calderbank gave excellent presentations during the course of the colloquium but for various reasons were unable to contribute to the edited volume. Kirsten McFarlane, Phillip Lasater, Cian Power, Estara Arrant, and Alison Salvesen assisted by chairing sessions. Judith Olszowy-Schlanger and César Merchán-Hamann graciously gave participants of the colloquium the opportunity to see some of the Bodleian Library's manuscript treasures up close.

We are grateful to the staff of Oriel College where the colloquium was hosted, in particular the Provost, Lord Neil Mendoza, who warmly welcomed us.

Finally, we wish to thank Geoffrey Khan for his willingness to accept this volume in the Semitic Languages and Cultures series, and the team at Open Book Publishers, who have guided us smoothly through the production process.

The Editors

# LIST OF CONTRIBUTORS

**Dr Davide D'Amico**
Postdoctoral Researcher at the University of Lorraine

**Dr Shlomi Efrati**
Heinrich-Hertz Fellow at the University of Münster's Institutum Judaicum Delitzschianum

**Prof. Robert Harris**
Professor of Bible and Ancient Semitic Languages at The Jewish Theological Seminary

**Regius Prof. Geoffrey Khan**
Regius Professor of Hebrew at University of Cambridge

**Dr Amrei Koch**
Faculty of Theology, Martin Luther University of Halle

**Dr Gavin McDowell**
CNRS Fellow, EPHE (Paris)

**Prof. Noam Mizrahi**
Associate Professor, Department of Bible, at Hebrew University of Jerusalem

**Dr Dorota Molin**
Lecturer in Classical Hebrew Language, University of Oxford

**Prof. Hindy Najman**
Oriel and Laing Professor of the Interpretation of Holy Scripture at Oriel College, University of Oxford

**Prof. Hector Patmore**
Associate Professor in the Research Unit Biblical Studies at the Faculty of Theology and Religious Studies of the KU Leuven

**Prof. Frédérique Michèle Rey**
Professor of Exegesis and Head of the Department of Theology at the University of Lorraine

**Dr Sophie Robert-Hayek**
Postdoctoral Researcher in Digital Humanities—Biblical Studies at University of Lorraine

**Dr Harald Samuel**
Lecturer in Hebrew and Old Testament at Eberhard Karls Universität Tübingen

**Prof. em. Willem Smelik**
Professor Emeritus of Hebrew and Aramaic Literature, University College London

**Dr Martin Tscheu**
Doctoral Researcher at Martin Luther University, Halle

**Dr Jeroen Verrijssen**
Postdoctoral Researcher at KU Leuven

# INTRODUCTION

*Hector M. Patmore, Hindy Najman, Stefan Schorch, Jeroen Verrijssen, Hanneke van der Schoor, Joseph Harrison and Ruthanne Brooks*

---

The current volume had its genesis in a set of conversations between Hindy Najman, Hector Patmore, and Stefan Schorch around their shared interest in how the realities of textual production, transmission, and performance affect the ways in which texts generate meaning. Those conversations eventually led to a colloquium entitled, 'Reading: Performance and Materiality in Hebrew and Aramaic Traditions', hosted at Oriel College, University of Oxford, from the 30th Oct to 1st Nov 2023. The colloquium was jointly sponsored by the Oriel Centre for the Study of the Bible, under the direction of Hindy Najman, and the European Research Council project, TEXTEVOLVE, led by Hector Patmore (funded under the European Union's Horizon 2020 research and innovation programme; grant agreement No. 818702). It is perhaps not without a tinge of irony that a colloquium in which questions of orality and textual fluidity were so prominent, has now fixed its text in its own material artefact, thereby becoming both subject and observer of the very process it examines. That artefact is the volume before you.

The colloquium's contributors were invited to respond to the following summary of the colloquium's aims:

> A manuscript, or any other written artefact, preserves the record of a text. But in order to be perceived as such, it requires a reader. Therefore, texts are products of reading no less than they are the work of an author or a scribe. Textuality emerges when a written artefact interacts with a host of further components, both textual and non-textual (oral traditions, knowledge of the language, the performative context, etc), which are shaped by the specific cultural contexts in which composition, transmission and reading take place.
>
> Reading and transmission presuppose a set of philological values by which variant texts and competing readings can be evaluated. The transmission of texts is therefore characterized by tensions between authority and creativity, preservation and innovation, understanding and misapprehension, knowledge and ignorance.
>
> This general perspective on texts is relevant to the emergence of the books that became the Hebrew Bible and to the transmission of the Hebrew Scripture. However, while the emergence and transmission of Biblical texts have been explored broadly from the perspective of writing and copying, the focus on reading has received much less scholarly attention.
>
> The conference, therefore, aims to investigate Jewish approaches to the reading of texts in Antiquity, with a focus on specific reading practices that were applied to Hebrew and Aramaic texts. While these reading practices are comparable in many respects to reading practices known from other cultural contexts (e.g., in terms of textual history, interpretation, or translation), they also reflect features that are characteristic of the Hebrew and Aramaic languages

and writing systems (e.g., characteristics of poetry, vocalization, and use of vocalization signs), as well as Jewish culture (e.g., Jewish identities, Jewish liturgies). The conference addresses this topic by considering questions such as:

- How did non-textual components determine reading?
- To what extent did materiality shape or limit readings?
- How did reading practices shape the texts themselves?
- Do reading practices reflect a shared sense of philology?
- What determined which form or version of a text was read and according to what conventions?

The papers collected in this volume offer diverse responses to these central themes. They were shared, discussed, and subsequently revised and expanded for publication. Each of the papers is briefly summarised below.

The volume opens with four papers that are concerned primarily with works of the Hebrew Bible. In his paper, 'Adaptation and Creativity in the Tiberian Reading Tradition of the Hebrew Bible', Geoffrey **Khan** traces the orthoepic features of the Masoretic Text to their origins in the proto-Masoretic reading practices of the Second Temple period. Drawing on a wide range of orthoepic measures, such as the vocalisation of consonantally identical words and the gemination of consonants, Khan argues that the orthoepic traditions are a clear example of the living tradition reflected in the reading practices of the Masoretes and their predecessors. Khan emphasises that these reading practices not only resisted influence from contact languages that would cause ambiguity, but consistently capitalised on new means of ensuring clarity. This chapter is a tour de force for thinking about practices of reading as exemplified in textual transmission, in late antiquity and medieval rabbinic traditions, preserving evidence of both interpretation and oral performance.

Harald **Samuel**, focusing in particular on the places in which the Tiberian vocalisation acts in an atypical way, provides a masterful analysis of the relationship between the consonantal framework of the Hebrew Bible and its vocalisation in his paper entitled 'The Double Nature of the Text of the Hebrew Bible'. While stressing throughout the generally conservative nature of the consonantal tradition, his exploration of the way that the reading traditions engage with such issues as stem shift, variations in the presence or absence of *matres lectionis*, and features such as the *energic nun* and pausal forms, provides not only an important argument for the vitality of the reading traditions but also sheds light on how elements of prosody can be reflected by the consonantal framework. Overall, he assesses the vitality of pronunciation traditions that indicate systematic grammatical developments. Although Jewish vocalisation traditions follow the consonantal framework of the Hebrew Bible quite strictly, changes in the verbal stems (*qal* to *nifʿal* or *hifʿil*) can be reflected in the vocalisation. His analysis of the orthography, changes in uses of the stems, the application or absence of *energic nun*, the vocalisation of stative and fientic verbs, and the non-assimilation of *he* in third-person singular suffixes, suggests that prosodic elements may be embedded both in the vocalisation traditions and in the consonantal framework itself. He draws important and significant attention to details often overlooked both in dictionaries and grammars. Samuel's profound appreciation for the history of the Hebrew language is essential for understanding the practices of reading and writing in the history of the rabbis and the masoretes.

Frédérique Michèle **Rey**, Sophie **Robert-Hayek**, and Davide **D'Amico**'s paper, 'Layout and Meaning: Stichography in Hebrew Manuscripts; The Case of Psalm 83 in Mas 1E and the Hebrew Manuscripts of Ben Sira', focuses on the impact that a manuscript's *mise en page* might have not only on what a text means, but also on how it might change as it is copied. Their focus is on the way in which texts have been divided into poetic units (stichs). Their first example is a copy of Psalm 83 from Masada. The scribe of this manuscript enforced a consistent layout of two stichs per line, even when a tristich occurs, resulting in a different pairing of the stichs than we find in the Masoretic Text. Even if done for purely aesthetic reasons, the layout imposes a different way of reading on the text. They then turn their attention to manuscripts of Ben Sira, some of which are arranged in stichs, while others present the text in continuous lines. They argue that certain textual changes (e.g., the addition of a stich) would only have been possible in a text transmitted in one layout (e.g., continuous) and not the other (e.g., stichographic), and create difficulties for copyists only when the layout of the text changes. As such their paper presents a clear example of how material factors could result in textual transformations.

In his study of the Septuagint of Ezekiel, 'The Vorlage of LXX Ezekiel: Orthographic Features, Phonetic Circumstances, and Reading Practice', Martin **Tscheu** explores how the ways in which Hebrew was read may have shaped the way in which the

Greek translator analysed the consonantal framework as well as the shape of the Hebrew *Vorlage* from which he worked. He discusses three phenomena. First, he presents cases in which he argues the translator has confused forms that would be graphically similar. Since these confusion would only arise in a Hasmonean, or perhaps even pre-Hasmonean Aramaic script, he argues that the variants arose because of the way the translator read the text, rather than because the consonantal framework of his *Vorlage* differed. Second, he suggests that the phonetic weakening of the gutturals may have resulted in the loss of guttural letters from the consonantal framework, creating ambiguities. The translator's attempts to resolve these ambiguities resulted in meanings that are different from that originally intended by the scribe of the Hebrew *Vorlage*, and also from that of the Masoretic text. Finally, he examines cases in which he believes that the translator's assumption that a guttural had been lost, led him to analyse the consonants incorrectly. Taken together, his assessment suggests that certain renderings of the Septuagint of Ezekiel are prompted by the virtual Hebrew *Vorlage* constructed in the mind of the reader, that is, the Greek translator.

The volume next turns its attention to works preserved among the Dead Sea Scrolls and related literature. Hindy **Najman**'s contribution, 'Reading and Articulation in Ancient Jewish Texts', examines the Thanksgiving Hymns (*Hodayot*), approaching the collection in a way that resists reducing the hymns to mere interpretation, commentary, or intertextual allusion. Instead, she stresses the way in which they invoke and creatively repurpose earlier materials in order to make them relevant and meaningful for new audiences. The *Hodayot* represent a response to what Najman has termed the generative "vitality" of scripture, extending and expanding it to build a new conceptual framework. At the same time, she draws attention to the way in which the first-person voice of the *Hodayot* turns the reader into a participant, who, by performing the text, is able to enter into the text's iterative meditation on their human essence in relation to God. The articulation of God's praise, so characteristic of the *Hodayot*, is a gift from God, but becomes a means of personal growth and development in relation to God. Ultimately Najman suggests that modern scholars, instead of approaching texts in ways that seek to disassemble them, might draw inspiration from the manner in which the *Hodayot* engages earlier texts.

In his chapter, 'Reading the Fifth Song of the Sabbath Sacrifice against the Loss of Its Performative Tradition', Noam **Mizrahi** considers indicators for a performative rendering of the Songs of the Sabbath Sacrifice, specifically in the fifth Song. By thoroughly analysing its poetic form, he illustrates the connection between the prosodic structure and the semantic content of the Song. Mizrahi notes that attention to rhythmic elements highlights the essential themes of the text and provides hints for its liturgical performance. In the face of a forgotten performative tradition that is of such great importance to the inherently liturgical Songs of the Sabbath Sacrifice, Mizrahi looks for the suggestions of performance that can be gleaned from the poetic form of the fifth Song. This dovetails very well with the essays of Khan and of Samuel. Focusing in particular on the potential rhythmic considerations that may have informed the writing of the text,

Mizrahi argues with great expertise and eloquence that, with the evidence that can be pieced together of the beliefs of the author(s) of the Songs, some hints of the original performance of the texts can be found, despite their fragmentary nature. This makes an important contribution to a broader understanding of poetics in ancient Judaism as well as to our understanding of what poetry can contribute to our understanding of reading and the liturgical performance of song.

Amrei **Koch** assesses the interplay between the written artefact and the impact of orally transmitted knowledge derived from the intellectual culture of the reader in her paper, '"Teaching the Sinners": A Motif and Its Application in 4Q372 1'. Koch establishes that the motif of "teaching the sinners" is first attested within texts that later came to form part of the Hebrew Bible (Deuteronomy, Psalms, prophetic literature), and she goes on to show how this motif is reconfigured in 4Q372 1 in reference to a reader's paratextual knowledge of the sapiential Joseph tradition in the Second Temple period. This piece contributes to thinking about pedagogy, about correction, and about the history of reception and the transformation of motifs from ancient Hebrew literature in the Dead Sea Scrolls. Moreover there are larger theological implications for how correction and perfection were regarded as cultivation in terms of halacha, prophecy, and wisdom tradition.

Dorota **Molin**, looks beyond the Qumran scrolls in her paper, 'Praise as Exorcism and Exorcism as Praise: Writing for Supernatural Audiences in the Hymns of the Maskil and Late-Antique Jewish "Magic"'. Her comparison of the Qumran Hymns of the Maskil, also known as the Songs of the Sage (4Q510–511), with a number of late-antique magical objects, brings together material in a way that challenges us to think again about how texts communicate and to whom. Molin shows that while these texts may have had human readers or listeners, the target audience was not exclusively, or even primarily, human. Rather, their aim was to communicate both with God and with demons—a "multi-audience orientation," as Molin puts it—hence elements of praise and exorcism are intertwined. Moreover, Molin emphasises that these texts were thought to be effective when performed. That performance may take different forms—public oral recitation in the case of the Qumran Hymns, the act of creating 'text-objects' in the case of the amulets and bowls—but in both cases it was in the performance that non-human audiences were believed to be reached. Molin's paper forms a bridge to the next section of the volume, which moves the focus to texts from the late Second Temple to the rabbinic period and beyond.

In his paper, 'Philology and the Evolution of the Palestinian Targum', Hector **Patmore** argues for an "evolutionary philology" approach to Jewish literature that embraces both the textual archetype and its subsequent iterations by exploring the textual evidence for scribal "philological values," particularly as exhibited in the Palestinian Targums. He situates this discussion by tracing two major approaches in modern philology: the genealogical approach, which focuses on the reconstruction of an archetype, and (so-called) 'material' or 'new' philology in response, which focuses on variance as an intrinsic and essential quality of texts and their transmission. He then pictures two axes through which we can envision how scribes viewed the works they produced: one axis representing the spectrum of producing a new work versus the same work, and another representing the usage of new wording versus retaining original wording. Patmore then shows that Jewish literature prior to the Gaonic period, including texts within the Palestinian Targum tradition, exhibit much diversity across these axes. This demonstrates a range of philological values held by scribes concurrently; as a result, Patmore asks us to reconsider how modern philological values have impacted which textual iterations scholars prioritise. Furthermore, attention to Targum provides us with essential information on how ancient and medieval Jews were reading and transforming traditions of text, interpretation, and ritual in ancient Judaism.

Willem **Smelik** rethinks the *raison d'être* of the Targums, specifically Targum Onqelos, in light of the fact that Hebrew was likely still a living language in the cultural contexts in which they were composed, in his paper, 'The Rabbinic Use for Translation'. What we now know of the language map of Roman Palestine, Smelik argues, suggests that switching between Hebrew and Aramaic would have begun as an "arbitrary and vernacular phenomenon." In such a setting, the function of an Aramaic translation need not be thought of as limited to making understandable a text that was otherwise impenetrable for its audience. All the evidence—rabbinic comments, the *mise en page* of Targum manuscripts, translation technique—presents the Targums as the counterpoint of the Hebrew text, partaking to some extent in its holiness, and forming with it a single "bilingual text" in oral performance (this in contrast to the Greek translations). By examining Targum Onqelos's translation technique, he is able to show how it offers a kind of 'thesaurus', an interpretative slant, and a more 'unified' text through the use of stereotypical translations. This enables a fuller, richer understanding of the Scriptures appropriate for different purposes, be that liturgy or study, and for varying degrees of language competence.

Shlomi **Efrati** tackles a closely related conundrum, addressing the intriguing question of why a text would continue to be read when its intended audience could no longer understand it. His paper, 'To Read or not to Read: Practising (Non-)Reading Targum in Medieval Europe', focusses on medieval practices of reading of the Targum to the Haftarot. Efrati seeks to nuance the conventional characterisation of Targum's liturgical use in terms of decline. Based on the testimonies of medieval authors and his own collation of medieval European manuscripts, he maps out how the Targum transitions from a tool of communication to an object of religious appreciation. Its diminishing functionality was matched by a heightening of its status, so that it continued to have a role in public worship. When the Targum was read increasingly infrequently in medieval Europe, it remained not as a fossilised relic, but rather continued, as Efrati puts it, to be a "living liturgical experience."

Jeroen **Verrijssen**'s contribution, 'On the Shores of the Red Sea: A Medieval Reconstruction of Palestinian Targum?', wrestles with many of the same puzzles as Efrati, while providing a very concrete example of the way reading practices can shape texts. He examines an expansion found in the different recensions of

Palestinian Targum. This expansion tells of four groups of Israelites each of whom proposes a different solution when they find themselves trapped between the Red Sea on one side and Pharaoh's troops on the other. Based on the examination of previously unstudied manuscripts of medieval festival-prayer books (*mahzorim*), Verrijssen first confirms the late Michael Klein's hypothesis that the text had become disordered when the whole expansion was moved from one verse to another. He is then able to go further and demonstrate why the transposition took place at all. The evidence he presents shows that, as the custom of reading Targum during the synagogue liturgy gradually died out, the Targum reading for Pesach was shortened by omitting the section that contained the 'four groups' expansion. The expansion, however, was thought worth retaining, so it was deliberately transposed to the section that continued to be publicly read, the Song of the Sea (Exod. 14.30–15.18). Thus, a conscious act of preservation created a new text.

Gavin **McDowell** provides a clear example of the ways in which one aspect of materiality, namely the availability of manuscripts, can determine the shape of a text in his article, 'Pseudo-Jonathan as a European Targum: Clues from *Pirqe de-Rabbi Eliezer*'. Building on his previous work, which established that Targum Pseudo-Jonathan used Pirqe de-Rabbi Eliezer as one of its sources, McDowell demonstrates that the manuscript(s) from which Targum Pseudo-Jonathan drew, though no longer extant, must have belonged to Pirqe de-Rabbi Eliezer's European textual-family. The local availability of manuscripts therefore determined the form that Targum Pseudo-Jonathan took. These results in turn bolster the view that Targum Pseudo-Jonathan itself is a late (twelfth century or later) European composition.

Finally, Robert **Harris** examines the approach to reading Scripture of works that would once have been thought to post-date Targum Pseudo-Jonathan by some centuries, but which may, in fact, be near contemporaneous. His paper, 'From פשטיה דקרא to פשוטו של מקרא: The Origins of *Peshat* Commentary in Eleventh and Twelfth Century Rabbinic Exegesis', illuminates the origins of medieval *peshat* commentary, by situating Rashi not only as an innovative reader of rabbinic scholars, but also as someone who interacted with his Christian environment. Harris highlights two important phrases employed in rabbinic exegesis associated as forerunners, the rabbinic Hebrew formula, פשוטו של מקרא, and the Aramaic formula, פשטיה דקרא. Harris demonstrates that while Rashi employed the previously-found Hebrew expression, his implementation evinced a new understanding and goal of expounding the 'plain meaning' of the text. Harris suggests that Charlemagne's eighth-century educational reforms in northwest Europe, bridging Greco-Roman heritage with Christian interests, and increasing shifts from an oral to a written culture, influenced new modes of interpretation as both Jews and Christians applied rhetorical training to exegesis. Thus, in conversation with Christian contemporaries who were transitioning from an allegoria mode of reading to *sensus litteralis*, Jewish interpreters adopted the phrase פשוטו של מקרא as they developed their new commentary genre. Celebrating innovation and creativity in medieval Jewish interpretation, Harris's evaluation challenges prior, rather reductionist assessments of Rashi's overarching contribution. In brief, Harris brings Rashi's overall contribution to the forefront as a practice of reading that should be understood as historically contingent, but nevertheless essential to rabbinic practices of reading and transmission.

In sum, the contributions to this volume deal with a number of different aspects of the topic, applying a range of approaches to the transmission of a diverse array of Hebrew and Aramaic texts covering a period of more than 1500 years. Yet despite this diversity, when taken together a common thread emerges: While "reading" is, of course, a concept of great importance for every textual culture, "reading practices" are typically bound to specific cultural, historical, linguistic and literary contexts, and as such cannot be separated from a given textual culture. Rather, "reading practices" are an essential part of a given textual culture. In this respect, the current volume hopes to substantially enrich the field of Hebrew and Aramaic philology by providing fundamental insights into "reading" as one central aspect of Jewish culture, which, although forming the inseparable counterpart to "writing," has often received less attention than it.

# ADAPTATION AND CREATIVITY IN THE TIBERIAN READING TRADITION OF THE HEBREW BIBLE

*Geoffrey Khan*

## 1.0. Preliminary Remarks

In the Second Temple period, written biblical manuscripts were read aloud in oral reading traditions, as we see clearly in the description of Ezra's public reading of the Torah in Neh. 8.1–8. This was the case throughout the first millennium CE down to the Middle Ages. These were memorised oral texts that were oral performances of the written text.

The surviving biblical manuscripts from Qumran clearly reflect the incipient stabilisation of one particular type of text. These texts from Qumran have been termed by Emanuel Tov "proto-Masoretic" or, in his more recent work, as "Masoretic-like" texts (Tov 2012, 107–9). This stabilised text formed the basis of the so-called Masoretic Text, which appears in the medieval biblical codices and is the source of modern printed editions of the Hebrew Bible.

When the written form of the text was stabilised, one particular reading tradition of this stabilised text was also stabilised.

This stabilisation of the written text and its associated oral reading were apparently carried out by the Temple authorities, and this endowed these traditions with authority. The reading tradition was transmitted in later generations after the Second Temple period as an authoritative oral performance of the authoritative written text, and eventually became committed to written form in the Middle Ages in vocalisation and accent signs.

The reading tradition that was fixed in the Second Temple period as the oral performance of the proto-Masoretic text may be termed the proto-Masoretic reading tradition.[1] It was a memorised oral tradition. The reading tradition reflected by the Tiberian vocalisation seen in medieval Masoretic Bible manuscripts, and which also appears in modern printed editions of the Bible, has its roots in this this tradition.

It is important to emphasise, however, that although the written text was fixed and the proto-Masoretic reading tradition gained authority and prestige, there was a pluriformity of oral reading traditions of the written text during the first millennium CE.

After the Second Temple period reading traditions of the Hebrew Bible were transmitted by later generations in various types, which differed from one another in a number of details. In broad terms, the differences between these types developed due

---

[1] Evidence for the existence in the Second Temple period of reading traditions that differed from this proto-Masoretic reading tradition can be identified in many renderings of the Septuagint, e.g., Isa. 9.7 Tiberian tradition: דָּבָר, Septuagint: θάνατον 'death', which reflects the reading דֶּבֶר.

*Adaption and Creativity in the Tiberian Reading Tradition* 17

to two factors, namely (i) the geographical region of transmission and (ii) the authority of the type. In the first millennium CE, after the destruction of the Second Temple, the main regional split of reading tradition types was between Palestine and Babylonia. Within Palestine there was a split between the authoritative Tiberian tradition of reading and the non-authoritative common tradition of Palestine, known as the Palestinian tradition. The three traditions, Tiberian, Babylonian and Palestinian, came to be represented by different vocalisation sign systems. The authoritative Tiberian tradition and also the Babylonian tradition, which was associated with the Babylonian centres of Jewish authority, are likely to have their roots in the proto-Masoretic reading tradition. The common Palestinian tradition of reading, however, is likely to have had its roots in non-authoritative popular reading traditions in Palestine and converged, imperfectly, with the authoritative Tiberian tradition. We should also mention the Samaritan oral reading tradition, which has continued from antiquity down to modern times (Ben-Ḥayyim 1958; 1968; 2000).

Figure 1: Relationship of Reading Traditions

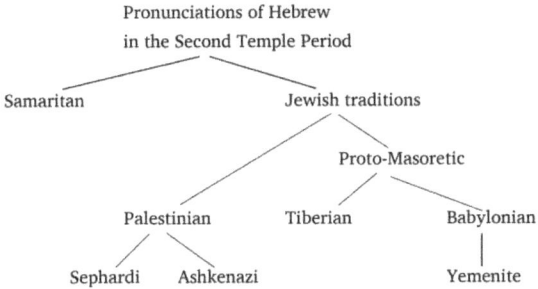

A feature of the proto-Masoretic reading tradition, reflected by the Tiberian and Babylonian vocalisation traditions, was the application of innovative adjustments for orthoepic purposes, i.e., adjustments that ensure a careful and accurate reading. The aim was to achieve a maximally careful oral reading, with optimal understanding and optimal articulation. This was achieved (i) by making phonetic adjustments to ensure that the written elements of the text were clearly distinguished and articulated and (ii) by making formal distinctions of homophonous words that were semantically distinct.

The measures taken to ensure accuracy of reading both preserved the reading and also endowed the reading with greater prestige due to its accuracy. Several features of orthoepy that appear in the Tiberian and Babylonian reading traditions can be shown to have their roots in the proto-Masoretic reading of the Second Temple period. Others appear to have developed during the oral transmission of these reading traditions during the first millennium CE.

In this paper I would like to examine the background of some of these orthoepic adjustments. My intention is to show that they arose (i) by interaction of the reading tradition with languages spoken by the transmitters of the reading tradition or (ii) by exploitation of morphological alternants within the reading tradition.

## 2.0. Interaction with Languages in Contact

### 2.1. Lengthening of Vowels to Preserve Gutturals

The vowel prefixes of the verbs הָיָה 'to be' and חָיָה 'to live' were pronounced long in the Tiberian pronunciation tradition, e.g.,

(1)   יִהְיֶ֫ה [jiːhˈjɛː] 'it will be' (Gen. 1.29)

(2)   יִחְיֶ֫ה [jiːħˈjɛː] 'he lives' (Eccl. 6.3)

Medieval Arabic transcriptions of the Tiberian reading written by Karaite scribes indicate that the vowel of the prefixes was regularly lengthened, e.g.,

(3)   بيهيا (BL Or 2549 fol. 87r, 6 | L [BHS]: יִהְיֶ֫ה Jer. 23.17 'it (ms) will be')[2]

(4)   تيحيو (BL Or 2549 fol. 120r, 10 | L [BHS]: תִּחְי֫וּ Jer. 35.7 'you (mpl) will live')

This lengthening of the vowel was an orthoepic measure to ensure that the guttural consonants were not weakened in these verbs in order to prevent them from being confounded. I have presented evidence elsewhere (Khan 2018) that this orthoepic measure in forms of the verbs הָיָה and חָיָה had deep historical roots that can be traced to the proto-Masoretic reading in Second Temple Palestine before the split of the Tiberian and Babylonian branches. The argument, in brief, is that all initial *he* and initial

---

[2] L = the manuscript conventionally referred to as 'Codex Leningradensis', i.e., The National Library of Russia, St. Petersburg, Firkovich B 19a A. This is the base manuscript of the BHS edition of the Hebrew Bible.

ḥet verbs originally had an [i] vowel in prefixes in the proto-Masoretic reading. This situation has been preserved in the Babylonian reading tradition, whereas in the Tiberian tradition the vowel generally underwent lowering to a *segol* or *pataḥ* (Yeivin 1985, 302), e.g.,[3]

(5) תִּהְדֹּ֫פוּ [tihdoːfuː] (L [BHS]: תֶּהְדֹּ֫פוּ Ezek. 34.21 'you will push')

(6) יִהְרֹ֫גוּ [yihroːʁuː] (L [BHS]: יַהֲרֹ֑גוּ Ps. 94.6 'they will kill')

The [i] has been preserved in the verbs הָיָה and חָיָה in the Tiberian tradition because it was lengthened for orthoepic reasons. This must have taken place before the vowel lowering took place in initial *he* and *ḥet* verbs at a remote historical period when such verbs originally had [i] in the prefixes before the Babylonian and Tiberian branches split.

This demonstrates that orthoepy was already a feature of the ancient reading and that care over the oral reading of the text went hand in hand with care over the copying of the written text at an ancient period, presumably within Temple circles.

The need for this orthoepic measure was the impact of non-Semitic languages, in particular Greek, on the recitation of the Hebrew Bible during the Second Temple period. There are reflections of the weakening of guttural consonants in some biblical manuscripts from Qumran, especially 1 QIsa[a], e.g.,

---

[3] Data supplied by Shai Heijmans.

# Adaption and Creativity in the Tiberian Reading Tradition 21

(7) *He* in place of *ḥeth* in the Masoretic Text (MT)

מהשוכים (1QIsaᵃ 35.27 | L [BHS]: מַחְשָׁךְ Isa. 42.16 'darkness')

ואהללה (1QIsaᵃ 37.6 | L [BHS]: וַאֲחַלֵּל Isa. 43.28 'and I will profane')

(8) *ʾAlef* in place of *he* in MT

אסיר (1QIsaᵃ 4.17 | L [BHS]: הָסֵר Isa. 5.5 'removing')

אנה (1QIsaᵃ 8.10 | L [BHS]: הִנֵּה Isa. 8.18 'behold')

In the Tiberian reading tradition, an epenthetic vowel is frequently inserted between a guttural and a following consonant, e.g., יַעֲלוּ 'they go up', הֶעֱלָה 'he brought up', טָהֳרָה 'cleansing'. This also was an orthoepic measure. Acoustically the epenthesis made the gutturals more perceptible when separated from the following consonant and this facilitated their preservation in the reading. The occurrence of epenthesis to increase the perceptual salience of consonants has been identified as a cross-linguistic function of epenthesis (Hall 2011, 1577–78).

The lengthening of the vowel of the prefix of verbs הָיָה and חָיָה can also be regarded as a type of epenthesis. I have termed this elsewhere as "metrical epenthesis" (Khan 2020, I:496–508). The lengthening had the status of a secondary stress. The clash of two prominent syllables of the secondary stress and the primary stress can be assumed to have induced a repair mechanism in the form of a short pause equivalent to a weak beat, in effect a metrical epenthetic or zero syllable, thus:

(9) יְהְיֶה [jiˑh.∅.ˈjɛː]

## 2.2. Vav

In the Tiberian tradition, the consonant ו was normally pronounced as a labio-dental [v] (Khan 2020, I:171). In ancient times, the Hebrew consonant ו was originally pronounced as a labio-velar [w]. Therefore, at some point in the history of Hebrew, the pronunciation of ו *waw* changed from [w] to [v]. This development occurred during the Roman and/or Byzantine period(s) as a result of contact with Greek (Kantor and Khan 2022), in which this sound developed around that time. This was most likely through the intermediary of Jewish Palestinian Aramaic, which was the vernacular language of the Jews of Palestine during the Byzantine period. There is evidence of the pronunciation of ו as a labio-velar [v] in Jewish Palestinian Aramaic in the interchange of ו and ב in the extant texts, e.g., הלביי in place of הלואי 'oh that!' (Breshith Rabbah, Sokoloff 1968).

It is significant that, judging by later vocalised texts, Jewish Palestinian Aramaic underwent further convergence with Greek sound patterns, in particular in the vowel system. Such a convergence can also be identified in the medieval Palestinian tradition of reading Hebrew. This convergence in the vowel system, however, was not extended to Tiberian Hebrew. One reason why only the [v] sound was extended to Tiberian Hebrew may have been the functional benefit associated with reading ו as [v] in the Tiberian tradition. The introduction of new sound patterns into a language through contact can serve a functional purpose and this, indeed, may be one of its motivating factors (Khan 2022). The pronunciation of ו as labio-velar [v] strengthened the pronunciation of the letter and so guarded against the possibility of its being slurred over or elided. It ensured a more careful reading. The acquisition of the [v] realisation of ו in Tiberian Hebrew would, therefore, have served an orthoepic purpose. The orthoepic advantage of the innovative strong pronunciation of ו as [v] licensed its acceptance into the otherwise highly conservative Tiberian tradition of reading.

## 2.3. Coding of Transitivity

The *qal* form of the verb is neutral as to transitivity, in that both transitive and intransitive verbs are used in this form. This lack of explicit coding of transitivity, therefore, potentially increases the burden of processing the meaning of the verb. An orthoepic measure was introduced into the reading of several originally *qal* forms in the Second Temple period to disambiguate their transitivity. This consisted of changing some intransitive *qal* forms to *nifʿal* forms and some transitive *qal* forms to *piʿel* forms so long as this could be achieved in the reading tradition without altering the fixed consonantal framework.

In Late Biblical Hebrew, certain intransitive verbs appear as *nifʿal* in the past suffix conjugation form (perfect) whereas they appear as *qal* in Classical Biblical Hebrew. The intransitive form of the verb 'to stumble' (כש״ל), for example, appears in the *nifʿal* נִכְשַׁל in the book of Daniel (וְנִכְשַׁל 'and he will stumble' Dan. 11.19) but in the *qal* form כָּשַׁל elsewhere. In the prefix conjugation (imperfect), however, the verb is vocalised as a *nifʿal* throughout the Bible. This is because the *ketiv* of the prefix conjugation (יכשל) is ambiguous as to the verbal conjugation and could, in principle, be read as *qal* or *nifʿal*. The Tiberian reading tradition treats the verbal forms as *nifʿal* where this would be compatible with the consonantal framework, but the occurrence of the *qal* form in the suffix conjugation in Classical Biblical Hebrew suggests that the verb was originally read as *qal* in all forms. This is clearly the case in the infinitive form of this verb וּבִכָּשְׁלוֹ (Prov. 24.17), where the consonantal framework lacks the initial *he* of the *nifʿal* (הִכָּשֵׁל) and so must have represented the *qal*, but it is nevertheless read as a *nifʿal*. The crucial point is that the replacement of the *qal* by the *nifʿal* is reflected by the consonantal framework itself in Late Biblical Hebrew in the book of Daniel.

The Tiberian vocalisation interprets as *piʿel* certain verbs that are likely to have been originally *qal*. The verb ג׳׳רש 'to drive out', for example, is normally vocalised as *piʿel* in the prefix and suffix conjugations (תְּגָרֵשׁ, גֵּרְשָׁה), in which the orthography is ambiguous between a *qal* or *piʿel* reading. In the participles, however, where the orthography of *qal* and *piʿel* would be distinct, the original *qal* is preserved (גֹּרֵשׁ, גֹּרְשָׁה).

A wider range of shifts of intransitive *qal* to *nifʿal* and of transitive *qal* to *piʿel* are attested in some manuscripts from Qumran and in various post-biblical Hebrew sources.[4] It is likely,

---

[4] For these issues relating to the vocalisation of verbal forms see Ginsberg (1934), Ben-Ḥayyim (1958, 237), Fassberg (2001) and Hornkohl (2023). For further re-interpretations of the Masoretic orthography in the Samaritan reading tradition see Ben-Ḥayyim (2000, 338–39) and Schorch (2004).

therefore, that this reflects a development in vernacular Hebrew in late antiquity,[5] e.g.,

(10) נשכב 'she lay down' (4QD 3 12) (Qimron 2018, 221) = Biblical Hebrew שָׁכְבָה

(11) Mishnah, Shabbat 32, 4
Genizah fragment: Oxford Heb.c.23.3–8 (Birnbaum 2008, 125):
לא יסָפֵּד בהן ישראל 'A Jew may not mourn with them (the flutes)'
Printed edition of the Mishnah (Vilna ed.): יספוד (qal)
Biblical Hebrew: לִסְפֹּד (qal)

(12) Nah. 3.4
4QpNah 3 II 7 (Fassberg 2001):
מרוב זנוני זונה טובת חן בעלת כשפים **הממכרת** גוים בזנותה
MT: מֵרֹב זְנוּנֵי זוֹנָה טוֹבַת חֵן בַּעֲלַת כְּשָׁפִים **הַמֹּכֶרֶת** גּוֹיִם בִּזְנוּנֶיהָ וּמִשְׁפָּחוֹת בִּכְשָׁפֶיהָ:
'And all for the countless whorings of the prostitute, graceful and of deadly charms, **who betrays** nations with her whorings, and peoples with her charms.'

(13) Gen. Rab. 945:4 (Fassberg 2001)
**שימר** יעקב אבינו את השבת
'Jacob, our father, **kept** the Sabbath' (= Biblical Hebrew שָׁמַר)

---

[5] For the vernacular background of the Tannaitic layer of Rabbinic Hebrew see Bar-Asher (2011, 515).

The vernacular influence with regard to this feature had a functional advantage. It brought about a formal expression of a semantic distinction and, therefore, facilitated interpretation. This vernacular influence was licensed in the otherwise conservative reading tradition to achieve this orthoepic enhancement.

## 2.4. קַרְנַיִם vs קְרָנַיִם

The dual of the noun קֶרֶן is vocalised קַרְנַיִם in Hab. 3.4, with the normal pattern of the dual, but קְרָנַיִם in Dan. 8 (verses 3, 6, 20), with the pattern of the stem of plural nouns. The dual form קְרָנַיִם in Dan. 8 has the meaning 'horns'. The form קַרְנַיִם in Hab. 3.4, which has the normal dual vocalic pattern, has the meaning 'rays (of light)'. This is the only other place where the word occurs in the biblical corpus as a common noun without a suffix and not in a construct. The difference in vocalisation, therefore, is likely to express a distinction in meaning between the two forms.[6]

The morphological pattern of the dual form קְרָנַיִם is found in early vocalised manuscripts of the Mishnah, e.g., MS Kaufmann, MS Antonin, MS Parma A, MS Parma B (Kister 1992, 47, n. 9; 1998, 246, n. 9), and so is likely to be a feature of vernacular Hebrew in late antiquity. This, therefore, is also a case of vernacular influence in the conservative reading being licensed for the orthoepic purpose of making a morphological distinction for the purpose of explicitly coding a semantic distinction.

---

[6] See the remarks of Yeivin (1985, 844, n. 74).

## 2.5. הָאֲמֵלָלִים vs אֻמְלָל (Neh. 3.34)

A further example of this process is the difference in vocalisation between אֻמְלָל 'feeble' (Ps. 6.3) and הָאֲמֵלָלִים 'the feeble' (Neh. 3.34). The vocalisation הָאֲמֵלָלִים in Neh. 3.34 reflects the one that is used in Rabbinic sources, reflected by the orthography אמיללים (Boyarin 1988, 63–64), and so is likely to reflect a vernacular morphology.

All cases of אֻמְלָל and its inflections are predicative, most with clear verbal inflection. הָאֲמֵלָלִים is the only nominal form with nominal inflection (functioning as an attributive adjective):

(14) וּפֹרְשֵׂי מִכְמֹרֶת עַל־פְּנֵי־מַיִם אֻמְלָלוּ (Isa. 19.8)
 'and those who spread a net upon the water will languish'

(15) אֻמְלַל אָנִי (Ps. 6.3)
 'I am languishing'

but:

(16) הַיְּהוּדִים הָאֲמֵלָלִים (Neh. 3.34)
 'the feeble Jews'

So, this morphological distinction, which has apparently come about by licensing influence from the vernacular language, had the orthoepic purpose of distinguishing the verbal (contingent) and nominal (time-stable) categories of a lexeme.

A parallel to this phenomenon is found in the morphology of participles in the Samaritan oral tradition. In this tradition participles that have a verbal function are in some cases distinguished morphologically from participles that have a nominal use. This can be illustrated by the participle of the verb קו״ם 'to rise'. When it has a nominal function, the participle has the form qaːm but when it has a verbal function it has the form qaːʔəm. The former is the more conservative form, which is found in the Tiberian tradition (קָם). The latter is an innovative restructuring modelled on the form of the participle in Aramaic (Florentin 1996; Ben-Ḥayyim 2000, 190). This arose when Aramaic was the vernacular of the Samaritan community. The vernacular influence was licensed to achieve this morphological distinction. The different functions are seen in the following:

(17) Deut. 33.11

    Tiberian MT:

    מְחַ֥ץ מָתְנַ֖יִם **קָמָ֑יו**

    Samaritan written tradition:

    מחץ מתני **קמיו**

    Samaritan Oral Tradition:

    ˈmaːʔesˤ maːˈteːni **ˈqaːmo**

    'Crush the loins of **those who rise against him**.'

(18) Gen. 37.7

    Tiberian MT:

    וְהִנֵּ֨ה **קָ֤מָה** אֲלֻמָּתִי֙ וְגַם־נִצָּ֔בָה

    'My sheaf rose and stood upright.'

    Samaritan written tradition:

    והנה **קמה** אלמתי וגם נצבה

    Samaritan Oral Tradition:

    ˈweːnna **qaːˈʔeːma** eːlimˈmaːti wˈgam neːˈsˤiːba

    'My sheaf rises (contingent, verbal) and stands upright.'

## 2.6. יָנִיחַ 'he gives rest' vs יַנִּיחַ 'he places'

A further example of the use of a morphological model of the vernacular language to express a semantic distinction is the morphological distinction between יָנִיחַ 'he gives rest' and יַנִּיחַ 'he places'. The former is the normal *hifʿil* form of II-w verbs. The latter is derived originally from the same root, but has undergone an innovative morphological restructuring, which reflects its construal as a weak I-n verb rather than a weak II-w verb. The morphological alternance between II-w and I-n construals of roots is found in early manuscripts of Rabbinic Hebrew. It is common, for example, in Rabbinic Hebrew texts with Babylonian vocalisation (Yeivin 1985, 647), e.g.,

(19)  d-w-ḥ: יֹדִיח (*yōḏīḥ*) vs הֹדִיח (*hiddīḥ*) 'rinse'
z-w-ʿ: היזיע (*hēzīʿ*) vs היזיעה (*hizzīʿō*) 'sweat'
ṭ-w-l: מטיל (*mēṭīl*) vs מטילין (*maṭṭīlīn*) 'cast, throw'

Examples of this alternance are found also in early manuscripts of the Mishnah with Tiberian vocalisation, e.g.,

(20) MS Kaufmann:
הֵזִיעַ vs הִזִּיעַ 'sweat'

The model for the morphologically alternant form יַנִּיחַ 'he places' in the Tiberian reading tradition, therefore, is likely to be the vernacular Hebrew of late antiquity.

## 3.0. Exploitation of Morphological Alternants within the Reading Tradition

### 3.1. Dagesh

The second source for innovative restructuring to express distinctions in meaning is morphological alternance internal to the Tiberian reading tradition. The first case of this that we shall consider is the use of gemination, reflected in the Tiberian tradition by a *dagesh* sign, to distinguish homophones. An example is the pair אֲבִיר 'powerful' referring to God, used in phrases such as אֲבִיר יַעֲקֹב 'the Mighty One of Jacob' (Gen. 49.24, Isa. 49.26, Isa. 60.16, Ps. 132.2, 5) vs אַבִּיר 'powerful', used to refer to humans.

The patterns קָטִיל and קְטִיל are sometimes morphological alternants in the Tiberian reading. This is seen, for example, in the alternants: אָסִיר ~ אַסִּיר 'prisoner'. Note also examples such as פְּרִיצֵי, פְּרִיצִים (construct pl), with 'virtual' gemination, vs פְּרִיץ (construct sg Isa. 35.9) 'violent, ravenous'. Furthermore, in some cases a קְטִיל form in the Tiberian reading of a particular word is read as a קַטִּיל form in the Babylonian tradition, reflecting morphological alternance in two branches of the proto-Masoretic tradition, e.g.,

(21) Ps. 102.21
   Tiberian: אָסִיר
   Babylonian: אסּיר

In the case of אֲבִיר vs אַבִּיר, this morphological alternance has been put to functional use as an orthoepic measure to distinguish meaning.

The use of gemination marked by *dagesh* to distinguish meaning in morphological alternants such as אָבִיר and אַבִּיר was extended to other contexts where no morphological alternants existed. When, for example, the negator לֹא is juxtaposed with the homophonous prepositional phrase לוֹ, a *dagesh* is added to the negator to distinguish the two, e.g.,

(22)  לֹא לוֹ יִהְיֶה הַזָּרַע (Gen. 38.9)
'The offspring would not be his'

(23)  עַל־רִיב לֹּא־לוֹ (Prov. 26.17)
'in an argument that is not his'

Another application of gemination reflected by *dagesh* in the Tiberian vocalisation to distinguish meaning that took place through such analogical extension can be identified in the prefix of *vayyiqtol* verbal forms. Originally this narrative construction was homophonous with the *veyiqtol* construction, which typically had a future modal sense. The purpose of the gemination of the prefix was to distinguish the indicative narrative function from the future modal function.

I have argued elsewhere (Khan 2021) that the narrative function of *vayyiqtol* developed by a semantic extension of the use of *veyiqtol* to express purpose, as in

(24)  וְעִבְדוּ אֶת־יְהוָה אֱלֹהֵיכֶם וְיָשֹׁב מִכֶּם חֲרוֹן אַפּוֹ׃ (2 Chron. 30:8)
ESV 'and serve the Lord your God, that his fierce anger **may turn away** from you.'

In some contexts, such constructions can express the result of a previous action rather than purpose, which is reflected by the translations of the versions, e.g.,

(25) וַיִּשְׁלַח אֵלָיו אֱלִישָׁע מַלְאָךְ לֵאמֹר הָלוֹךְ וְרָחַצְתָּ שֶׁבַע־פְּעָמִים בַּיַּרְדֵּן וְיָשֹׁב
בְּשָׂרְךָ לְךָ וּטְהָר׃ (2 Kgs 5.10)

ESV 'And Elisha sent a messenger to him, saying, "Go and wash in the Jordan seven times, and your flesh **shall be restored**, and you shall be clean."'

LXX καὶ **ἐπιστρέψει** ἡ σάρξ σού σοι 'and your flesh will return to thee'

By a semantic extension of this function of *veyiqtol* to express sequential actions, the narrative function of the construction developed.

The fact that *dagesh* in the *vayyiqtol* form, as well as the other cases of *dagesh* for distinguishing meaning discussed so far, occurs in the Tiberian tradition and in the Babylonian tradition suggests that it developed during the Second Temple period in the proto-Masoretic reading traditions before its Tiberian and Babylonian transmissions became geographically divided. This reflects a general Second Temple development in the proto-Masoretic reading tradition involving the introduction of strategies to increase care in pronunciation and clarity of interpretation. Reading traditions that were not direct heirs to the proto-Masoretic reading also exhibited such strategies, but they did not always coincide with the proto-Masoretic tradition. With regard to the *dagesh* of *vayyiqtol*, it is significant to note that the Samaritan reading tradition does not have gemination of the prefix. In the Samaritan tradition, where possible, i.e., in *qal* I-*y* verbs, a different strategy was adopted for distinguishing *vav* + *yiqtol* with a past consecutive meaning, namely the mapping of the *qaṭal* vocalic pattern onto the verbal form, e.g., wˈtaːrad 'and she went

*Adaption and Creativity in the Tiberian Reading Tradition* 33

down' (Tiberian וַתֵּ֫רֶד), by analogy with the pattern ˈqaːtˤal, versus ˈteːrad 'she goes down' (non-past, Tiberian תֵּרֵד, תֵּ֫רֶד).

In the Greek transcription of the Hexapla, moreover, the *dagesh* of *vayyiqtol* is reflected to a far lesser extent than in the Tiberian and Babylonian traditions (Kantor 2020). Furthermore, there are sporadic examples in the Babylonian tradition of constructions where a form that is *veyiqtol* modal future in Tiberian is read as *wayyiqtol*, suggesting that the gemination of the prefix was a matter of interpretation of tradition, rather than an original feature of the form, e.g.,

(26) Jer. 23.22
Babylonian (Yeivin 1985, 1063–68):
וִישְׁמִעוּ *wayyašmiʿu*
'and they made hear'
Tiberian MT:
וְיַשְׁמִעוּ
'and let them make heard'

(27) Babylonian (Yeivin 1985, 1063–68):
וְאַשְׁמִיעֵם *wəʾašmiʿem*
'and I announced them'
Tiberian MT:
וְאַשְׁמִיעֵם
'that I may announce them'

The use of *dagesh* to distinguish the meaning of homophones or polysemous words is more frequently encountered in the Babylonian tradition of Biblical Hebrew (Yeivin 1985, 355–63). In Babylonian vocalisation, a *dagesh* (known as *digsha* in the Babylonian tradition) is represented by a superscribed minute *gimel* and *rafe* (known as *qipya*) is represented by a superscribed minute *qof*. An example is the word כהנים, which is marked with a *dagesh* when it refers to 'priests of foreign gods' (Yeivin 1985, 358), e.g.,

(28) הכֹּהֲנִֽים (L [BHS]: הַכֹּהֲנִ֔ים Zeph 1.4 'the priests')
כֹּהֲנִֽים (L [BHS]: וַתַּעֲשׂ֨וּ לָכֶ֤ם כֹּֽהֲנִים֙ כְּעַמֵּ֣י הָאֲרָצ֔וֹת 2 Chron. 13.9 'and you will make for yourselves priests like the peoples of the lands')

These cases of orthoepic *dagesh* to distinguish meaning that do not occur in the Tiberian tradition must have developed in the Babylonian tradition after it split from the proto-Masoretic tradition.

## 3.2. Alternants of Weak Roots

Another type of morphological alternance that has been exploited to express distinctions in meaning is reflected by the form חָיֽוֹת in in the Tiberian reading tradition of Exod. 1.19:

(29) כִּ֣י לֹ֧א כַנָּשִׁ֛ים הַמִּצְרִיֹּ֖ת הָֽעִבְרִיֹּ֑ת כִּֽי־**חָי֣וֹת** הֵ֔נָּה בְּטֶ֨רֶם תָּב֧וֹא אֲלֵהֶ֛ן הַמְיַלֶּ֖דֶת וְיָלָֽדוּ׃

ESV 'Because the Hebrew women are not like the Egyptian women, for they are vigorous and give birth before the midwife comes to them.'

The form חָיֽוֹת in the Tiberian reading tradition in this verse is typically interpreted in English Bible versions as meaning 'vigorous' (ESV, NIV) or 'lively' (KJV, JPS).

Interpretations of the form in ancient versions include τοκάδες 'in childbirth' (Aquila), μαῖαι 'midwives' (Symmachus), *obsetricandi habent scientiam* 'having knowledge of delivering children' (Vulgate), חֲכִימָן 'wise (i.e., lively in mind)' (Targum Onqelos), זריזן וחכימן בדעתיהן 'lively and wise in their knowledge' (Targum Pseudo-Jonathan). Rabbinic sources interpret the form as meaning 'midwives' (מילדות) or 'wild animals (חיות השדה) (*Shemot Rabba*, ed. Vilna), i.e., they do not require midwives.[7] All of these interpretations are compatible with the reading חָיוֹת. The meaning 'wild animals' is a common meaning of Biblical Hebrew חַיּוֹת. The word חָיוֹת is used with the meanings 'in childbirth' and 'midwives' in Rabbinic Hebrew (Jastrow 1903, 451–52) and this corresponds to the same range of meanings in Aramaic (Driver 1955). Moreover, the Samaritan oral tradition of the word in question in this verse is ˈʕajjot:

(30) ˈkiː ˈlaː kɑːˈʔinʃəm ammisˤˈrijjot ɑːbˈrijjot ˈkiː ˈ**ʕajjot** ˈinna

The morphological form ˈʕajjot in the Samaritan oral tradition of Exod. 1.19 corresponds to the Tiberian morphological form חָיוֹת. Compare, for example:

(31) Lev. 14.4:
Tiberian MT:
שְׁתֵּי־צִפֳּרִים חַיּוֹת
Samaritan Oral Tradition:
ˈʃitti sˤibˈbuːrəm ˈʕajjot
'two live birds'

It is likely, therefore, that the Samaritan form is a reflex of the original morphological form in this verse, and the early in-

---

[7] Online Responsa Project (responsa.co.il).

terpretations presented above would, as remarked, all be compatible with this. The form חָיוֹת in the Tiberian reading tradition seems to have arisen by a restructuring of an original חַיּוֹת. This restructuring conforms to the principles that have been identified in the examples adduced in §2.5. of this paper, whereby it distinguishes a contingent property from a time-stable property. If this is the case, it is likely to reflect the ancient interpretation of 'in childbirth' (contingent) in contrast to חַיּוֹת 'alive' (time-stable).[8]

The innovative morphological form חָיוֹת appears to have been based on morphological alternance in weak roots. The lexeme 'live' itself exhibits alternance, in that the normal form of the adjective reflects a final geminate root (חַי ms, חַיָּה fs, חַיִּים mpl, חַיּוֹת fpl) whereas the verb exhibits a III-y root (חָיָה, יִחְיֶה). The form חָיוֹת could have been construed as a fpl of a stative participle with the III-y form חָיֶה, corresponding to the pattern of stative participles such as כָּבֵד.

In principle, חָיוֹת may also have been construed as the fpl participle of a II-weak root, such as קָם ms, קָמוֹת. The model for this would have been morphological alternance between final geminate and II-w roots such as the following:

(32) צוּר 'to tie up', by-form of צרר

לָבוּר 'to examine' (Eccl. 9.1), by-form of ברר

יָרוּץ 'he breaks' (Isa. 42.4), by-form of רצץ

In addition to the existence of such alternants within the reading tradition, it is relevant to note that in the Pesharim from

---

[8] This interpretation was favoured by Driver (1955), though he did not explain the vocalisation of the form in way that I am proposing here.

Qumran, words that we nowadays would identify as II-w and final geminate roots are sometimes conflated in interpretations. Consider the following passage from the Habakkuk Pesher:

(33) Habakkuk Pesher
Tiberian MT:
וְצוּר לְהוֹכִיחַ יְסַדְתּוֹ (Hab. 1.12)
ESV You, O Rock, have established them for reproof
Pesher:
אשר שמרו את מצוותו בצר למו
'Since they (his elect) have kept his commandments in their time of suffering'

Here the interpreter associates the word צוּר with the word צַר 'sorrow'. According to our modern analysis, the former has a medial weak radical (II-w) and the latter is derived from a final geminate root (צר״ר). The ancient interpreter was not aware of the theory of triradical root structure, but he based his interpretation on the similarity between the forms. We would say today that he treated the forms as morphological alternants of the same lexeme. He exploited this alternance for exegetical purposes. This would be analogous to the exploitation of morphological alternants for innovative restructuring to express distinctions in meaning within otherwise homophonous forms in the Tiberian reading tradition.

It is also worth noting that that the process of innovation that resulted in the form חָיוֹת has a parallel in the poetics reflected by the language of late antique Hebrew liturgical poetry known as *piyyuṭ*. In the language of *piyyuṭ* there was a tendency to conjugate all Biblical Hebrew weak verbs as II-weak, e.g., עָשׂ 'he did'

(II-weak) < עָשָׂה ;עָשׂ 'he set out' (II-weak) < נָסַע ;קַח 'he took' (II-weak) < לָקַח ;רָד 'he descended' (II-weak)< יָרַד (Rand 2013). Here morphological alternance of weak roots was used for innovative restructuring for poetic effect.

## 4.0. Concluding Remarks

Orthoepic measures in the Tiberian reading traditions had the aim of ensuring careful and accurate reading. Two main sources for such orthoepic features can be identified, viz. interaction with languages in contact and morphological alternance within the reading tradition. The development of many of these features can be reconstructed to the proto-Masoretic reading of the Second Temple period, from which the Tiberian and Babylonian traditions were derived historically.

The Tiberian reading tradition resisted influence from contact languages where this would reduce semantic distinctions, e.g., the weakening of gutturals and the reduction of vowel system. The reading tradition exploited features in contact languages to enrich the reading tradition for the sake of making semantic distinctions and ensuring careful articulation.

The distinction of forms of morphological alternants within the reading tradition was exploited to express semantic distinctions. This process was developed by analogical extensions of features of attested alternatives to a wider range of forms, as we have seen with regard to extension of the use of gemination (marked by dagesh in the vocalisation) for semantic distinction.

Such phenomena of resistance and functional exploitation of elements in languages in contact are features of living languages in contact (see, for example, Khan 2022). Exploitation of morphological variation within a lexeme to express distinction in meanings can be compared to the well-known phenomenon of lexical doublets in spoken languages. The development of the orthoepic features discussed in this paper, therefore, reflect the fact that the oral reading of the Hebrew Bible was a living tradition exhibiting growth that is characteristic of living languages.

## References

Bar-Asher, Moshe. 2011. 'Mishnaic Hebrew'. In *The Semitic Languages: An International Handbook,* edited by Stefan Weninger, Geoffrey Khan, Michael P. Streck, and Janet C. E. Watson, 515–22. Berlin-Boston: De Gruyter.

Ben-Ḥayyim, Zeev. 1958. 'The Samaritan Tradition and Its Relationship to the Language Tradition of the Dead Sea Scrolls and to Rabbinic Hebrew'. *Lešonénu* 22: 223–245. [Hebrew]

———.1968. 'The Contribution of the Samaritan Inheritance to Research into the History of Hebrew'. *Proceedings of the Israel Academy of Sciences and the Humanities* 3 (5): 162–74.

———. 2000. *A Grammar of Samaritan Hebrew: Based on the Recitation of the Law in Comparison with the Tiberian and Other Jewish Traditions*. Jerusalem: Hebrew University Magnes Press; Winona Lake: Eisenbrauns.

Birnbaum, Gabriel. 2008. *The Language of the Mishna in the Cairo Geniza: Phonology and Morphology*. Jerusalem: The Academy of the Hebrew Language. [Hebrew]

Driver, Godfrey R. 1955. 'Hebrew Mothers (Exodus i 19)'. *Zeitschrift für Alttestamentliche Wissenschaft* 67: 246–48.

Fassberg, Steven. 2001. 'The Movement from Qal to Pi"el in Hebrew and the Disappearance of the Qal Internal Passive'. *Hebrew Studies* 42: 243–55.

Florentin, Moshe. 1996. 'עיונים בתורת הצורות של עברית השומרונים: בידולים סמנטיים באמצעים מורפולוגיים'. *Lěšonénu* 59: 217–41.

Ginsberg, Harold Louis. 1934. 'From behind the Massorah'. *Tarbiz* 5: 208–223. [Hebrew]

Hall, Nancy. 2011. 'Vowel Epenthesis'. In *The Blackwell Companion to Phonology*, edited by Marc van Oostendorp, Colin J. Ewen, Elizabeth Hume, and Keren Rice, 1576–96. Malden, MA: Wiley; Oxford: Blackwell.

Hornkohl, Aaron D. 2023. *The Historical Depth of the Tiberian Reading Tradition of Biblical Hebrew.* Cambridge Semitic Languages and Cultures 17. Cambridge: University of Cambridge & Open Book Publishers.

Jastrow, Marcus. 1903. *Dictionary of the Targumim, the Talmud Babli and Yerushalmi, and the Midrashic Literature.* London: Luzac.

Kantor, Benjamin, and Geoffrey Khan. 2022. 'Waw to Vav: Greek and Aramaic Contact as an Explanation for the Development of the Labio-Dental [v] from the La-Bio-Velar [w] in Biblical Hebrew'. *Zeitschrift der Deutschen Morgenländischen Gesellschaft* 172: 27–55.

Khan, Geoffrey. 2018. 'Orthoepy in the Tiberian Reading Tradition of the Hebrew Bible and Its Historical Roots in the Second Temple Period'. *Vetus Testamentum* 68: 1–24.

———. 2020. *The Tiberian Pronunciation Tradition of Biblical Hebrew: Including a Critical Edition and English Translation of the Sections on Consonants and Vowels in the Masoretic Treatise Hidāyat al-Qāriʾ 'Guide for the Reader'*, 2 vols. Cambridge Semitic Languages and Cultures 1. Cambridge: University of Cambridge & Open Book Publishers. doi.org/10.11647/OBP.0163.

———. 2021. 'The Coding of Discourse Dependency in Biblical Hebrew Consecutive Weqaṭal and Wayyiqṭol'. In *New Perspectives in Biblical and Rabbinic Hebrew*, edited by Aaron D. Hornkohl and Geoffrey Khan, 299–354. Cambridge Semitic Languages and Cultures 7. Cambridge: University of Cambridge & Open Book Publishers. https://www.openbookpublishers.com/product/1392

———. 2022. 'Phonological Enrichment in Neo-Aramaic Dialects through Language Contact'. In *Historical Linguistics and Endangered Languages: Exploring Diversity in Language Change*, edited by Patience Epps, Danny Law, and Na'ama Pat-El, 41–55. Studies in Historical Linguistics. Amsterdam: John Benjamins.

Qimron, Elisha. 2018. *A Grammar of the Hebrew of the Dead Sea Scrolls*. Jerusalem: Ben-Zvi Institute.

Rand, Michael. 2013. 'Paytanic Hebrew'. In *Encyclopedia of Hebrew Language and Linguistics*, edited by Geoffrey Khan, Shmuel Bolozky, Steven E. Fassberg, Gary A. Rendsburg, Aaron D. Rubin, Ora R. Schwarzwald, and Tamar Zewi, 3:55–60. Boston: Brill.

Schorch, Stefan. 2004. *Die Vokale des Gesetzes: die Samaritanische Lesetradition als Textzeugin der Tora*. Beihefte zur Zeitschrift für die Alttestamentliche Wissenschaft 339. Berlin: De Gruyter.

Sokoloff, Michael. 1968. 'The Hebrew of "Bĕréšit Rabba" According to Ms. Vat. Ebr. 30'. *Lĕšonénu* 33: 25-42 [Hebrew].

Tov, Emanuel. 2012. *Textual Criticism of the Hebrew Bible*, 3rd ed. Minneapolis: Fortress Press.

Yeivin, Israel. 1985. *The Hebrew Language Tradition as Reflected in the Babylonian Vocalization*. Jerusalem: The Academy of the Hebrew Language. [Hebrew]

# THE DOUBLE NATURE OF THE TEXT OF THE HEBREW BIBLE[1]

## Harald Samuel

The relationship between the consonantal framework of the Hebrew Bible and its vocalisation has been a topic fraught with dogmatic interests and presuppositions since at least the Reformation period, when it played a prominent role in discussions about the 'reliability' of the textual tradition and, thus, the weighing of scripture *versus* tradition (Schnedermann 1879; Sæbø 2008). Of course, the underlying problem has been discussed since antiquity as, for example, quotes from the Rabbinic tradition and the Church fathers indirectly show—quotes compiled by the same authors involved in those sixteenth- and seventeenth-century controversies. Yet it made no small difference that the quest for the antiquity of the oral tradition was now mingled with the quest for the origins of its written form, i.e., the vowel signs and accents.

---

[1] Warm thanks go once more to my dear friend Paul M. Kurtz for his help avoiding Denglish as well as to the careful reviewers and editors for their helpful suggestions. The article profited furthermore from numerous conversations with Erhard Blum.

While it would be a considerable oversimplification to assume unilinear relations between certain dogmatic and philological positions, one may note that some non-philological presuppositions seem to live on in different scholarly traditions (consider the conspicuous usage of the category of 'reliability' in several article titles). It could be a rewarding, but also potentially sobering enterprise to trace the offshoots of the allegedly bygone early modern discussions into the nineteenth and twentieth centuries. And yet, it is not a naïve sentiment, I believe, to say that in recent decades, questions more strictly philological have come to the fore that seek to integrate the 'new' materials from the Cairo Genizah and especially the Dead Sea Scrolls into a more nuanced picture of the history of the Hebrew language and its diverse pronunciation traditions. We seem to be in a much better position now to appreciate the astonishing conservatism embedded within the Masoretic tradition[2]—especially in its Tiberian version—and at the same time to be aware of the vitality of the tradition, including subtle linguistic expressions of exegesis as well as more systematic grammatical developments.

My main interests in this paper are grammatical developments.[3] I will look for reflections of recurring differences between

---

[2] See numerous articles by Geoffrey Khan (e.g., Khan 2018), as well as Hornkohl 2023.

[3] The presentation underlying this paper had a twisted history. Shortly before the conference, a brilliant article by Chanan Ariel was prepublished online by *Vetus Testamentum* (see now Ariel 2024). It covered a huge share of the examples I had originally amassed for this paper.

the Tiberian vocalisation tradition, on the one hand, and the intended grammatical system(s) of the consonantal framework, on the other hand. Often, such differences are also reflected by more or less systematic distinctions *between* vocalisation traditions and also systemic inconsistencies *within* one tradition. The paradox we deal with is therefore the double nature of the vocalisation tradition, which is independent of the written consonantal framework, yet inseparable from it.

## 1.0. How to Proceed: Spelling and Pronunciation

Before I can proceed with actual examples, it will be necessary to elucidate and justify two basic assumptions underlying my approach:

1) Despite the obvious general flexibility in the use of *matres lectionis*,[4] some grammatical categories overwhelmingly demand the usage of a *mater lectionis*.[5] The spelling tradition in the

---

While I reworked my hypothesis, it should now be read in correspondence with Ariel's article. All the more I would like to thank him for several useful observations.

[4] E.g., in the (non-)use of ו in *qal* participles or the ending of the inf. cs. in ל"י\ו verbs.

[5] E.g., verbs in the *nifʿal* and *hifʿil* stems as well as prefixed nouns derived from פ"ו roots where the ו originally had consonantal value and where typically a ו is therefore also written, unlike in the previous cases. Exceptions to this tendency are either reflections of a linguistic development, as in the case of the conspicuous *defective* spellings of the verb יס"ף in the *hifʿil* stem (see below), or—typically late—scribal conven-

Masoretic Text (MT) is generally much more systematic and consistent than James Barr was willing to accept,[6] even though his criticism of previous works on spelling practices is more than justified (see especially Barr 1988).[7]

2) The Jewish vocalisation traditions—unlike the Samaritan reading tradition—*generally seem* to follow the consonantal framework quite strictly[8] (though they do not always do so, a point to which we return below).

Let me elucidate this with some examples:

a) The Hebrew name of the city known as Jericho in English translations has two variants: When written with י, it is vocalised with *ḥireq* as יְרִיחוֹ (mainly in the Book of Joshua and in 2 Kings 2). However, when spelled without י, the vocalisation יְרֵחוֹ shows *ṣere* (in the remaining books,

---

tions, as in the case of the noun תולדות, which in Chronicles is consistently spelled without the first ו, or תוצאות which only in the Book of Joshua is consistently spelled defectively.

[6] It should be noted that some medieval manuscripts seem to deviate consistently from the Masoretic main tradition with respect to specific grammatic categories, e.g., the Codex Reuchlinianus. This phenomenon deserves more attention as an indirect expression of medieval grammatical thinking.

[7] Without going into detail, to my mind the fundamental problem of Andersen and Forbes' *Spelling in the Hebrew Bible*, sharply criticised by Barr, is the philologically faulty categorisation of several spelling features (Barr 1988).

[8] However, the traditional picture about the relationship between spelling and recitation in the Samaritan tradition needs a fresh and more nuanced treatment (Stefan Schorch, oral communication).

including the Pentateuch, Chronicles, and Ezra–Nehemiah, i.e., there is no obvious chronological pattern). See also Judg. 1.31 אֲפִיק *versus* the standard אֲפֵק (e.g., Josh. 19.30).

b) Personal names with a theophoric element like אב or צור may or may not contain a connecting vowel /i/. For many such names, both variants exist. It is most relevant that in almost all cases, the vocalisation depends on the spelling. If the name is spelled with י, it contains the vowel; if the letter is absent, the vowel is absent as well, e.g., Ab(i)ner (אַבְנֵר/אֲבִינֵר) in 1 Sam. 14.50 and 51 or El(i)zaphan ben Uzziël in Exod. 6.22, Lev. 10.4 (אֶלְצָפָן) *versus* Num. 3.30 (אֱלִיצָפָן). Even more interesting is the name Amnon (אַמְנוֹן), which appears once (2 Sam. 13.20) as אֲמִינוֹן, since this name follows a different naming pattern and the י there is quite difficult to explain. What matters, however, is the fact that the vocalisation strictly adheres to the spelling. Apparently, consistency in the correspondence between spelling and pronunciation was more important than consistency in naming one and the same person.

c) Obviously, the transmission of names may follow its own rules. In other words, this does not affect the morphological level of the language. Yet we can observe a very similar tendency with the *hifʿil* forms of the verb בו"א. As this root is hollow, we expect the second- and first-person forms of the suffix conjugation to contain the connecting vowel /o/, thus הֵבֵיאתָ, הֲבִיאוֹתִי, הֲבִיאֹתָם, הֲבִיאֹנֻם. Such forms indeed exist. But, (maybe) due to the fact that this root is additionally a ל"א root, we also find forms like הֲבֵאתֶם, הֲבֵאתִי, הֲבֵאתָ. The choice between the two forms is mainly determined by the spelling. If we have *plene* spellings with י (rarely with ו for the connecting vowel), we find the former type of vocalisation; if the spelling is *defective*, we find the latter.[9] We should note that there is a lot of textual variation, already among the Dead Sea Scrolls and also among the medieval manuscripts, i.e., the tradition is quite flexible in this case. We should furthermore note that there might be a diachronic pattern, i.e., the Samaritan tradition and Rabbinic Hebrew know basically (with exceptions) only the forms without the connecting vowel. Furthermore, we have a few 'problematic' cases where MT records a י but the vocalisation still prefers the forms without the connecting vowel, like Num. 14.31 וְהֵבֵיאתִי.[10] Thus, the situation is not unequivocal. Yet statistically speaking, a certain tendency is clear: if possible, the vocalisation tradition prefers the forms without the connecting vowel, especially in the ambiguous, defectively spelled forms. But here and there, even forms with י are not vocalised with a connecting vowel, i.e., the י serves as a vowel letter for *ṣere*, which stretches the spelling conventions of

---

[9] Exceptions are 1 Sam. 1.22 וַהֲבִאֹתִיו and Jer. 25.9 וַהֲבֵאתִים.

[10] See also 2 Kgs 9.2 וַהֲבֵיאתָ, 19.25 הֲבֵיאתִיהָ ‖ Isa. 37.26 הֲבֵאתִיהָ (1QIsa$^a$ הביאותיה, 19-ל הביאתיה), 43.23 הֵבֵיאתָ (1QIsa$^a$ הביאותה, var. הבאת), and Jer. 25.13 *qᵉri* וְהֵבֵאתִי but *kᵉtiv* והבאיתי (thus M$^L$) or והבאותי (thus M$^A$). Cf. Deut. 21.12 וַהֲבֵאתָהּ with its equivalent והביאותה in the Temple Scroll.

Biblical Hebrew, since ׳ usually serves as vowel letter for ṣere where a diphthong existed previously (cf. Qimron 2018, 246–48 [C3.6.2.4] for a different evaluation of the evidence).

d)  This latter stretch of the spelling conventions can also be found in the noun פליטה/פלטה. We find both spellings of the word, with ׳ (24 times) and without ׳ (4 times) according to BHK/BHS,[11] yet the vocalisation always has ṣere. Since the nominal pattern qᵊtelā (*qatilat) is otherwise consistently spelled without ׳ and since spellings with ׳ instead suggest the nominal pattern qᵊtīlā (*qatīlat) (cf. Bauer and Leander 1922, 466 [§61j‴]) and the expected long vowel in the Samaritan tradition's fēlīta),[12] the form פְּלֵיטָה instead of either פְּלֵטָה or פְּלִיטָה is a statistical anomaly that needs to be explained. While the spelling of ׳ for an originally short ṣere is conspicuous within Biblical Hebrew, one should remember it is permissible in later spelling traditions. Furthermore, the pattern qᵊtīlā—while still rare in Biblical Hebrew—became prominently used for verbal nouns in Rabbinic Hebrew. My hunch is that since the word פליטה in Biblical

---

[11] In Jer. 50.29, however, the Aleppo Codex has a ׳, and in Ezek. 14.22 several other manuscripts also attest the spelling with ׳.

[12] An additional curious case is the noun חֲשֵׁיכָה in Ps. 139.12, otherwise (5×) spelled without ׳. Since the following word is אוֹרָה instead of אוֹר which one would expect in prose, one may assume that חשיכה is a poetic biform of חשכה belonging to a different nominal pattern. Cf. furthermore Barth (1894, 314 n. 2).

Hebrew is not a verbal noun, it probably felt 'wrong' in later times (in the first half of the first millennium?) to use it in the *qᵊtīlā* pattern (cf. Mor 2015 for similar examples).

Attentive readers will have remarked, and may therefore want to object, that examples a) and b) differ from c) and d). While the former two show strict adherence to the consonantal framework at the expense of onomastic consistency in isolated cases, the latter two attest to creative usage of the ambiguities of the consonantal framework to make room for grammatical or lexical changes. However, the changes are still bound to the consonantal framework. In other cases, as we will see, this may lead to the creation of synchronically split paradigms when only one subset of forms is ambiguous and therefore renders a reflection of the grammatical change possible, while the remainder of forms unambiguously demands the older subset of forms. Paradoxically, it is this incomplete change that highlights the conservatism of the unchanged forms.

## 2.0. Changes in the Verbal Stem System

Stem shifts in the verbal system are by now a relatively well-known phenomenon,[13] basically affecting verbs in the *qal* stem which are instead (or additionally) used in the *nifʿal*, *piʿel*, or *hifʿil*

---

[13] I elaborated the topic in an unpublished paper at Cambridge in May 2018, where I also look at the semantic properties of the verbs in an attempt to explain why they shift to either of the three derived stems. See also Samuel (2019, §3.2.3.3), and now Hornkohl (2023, 183–318).

without any difference in meaning.[14] I merely wish to add a few details and to highlight the systematic points.

In the Hebrew Bible, the verb כש"ל forms the suffix conjugation in the *qal* as well as in the *nifʿal* stem, though the latter occurs only in the book of Daniel, i.e., in a rather late[15] text. These forms are consonantally unambiguous, whereas all the consonantally ambiguous forms of the prefix conjugations are vocalised according to the *nifʿal* paradigm. Even though the distribution of the split paradigm is not exclusive, it is statistically telling: There is a diachronic shift from *qal* to *nifʿal*. If we look at the examples in detail, further peculiarities emerge:

(1) Isa. 40.30 reads a *figura etymologica* כָּשׁוֹל יִכָּשֵׁלוּ with apparent stem shift. Thanks to the non-reduction of the thematic vowel and the excessive *plene* spelling, 1QIsaᵃ helpfully reads the finite verbal form as יכשולו, i.e., clearly *qal*—at least on one occasion, the Qumran fragments do not break off immediately before the most interesting parts!

---

[14] For '*nifʿal*-isation' and '*piʿel*-isation' see the chapter by Geoffrey Khan in this volume. Cf. Zurawel (1984), Fassberg (2001; 2011), and Samet (2021). For a potentially parallel phenomenon in (Biblical) Aramaic, see Fassberg (2014).

[15] The attribute "late", which I simply use for want of a better alternative, is not meant to continue the highly problematic notions engrained in the infamous idea of *Spätjudentum*. Unfortunately, the common rhetoric of Classical Hebrew as the Golden Age of the Hebrew language perpetuates such problematic notions of peak and decay.

(2) Hos. 5.5 וְאֶפְרַיִם יִכָּשְׁלוּ בַּעֲוֺנָם כָּשַׁל גַּם־יְהוּדָה עִמָּם juxtaposes—according to the vocalisation—*qal* (suffix conjugation) and *nifʿal* (prefix conjugation) without any semantic difference.

(3) Most revealing, however, is the form וּבִכָּשְׁלוֹ in Prov. 24.17. Elision of intervocalic ה in such forms is impossible in Biblical Hebrew[16] but widely known from Rabbinic Hebrew and already attested in Qumran, especially in 1QpHab (Qimron 2018, 178–80 [C2.1.7.2]). In other words, the consonantal framework clearly demands reading a *qal* infinitive according to the classical (Biblical) standard, yet the spelling practices known from Rabbinic Hebrew enable later tradents to vocalise this form in accordance with their lexico-grammatical preferences. A Babylonian vocalised manuscript has the ה even included in the consonantal framework; i.e, the reading tradition has entered the written text.[17]

In light of the Daniel passages, the shift from *qal* to *nifʿal* must have started already in the Maccabean period, i.e., in the latest phase of the emergence of books that became biblical, unless we assume that the consonantal framework of Daniel was less stable in its transmission than other books, which would suggest that late forms could enter the consonantal framework even some time after the composition of the book. It seems to me one should not exclude such a possibility for isolated cases (see the

---

[16] Against Rendsburg (1982), the few so-called *laqṭīl* forms are best explained in the same light, and see below.

[17] See also m. Avot 4.19 where Proverbs is quoted and the manuscripts read ובכשלו, וב[ה]כשלו, ובהכשלו, and even וביכשלו, cf. Sharvit (2004).

example above), but it is rather unlikely that this affected almost systematically a group of forms.[18] This historical development in the Hebrew of the time influenced the oral tradition: whenever possible, the verbal forms were read as *nifʿal*, yet the written tradition had already set a boundary. Consonantally unambiguous forms were not altered (except, maybe, in isolated cases) and instead read as *qal*, and thus a largely split paradigm emerged.[19]

The most significant difference of the intransitive verb נג"ש from כש"ל regards its first root letter, the assimilation of which in different positions therefore leads to a different distribution of *qal* and *nifʿal* forms within the verbal paradigm. The *nifʿal* features only forms of the suffix conjugation and a participle, while the *qal* knows only the prefix conjugation and related forms, i.e., imperatives and the construct infinitive. Once more, the vocalisation tradition does not interfere with the text. Rather, it only uses the ambiguities of the consonantal framework in a creative way so the diachronic changes in the development of the Hebrew language are reflected. The first clear *nifʿal* form of נג"ש is to be found among the Dead Sea Scrolls: the construct infinitive בהנגשו

---

[18] In this context, I would like to mention that also the Song of Hannah, sometimes classified as Archaic Biblical Hebrew, features the *nifʿal* participle וְנִכְשָׁלִים in 1 Sam. 2.4, as does Zech. 12.8 הַנִּכְשָׁל. If the emergence of the *nifʿal* forms in Daniel is indicative for the history of the Hebrew language, I see little reason to doubt that the same is true for 1 Sam. 2 and Zech. 12—unless participles are somehow an exception.

[19] Holger Gzella's attempt to explain suppletive paradigms by a combination of the TAM system with the system of the verbal stems (Gzella 2016) is attractive, though impossible in light of the following example which shows the opposite distribution of forms.

in 4Q414 || 4Q512 which resembles Prov. 24.17 וּבְכָּשְׁלוֹ. If one assumes that the tendency to read the ambiguous forms whenever possible as *nifʿal* originated again in the Graeco-Roman period, it may not be superfluous to remark that the Samaritan reading tradition generally treats the verb as *qal* and thus does not share this development with the Jewish tradition.[20]

What has been said about the root נג"ש can be repeated for נת"ך: the verb is used in the *qal* stem, but whenever possible a *nifʿal* vocalisation is laid onto the consonantal framework, e.g., תִּתַּךְ in Jer. 42.18 and נִתַּךְ in the same verse, without any semantic difference. The first clear attestation for *nifʿal* is found among the Dead Sea Scrolls: ינתך in 4Q424 and the tendency for 'nifʿal-isation' is again not shared by the Samaritan tradition which treats Exod. 9.33 נתך, the only relevant example from the Pentateuch, as *qal* as against the *nifʿal* נִתַּךְ of the Tiberian text.

The two following examples concern the shift from *qal* to *hifʿil*. We can detect these examples again because of the curious distribution of forms within the paradigm, since basically we have split paradigms. For נח"ה, the *qal* covers the suffix conjugation and the imperative, whereas the ambiguous forms of the prefix conjugations are covered by the *hifʿil*. However, we do find consonantally unambiguous *hifʿil* forms in Neh. 9, certainly a late text, and also in Gen. 24.48 הִנְחַנִי next to the *qal* נָחַנִי in v. 27. Even though Gen. 24 is certainly not one of the oldest chapters in the Pentateuch, the occurrence of the *hifʿil* here could signal

---

[20] Unfortunately, כש"ל occurs only once in the Pentateuch in Lev. 26.37 וְכָשְׁלוּ, but no ambiguous form that could be vocalised as *nifʿal* is attested, thus there is no relevant information from the Samaritan tradition.

that the shift from *qal* to *hifʿil* started earlier than the above shifts from *qal* to *nifʿal*; however, it is equally possible that this one late form crept into the text during its transmission. Isolated cases are hardly solid ground to build hypotheses upon. Maybe more interesting is Exod. 13.21 לִנְחֹתָם, another case where the consonantal framework suggests *qal*, but in light of later developments of the language, it was possible to read this text as *laqṭil* infinitive, indicating the direction of the linguistic development.[21]

The verb יס"ף shows a comparable peculiarity.[22] Again, the suffix conjugation uses mainly *qal* formations, whereas the prefix conjugation is vocalised as *hifʿil* with the minor problem that the *hifʿil* should be written with ו but most forms do not show the etymologically correct ו, i.e., they were intended as *qal* forms of the type וַיֶּסֶף.[23] A quite revealing case is a comparison between 1 Kgs 10.7 הוֹסַפְתָּ and its verbatim parallel 2 Chron. 9.6 יָסַפְתָּ, where Chronicles features the typologically older *qal* variant. Another fascinating passage is 2 Kgs 20.6 וְהֹסַפְתִּי, paralleled by Isa.

---

[21] See n. 16 above. The Samaritan tradition apparently derives this form from the root נו"ח (regardless of the spelling as either לנחתם or להנחתם). A parallel case is Deut. 1.33 לַחֲנֹתְכֶם with Samaritan Pentateuch (SP) להחנ(ו)תכם. I thank Stefan Schorch for the clarifications concerning the Samaritan tradition beyond Ben-Ḥayyim's grammar.

[22] See already Schorch (2004, 108): "Zudem hat sich im Samaritanischen Hebräisch die schon in der tiberiensischen Überlieferung in bezug auf das vorliegende Verb zu beobachtende Tendenz, in der AK Formen des *q.* und in der PK Formen des *hif.* zu verwenden, vollends durchgesetzt."

[23] See now also Hornkohl (2024) for the data. However, I disagree emphatically with his historical evaluation.

38.5 הִנְנִי יֹסֵף. The latter is quite unusual since after הנני one expects a participle, which could be יֹסֵף *qal*, whereas in 2 Kgs the *we-qaṭal* of the *hifʿil* stem is unusually spelled defectively. One is therefore tempted to assume that an original ויספת was erroneously copied as והספת due to the similarity between ה and י in the ancient Hebrew script *and* under the influence of the linguistic innovation to use the verb in the *hifʿil* stem.

Additional interesting examples could be given, but the principle remains the same in all cases. Linguistic updating via the oral tradition occurs mostly in those places where the consonantal framework is ambiguous and enables such a reading, even when this may lead to inconsistencies like split or suppletive paradigms. The consonantal framework may show repercussions of the oral tradition in rare cases, but overall, this is rather the exception and the consonantal framework seems stable. One needs to be careful here, not to fall into a logical trap: it is only because there is a relative stability of the consonantal framework that we are able to see this kind of statistical anomaly at all.[24]

---

[24] A rare case of an attested linguistic update within the consonantal framework is Gen. 40.15 with the reading גֻּנֹּב גֻּנַּבְתִּי in MT but the variant גנוב נגנבתי in SP. The Jewish reading tradition could understand the original *qal* passive as a *puʿʿal* without any change of the consonantal framework, while the Samaritan tradition replaced the obsolete *qal* passive by a *nifʿal* form, which necessitated an alteration of the consonantal framework. How old that change is, is impossible to determine.

## 3.0. Creative Reinterpretation of Obsolete Elements

The rules for applying the so-called *energic* (or intrusive, epenthetic, or inserted) *nun*[25] are one of the mysteries not so much of Hebrew grammar but of Hebrew grammar writing. The basic rules were already established by Mayer Lambert more than 100 years ago (Lambert 1903), but somehow ignored by several standard grammars or subsequently obscured. Thus, the topic does not belong to the shared common knowledge in the field but is taken for granted by some scholars, yet is a complete novelty for others.

In short: the *energic nun* in forms of the prefix conjugation occurs only with the long *yiqṭol*. We generally do not find the *energic nun* in *wayyiqṭol* forms,[26] and—as far as we can check by other morphological or syntactic criteria—all other forms without the *energic nun* are short forms of the prefix conjugation (jussives),[27] while the ones with *energic nun* are long forms. The cohortative, even though it forms a suppletive paradigm together

---

[25] As against the so-called *paragogic nun*.

[26] For the few exceptions see Bloch (2007, 144 n. 12).

[27] The latter point is corroborated by the inscriptional evidence. The three times attested jussive "may YHWH bless you" is spelled phonetically יברך with a single *kaph*, see Ariel and Yuditsky (2015/16 [5776]). A long *yiqṭol* with *energic nun* would necessarily have been spelled with two *kaph*s. Thus, rather the spelling יברכך in Num. 6.24 requires explanation. I suggest to understand it as an etymologising spelling.

with the imperative and jussive,[28] usually carries the *energic nun*.[29] This distribution of the *energic nun* is very coherent. The grammatical rule just described is occasionally stretched to its limits in the Psalter and clearly does not work in the Book of Job.[30] Yet these exceptions do not invalidate its general significance.

Recognising this rule, or at least this basic relationship between long and short forms of the prefix conjugation and the application or non-application of the *energic nun* in front of certain suffixes, has been hampered in the past by the limits of the consonantal framework and peculiarities of the vocalisation, respectively. The consonantal framework shows the *energic nun* only in the case of the third person singular suffixes, while in the second- and first-person suffixes, a potential *energic nun* is visible only in

---

[28] The few imperatives with energic nun before third person singular suffixes are apparently the suffixed counterparts of the adhortative. The lengthened jussive, though extremely rare (see Blum 2008, 107–9 on Isa. 5.19), suggests the possibility that a suffixed lengthened jussive with energic nun existed as well. However, it would have been morphologically indistinguishable from a regular long *yiqtol* with suffix. I thank Erhard Blum for his insistence on this phenomenon.

[29] Thus, forms like Gen. 45.28 אֵלְכָה וְאֶרְאֶנּוּ or 37.27 לְכוּ וְנִמְכְּרֶנּוּ are expected whereas the non-use of the *energic nun* in Gen. 37.20 לְכוּ וְנַהַרְגֵהוּ וְנַשְׁלִכֵהוּ needs an explanation. See also Jer. 18.18 לְכוּ וְנַכֵּהוּ with the variant ונכנהו in 4QJer<sup>a</sup>.

[30] The verbal system in Job needs a fresh treatment that stresses its independence from the other books of the Hebrew Bible. See preliminarily Lauber (2016), and a hitherto unpublished paper by Holger Gzella, '*Yiqtol* as a Preterite in Job: An Unsolved Problem?', given in Oxford in November 2022.

the vocalisation. The rules are clear in the former case, while the latter two attest a different distribution of the form.[31] We see examples of long *yiqtol* forms without the expected *energic nun* (4–7) as well as (a few) jussives surprisingly with *energic nun* (8–9).

(4)  Gen. 3.15  הוּא **יְשׁוּפְךָ** רֹאשׁ וְאַתָּה תְּשׁוּפֶנּוּ עָקֵב

(5)  Deut. 31.6 [32]  לֹא **יַרְפְּךָ** וְלֹא יַעַזְבֶךָּ

(6)  1 Sam. 23.17  אַל־תִּירָא כִּי לֹא **תִמְצָאֲךָ** יַד שָׁאוּל

(7)  Gen. 19.19  פֶּן־**תִּדְבָּקַנִי** הָרָעָה וָמַתִּי

(8)  Num. 6.25  יָאֵר יְהוָה ׀ פָּנָיו אֵלֶיךָ **וִיחֻנֶּךָּ**

(9)  Prov. 4.6  אַל־תַּעַזְבֶהָ וְתִשְׁמְרֶךָּ אֱהָבֶהָ וְתִצְּרֶךָּ׃

The most natural conclusion is that evidence from the consonantal framework with a clear distribution of the *energic nun* with suffixes of the third-person singular, on the one hand, and the vocalisation tradition in case of the second- and first-persons singular, on the other, cannot be treated on a par. Rather, historical developments have resulted in a redistribution of the *energic nun*, the rules of which must be clarified.

A short survey supports the impression of the examples above: namely, that the (non-)use of the *energic nun* depends on prosodic features. Irrespective of the morphosyntactic context, the majority of forms with *dagesh* are in pause, while the forms

---

[31] The *energic nun* is practically absent in combination with the first-person singular suffix. One notable exception is the form תְּבָרֲכַנִּי in Gen. 27.19, 31. For Prov. 1.28 יִקְרָאֻנְנִי, יְשַׁחֲרֻנְנִי, and יִמְצָאֻנְנִי and related cases cf. Gzella (2007).

[32] See also Deut. 31.8 as well as Josh. 1.5.

without *dagesh* are contextual forms. Especially telling are 'minimal pairs' as in (5) but also (4) and (9).

Admittedly, there are exceptions, i.e., not every pausal form has the expected *dagesh*:

(10) Gen. 15.4 [33] אֲשֶׁר יֵצֵא מִמֵּעֶיךָ הוּא יִירָשֶׁךָ

(11) Deut. 4.31 לֹא יַרְפְּךָ וְלֹא יַשְׁחִיתֶךָ

It is possible that said redistribution was still at an incipient stage and thus never fully implemented. However, the general tendency remains clear, and the exceptions do not seem to be weighty enough to belie the above assumption. Additionally, a thorough review of the text-critical evidence, which is beyond the confines of this paper, might add examples that show a certain degree of inconsistency.

From the historical point of view, it is worth noting that the Secunda occasionally shows a difference to MT. Compare, for example, Ps. 30 (29LXX).10:

(12) μεββεσε βδαμι βρεδεθι ελ σααθ αϊωδεχχα αφαρ αϊεγγιθι {*αϊεγγιδ} εμεθθαχ;

with MT,

(13) מַה־בֶּצַע בְּדָמִי בְּרִדְתִּי אֶל שָׁחַת הֲיוֹדְךָ עָפָר הֲיַגִּיד אֲמִתֶּךָ

where only the Secunda has the historically expected reflex of the *energic nun* (see Yuditsky 2017 and Maurizio 2023).

Eventually, one should add that the *dagesh* in pause spread to forms where an *energic nun* has no historical justification at all, e.g.:

---

[33] Cf. the contextual form לֹא יִירָשְׁךָ זֶה in the first half of the verse.

(14) *wayyiqtols*: Isa. 49.7 [34]וַיִּבְחָרֶךָ, Ps. 81.8 וְאָעִ֣ידָה בָּ֑ךְ, Prov. 7.15 וָֽאֶמְצָאֶֽךָּ

(15) *we-qatal*: Deut. 24.13 וּבֵרֲכֶֽךָּ

(16) Infinitives: e.g., Deut. 23.5 [35]לְקַֽלְלֶֽךָּ ... וַאֲשֶׁר֩ שָׂכַ֨ר עָלֶ֜יךָ אֶת־בִּלְעָ֗ם

(17) Participles: e.g., Deut. 12.14 [36]מְצַוֶּֽךָּ וְשָׁ֣ם תַּעֲשֶׂ֔ה כֹּ֛ל אֲשֶׁ֥ר אָנֹכִ֖י

(18) Prepositions: Gen. 41.40 רַ֥ק הַכִּסֵּ֖א אֶגְדַּ֥ל מִמֶּֽךָּ (as opposed to contextual מִמְּךָ), and even the

(19) Presentative particle: Ps. 139.8 הִנֶּֽךָּ (as opposed to contextual הִנְּךָ)

Almost all cases with *dagesh* have in common that they are pausal forms.[37] To be clear, again, not all pausal forms feature the *dagesh*. Thus, as said, the process of reanalysis—the details of which still elude me—might simply have been incomplete when the recitation tradition became part of the written tradition.

## 4.0. Internal Inconsistencies and Pausal Forms

Slightly more complex, and no less interesting, are cases where the inconsistency in vocalisation pattern alone might hint at some developments, without any help from the consonantal framework.

---

[34] For Isa. 49.7, manuscript Eb 10 notes *raphe* pronunciation.

[35] Additionally, Deut. 4.6 and Job 33.32.

[36] See further Deut. 8.5, 12.28, and Job 5.1.

[37] One exception is Ps. 81.8 which carries a conjunctive accent. However, the verse might easily be a case where the accents and the vocalisation reflect different syntactic analyses.

Standard grammars and textbooks usually tell us that stative verbs follow a different pattern from fientive verbs, e.g., כב"ד vs. כת"ב, with /a/ imperfect instead of the typical /o/. The inconvenient truth is that stative verbs suffer from paradigm pressure of the fientive verbs, and they are sometimes vocalised with /o/ as the thematic vowel in the imperfect as well. Other stative verbs follow the fientive pattern in the suffix conjugation. Obviously, due to vowel reduction most of the forms do not evince any difference at all, which might have raised the paradigm pressure even more.

A case in point is the root חפ"ץ. It could be a prime example of a stative verb, yet the prefix conjugation has /o/ as the thematic vowel, and Sirach already shows forms with respective *plene* spelling. Interestingly, however, the pausal forms of the verb show *qameṣ* instead. Obviously, *qameṣ* does not result from pausal lengthening of /o/, but of /a/, *pataḥ*. Thus, indirectly, the pausal forms preserve the old stative /a/-imperfect, whereas the context forms attest the shift to the fientive /o/-imperfect.

Potentially, a similar case can be found with the root שמ"מ. The forms of the prefix conjugation of this geminate root generally follow the fientive pattern, like Ps. 40.16 יִשֹּׁמּוּ. And yet the pausal form תֵּשַׁם in Gen. 47.19 reflects the stative pattern. Admittedly, this root is a complicated case, since there might be a (secondary?) semantic distinction between 'lay desolate' (Ps. 40.16) and 'to be appalled' (Gen. 47.19).

The case of קר"ב is the reverse. The prefix conjugation forms and imperatives feature /a/ as the thematic vowel like any other good stative verb. The suffix conjugation, on the other hand, is usually vocalised as fientive verb, with *paṭaḥ*. i.e., the third masculine singular reads קָרַב, not קָרֵב, which is reserved for the participle. Unfortunately, there is only one relevant pausal form,[38] which is Zeph. 3.2 קָרֵבָה with *ṣere*. It seems the pausal form preserved the older linguistic state of affairs with a separate paradigm for stative verbs, while the contextual forms were apparently more susceptible to linguistic change and paradigm pressure from the fientive verbs.

In other words, I would argue that the notation of the vowels offers us a rare glimpse into performative aspects of reading. The vowels record not only the grammatical structure but indirectly also aspects of prosody. That is a very different understanding of recording vowels in the alphabetic writing systems I am familiar with, where the written form of a word does not change according to its position in the sentence.[39] This observation is not radically new, of course, but it should affect our descriptive grammatical categories more than hitherto.

---

[38] Deut. 2.37 קָרַבְתָּ is not pertinent.

[39] Elision of vowels marked by an apostrophe as in English 'don't', French 'c'était', German 'ist's', or Italian 'un'altra' might be comparable to some extent, insofar as these contractions can depend on the position within a sentence. However, I am not aware of any reflection of a change in vowel quality due to prosody.

## 5.0. Prosodic Elements in the Consonantal Spelling?

So far, we have looked at pausal forms where prosody changes the vowel quality, which are only visible thanks to the vocalisation. There is no indication in the consonantal framework. In other instances, pausal forms attest a different stress pattern, e.g., the long *yiqtol* forms and imperatives with vocalic endings. Thus, they preserve the thematic vowel otherwise reduced to *shewa*. If the thematic vowel is an /o/, the consonantal framework may here and there reflect the pausal form as well thanks to *plene* spelling. However, this is a very rare phenomenon in MT. One of the few instances is the *ketiv* מלוכה in Judg. 9.8 as against the *qere* מְלְכָה. Such spellings are much more common in the typical Qumran spelling practice, and there not just in pause. The Dead Sea Scrolls preserve a pre-Masoretic state of affairs where the vowel reduction in these cases has not yet taken place. Put differently: the *defective* spelling of (proto-)MT made it possible to read one and the same form as either a contextual or as pausal form. Consequently, the post-Qumranic stress shift to the ultima and the corresponding vowel reduction that happened in the (Tiberian)[40] reading tradition could be applied to the consonantal framework without leaving any visible traces. The few cases like Ps. 26.2 or Judg. 9.8 could be sufficiently dealt with by *qere* notes.

Naturally, the question remains whether there were pausal forms that also affected the consonants and which therefore left

---

[40] Notably, the Babylonian vocalisation partially preserves the older stress patterns, see Khan (2013) or Heijmans (2016).

traces in the earlier tradition. It seems to me that exceptional non-assimilation of the initial ה of the third-person masculine singular suffixes or the occasional non-assimilation of *energic nun* to a following consonant may hint at such early reflections of prosody. The few potential examples for the latter are:

(20) Exod. 15.2 וַאֲרֹמְמֶנְהוּ, Jer. 22.24 אֶתְּקֶנְךָּ, Ps. 72.15 יְבָרֲכֶנְהוּ, or Job 4.12 מֶנְהוּ

While these are all pausal forms, most pausal forms simply show the regular assimilation.[41] The data corpus is too small to get a clear view of the trajectory. If non-assimilation was once a more common feature of the language, next to nothing survived in MT. It is telling, though, that of the two relevant forms with *energic nun* in the epigraphic record only one shows assimilation.[42]

Non-assimilation of the initial ה of the third-person masculine[43] singular suffixes to a preceding ת is slightly more common, though still not abundantly attested. Of the 28 examples in sum,

---

[41] Non-pausal forms include Deut. 32.10 יְסֹבְבֶנְהוּ and יִצְּרֶנְהוּ. It might be that the non-assimilation here preserves an archaic phenomenon within the poetic register.

[42] See the imperative ושלחנו in Arad 4 l. 2 and the long *yiqtol* אתננהו in Lachish 3 l. 12, and cf. Bloch (2017, 94–6) for a thorough discussion of the difficult form in Lachish 3.

[43] There are also five cases with the third-person feminine suffix: 1 Sam. 1.6; Isa 34.7; Jer. 49.24; Ezek. 14.15; and Ruth 3.6. All but Ezek. 14.15 וְשִׁכְּלָתָה are in context, and they all show assimilation. That, however, is a matter of the vocalisation, the unassimilated counterpart would have been *וְשִׁכְלָתֶהָ and thus have shown the same consonantal framework.

eleven cases of assimilation are attested in context[44] and fourteen cases of non-assimilation are attested in pause,[45] for example:

(21) Zech. 5.4 וְכִלַּ֫תּוּ vs. 2 Chron. 22.11 הֱמִיתָ֫תְהוּ

Only three cases do not fit the proposed pattern.[46] Whether these are statistically significant enough to disprove the attempt or can still count as minor anomalies is difficult to decide. I prefer the latter interpretation. But in any case, we see at best remnants of an older system which record a distinct, non-assimilating pronunciation as a prosodic feature.[47]

## 6.0. Summary

My main interest has been the relationship between the consonantal framework and the vocalisation traditions, mainly the Tiberian vocalisation. The two represent different developmental phases of the Hebrew language, very conservative features of the

---

[44] 1 Sam. 1.24, 16.14; Zech. 5.4; Prov. 7.21, 31.1; Job 20.9, 21.18, 27.20, 28.7, 33.20; Ruth 4.15.

[45] Gen 37.20, 33; Judg. 9.54, 14.17, 20.42; 1 Sam. 18.28; Isa. 59.16; Jer. 50.43; Ezek. 19.5, 12, 24.7, 31.4; Ps. 105.19; 2 Chron. 22.11. I count Judg. 14.17 הֱצִילַ֫תְהוּ and Jer. 50.43 הֶחֱזִיקַ֫תְהוּ as (minor) pausal forms.

[46] Ezek. 15.5 אֲכָלָ֫תְהוּ and Prov. 31.12 גְּמָלַ֫תְהוּ are not in pause and would thus be expected to show assimilation. Ezek. 24.7 שְׁפָכַ֫תְהוּ is also not in pause but may have been influenced by the spelling of the immediately preceding שָׂמָ֫תְהוּ in the same verse.

[47] There are a few related features like the preservation of the ל״י/ו in pause which I plan to tackle in a different contribution.

Tiberian tradition notwithstanding. While some of these developments affect morphology and morphosyntax in general, others specifically reflect features of prosody insofar as the morphology is affected. The latter category is especially important for me since prosody is often poorly reflected in traditional grammars, even though it shows most clearly the vitality of the transmission of tradition. My plea is that grammars, lexicons, and textbooks should treat prosody much more prominently.

All in all, the Jewish vocalisation traditions closely follow the consonantal framework, even though some of the readings need to bend the spelling norms slightly. However, the generally conservative orthography of MT leaves room for ambiguity and thus sometimes linguistic updating of the written form of the language. We can compare this to the typical Qumran scribal practice, where progressive and extensive use of vowel letters often helps to disambiguate and—as I hypothesise—also aims to preserve linguistic features that were on the verge of disappearing from the Hebrew language.[48] Most important for the context of this volume and a somewhat surprising discovery for me is the possibility that elements of prosody may, in some cases, have already been embedded in the consonantal framework.[49]

---

[48] These preliminary chronological observations dovetail nicely with the much more detailed observations on the vocalisation tradition(s) of Biblical Aramaic in Suchard (2019; 2021).

[49] Geoffrey Khan kindly referred me to the use of resumption pronouns to express pause as a related phenomenon (see Khan 1988, 84, 92).

## References

Ariel, Chanan. 2024. 'Changes in Biblical Orthography Reflecting the Development of the Language. The Verbal Tense System vs. the Verbal Stem System'. *Vetus Testamentum* 74 (4–5): 465–85.

Ariel, Chanan, and Alexey (Eliyahu) Yuditsky. 2015/16 (5776). ['יברך: עדות על תצורת הפועל בימי הבית הראשון ['ברך: Morphological Evidence for a First Temple Hebrew Verb']. *Lěšonénu* 78 (3): 239–46.

Barr, James. 1988. 'Review of *Spelling in the Hebrew Bible*, by Francis I. Andersen and Dean A. Forbes.' *Journal of Semitic Studies* 33 (1): 122–31.

Barth, Jakob. 1894. *Die Nominalbildung in den semitischen Sprachen*, 2nd edition. Leipzig: J. C. Hinrichs.

Bauer, Hans, and Pontus Leander. 1922. *Historische Grammatik der Hebräischen Sprache des Alten Testaments*. Halle: Max Niemeyer.

Bloch, Yigal. 2007. 'From Linguistics to Text-Criticism and Back: *Wayyiqṭōl* Constructions with Long Prefixed Verbal Forms in Biblical Hebrew'. *Hebrew Studies* 48: 141–70.

———. 2017. 'Aramaic Influence and Inner Diachronic Development in Hebrew Inscriptions of the Iron Age'. In *Advances in Biblical Hebrew Linguistics. Data, Methods, and Analyses*, edited by Adina Moshavi and Tania Notarius, 83–112. Linguistic Studies in Ancient West Semitic 12. Winona Lake: Eisenbrauns.

Blum, Erhard. 2008. 'Das althebräische Verbalsystem – eine synchrone Analyse'. In *Sprachliche Tiefe – Theologische Weite*, edited by Oliver Dyma and Andreas Michel, 91–142. Biblisch-Theologische Studien 91. Neukirchen-Vluyn: Neukirchener.

Fassberg, Steven E. 2001. 'The Movement from *Qal* to *Pi"el* in Hebrew and the Disappearance of the *Qal* Internal Passive'. *Hebrew Studies* 42: 243–55.

———. 2011. 'The Shift from *Qal* to *Piel* in the Book of Qoheleth'. In Ἐν πάσῃ γραμματικῇ καὶ σοφίᾳ: *Saggi di linguistica ebraica in onore di Alviero Niccacci, OFM*, edited by Gregor Geiger, 123–27. Analecta 78. Jerusalem: Terra Santa.

———. 2014. נִטְעֵי אִילָן ?מעבר מבניין פְּעַל לבניין פִּעֵל בארמית המקרא In: מחקרים בלשון העברית ובאחיותיה מוגשים לאילן אלדר [*Niṭʻe Ilan. Studies in Hebrew and Related Fields Presented to Ilan Eldar*], edited by Moshe Bar-Asher and Irit Meir, 153–57. Jerusalem: Carmel.

Gzella, Holger. 2007. 'Unusual Verbal Forms in the Book of Proverbs and Semantic Disambiguation'. In *Studies in Hebrew Literature and Jewish Culture, presented to Albert van der Heide on the Occasion of his Sixty-Fifth Birthday*, edited by Martin F. J. Baasten and Reinier Munk, 151–68. Amsterdam Studies in Jewish Thought 12. Dordrecht: Springer.

———. 2016. 'Die Ausbildung suppletiver Verbalparadigmen im Aramäischen und Hebräischen'. In *Nächstenliebe und Gottesfurcht. Beiträge aus alttestamentlicher, semitistischer und altorientalistischer Wissenschaft für Hans-Peter Mathys zum 65. Geburtstag*, edited by Hanna Jenni and Markus Saur, 115–27. Alter Orient und Altes Testament 439. Münster: Ugarit.

Heijmans, Shai. 2016. 'Babylonian Tradition'. In *A Handbook of Biblical Hebrew*, edited by W. Randall Garr and Steven E. Fassberg, 133–45. Winona Lake: Eisenbrauns.

Hornkohl, Aaron D. 2023. *The Historical Depth of the Tiberian Reading Tradition of Biblical Hebrew*. Semitic Languages and Cultures 17. Cambridge: Open Book.

———. 2024. *Diachronic Diversity in Classical Biblical Hebrew*. Semitic Languages and Cultures 29. Cambridge: Open Book.

Khan, Geoffrey. 1988. *Studies in Semitic Syntax*. London Oriental Series 38. Oxford: Oxford University Press.

———. 2013. 'Vocalization, Babylonian'. In *Encyclopedia of Hebrew Language and Linguistics*, edited by Geoffrey Khan et al., III:953–63. Leiden: Brill.

———. 2018. 'Orthoepy in the Tiberian Reading Tradition of the Hebrew Bible and Its Historical Roots in the Second Temple Period'. *Vetus Testamentum* 68 (3): 378–401.

Lambert, Mayer. 1903. 'De l'emploi des suffixes pronominaux avec *noun* et sans *noun* au futur et a l'impératif'. *Revue des Études Juives* 46 (92): 178–83.

Lauber, Stephan. 2016. 'Die Kurzform der Präfixkonjugation in der Ijob-Dichtung. Beobachtungen zu Verwendung und Reichweite'. In *In Memoriam Wolfgang Richter*, edited by Hans Rechenmacher, 239–52. Arbeiten zu Text und Sprache im Alten Testament 100. St. Ottilien: EOS.

Maurizio, Isabella. 2023. *Le contexte linguistique et la tradition de langue hébraïque de la* Secunda *(Deuxième colonne des* Hexaples *d'Origène)*. PhD Dissertation, Università di Bologna.

Mor, Uri. 2015. 'The Verbal Noun of the Qal Stem in Rabbinic Hebrew Traditions and *Qĕṭēlâ/Qĕṭîlâ* Alternations'. Journal of Jewish Studies 66 (1): 79–96.

Qimron, Elisha. 2018. *A Grammar of the Hebrew of the Dead Sea Scrolls*. Jerusalem: Yad Yizhak Ben-Zvi.

Rendsburg, Gary. 1982. '*Laqṭîl* Infinitives: *Yiphʻil* or *Hiphʻil?*' Orientalia 51 (2): 231–38.

Sæbø, Magne (ed.). 2008. *Hebrew Bible/Old Testament, vol. 2. From the Renaissance to the Enlightenment.* Göttingen: Vandenhoeck & Ruprecht.

Samet, Nili. 2021. 'The Morphology of the Biblical Root *ḥ-b-q*: A Diachronic Analysis'. *Journal of the American Oriental Society* 141 (3): 661–67.

Samuel, Harald. Forthcoming. *Linguistic Dating: Fallstudien zu einer umstrittenen Methode.* (Habilitationsschrift, George-August-Universität Göttingen. 2019.) Beihefte zur Zeitschrift für die alttestamentliche Wissenschaft. Berlin: De Gruyter.

Schnedermann, Georg Hermann. 1879. *Die Controverse des Ludovicus Cappellus mit den Buxtorfen. Über das Alter der hebräischen Punctation. Ein Beitrag zu der Geschichte des Studiums der hebräischen Sprache.* Leipzig: Hinrichs.

Schorch, Stefan. 2004. *Die Vokale des Gesetzes. Die samaritanische Lesetradition als Textzeugin der Tora 1. Das Buch Genesis.* Beihefte zur Zeitschrift für die alttestamentliche Wissenschaft 339. Berlin: Walter de Gruyter.

Sharvit, Shimon. 2004. מסכת אבות לדורותיה: מהדורה מדעית, מבואות, נספחים [*Tractate Avoth Through The Ages. A Critical Edition, Prolegomena and Appendices*]. Jerusalem: Bialik Institute.

Suchard, Benjamin D. 2019. 'Sound Changes in the (Pre-)Masoretic Reading Tradition and the Original Pronunciation of Biblical Aramaic'. *Studia Orientalia Electronica* 7: 52–65.

———. 2021. 'The Origins of the Biblical Aramaic Reading Tradition'. *Vetus Testamentum* 71 (1): 105–19.

Yuditsky, Alexey (Eliyahu). 2017. דקדוק העברית של תעתיקי אוריגנס [*A Grammar of the Hebrew of Origen's Transcriptions*]. Texts and Studies, New Series 16. Jerusalem: The Academy of the Hebrew Language.

Zurawel, Talma. 1984. נטישת בניין קל בעברית נוסח שומרון: לבירורה של סוגייה בדקדוק ההסטורי של העברית [The *Qal* Conjugation in Samaritan Hebrew]. *Massorot* 1: 135–51.

# LAYOUT AND MEANING: STICHOGRAPHY IN HEBREW MANUSCRIPTS; THE CASE OF PSALM 83 IN MAS 1E AND THE HEBREW MANUSCRIPTS OF BEN SIRA

*Frédérique Michèle Rey, Sophie Robert-Hayek and Davide D'Amico*

---

The layout of a manuscript—such as the use of margins, columns, spacing, marginal notes, and decorative elements—actively shapes the reader's reading experience and interpretation of the content in front of them, for the act of understanding cannot be dissociated from the visual effect created by the manuscript's physical characteristics. From this perspective, manuscripts are not just conveyors of words but dynamic, multi-layered objects where form and meaning are deeply interwoven.

As we will show in this paper, using as case studies Ps. 83 in Mas 1e and the nine Ben Sira Hebrew manuscripts—from the first century BCE to the medieval period—part of the transmission of the text, and consequently its interpretation, heavily relies on the arrangement of the text itself, as much as its content. Because scribes can be considered as both readers and writers, they engage with the text on the basis of their own interpretation and choose in consequence the layout for the copied manuscript, which in turn impacts the reader of the manuscript.

Based on our two case studies, we aim to demonstrate that even if no Hebrew letter changes from one manuscript to another, the layout of the text on the page has a radical impact on its meaning and the way it is read. From this perspective, each particular arrangement of the text produces a new text, even if the letters have not changed at all. To illustrate our point, we will focus on the question of the stichographic[1] or non-stichographic layout of manuscripts. We aim to show how this layout of the text on the page implies a process of interpretation and a specific poetic effect, both at the level of the composition of the text on the page by the scribes, and at the level of the readers who perceive the text through this layout.

The paper is organised as follows: (1) In the first part, an overview will be given of the state of research on stichography in Hebrew manuscripts. (2) The example of Ps. 83 in Mas 1e, our first case study, will be used to show how this arrangement has a fundamental impact on the poetic interpretation of the text. (3) Our second case study, the Hebrew witnesses of Ben Sira, will present the implications of stichography organisation of the textual material. Finally, (4) we will draw some conclusions from the observations we have been able to make.

---

[1] We borrow the term 'stichography' from James L. Kugel, which distinguishes it from the more common 'stichometry'. The former focuses on the material representation of the text, the latter on a notion of meter, which is poorly suited to Hebrew poetry (Kugel 1981, 119).

## 1.0. Materiality, Text Perception and Textual Transmission: Stichographic Presentation and Understanding

In terms of critical editions (or modern translation), the way the text is represented on the page is a fundamental choice on the part of the editor. In the case of poetry, for example, representing a text in verse can be strongly biased by our own conception of what poetry should be (Placial and Rey, forthcoming).

Neither a Lachmanian eclectic edition nor a Bédierist single-manuscript edition is adequate to account for the singularity and variance of page layouts in manuscript traditions. In this study, we would like to take a position that considers each manuscript in its individuality, but also as iterations of a work in constant flux. Variance can only be fully understood in terms of the relationship between manuscripts. In this respect, the *stemma codicum* of manuscripts, when it can be traced, is no longer intended as a means of reconstructing the archetype of the entire manuscript tradition, but as a way of understanding the successive transformations of texts in the course of their transmission, by studying their variance over time, whether textual or material (Rey et al. forthcoming).[2]

One of the traits manuscripts bear in this ever-evolving tradition is the layout of the text on the page, which reflects not only the scribe who composed it but also the way the text is or could have been read. In this respect, Ben Sira's manuscripts are exemplary. Each manuscript has specific characteristics. For

---

[2] For more detail on such a position in studies of medieval literature: Altschul (2006); Leonardi (2014); and Leonardi et al. (2022).

example, while Manuscript C is presented as an anthology of Ben Sira's book, representing a specific selection and order of sentences, Manuscript B is characterised by its numerous marginal notes, which are the result of the collation of at least one other manuscript, as is clearly indicated by the last marginal note written in Persian. This presentation of the text testifies to the desire to preserve different textual traditions on the same manuscript without merging them. In fact, the presence of numerous doublets, the result either of the conflation of different textual traditions or of literary creativity, reflects the desire to accumulate variance in the text itself.

Out of all these different characteristics, we would like to focus our attention on the stichographic representation of texts. The topic has been extensively studied by scholars in relation to the Dead Sea Scrolls. Different forms of text segmentation can be observed on the manuscripts, and Emanuel Tov is credited with the first attempt at a typology. Tov's initial studies have been extended by a number of analyses focusing on more specific points (cf. Tov 2004, 156–67; 2008, 409–20). Kipp Davis addressed the question of 'Psalms scrolls' structured into a narrow columnar format (Davis 2017). Anna Krauß and Friederike Schücking-Jungblut are particularly interested in the layout of Psalms manuscripts. They conclude that the stichographic arrangement is chosen to emphasise the linguistic structure of a text (Krauß and Schücking-Jungblut 2020). The most extensive study on the subject is certainly the monograph by Shem Miller, who is particularly interested in the literary function of stichography and its close relationship with orality (Miller 2019; cf. Miller 2015 and 2017).

To these studies specifically dedicated to the Dead Sea Scrolls, we must add studies on Hebrew poetry, and in particular James Kugel's seminal work, *The Idea of Biblical Poetry: Parallelism and its History,* which devotes several dense pages to the subject. For Kugel, the practice of stichography is closely linked to the representation of parallel structures (*parallelismus membrorum*), but also to a desire to set certain texts apart for aesthetic reasons (Kugel 1981, 119–27; cf. Dobbs-Allsopp 2015).[3]

In the case of the nine manuscripts of Ben Sira, with the exception of the manuscript with the rhyming paraphrases (see Rey and Reymond 2024), only the typology of two stichs per line separated into two columns is attested.[4] We will therefore only focus on this model. By placing two stichs per line, the scribe imposes a way of reading the text as a combination of two pairs that make sense in a coordinated manner, at least visually.

## 2.0. Psalm 83 in Mas 1e

Our first case study consists of the discussion of a Masada manuscript of the Psalter. Mas 1e is presented in two columns, with one stich per column. In the case of Ps. 83, the scribe places the 'title' of the psalm, שיר מזמור לאסף, in the right-hand column and verse 1a in the left-hand column of the first line. As a result, the combination of the psalm's sentences differs from that indicated

---

[3] For a discussion of the complex relationship between stichography and the definition of Hebrew poetry see Placial and Rey (forthcoming).

[4] In rabbinic literature, this model is designed as "small brick over small brick, large over large," see b. Meg. 16b and y. Meg. 3.7, and Kugel (1981, 121).

by the Masoretic punctuation (see figure 2 for a translation of the text as it appears in Mas 1e compared to the Masoretic Tradition [MT]).

Figure 1: Mas 1e.[5]

---

[5] Photo by Shai Halevi. Courtesy of the Israel Antiquities Authority.

## Figure 2: Comparison of Ps. 83 in Mas 1e and in MT

**Psa 83 (Mas 1e, transl. NRSV slightly modified)**

1 A Song. A Psalm of Asaph.
2 O God, do not keep silence.

  Do not hold your peace or be still, O God,
3 because now your enemies are in tumult.

  And those who hate you have raised their heads,
4 against your people, they lay crafty plans.

  And they consult together against those you protect,
5 they say, "Come, let us wipe them out as a nation,

  And Let the name of Israel be remembered no more;"
6 because they conspire with one accord;

  Against you they make a covenant,
7 the tents of Edom and the Ishmaelites,

  Moab and the Hagrites,
8 Gebal, Ammon and Amalek,

  Philistia with the inhabitants of Tyre,
9 also Assyria has joined them.

  They are the strong arm of the children of Lot. Selah
10 Do to them as to Midia, as to Sisera

  As Jabin at the Wadi Kishon,
11 who were destroyed at En-dor.

  They became dung for the ground,
12 Make their nobles as Oreb and as Zeeb.

  And as Zebah and as Zalmunna, all their princes
13 who said, "Let us take for us

  the pastures of God.
14 God, make them like whirling,

  Like chaff before the wind
15 Like fire consumes the forest.

  And as the flame sets the mountains ablaze,
16 so pursue them with your tempest.

  And with your hurricane terrify them,
17 Fill their faces with shame.

**Psa 83 (TM, transl. NRSV slightly modified)**

1 A Song. A Psalm of Asaph.

2 O God, do not keep silence,
  do not hold your peace or be still, O God.

3 Because now your enemies are in tumult,
  and those who hate you have raised their heads.

4 Against your people, they lay crafty plans,
  and they consult together against those you protect.

5 They say, "Come, let us wipe them out as a nation,
  and Let the name of Israel be remembered no more."

6 Because they conspire with one accord,
  against you they make a covenant.

7 The tents of Edom and the Ishmaelites,
  Moab and the Hagrites,

8 Gebal and Ammon and Amalek,
  Philistia with the inhabitants of Tyre.

9 Also Assyria has joined them,
  they are the strong arm of the children of Lot. Selah

10 Do to them as to Midia,
  as to Sisera, as Jabin at the Wadi Kishon.

11 Who were destroyed at En-dor,
  They became dung for the ground.

12 Make their nobles as Oreb and as Zeeb,
  and as Zebah and as Zalmunna, all their princes.

13 Who said, "Let us take for us
  the pastures of God.

14 God, make them like whirling
  like chaff before the wind.

15 Like fire consumes the forest,
  and as the flame sets the mountains ablaze.

16 So pursue them with your tempest,
  and with your hurricane terrify them.

17 Fill their faces with shame...

In other psalms, the scribe places the title in the middle of the column, independent of the rest of the psalms, as in Ps. 82 (מזמר לאסף, figure 1, line 3). This demonstrates that the position of the title of Ps. 83 in the first column is a deliberate choice by the scribe to organise this psalm in this very specific way. The same phenomenon of what we may call a 'cyclic permutation' appears when, according to the Masoretic punctuation tradition, the poem includes a tristich. Indeed, the two stichs per line layout does not allow the construction in tristich, unless leaving a *vacat* after the third stich. Otherwise, it will cause a shift in the overall composition, making the third stitch the first of the next pair, and so on.

Talmon (1996, 307) notes that "MasPs[a] preserves the two half-columns structure throughout, altogether disregarding the resulting loss of content parallelism of the stichs in a line." Similarly, Krauß and Schücking-Jungblut (2020, 19) emphasise the aesthetic value of presentation at the expense of parallelistic structure. They remark:

> Mas 1e is arranged… in columns with two separated stichs per line. Even when a tristichon occurs, the scribe does not deviate from this strategy. Thus, not every verse begins in a new line but rather shares a line with another verse after every second verse with three stichs. This strict arrangement of columns with two stichs per line does still structure the text in smaller sense units but the larger units–that is: verses–are not visualized through this kind of arrangement.

Krauß, Schücking-Jungblut, Talmon and Kugel suggest that Mas 1e does not respect in its layout the correct organisation of the distichs imposed by *parallelism membrorum* or by verses. However, in agreement with Shem Miller (2019, 130–32), it is possible to regard the text thus arranged as imposing a legitimate semantic organisation, albeit one different from that later preserved by the Masoretic punctuation tradition. Moreover, whether the initial intention was purely aesthetic or not, the effect on the reader is similar: the units of meaning are guided by the layout of the text and not by an *a priori* idea of the correct order or of what ancient Hebrew poetry should be. Presented in this way, the text makes perfect sense and highlights poetic constructions different from those retained by the Masoretic tradition.

It is beyond the scope of this article to present the poetic structure of Mas 1e. A brief presentation of the first verses will suffice to capture the idea.

Table 1: Paralleling Ps. 83.1–4 between Mas 1e and MT

|  | Mas 1e | MT |  |
|---|---|---|---|
| 1. |  | שִׁיר מִזְמוֹר לְאָסָף: |  |
|  | שיר מזמור לאסף |  |  |
| 2. |  | אֱלֹהִים אַל־דֳּמִי־לָךְ |  |
|  | אלהים אל דמי לך | אַל־תֶּחֱרַשׁ וְאַל־תִּשְׁקֹט אֵל: |  |
|  | אל תחרש ואל תשקט אל |  |  |
| 3. |  | כִּי־הִנֵּה אוֹיְבֶיךָ יֶהֱמָיוּן |  |
|  | כיא הנה אויבך יהמיון | וּמְשַׂנְאֶיךָ נָשְׂאוּ רֹאשׁ: |  |
|  | ומשנאיך נשאו ראש |  |  |
| 4. |  | עַל־עַמְּךָ יַעֲרִימוּ סוֹד |  |
|  | על עמך [יע]ר[ימו ס]וד | וְיִתְיָעֲצוּ עַל־צְפוּנֶיךָ: |  |

- In the verse 2 of MT, the text is constructed as a synonymous parallelism. Each stich has a double vetitive (אל) with God as subject and a verb evoking the silence.

- In the text of Mas 1e, stich 2b is associated with 3a building an antithesis between God's peace and silence *versus* the tumult of the enemies. The conjunction כי marks the articulation of the two pairs as often in Hebrew poetry, v. 3a being indeed the causal proposition of 2b: why God must not be still? Because enemies are in tumult. This is perfectly coherent from a syntactic and stylistic point of view.
- In the verse 3 of MT, the two stichs are built in synonymous parallelism: 'your enemies' (אויביך) // 'those who hate you' (ומשנאיך) and 'are in tumult' (יהמיון) // 'raised their hands' (נשאו ראש).
- In the Masada organisation, the second pair is also perfectly coherent: first, 'those who hate you' (ומשנאיך) is the subject of the verbs of the two stichs in semantic parallelism: they 'raised their head' (נשאו ראש) and they 'lay crafty plans' ([יע]ר[ימו ס]וד); second, the first expression of each stich is antithetic: 'those who hate you' (ומשנאיך) vs 'your people' (עמך).

In the absence of Masoretic punctuation and an anachronistic notion of verse, it is the two-column layout of the text combined with the syntax that imposes its rhythm and meaning. This simple observation invites us to rethink the organisation of texts, beyond the verse and the Masoretic organisation. For example, every time we are confronted with a 'tristich' in a poem, we can imagine that it is actually a distich (2 tristichs are also 3 distichs). What we think of as the third distich would actually be the first of the next pair, implying a cyclic permutation of all the following pairs according to Masoretic punctuation.

It goes without saying that these questions only arise when the scribe arranges the text in two columns with one stich per column; the question is wholly different with a text written in continuous script, as in 11QPsa, for example.

## 3.0. Stichography in the Ben Sira Manuscripts

Going back to Ben Sira Hebrew manuscripts, five are arranged in stichography (2Q18, Masada, B, B margin, E and F), while the other four arrange the text in continuous lines (11QPs[a], A, C, and D). These two forms of text presentation are attested in both medieval manuscripts and those from antiquity.[6] Since both layouts survive in different branches and at different stages of the stemma (Rey et al. forthcoming), we must assume that some scribes deliberately chose to change the presentation of the text in one direction or the other as they passed it down.

## 3.1. Stichography in 2Q18 and Masada

The most ancient examples of stichographic presentations of the text of Ben Sira are found in 2Q18 and the Masada manuscript. Stichographic layout—in the absence of any sort of punctuation—shows that, in the first century BCE, the scribes of Masada and 2Q18 considered the text of Ben Sira as a succession of sentences constructed as pairs. It prohibits all forms of tristichs unless textually indicated by a free empty half line. In the whole of the Masada manuscript this layout is attested only once, in Sir.

---

[6] 2Q18 and Masada date from the 1st century BCE, while 11QPs[a] dates from the early 1st century CE.

42.24. This sole example of blank stich on the manuscript is a good indication that the scribe made conscious choices regarding the layout of the text. Apart from this particular case, the text shows no exceptions, with every line from Sir. 39.27 to 44.17 regularly organised as a pair of stichs. Whatever the definition of Hebrew poetry or *mashal*, the text of Ben Sira is graphically presented, here, through two elements, A and B, connected to one another, at least graphically (Kugel 1981, 69; Vayntrub 2019, 57–59).

As manuscript 2Q18 is very fragmentary, it is difficult to draw any conclusions apart from the fact that its layout corresponds to the punctuation of the text preserved in Manuscript A.

### 3.2. Stichographic Layout of Manuscript B

We now turn our attention to the stichographic presentation of Manuscript B. With the exception of a few titles centred between the two columns of text, the scribe never deviates from the rule of two stichs per line. How, then, does the scribe proceed in the case of tristichs? The situation is relatively frequent, but at no time is there an isolated stitch in the manuscript presentation. In numerous cases, the scribe tightens letters' size to fit the three stichs onto a single line. This reveals that the scribes are clearly aware of the incongruity of the situation and the importance of not inserting a shift in the organisation of the text. A good example of this phenomenon is Sir. 37.1–2.

## 3.2.1. Sir. 37.1–2

Figure 3: Sir. 37.1 (Or. 5518.1 recto l. 6–10, courtesy to the British Library)

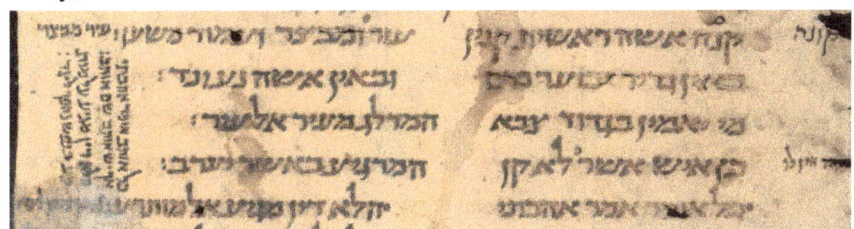

In Sir. 37.1, the main text of Manuscript B preserves three stichs written on one line:

כל אומר אמר אהבתי    הלא דין מגיע אל מות רע כנפשך נהפך לצר:

1. Everyone who speaks says, "I love."
2. Is it not a sadness approaching death—a companion like your very self who turns into an enemy?

However, the text is also preserved in the margin of Manuscript B in two distichs (as it is also the case for this verse in Manuscript C, the Greek and the Syriac):[7]

1. כל אוהב אומר אהבתי
   אך יש אוהב שם אוהב:
2. הלא דין מגיע על מות
   רע כנפש נהפך לצר:

1. Every friend says, "I love"
   but there is the friend (who is only) a friend in name.
2. Is it not a sadness approaching death—

---

[7] For the marginal readings of Manuscript B, see among others: Rey and Dhont (2019, 97–124).

a companion like your very self who turns into an enemy?

We can clearly see how the scribe of Manuscript B adapted their writing to keep the tristich on one line so as not to provoke a cyclic permutation of the next sentences. It also shows that the stichographic representation of Manuscript B was certainly reconstructed *a posteriori*, probably on the basis of a text that did not have a stichographic representation that allowed such freedom in textual organisation.

Numerous examples are found (Sir. 15.20; Sir. 31.16; Sir. 31.22; Sir. 31.31 [// MS F]; Sir. 32.1 [// MS F];[8] Sir. 32.4 [// MS F]; Sir. 37.2 [// MSS C and D]; Sir. 44.11–12; Sir. 45.26; Sir. 44.17). As is the case in the numerous tristichs in Manuscript A, they are always the place and result of complex textual transformations (see section 3.3).

These examples, directly perceptible in the materiality of the text, are visible traces of the text's development over time. In many cases, however, stich shifts and re-compositions of semantic pairs have been definitively incorporated into the body of the text, remain perceptible only by comparison with ancient Greek, Syriac and Latin versions, and explain the frequent discrepancies in verse numbering.

---

[8] Sir. 31.31 and 32.1 present the same tristich on a single line in Manuscript B and Manuscript F, although the two manuscripts do not belong to the same branch of the stemma. Nevertheless, the fragmentary state of Manuscript B for these verses does not allow us to draw any further conclusions.

## 3.2.2. Sir. 42.23–43.1

Consider, for example, the case of Sir. 42.23ff. Compared with the Masada text, manuscript B does not include (at least not at this location) verse 24, which is exceptionally arranged in three stichs in the Masada manuscript, the last stich being followed by a blank space. Nor does Manuscript B preserve the second stich of verse 23 (attested only in the margin), which is replaced with the first stich of Masada's verse 25, creating an obvious shift at the beginning of chapter 43. Indeed, Sir. 43.1a is now connected with 42.25b. Consequently, the following sentences are constructed in a totally different way from Masada's text.

**Masada (Sir. 42.23–43.1)**

| | | |
|---|---|---|
| [ו]כל צרך והכל נשמר | הכל חי ועמ[ד] לעד | 23. |
| [זה] לעמת זה | כלם שנ[ים] | 24. |
| vacat | ולא עשה מהם [שוא] | |
| [ו]מי ישבע להביט הודם | זה על זה חלף טובם | 25. |
| עצם שמים מֹ[בי]טֹ נֹהֹוֹרֹוֹ | תאר מרום ורקיע לטהר | 43.1a |

23. All live and endure forever;
    (their) every need—everything is provided for.
24. All of them, diff[erent]
    opposite
    he made none of them [in vain]
    vacat
25. This one to the next, their beauty is surpassing
    who could be sated at seeing their splendour?
 1. The beauty of the height(s) and of the firmament (is)
    pristine indeed;
    heaven itself em[it]s its shining.

## Manuscript B (Sir. 42.23–43.1)

וקים 23a/25a הוא ח[י ו]עמד לעד      זה על זה חלף טובו:
                                        (23b) לכל צרוך הכל נשמע:

25b/43.1a וימי ישב[ע] ל[ה]ב[י]ט הדם   תואר]      [לטוהַר:

23a. He is a[live and] remaining (margin: enduring) forever,

25a. This one to the next, his beauty is surpassing.
    (margin: *23b* For every need, all is considered.)

25b. And, who can get their fi[ll] at [se]eing their glory?

1a. Beauty[ ] (are) pristine.

This example clearly shows how the addition or omission of a stich causes a complete re-composition, not only of the verse in question, but of all the stichs that follow. As a result of this phenomenon, the new pairs of meanings are created.

## 3.3. Non-Stichography in Manuscript A: Creation of Tristichs and Shift of the Following Stichs

In the case of manuscript not written in stichography, like Manuscript A, one of the difficulties is the precise definition of 'stich'.[9] A good example of this imprecision is the case of Mas Sir. 42.24, mentioned previously, where the scribe lays out the text in three stichs, requiring the scribe to leave a blank space in the second

---

[9] We use *stich* as a synonym of *colon* and in the case of stichographic layout as the first and second part of the line divided by a white space. For terminology, see Dobbs-Allsopp (2015, 20–29).

column, where the Greek tradition—which agrees completely with the Hebrew—makes it a distich.[10]

### 3.3.1. Sir. 4.3–6

Among the many transformations witnessed in the Ben Sira manuscripts, one of the most obvious is the creation of doublets (Rey 2021). Let consider the case of Sir. 4.3-4, found only in Manuscript A which is written in non-stichography, but whose textual units are delimited by *sof passuq*. In comparison with the Greek and Syriac version, Manuscript A has a supplementary stich that seems to be the result of a collation of two textual traditions, one attested by the Greek, the other more or less by the Syriac. The insertion of this 'extra' stich by one scribe creates a shift in all the pairs of the following verses, creating a completely different poem with different poetical combination, exactly as in our example of Ps. 83 from Mas 1e. By contrast, the Greek has two additional stichs (4b and 5a) that are missing in the Hebrew and the Syriac. Consequently, the three versions present different combinations of pairs in verses 3–5, finally realigning from verse 6 onwards (marked by a small *vacat* in the Hebrew manuscript).

---

[10] It is clearly visible on Codex Vaticanus, for example, which lays out the text of Ben Sira in stichography (folio 882, ll. 20–22). For stichography in Greek Bible manuscripts, see Swete and Thackeray (1900, 348–50).

**Hebrew Text** (Greek numeration of verses in parenthesis)

3. אל תחמיר מעי דך
וקרב עני אל תכאיב:
4. אל תמנע מתן ממסכינך
ולא תבזה שאולות דל
5. לא תתן לו מקום לקללך:
6. vacat צועק מר רוח בכאב נפשו
ובקול צעקתו ישמע צורו:

    3. Do not inflame the emotions of the oppressed,
(>G, S) and do not pain the bosom of the poor.
    4. (3b) Do not refuse a gift to the destitute who is near you,
      (4a) and you should not despise the requests of the impoverished,
    5. (5b) so as not to give them occasion to curse you.
    6. *vacat* (When) one of bitter spirit cries out in the pain of their soul,
their rock hears the sound of their cry.[11]

**Greek Text** (Hebrew numeration of verses in parenthesis)

3. καρδίαν παρωργισμένην μὴ προσταράξῃς
καὶ μὴ παρελκύσῃς δόσιν προσδεομένου.
4. ἱκέτην θλιβόμενον μὴ ἀπαναίνου
καὶ μὴ ἀποστρέψῃς τὸ πρόσωπόν σου ἀπὸ πτωχοῦ.
5. ἀπὸ δεομένου μὴ ἀποστρέψῃς ὀφθαλμὸν
καὶ μὴ δῷς τόπον ἀνθρώπῳ καταράσασθαί σε·
6. καταρωμένου γάρ σε ἐν πικρίᾳ ψυχῆς αὐτοῦ
τῆς δεήσεως αὐτοῦ ἐπακούσεται ὁ ποιήσας αὐτόν.

---

[11] Translation Eric D. Reymond and Frédérique Michèle Rey.

3. An angry heart do not trouble,
4a. and do not delay giving to one in need.
4. (4b) A suppliant in distress do not keep rejecting,
(>H, S) and do not turn your face away from the poor.
5. (>H, S) From one who begs do not turn away an eye,
(5) and do not give him occasion to curse you.
6. For if one curses you in bitterness of his soul,
the one who made him will hear his petition.[12]

**Syriac Text**

3. ܡܥܘ̈ܗܝ ܕܐܢܫܐ ܡܣܟܢܐ ܠܐ ܬܟܐܒ.
ܘܠܐ ܬܟܠܐ ܡܘܗܒܬܐ ܡܢ ܨܪܝܟܐ.
4. ܒܥܘܬܗ ܕܡܣܟܢܐ ܠܐ ܬܫܒܘܩ.
5. ܘܠܐ ܬܬܠ ܠܗ ܐܬܪܐ ܕܠܠܛܟ·
6. ܠܐܛ ܗܘ ܒܪ ܡܪܝܪ ܢܦܫܐ
ܡܢ ܟܠܗ ܢܦܫܗ· ܘܩܠ ܒܥܘܬܗ ܫܡܥ ܒܪܘܝܗ.

3. Do not make the emotions of the poor man suffer
And do not withhold a gift from the needy
4. Do not ignore a request of the poor
5. and do not give him an occasion to curse you.
6. He curses because he is completely embittered
but his Creator hears the sound of his cry.[13]

If one of the two stichs of the verse 3 has been added secondarily—whatever the aetiology—we have to conclude that the scribe has taken an active part into the poetic construction of the text by creating a beautiful chiastic parallelism (verb – complement

---

[12] Translation Benjamin G. Wright, NETS.

[13] Translation Nuria Calduch Benages, Joan Ferrer, and Jan Liesen (modified).

*versus* complement – verb) full of biblical echoes.[14] The Hebrew is clearly structured by *'vav'* that articulate stich pairs and, later, by the addition of *sof passuq*. In the present context, the addition of one stich in verse 3 does not create a tristich in this verse. Rather, the scribe carries the shift over to the next verse, generating a new synonymous parallelism in vv. 4a and 4b where the two complements echo each other ('the destitute who is near you' [ממסכינך] // 'the requests of the impoverished' [שאולות דל]) as well as the two verbs ('Do not refuse' [אל תמנע] // 'you should not despise' [לא תבזה]). However, it seems clear that such a stich addition would only be possible in a non-stichographic layout.

## 3.3.2. Sir. 14.11–14

A second example can be found in Sir. 14.11–14. The scribe's punctuation and the insertion of a *vacat* in the middle of verse 13 (according to the Greek) suggest the following organisation, which is somewhat counterintuitive to Hebrew syntax:

**Hebrew Text**

| | | |
|---|---|---|
| ואם יש לך היטיב לך | בני אם יש לך שָׁרֵוֹת נפשך ולאל ידך הדשן: | 11. |
| ולא מות יתמהמה: | זכור כי לא בשאול תענוג | 12ab. |
| בטרם תמות היטב לאוהב: | וחוק לשאול לא הגד לך | 12c/13a. |
| vacat | | |
| אל תמנע מטובת יום· | והשיגת ידך תן לו | 13b/14a. |
| וחמוד רע אל תחמוד: | ובה לקח אח אל תעבר | 14bc. |

---

[14] מעה and קרב are connected in Lam. 1.20 (which also use the association of מעה and חמר, see also Lam. 2.11), Isa. 16.11 and Job 20.14; and for the link between דך and עני echoes Ps. 74.21.

11. My child, if you have the means, serve your soul
    if you have the means, do good to yourself
    and according to your abilities, satisfy yourself.
12. Remember that there is no pleasure in Sheol
    and that death does not delay.
13. before dying, do good to (your) friend. *vacat*
    And as much as you are able, give to them.
14. do not refuse the happiness of a day
    and do not neglect to bring a brother into it
    and do not desire what your companion desires.[15]

The text is full of doublets that are missing in the Greek and Syriac texts:

**Greek Text**

11. Τέκνον, καθὼς ἐὰν ἔχῃς, εὖ ποίει σεαυτὸν
    καὶ προσφορὰς κυρίῳ ἀξίως πρόσαγε·
12. μνήσθητι ὅτι θάνατος οὐ χρονιεῖ
    καὶ διαθήκη ᾅδου οὐχ ὑπεδείχθη σοι·
13. πρίν σε τελευτῆσαι εὖ ποίει φίλῳ
    καὶ κατὰ τὴν ἰσχύν σου ἔκτεινον καὶ δὸς αὐτῷ.
14. μὴ ἀφυστερήσῃς ἀπὸ ἀγαθῆς ἡμέρας,
    καὶ μερὶς ἐπιθυμίας ἀγαθῆς μή σε παρελθάτω.

11. Child, even as you have, treat yourself well,
    and bring offerings to the Lord worthily.
12. Remember that death will not tarry,
    and the covenant of Hades has not been shown to you.

---

[15] Translation Eric D. Reymond and Frédérique Michèle Rey.

13. Before you die, treat a friend well,
    and, according to your strength, reach out, and give to him.
14. Do not withdraw from a good day,
    and do not let a share of a good desire pass you by.[16]

**Syriac Text**

11. ܐܢ ܐܝܬ ܠܟ ܒܪܝ، ܫܡܫ ܢܦܫܟ.
ܘܐܢ ܐܝܬ ܠܟ ܐܛܐܒ ܠܟ
12. ܐܬܕܟܪ ܕܥܕܡܐ ܠܗܫܐ ܡܘܬܐ ܠܐ ܚܙܝܬ.
ܘܓܙܪܬ ܫܝܘܠ ܠܐ ܐܬܚܘܝܬ ܠܟ.
13. ܥܕ ܠܐ ܬܡܘܬ ܐܛܐܒ ܠܪܚܡܟ:
ܘܡܕܡ ܕܫܐܠ ܠܟ ܗܒ ܠܗ.
14. ܠܐ ܬܬܟܠܐ ܡܢ ܛܒܬܐ ܕܝܘܡܐ.
ܘܪܓܬܐ ܣܢܝܬܐ ܠܐ ܬܪܓ.

11. If you have (something), my son, attend to yourself
    and if you have (something), do well to yourself.
12. Remember that up till now you did not see death
    and the decree of Sheol was not visible for you.
13. Before you die, do good to your friend
    and what he asks of you, give (it) to him.
14. Do not refrain from the good which (you can do) today and do not covet an odious desire.[17]

Clearly, this passage underwent numerous transformations during its transmission. A scribe punctuates v. 11 as a tristich, which is unusual and not in concord with a stichographic layout. This verse is obviously the conflation of two textual traditions. Indeed,

[16] Translation Benjamin G. Wright, NETS.

[17] Translation Nuria Calduch Benages, Joan Ferrer, Jan Liesen.

the stichs 11ab are reflected with a variation of the word order in the Syriac translation (11ab: בְּנִי אִם יֶשׁ לְךָ שָׁרֵות נַפְשֶׁךָ וְאִם יֵשׁ לְךָ ܐܢ ܐܝܬ ܠܟ ܒܪܝ ܗܒ ܢܦܫܟ. ܘܐܢ ܐܝܬ ܠܟ ܐܛܐܒ ܠܢ versus היטיב לך), while the stichs 11bc are represented by the Greek version. The stich 11b בני... אם יש לך היטיב לך corresponds to Τέκνον, καθὼς ἐὰν ἔχῃς, εὖ ποίει σεαυτὸν also attested as such in b. ʿErub. 54a (בני אם יש לך היטב), whereas in stich 11c through Greek in reflected is [18]ולא καὶ... κυρίῳ, while הדשן is echoed in the term προσφοράς.

The first two stichs (12a and 12b) of the tristich 12a–c are also clearly the result of a conflation of various textual traditions. Both Greek and Syriac have only the distich 12b and 12c. The stich 12a (זכור כי לא בשאול תענוג) is a doublet of Sir. 14.16a (כי אין בשאול לבקש תענוג), but its place before 12bc is also attested in the citation of b. ʿErub. 54a, which organises verse 12 as two pairs of stichs.

The Steinsaltz edition provide the following text:

שאין בשאול תענוג
ואין למות התמהמה
ואם תאמר אניח לבני
חוק בשאול מי יגיד לך

MS Vat. ebr. 109, fol. 28v, l. 4 offers a slightly different text, but preserves the same order of stich:

כי אין בשאול תענוג למות התמהמה ואם תאמר אניח לבניי ולבנותיי חוק בשאול מי יגיד לך.

---

[18] The syntax of ולא ידך is slightly different from the classical usage—supposedly יש לאל יד, see Sir. 5.1 and Gen. 31.29—which may explain the Greek translator's confusion.

In Manuscript A, however, a scribe has placed a *sof passuq* at the end of stich 12b, punctuating the text in distich as required by a stichographic layout. As a result, 12a and 12b are joined, and the following stichs are offset from the Greek and Syriac versions. Stich 12c is then strangely joined to stich 13a. This organisation of the text is confirmed by the *vacat* that disconnects 13a from 13b. From verse 15 onwards, all the versions are realigned, since verse 14 also contains an additional stich. The latter, in the same way, is the result of the conflation of two textual traditions, one (v. 14b) more or less reflected by the Greek tradition[19] and the other (v. 14c) by the Syriac tradition (וחמוד רע אל תחמוד:) corresponds very exactly to ܘܠܐ ܬܚܡܘܕ ܠܐ ܪܚܡܟ). A beautiful example of the idea that two tristichs can also be two distichs.

Similar situations where Hebrew stich pairs are reorganised by the addition or omission of a clause that cannot be adapted to a stichographic presentation are not an isolated phenomenon.[20]

## 4.0. Conclusion

This article was dedicated to the analysis of the implications of the text layout on the page in stichography or non-stichography and the consequences of switching from one model to the other.

As the stichographic layout requires more paper or leather than a full-line text it is more expensive to produce. As a result,

---

[19] The Hebrew does not correspond exactly to the Greek but both versions can be explained in relation to each other, see for example the solution proposed by Lévi (1901, 104).

[20] See also Sir. 3.28; 4.17; 11.25; 12.11; 12.14; 13.2; 13.17; 14.11; 14.14; 15.14; 16.15.

it already conveys essential information to the reader about the importance of the copied text. The codicological quality of Manuscript B is close to that of the Masoretic biblical manuscripts, testifies to this in more ways than one. But beyond the obvious aesthetic function of presenting the text on the page, the stichographic layout closely associates two sentences, creating a specific syntactic, semantic and poetic link between them. This is not the case in a text written without stichography, especially in the absence of any punctuation, where each sentence can be understood through a variety of connections with the texts that precede or follow it, or through the constitution of larger units. The very definition of the theoretical notion of 'stich' for an unpunctuated text is in itself a complex, even problematic issue.

Moreover, on the basis of several examples, we were able to show that the layout of the text in two stichs per line creates a strong constraint for the poet: the impossibility of integrating a tristich without generating a cyclic permutation of all the following stichs. Of course, this constraint disappears as soon as the text is no longer presented in stichography. But although the stichographic model is attested in the oldest manuscripts, we have been able to show from both Manuscript B and Manuscript A that the scribes may have oscillated from one model to another during the transmission of the text. As a result, while difficult to introduce in a stichographic presentation, tristichs have appeared in the textual tradition generally by conflation of different textual traditions. The scribe of Manuscript B tries to accommodate them as best they can without disrupting the sequence of subsequent stichs. Conversely, in Manuscript A, certain syntactically counterintuitive punctuation marks seem to reflect a time when the text was presented as in stichography. While the scribe of Manuscript B—or the earlier scribe in the branch of Manuscript A—tries to avoid cyclic permutations, these later ones are clearly attested. They lead to a completely new syntactic, semantic and poetic composition without changing any letter of the transmitted text. Finally, like the transformation and evolution of the consonantal text or of its vocalisation traditions through its textual transmission, the layout of the text takes an entire part of its life, its meaning, and its poetical structure.

To conclude, the question of text layout also affects modern editions, which vary greatly in their representation of poetry (or what they consider as poetry) and the very Western idea that poetry should be presented in verse/stich. When Eric Reymond and Frédérique Michèle Rey designed the critical edition of the Hebrew Manuscripts of Ben Sira, they had a methodological dilemma that is indicative of this problem: should we present non-stichographic manuscript as they are preserved in the manuscript or in stichography like Masada and B? We opted for the second solution, precisely because of the effect it would have on the reader: enhancement of sentence pairs, ease of reading, ease of cross-referencing notes, ease of comparison with other manuscripts, and so on. But the other solution is still on our mind and we still have a touch of regret: how would a text of Ben Sira in continuous script affect the reader differently?

## References

Altschul, Nadia. 2006. 'The Genealogy of Scribal Versions: A Fourth Way in Medieval Editorial Theory'. *Textual Cultures: Text, Contexts, Interpretation* 1 (2): 114–36.

Davis, Kipp. 2017. 'Structure, Stichometry, and Standardization: An Analysis of Scribal Features in a Selection of the Dead Sea Psalms Scrolls'. In *Functions of Psalms and Prayers in the Late Second Temple Period*, edited by Mika S. Pajunen and Jeremy Penner, 153–84. Beihefte zur Zeitschrift für die alttestamentliche Wissenschaft 486. Berlin: De Gruyter.

Dobbs-Allsopp, F. W. 2015. *On Biblical Poetry*. New York: Oxford University Press.

Krauß, Anna H., and Friederike Schücking-Jungblut. 2020. 'Stichographic Layout in the Dead Sea Psalms Scrolls: Observations on Its Development and Its Potential'. In *From Scrolls to Scrolling: Sacred Texts, Materiality, and Dynamic Media Cultures*, edited by A. Anderson Bradford, 13–33. Judaism, Christianity, and Islam—Tension, Transmission, Transformation 12. Berlin: De Gruyter.

Kugel, James L. 1981. *The Idea of Biblical Poetry: Parallelism and Its History*. Baltimore: Johns Hopkins University Press.

Leonardi, Lino. 2014. 'Filologia Della Ricezione: I Copisti Come Attori Della Tradizione'. *Medioevo Romanzo* 38 (1).

Leonardi, Lino, Laura Minervini, and Eugenio Burgio. 2022. *Filologia Romanza: Critica Del Testo, Linguistica, Analisi Letteraria*. Prima edizione Mondadori Università. Firenze: Le Monnier Università.

Lévi, Israël. 1901. *L'Ecclésiastique, ou la Sagesse de Jésus, fils de Sira*. Bibliothèque de l'école des Hautes études. Sciences religieuses 10.2. Paris: E. Leroux.

Miller, Shem. 2015. 'The Oral-Written Textuality of Stichographic Poetry in the Dead Sea Scrolls'. *Dead Sea Discoveries* 22 (2): 162–88.

———. 2017. 'Multiformity of Stichographic Systems in the Dead Sea Scrolls'. *Revue de Qumrân* 29 (2): 219–45.

———. 2019. *Dead Sea Media: Orality, Textuality and Memory in the Scrolls from the Judean Desert*. Studies on the Texts of the Desert of Judah 129. Leiden: Brill.

Placial, Claire, and Frédérique Michèle Rey. Forthcoming. 'Trouble dans le genre (littéraire)—de la stichométrie au vers, qu'est-ce que la poésie biblique?' In *La traversée des textes: Mélanges offerts à Jean-Jacques Lavoie*, edited by Isabelle Lemelin, Anne Letourneau, and Olga Hazan. Turnhout: Brepols.

Rey, Frédérique Michèle. 2021. 'Doublets in the Hebrew Manuscript B of Sirach'. In *Sirach and Its Contexts: The Pursuit of Wisdom and Human Flourishing*, edited by Samuel L. Adams, Greg S. Goering, and Matthew J. Goff, 126–48. Supplements to the Journal for the Study of Judaism 196. Leiden: Brill.

Rey, Frédérique Michèle, and Marieke Dhont. 2019. 'Scribal Practices in Ben Sira Manuscript B'. In *Discovering, Deciphering and Dissenting: Ben Sira Manuscripts after 120 Years*, edited by James K. Aitken, Renate Egger-Wenzel, and Stefan C.

Reif, 97–124. Deuterocanonical and Cognate Literature Yearbook 2018. Berlin: De Gruyter.

Rey, Frédérique Michèle, and Eric Reymond. 2024. *A Critical Edition of the Hebrew Manuscripts of Ben Sira: With Translations and Philological Notes*. Supplements to the Journal for the Study of Judaism 217. Leiden: Brill.

Rey, Frédérique Michèle, Sophie Robert-Hayek, and Davide D'Amico. Forthcoming. 'Stemma Codicum: Urtext or Textual Variance. The Stemma of the Hebrew Manuscripts of Ben Sira as Test Case'. In *Urtext, Archetype, Fluidity or Textual Convergence*, edited by Frédérique Michèle Rey, Sophie Robert-Hayek, and Stefan Schorch. Leuven: Peeters.

Swete, Henry Barclay, and H. St J. (Henry St John) Thackeray. 1900. *An Introduction to the Old Testament in Greek*. Cambridge: Cambridge University Press.

Talmon, Shemaryahu. 1996. 'Fragments of a Psalms Scroll–MasPs$^a$ Ps 81:2b-85:6a (1039–160; Mas1e; Final Photo 5255)'. *Dead Sea Discoveries* 3 (3): 296–314.

Tov, Emanuel. 2004. *Scribal Practices and Approaches Reflected in the Texts Found in the Judean Desert*. Studies on the Texts of the Desert of Judah 54. Leiden: Brill.

———. 2011. 'The Background of the Stichometric Arrangements of Poetry in the Judean Desert Scrolls'. In *Prayer and Poetry in the Dead Sea Scrolls and Related Literature: Essays in Honor of Eileen Schuller on the Occasion of Her 65th Birthday*, edited by Jeremy Penner, Ken M. Penner, and Cecilia Wassen, 409–20. Studies on the Texts of the Desert of Judah 98. Leiden: Brill.

Vayntrub, Jacqueline. 2019. *Beyond Orality: Biblical Poetry on Its Own Terms*. The Ancient Word. London: Routledge.

# THE *VORLAGE* OF LXX EZEKIEL: ORTHOGRAPHIC FEATURES, PHONETIC CIRCUMSTANCES, AND READING PRACTICE

*Martin Tscheu*[*]

This paper explores the extent to which renderings found in LXX Ezekiel provide information about the materiality of their *Vorlage*, and whether these Greek readings are indicative of practices and techniques of reading Hebrew texts that were inherent to the translation process.

The first part of this study will present examples that allow conclusions to be drawn about the paleographic and orthographic features of the Hebrew *Vorlage(n)* of LXX Ezek. The second part considers examples of phonetically induced spellings in the *Vorlage*. The third and last part presents the reconstruction of

---

[*] Special thanks for their manyfold corrections and contributions go to the reviewers of this article, Johanna van der Schoor and Hector Patmore (Leuven). Stefan Schorch (Jerusalem), the supervisor of my doctoral dissertation at Martin-Luther-Universität Halle–Wittenberg, contributed significantly to the stringency of the text. My gratitude further extends to Bradley Marsh (Hurst, Texas) and Eibert Tigchelaar (Leuven) for their contributions and insightful critiques.

a specific reading technique of Hebrew consonantal frameworks that underlies the Greek translation in the Book of Ezekiel. The paper concludes by considering the implications of the results obtained for the homogeneity of LXX Ezek.

## 1.0. Paleography of the Hebrew *Vorlage* of LXX Ezekiel

### 1.1. Ezekiel 48.35

The very last words of the book read, according to the Masoretic Text (MT):[1] "And the name of the city from that time on shall be, The LORD Is There," whereas LXX according to NETS renders: "And the name of the city after whatever day it comes to be, shall be its name."

> MT: וְשֵׁם־הָעִיר מִיּוֹם יְהוָה שָׁמָּה׃
> LXX: καὶ τὸ ὄνομα τῆς πόλεως, ἀφ' ἧς ἂν ἡμέρας γένηται, ἔσται τὸ ὄνομα αὐτῆς.

The text of this subscript in the LXX seems to be enigmatic, but to express an enigma might actually be the aim of the Greek. The name of the city will only be revealed once the city and its temple 'comes to be' ἀφ' ἧς ἂν ἡμέρας γένηται, i.e., when the city and the temple will be restored, but the name of the city is declared an apocalyptic mystery. Of note, all manuscripts classified by Ziegler as pre-hexaplaric, i.e., *Codex Vaticanus* (B; 4th cent. CE), Papyrus 967 (P967; around 200 CE), the Old Latin palimpsest *Codex*

---

[1] The translations provided in the following are based on NRSV for MT and on NETS (New English Translation of the Septuagint) for LXX.

*Wirceburgensis* (La^W; 5th cent. CE) and, moreover, the main witnesses of the Antiochian text attest to the said formulation.² The rest of the Greek manuscripts included in the Göttingen edition contain the textual plus κυριος εκει, which parallels MT יְהוָה שָׁמָּה and appears to have been added to the older textual tradition and concurs with the hexaplaric witnesses.³

The most plausible explanation for the emergence of the Greek rendering is based on the assumption that the two letters ו and י in the translator's *Vorlage* were graphically similar or even indistinguishable. In addition, the translator could obviously not rely on a reading tradition of the book, nor on any paratextual knowledge of the book's subscript, since it would otherwise be incomprehensible that he rendered the Tetragrammaton in his *Vorlage* as a 3ms *yiqtol* form of the root הי״י, i.e., *יהיה instead of יהוה. Already Carl H. Cornill (1886, 544) posits a misreading on part of the translator in in this case instead of a *Vorlage* deviating from the consonantal framework found in MT:[4]

---

[2] Among the witnesses of the Antiochian text the pre-hexaplaric reading is preserved in the *Codex Venetus* (V; 8th cent. CE), Theodoret of Cyrus' commentary on the Book of Ezekiel (5th cent. CE), and the minuscule MSS 22, 46, 48, 51, 96, 231, 763. In addition, the two minuscule MSS 26 and 106 that belong to the Alexandrian text type also attest to the older version of the verse.

[3] Cf. the reading in *Codex Marchalianus* (Q; 6th cent. CE) κυριος εκει εσται το ονομα αυτης 'the Lord is there will be its name' which concurs with Syrohexaplar ܡܪܝܐ ܬܡܢ ܢܗܘܐ ܫܡܗ.

[4] The reading of the *Vorlage* on which the Greek rendering is based is referred to in the following as *^read LXX.

MT: יְהוָה שָׁמָּה
*read*LXX: *יהיה שמה
LXX: ἔσται τὸ ὄνομα αὐτῆς

On the basis of these considerations, a further conclusion can be drawn: the divine name was not written in ancient Hebrew letters as McGregor (1985, 86–87) reconstructs, but in Aramaic script.

Summing up, even if wording and meaning of the verse are clearly different in the LXX vis-à-vis MT, the Greek rendering is probably based on the same consonantal framework, and the translator aimed for a quite literal rendering of the Hebrew text.

The following cases from the Greek text of the Book of Ezekiel originate in a similar situation, i.e., they result in a divergence of the Greek translation from the Hebrew textual tradition, emerging in the course of reading. The phenomenon under scrutiny here is therefore a further case of 'dissimilatory reading', which was operative also in the transmission of the Hebrew Bible.[5]

## 1.2. Ezekiel 48.10

The verse concerns the definition of the priest's share in the eschatological land allotment, which ends with the following subscript, according to MT: "and the sanctuary of the Lord shall be in the middle of it (i.e., the holy portion)." In LXX, however, the same passage reads as follows: "and the mountain of the holies shall be in his midst."

---

[5] The term was introduced by Stefan Schorch (see Schorch 2016, 109–28).

MT: וְהָיָה מִקְדַּשׁ־יְהוָה בְּתוֹכוֹ
LXX: καὶ τὸ ὄρος τῶν ἁγίων ἔσται ἐν μέσῳ αὐτοῦ

Although again the difference between the two versions is considerable, its explanation is evident. Instead of י in והיה the Greek translator read ר, leading to *והר, the following ה of the *Vorlage* was perceived as an article prefixed to the next word, i.e., *המקדש,[6] and instead of the Tetragrammaton he again read *יהיה, rendering ἔσται. Except for the two cases for this misreading of the Tetragrammaton in Ezekiel mentioned in this article, there are no further occurrences of this phenomenon in the book. This is probably due to the fact that the Tetragrammaton appears otherwise generally within coined phrases, or in prophetic speech formulas. It should be noted, however, that the boundaries between יהוה and יהיה are blurred also in the Greek translation of Isaiah, which reflects no less than four cases of a similar misreading (Isa. 4.5, 8.18, 28.21, 49.1 [Seeligmann 2004, 216]) as well as in LXX Joel 4.11.[7]

MT: וְהָיָה מִקְדַּשׁ־יְהוָה בְּתוֹכוֹ
*LXX: והיה מקדש יהוה בתוכו
*readLXX: והר המקדש יהיה בתוכו
LXX: καὶ τὸ ὄρος τῶν ἁγίων ἔσται ἐν μέσῳ αὐτοῦ
(i.e., in 'what is set apart': ἀφορισμός)

---

[6] With the exception of three cases in sg. in Ezek. 45.4, 18 and 48.8 Hebrew מקדש is mostly rendered by nominalised forms of ἅγιος in pl. (Ezek. 43.21, 44.1, 5, 7, 8, 9, 11, 15, 16, 47.12, 48.10). Against the other witnesses of LXX Ezek. P967 provides a singular form in Ezek 48.10 only.

[7] I thank Bradley Marsh for providing the example from LXX Joel.

The explanation provided for the Greek rendering relies on two assumptions: First, not only the letters ו and י, but also ר were graphically similar in the Hebrew *Vorlage*. Second, the Greek translator again misread the Tetragrammaton as an imperfect of היה. Therefore, similar to the first example, the Hebrew *Vorlage* of LXX was probably identical to MT in terms of the consonantal framework.

## 1.3. Ezekiel 41.25 and 26

In the description of the main temple building MT mentions an 'עָב of wood,' in 41.25, and in the following verse the plural עָבִים appears. Both the etymology and the meaning of עָב is unclear:

> MT: וְעָב עֵץ אֶל־פְּנֵי הָאוּלָם מֵהַחוּץ
> 'and there was an עָב of wood in front of the vestibule outside'
>
> MT: וְצַלְעוֹת הַבַּיִת וְהָעֻבִּים
> 'and the side chambers of the temple and the עבים'

The Targum translates עָב as 'lintel'—סקופה—which is probably contextually inferred from the aforementioned 'door wings of the sanctuary' (דַּלְתוֹת הַהֵיכָל) in 41.25 and corresponds to the Targum's rendering of עָב in 1 Kgs 7.6. Similarly, Rabbinic sources interpret עובים as מְרִישׁוֹת 'beams' (e.g., b. B. Qam. 67a). The Peshitta translates ܡܛܠܠ ܒܩܝܣܐ 'panelled with wood',[8] and Jerome

---

[8] The rendering of וְעָב עֵץ as ܡܛܠܠ ܒܩܝܣܐ in the Peshitta corresponds to the translation of עֵץ שָׁחִיף as ܩܝܣܐ ܣܚܝܦܐ in Ezek. 41.16, which probably describes the wooden cladding of the building to the east of the היכל.

renders *grossiora ligna* 'thicker wood,' obviously connecting עָב with the root עב"י 'to be thick.'[9]

In opposition to this, the Greek rendering of עָב in 41.25 and of עָבִים in 26 does not follow either of these interpretative paths and reads as follows:

> LXX: [25] καὶ σπουδαῖα ξύλα κατὰ πρόσωπον τοῦ αιλαμ ἔξωθεν [26] ...καὶ τὰ πλευρὰ τοῦ οἴκου ἐζυγωμένα.
> '[25] and there was excellent wood (σπουδαῖα ξύλα) facing the ailam outside, [26]...and the joined (ἐζυγωμένα) sides of the house.'

All the witnesses of LXX except for P967[10] provide the adjective σπουδαῖος 'excellent' or 'precious' where we would expect a rendering of עָב to stand. The plural עָבִים is rendered as ἐζυγωμένα, an attributive participle describing the sides of the temple being 'joined' or 'yoked' to the nave. In contrast to the other versions, the Greek renderings of עָב and עָבִים are not immediately evident from the context, and the translation of עָב as σπουδαῖα does not correspond with the rendering of the plural עָבִים as ἐζυγωμένα. Nevertheless, the suggestion of a completely free-handed rendering is not convincing either, since rare architectural terms in the Second Temple vision are otherwise typically rendered by Greek transcriptions (cf. the frequently occurring renderings of תָּא as θεε Ezek. 40.7, אוּלָם and אֵילָם both as αιλαμ Ezek. 40.7, 21, probably due to the indistinguishability of ו and י in *LXX, and אַיִל as

---

[9] Cf. the rendering of עָב in 1 Kgs 7.6 by LXX as πάχος ('thickness').

[10] For an evaluation of the variant reading καλα in P967, see the following footnote.

αιλ*, Ezek. 40.21), which suggests that the translation technique was generally literal in this regard.

The most likely explanation for both Greek translations refers again to paleographical characteristics of the Hebrew *Vorlage*. As for עַב in verse 25, the Greek translator seems to have read *טָב, i.e., Aramaic 'good,'[11] leading to the following reconstruction:

| MT | *LXX | *read LXX | LXX |
|---|---|---|---|
| וְעָב עֵץ | ועב עץ | וטָב עץ | καὶ σπουδαῖα ξύλα |

Moreover, the morphology of the plural עֵבִים in verse 26 demands singular forms like עִיב or עוּב which suggests that the singular of the word in verse 25 of the Hebrew Vorlage might also have been spelled *וּעוב, i.e., with *waw* as mater lectionis. This latter spelling provides an even easier explanation how the translator arrived at

---

[11] It should be noted that the word טוב is never spelled without *waw* in MT and the Qumran Hebrew scrolls, although defective spelling is attested in the fs (Deut. 6.18; 8.10; 11.17) and the plural (e.g., Gen. 6.2; 2 Sam. 25.15). The other renderings of Hebrew טוב attested by Ezek. (LXX) are ἀγαθός (Ezek. 34.14, 36.31), καλός (Ezek. 17.8, 20.25, 24.4, 34.18) and ἐναντία rendering לא־טוב in Ezek. 18.18. In P967, the LXX-Hapax σπουδαῖος corresponds to the semantically close but far more common adjective καλός. Similarly, P967 offers the variant κατα στιχιον ("according to a row") in Ezek. 41.25 instead of the passive participle ἐστιχισμέναι ("set in a row") based on the verb στιχίζω, which is not attested in any other ancient Greek source. In Ezek. 45.20 the LXX-Hapax ἀπόμοιρα corresponds in the text of P967 to the common Pentateuchal designation for a cult levy ἀφαίρεμα. The mentioned variants suggest that P967 attests to a hermeneutical reworking aiming to replace rare forms by common synonyms and phrases in the last chapters of LXX Ezek.

his translation, since he might have read *read וּטוֹבּ. The reconstructed Hebrew variant *וְעוּב can also be viewed as a text-historically older form in comparison to the MT-reading עָב, given that the latter can be explained as an adaption to the noun עַב attested in 1 Kgs 7.6.

| MT | *LXX | *readLXX | LXX |
|---|---|---|---|
| וְעָב עֵץ | ועוב עץ | וטוב עץ | καὶ σπουδαῖα ξύλα |

The conclusion that the translator read ט[ו]ב instead of ע[ו]ב also provides an explanation of the otherwise surprising fact that he did not establish any lexical connection between verse 25 and עבים in verse 26.

As noted, the equivalent of MT ἐζυγωμένα is also found in 1 Kgs 7.43 (7.6), the only other verse in the Hebrew Bible where the word עַב is mentioned. The verse describes the dimensions of the 'Hall of Pillars' and mentions a further porch as well as pillars provided with an עב before the 'Hall of Pillars'.

MT: וְאֵת אוּלָם הָעַמּוּדִים עָשָׂה... וְאוּלָם עַל־פְּנֵיהֶם וְעַמֻּדִים וְעָב עַל־פְּנֵיהֶם:

'He made the Hall of Pillars... and there was a porch in front of them and pillars and an עב in front of them.'

The Greek in 1 Kgs 7.43 reflects an understanding of the word עַב as stemming from the root ע״בי resulting in the translation as πάχος 'thick,' whereas the participle ἐζυγωμένα 'yoked together' has no equivalent in MT.

MT: וְאֵת אוּלָם הָעַמּוּדִים עָשָׂה... וְאוּלָם עַל־פְּנֵיהֶם וְעַמֻּדִים **וְעָב** עַל־פְּנֵיהֶם:

LXX: καὶ τὸ αιλαμ τῶν στύλων... **ἐζυγωμένα** αιλαμ ἐπὶ πρόσωπον αὐτῶν, καὶ στῦλοι **καὶ πάχος** ἐπὶ πρόσωπον αὐτῆς τοῖς αιλαμμιν.

'And the Ailam of the Pillars was... linked together (i.e., with the Ailam of the Pillars)[12] was an ailam in front of them, and pillars and thickness before it for the ailammin.'

Since neither the participle nor any form of the verb ζυγόω are attested beyond LXX 1 Kgs 7.43 and Ezek. 43.26, the concordant attestation in the two verses can hardly be attributed to coincidence.

Due to the lack of an equivalent for ἐζυγωμένα in LXX 1 Kgs 7.43, the latter may be the result of what Michael Klein (2011, 78–81) has termed 'associative translation', which combines an etymological analysis of the form ויצע with the equivalent of an associated translation found in Ezek. 43.26.[13] The reason for taking up the equivalent ἐζυγωμένα probably was to specify the architectural connection between the Hall of Pillars and the additional porch, the pillars, and the thickness in front of it, which is not elaborated in MT 1 Kgs 7.6.

---

[12] NETS refers the participle to the length and width of the Hall of Pillars, which is not very likely, since LXX does not mark the following 'ailam in front of them' as a new clause with a copula as MT does.

[13] I would like to thank Hector Patmore (Leuven) for drawing my attention to the phenomenon of 'associative translations' and for referring me to Klein's study.

In Ezek. 43.26 the rendering ἐζυγωμένα could again proceed from a misinterpretation of paleographically similar letters. However, the starting point here would not be the consonantal framework attested by MT, but a *plene* spelling of the short /u/ in the plural form, as is common in the Hebrew Qumran scrolls (see Qimron 2018, 135):

| MT | *LXX | *readLXX | LXX |
|---|---|---|---|
| וְהָעֻבִּים | והעובים | [1]והערבים | ἐζυγωμένα |

As can be seen from this reconstruction, the Greek translator mistook the ו in his *Vorlage* for a ר and derived the word as a passive form of the root ער״ב 'to mix,' as is the case with regard to the forms of the root in Ezek. 27.27, which are rendered by σύμμεικτος:

MT: וְעֹרְבֵי מַעֲרָבֵךְ

'the dealers of your merchandise'

LXX: καὶ οἱ σύμμικτοί σου ἐκ τῶν συμμίκτων σου

'and your sundries from your sundries'

By rendering his reading *readוהערבים as ἐζυγωμένα in Ezek 43.26, the translator has adapted his translation of ער״ב to an architectural context and ignored the copula in his translation for syntactical reasons.

The conclusion that the letters ו, י, ר, and for that matter also ד, in the *Vorlage* of Greek Ezekiel were graphically similar, receives further support from the following variants.

## 1.4. Ezekiel 32.27

According to MT, 'Meshech and Tubal will not lie with the fallen warriors from the uncircumcised (מֵעֲרֵלִים)' whereas according to the LXX 'they will lie with giants fallen long ago (ἀπὸ αἰῶνος)'.

> MT: וְלֹא יִשְׁכְּבוּ אֶת־גִּבּוֹרִים נֹפְלִים מֵעֲרֵלִים
> LXX: καὶ ἐκοιμήθησαν μετὰ τῶν γιγάντων τῶν πεπτωκότων ἀπὸ αἰῶνος

The expression מֵעֲרֵלִים 'from the uncircumcised' corresponds to ἀπὸ αἰῶνος 'long ago', being again the result of the translator's confusion of ו and ר, and probably a defective spelling of the plural ending in the *Vorlage*, which can be reconstructed as *read*מֵעוֹלָם.

| MT | *LXX | *readLXX | LXX |
|---|---|---|---|
| מֵעֲרֵלִים | מערלם | מעולם | ἀπὸ αἰῶνος |

## 1.5. Ezekiel 28.15

In the judgement speech against the King of Tyre, MT states: "You were blameless in your ways (בִּדְרָכֶיךָ) from the day that you were created," whereas LXX renders: "You were born blameless in your days (ἐν ταῖς ἡμέραις σου) from the day you were created."

> MT: תָּמִים אַתָּה בִּדְרָכֶיךָ מִיּוֹם הִבָּרְאֶךָ
> LXX: ἐγενήθης ἄμωμος σὺ ἐν ταῖς ἡμέραις σου ἀφ᾽ ἧς ἡμέρας σὺ ἐκτίσθης

Following Hector Patmore (2012, 162), the Greek rendering ἐν ταῖς ἡμέραις σου in the first half of this sentence is probably influenced by the following expression ἀφ᾽ ἧς ἡμέρας, which renders Hebrew מיום. Patmore concluded that this influence occurred at the level of translation of the phrase. In my view, it is more probable that this influence was operative already in the reading of the *Vorlage* that was the point of departure for the Greek translation (a position Patmore considers, but ultimately dismisses). In fact, ἐν ταῖς ἡμέραις σου was probably derived from a Hebrew *Vorlage* that was identical with the consonantal framework of MT. Due to the paleographical characteristics of the *Vorlage*, the letter sequence דר looked similar to י, a semi-ligature of כ and י looked similar to ם, which appears to have caused the translator's reading *ביומך instead of בדרכיך. The plural rendering in the Greek can be explained by the aim to produce an idiomatic Greek phrase referring to a 'life span' (see e.g., Matt. 2.1, 11.12, 23.30, 24.37; Luke 1.5, 18, 73, 4.25, 17.26, 28).

| MT | *LXX | *readLXX | LXX |
|---|---|---|---|
| בִּדְרָכֶיךָ | בדרכיך | ביומך | ἐν ταῖς ἡμέραις σου |

## 1.6. Ezekiel 37.8

In the vision of the dry bones, skin becomes "covered upon" the flesh and the sinews, according to MT, whereas the "skin came up upon," according to LXX.

MT: וַיִּקְרַם עֲלֵיהֶם עוֹר מִלְמָעְלָה
LXX: καὶ ἀνέβαινεν ἐπ' αὐτὰ δέρμα ἐπάνω

Instead of MT וַיִּקְרַם, LXX is likely to be based on the reading *ויקום, confusing this time ר in its *Vorlage* with ו. This case does not prove a *plene* spelling in the *Vorlage*, but the translator's expectation of a short /o/ being spelled by a *waw* as *mater lectionis*. A comparable spelling of short /u/ with a *mater lectionis* was in fact attested by the *Vorlage* of LXX Ezek. with regard to the aforementioned plural *עובים, according to my reconstruction.

| MT | *LXX | *read LXX | LXX |
|---|---|---|---|
| וַיִּקְרָם | ויקרם | ויקום | καὶ ἀνέβαινεν |

In light of the frequent ו–י confusion, and following the typological sequencing of the Aramaic script proposed by Frank Moore Cross (1998, 386–401), one might be led to assume that the Hebrew *Vorlage* of LXX Ezek. applied a late Hasmonean formal book hand. However, manuscripts from the third cent. BCE, like 4Q Sam[b], and from the first part of the second cent. BCE, like 4Q Deut[a], are also copied in scripts in which ו and י are often difficult to distinguish. By contrast, the confusion of ד and ר with ו and י would require a script where the head of ר and ד are still narrow, which rather points to an older pre-Hasmonean hand. However, depending on the type and execution of the Hasmonean hand as well as the use of the pen, younger scrolls like 4Q Deut[a] and 4Q Job[a] can still exhibit narrow heads for the letters ד and ר.[14]

## 2.0. Phonetically Induced Spellings in the *Vorlage*

From the examples of paleographically induced readings in the Greek text, I will now turn to two renderings that point to spelling

---

[14] In a first draft of this paper, I attempted to establish that the script of the *Vorlage* was Late Hasmonean on the basis of Cross' (1998, 379–402) paleographical sequencing. I would like to thank Eibert Tigchelaar (Leuven) for pointing out to me the difficulties of my attempt to date the *Vorlage(n)* of LXX Ezek. based on letter confusions by referring me to the said fragments and their characteristics.

mistakes in the Hebrew *Vorlage* induced by the phonetic weakening of gutturals.

## 2.1. Ezekiel 44.20

In the instruction regarding the priests' haircuts, MT and LXX agree on the first prohibition that priests should not "shave their heads." However, regarding the second prohibition MT stipulates that priests "should not let their locks grow long," while LXX transmits a quite contradictory statement: "they shall not strip off their hair":

MT: וְרֹאשָׁם לֹא יְגַלֵּחוּ וּפֶרַע לֹא **יְשַׁלֵּחוּ**

LXX: καὶ τὰς κεφαλὰς αὐτῶν οὐ ξυρήσονται καὶ τὰς κόμας αὐτῶν οὐ **ψιλώσουσιν**

Since the LXX hapax ψιλόω generally refers to the removal of hair by plucking or rubbing, it might seem reasonable to interpret the Greek rendering as contextual translation that refers to contemporary Greek mitigating rites of mourning and distress, which should thus be declared forbidden for priests. However, the extrabiblical Greek sources use exclusively the verb τίλλω in these contexts.[15]

Another explanation for the background of the Greek rendering in Ezek. 44.22 has been suggested by John W. Olley (2009, 527), who sees here Pentateuchal influence, specifically from Lev 21.5, which prohibits Aaronite priests from shaving in

---

[15] See Liddell, Scott, and Jones, "τίλλω," 1792; "ψιλόω," 2024. Cf. also the usage of τίλλω to describe the mitigating act in Ezra 9.3.

connection with mourning rites and resembles the wording of the first prohibition in Ezek. 44.20.

> LXX: καὶ φαλάκρωμα οὐ ξυρηθήσεσθε τὴν κεφαλὴν ἐπὶ νεκρῷ καὶ τὴν ὄψιν τοῦ πώγωνος οὐ ξυρήσονται.
> 'And you shall not have a bald spot shaven upon your head for the dead, nor shall they shave the appearance of their beard.'

The Pentateuchal influence on the Greek rendering of the instructions for the Zadokite priests in Ezek. 44.17–31 is indeed evident in several cases, namely the adoption of terms like περισκελής 'leggings' (Ezek. 44.18; see Olley 2009, 527), πρωτογένημα 'firstfruit', and πρωτότοκος 'firstborn' (Ezek. 44.30; Tov 1999, 186), which are at least rare words and maybe even neologisms coined in the Greek Pentateuch. The phrase καὶ ἐπὶ ψυχῇ ἀνθρώπου 'and over a soul of a human' in LXX Ezek. 44.25, introducing the instruction on corpse impurity, differs from MT וְאֶל־מֵת אָדָם 'and to corpse of a human', but agrees with Num 9.6–7 as well as 19.11 and 13, which similarly deal with corpse impurity. The formulation in LXX Ezek. 44.25 thus probably serves as an intertextual marker, aiming to identify the seven days for purification of the priest prescribed in the following verse 26 with the seven-day ritual as described in Num 19. In the light of this broad evidence for influence from corresponding texts from the Pentateuch, the very fact that the verbal form ψιλώσουσιν has no correspondence in the wording of the Greek Pentateuch argues against the assumption that the rendering can be attributed to Pentateuchal influence.

Against this background, the Greek rendering ψιλώσουσιν cannot be attributed to the influence of the Greek Pentateuch, nor can it be explained as a dissociation from Greek Hellenistic rites and traditions, and a different explanation is required. Most probably, the Greek translator recognised a verb of the root של״ל, which appears in Ruth 2.16, where Boaz commands his servants to make sure 'to pull out' (שֹׁל־תָּשֹׁלּוּ) parts of the bundles of sheaves gathered in the harvest to leave them in the field for Ruth. As an alternative origin of the Greek rendering, the translator might have read the Aramaic verbal root של״י 'to draw out', which is attested in several dialects of late antique Aramaic.[16]

This assumption obviously implies that the letter ח of the verbal form of של״ח was missing in the *Vorlage*. The letter's omissions, misplacements, and replacements by א and ה in spellings of the Hebrew Qumran scrolls (see Qimron 2018, 107–9) as well as the Samaritan pronunciation *yēšallā'u* make the possibility of a phonetically induced misspelling in the *Vorlage* in this case likely.

| MT | *LXX | *read LXX | LXX |
|---|---|---|---|
| יְשַׁלֵּחוּ | ישלו | יְשֹׁלּוּ | ψιλώσουσιν |

Defective spelling of a weakened guttural seems to have been present also in further places of the Hebrew *Vorlage* of Greek Ezekiel, e.g., in Ezek. 42.11.

---

[16] See CAL (https://cal.huc.edu; accessed 26 February 2024), sub voce של״י.

## 2.2. Ezekiel 42.11

In this verse, the Greek phrase κατὰ τὰ μέτρα τῶν ἐξεδρῶν 'like the measurements of the halls' suggests that the *Vorlage* was כמד[ו]ת הלשכות, as opposed MT כְּמַרְאֵה הַלְּשָׁכוֹת 'like the appearance of the chambers'. Throughout LXX Ezek., מראה is translated six times as ὅρασις (Ezek. 40.3, 41.21, 43.3[4]) and in one case as ὄψις (Ezek. 41.21), whereas the word מדה coherently corresponds to Greek μέτρον (Ezek. 40.32, 41.21, 42.11, 43.34). Since a confusion between ר and ד is again obvious and a confusion of ה and ת is at least conceivable in this case, one can assume that LXX testifies to a *Vorlage*, in which the א of מראה was dropped.

| MT | *LXX | *readLXX | LXX |
|---|---|---|---|
| כְּמַרְאֵה הַלְּשָׁכוֹת | כמרה הלשכות | כמדת הלשכות | κατὰ τὰ μέτρα[17] τῶν ἐξεδρῶν |

Admittedly, this assumption is challenged by the fact that the א in מראה probably retains its value as a glottal stop in Qumran Hebrew, as suggested by the observation that in all the 61 attestations of מַרְאֶה (or מַרְאָה) in the scrolls, the א is indeed not dropped even once. However, the Samaritan Hebrew pronunciation *mårī* demonstrates that the weakening of aleph was at least susceptible to omission in spelling in certain strands of late Second Temple Hebrew. According to Ze'ev Ben-Ḥayyim (2000, 69), the Samaritan pronunciation emerged from the introduction of a vowel glide before the glottal stop (*marʲʾi*), which turned into a full vowel (*mårīʾi*), and finally led to the reduction of the two last

---

[17] Cf. the rendering of כמדת השער in Ezek. 40.21 as a plural κατὰ τὰ μέτρα in the Greek.

syllables resulting in a hyper-long vowel (må̄rī). In a manner analogous to the present case Noam Mizrahi (2012, 57–83) identifies the reading הַמְלָאָכִים in *Codex Aleppo* for 2 Sam. 11.1 to be a preserved deviation from the standard pronunciation of the word הַמַּלְאָכִים 'the messengers' in MT, which resulted from the elision of the word medial glottal stop similar to the Samaritan Hebrew pronunciation of the word (må̄ lå̄k).[18]

In any case, according to this reconstruction, the spelling of the Hebrew *Vorlage* of LXX Ezek. contained clear cases, in which the weakening of gutturals led to the loss of gutturals in the consonantal framework.

## 3.0. The Translator's Reading Technique

The spelling features of the *Vorlage* are also reflected by the reading technique employed by the translator to decipher the consonantal framework of his *Vorlage*. This will be demonstrated with three cases.

### 3.1. Ezekiel 24.17 and 26

In Ezek. 24.15–24, YHWH announces to the prophet that the loss of his beloved wife will become a symbol for the exiled Judeans, who will lose their sons and daughters in the impending destruction of Jerusalem. Just as the prophet is forbidden to mourn and to perform mourning rites for his wife by YHWH's command in Ezek. 24.16–17, so the exiled Judeans will also not be able to

---

[18] I thank Stefan Schorch (Jerusalem) for drawing my attention to the said variant in the *Codex Aleppo* and Mizrahi's analysis of it.

perform mourning rites for their sons and daughters, according to the announcement in Ezek. 24.22–23. In MT, the enlisted mourning rituals that the prophet must abstain from and that will be impossible also for the Judeans to perform, includes a stipulation to keep the head covered by a turban.

Ezek. 24.17

> MT: הֵאָנֵק דֹּם מֵתִים אֵבֶל לֹא־תַעֲשֶׂה פְּאֵרְךָ חֲבוֹשׁ עָלֶיךָ
> 'Groan quietly; make no mourning for the dead, bind thy turban upon thee.'

Ezek. 24.23

> MT: וּפְאֵרֵכֶם עַל־רָאשֵׁיכֶם
> 'your turban will be on your heads'

In verse 17, the Greek translation differs considerably from the MT both in terms of the underlying wording and in terms of the identified syntax of its *Vorlage*:

> LXX: στεναγμὸς αἵματος, ὀσφύος, πένθους ἐστίν· οὐκ ἔσται τὸ τρίχωμά σου συμπεπλεγμένον ἐπὶ σὲ
> 'It is a groan of blood, of a loin, of mourning; your hair shall not be plaited upon you'

The rendering of the verse once again clearly demonstrates that the Greek translation is not based on a Hebrew reading tradition. The Greek translator arrived at his translation through reading the consonantal framework דם as the noun *דָּם, i.e., 'blood,' instead of the imperative דֹּם 'groan,' and *מתנים 'loins,' instead of מתים as contained in MT. In addition, he took the second imperative חבוש from his *Vorlage* for a passive participle (*חָבוּשׁ). In order to make sense of the emergent reading, he further related the negated verbal form לא תעשה to the following phrase and translated it freely as οὐκ ἔσται.

MT: הַאֲנֵק דֹּם מֵתִים֙ אֵ֣בֶל לֹֽא־תַעֲשֶׂ֔ה פְאֵרְךָ֙ חֲב֣וֹשׁ עָלֶ֔יךָ

*read*LXX: האנק דם מתנים אבל לא תעשה [פארך] חבוש עליך

LXX: στεναγμὸς αἵματος, ὀσφύος, πένθους ἐστίν· οὐκ ἔσται τὸ τρίχωμά σου συμπεπλεγμένον ἐπὶ σὲ

The determination of the relationship between the Greek τὸ τρίχωμά σου 'your hair' and equivalent פארך found in MT requires further inquiry, especially since in 24.23 Hebrew וּפְאֵרֵכֶם is again translated with 'your hair,' albeit using here κόμη instead of τρίχωμα:

Ezek. 24.23

MT: וּפְאֵרֵכֶ֖ם עַל־רָאשֵׁיכֶ֑ם

LXX: καὶ αἱ κόμαι ὑμῶν ἐπὶ τῆς κεφαλῆς ὑμῶν

'and your hair shall be on your head'

The key for understanding the Greek rendering in Ezek. 24.17 and 24.23 lies in the fact that the Greek text of verse Ezek. 44.18 translates the Hebrew word פְאֵר quite aptly as κίδαρις 'turban', whereas in Ezek. 44.20 a plural of Greek κόμη translates the Hebrew collective noun פֶּרַע 'hair' in an equally accurate manner.

Given the broad attestation of forms with dropped א in intervocalic position in Qumran manuscripts and in light of the attested defective spelling of the plural *constructus* פרי in 1QM 7:11, the translator was probably faced with the defective forms פרך (Ezek. 24.17) and פרכם (Ezek. 24.23) in his *Vorlage*. Recognising these forms as being defective, however, he identified פרך and פרכם as forms of the noun פֶּרַע, on the basis of a hypercorrection of the guttural ע instead of א.

|  | MT | *LXX | *readLXX | LXX |
|---|---|---|---|---|
| Ezek. 24.17 | פְּאֵרְךָ | פרך | פר[ע]ך | τὸ τρίχωμά σου |
| Ezek. 24.23 | וּפְאֵרֵכֶם | ופרכם | ופר[ע]כם | καὶ αἱ κόμαι ὑμῶν |

## 3.2. Ezekiel 47.22

The section on land allotment in Ezek. 47 entails a statute for the inclusion of resident foreigners, the גרים:

In verse 22, MT reads: "with you they (i.e., the resident foreigners) shall receive (אִתְּכֶם יִפְּלוּ) an inheritance among the tribes of Israel." According to the LXX, however, the foreign guests "shall eat with you (μεθ ὑμῶν φάγονται) by inheritance in the midst of the tribes of Israel" with the Israelites.

MT: אִתְּכֶם יִפְּלוּ בְּנַחֲלָה בְּתוֹךְ שִׁבְטֵי יִשְׂרָאֵל

LXX: μεθ ὑμῶν φάγονται ἐν κληρονομίᾳ ἐν μέσῳ τῶν φυλῶν τοῦ Ισραηλ

As assumed by Daniel M. O'Hare (2010, 40), the Greek translator obviously read a verbal form of the root אכ"ל instead of נפ"ל. The wording of MT in 47.22 seems somewhat unusual. In texts on land allotments the grammatical subject of forms of נפ"ל *hifʿil* is usually the person who is granted the allotment, as is the case in the first half of verse 47.22 with the form תַּפִּלוּ. If the verb is used in the *qal*, the allotted portion becomes the grammatical subject, as in Ezek. 47.14. The fact that in Ezek. 47.22 the person obtaining the allotment appears as subject of the verb in *qal* is therefore peculiar, but since the Greek translation is not based on a fixed reading tradition, he certainly could have opted to read the form as *hifʿil*. However, taking into consideration a graphic similarity between כ and פ by itself is not sufficient to explain how the translator derived his rendering from the consonantal framework in front of him.

| MT | *LXX | *read LXX | LXX |
|---|---|---|---|
| יֹפְלוּ | יפלו | יֹ[א]כלו | φάγονται |

The Greek rendering shows that the translator most probably reckoned with a spelling of *yōḵelu*, that was lacking a graphical representation of the letter א. Similar spellings of *verba primae aleph* are of course frequent in Qumran manuscripts (see Reymond 2014, 200; Qimron 2018, 199–200), and they are even found in MT.[19]

## 3.3. Ezekiel 43.10

The suggestion that the translator anticipated a defective spelling of א in the above-mentioned case receives further support from another similar case, e.g., Ezek. 43.10:

| MT | *LXX | LXX |
|---|---|---|
| וּמָדְדוּ | [*ומראהו] | καὶ τὴν ὅρασιν αὐτοῦ |
| אֶת תָּכְנִית׃ | | καὶ τὴν διάταξιν αὐτοῦ |

The Greek text contains a double object—τὴν ὅρασιν αὐτοῦ 'its appearance' and τὴν διάταξιν αὐτοῦ 'its plan'—but a comparison with the Hebrew *Vorlage* reveals that the first of the two noun phrases is based upon the misreading of a Hebrew verb.

Instead of the MT reading ומדדו, the Greek rendering καὶ τὴν ὅρασιν αὐτοῦ seems to presuppose that the translator did read his *Vorlage* as *ומראהו (see Zimmerli 1969, II:1073). Again, the

---

[19] For defective spellings of פ״א imperfect forms in MT, see 2 Sam. 6.1; Isa. 13.20, Ps. 104.29, and cf. also MT Ezek. 42.5 יֹכְלוּ.

graphic similarity between ד and ר played a role in this productive misreading, but it is by no means sufficient to derive the Greek reading from the consonantal framework as preserved in MT, and further factors must have been involved.

First, when 3ms pronouns are attached to a ל"י noun, the ה of the suffix is frequently dropped in Qumran Hebrew and beyond (see Qimron 2018, 272–73). Second, due to weakening, א is also frequently dropped in Qumran Hebrew spelling in intervocalic position as well as in the beginning of a syllable (see Kutscher 1974, 505–6; Qimron 2018, 100–102). Following the reconstruction proposed above, a defective spelling of מראה was probably attested in the *Vorlage* of *LXX Ezek. 42.11: כמרה *הלשכות. And finally, *verba mediae geminatae*, like מד"ד, can be used either in the *qall*-pattern or in late Second Temple Hebrew even in the *qūl*-pattern, instead of the *qalal*-pattern (see Kutscher 1974, 344; Ben-Ḥayyim 2000, 154–56). It is therefore plausible to suggest that the Hebrew *Vorlage* of the Greek translator contained the form ומדו, vis-à-vis MT ומדדו, and this was read by the Greek translator as *read[א]ומר, due to a confusion of ד with ר, and, by way of hypercorrection, an added א.

| MT | *LXX | *readLXX | LXX |
|---|---|---|---|
| וּמָדְדוּ | ומדו | ומר[א]ו | καὶ τὴν ὅρασιν αὐτοῦ |

The examples show that the translator is likely to have followed internalised orthographical conventions of spelling and morphology, otherwise known from the Qumran scrolls, and that he adopted these as the basis for his reading of the consonantal framework he was confronted with. In fact, therefore, his reading technique produced something which may be called 'virtually augmented readings'—proceeding from a Hebrew *Vorlage* that in fact contained a quite different consonantal framework, but was open to interpretation, due to an ambiguity that was caused by the spelling conventions relating to (weakened) gutturals in late Second Temple Hebrew texts.

## 4.0. Conclusion

The Greek translation of Ezek. seems to have aimed generally at a literal rendering of its Hebrew *Vorlage*. Against this background, the fact that the Greek text contains single renderings that deviate from their Hebrew *Vorlage* to a considerable degree stands out and requires explanation. The evidence emerging from the cases analysed in the first and second part of this study, i.e., palaeographical ambiguities in the *Vorlage*, divergent *plene*- and defective-spellings, traces of misspellings, often under the influence of the phonetic weakening that affected gutturals in the Hebrew of the late Second Temple period, lead in many cases to the production of variant readings in LXX Ezek. The cases discussed in the third part reveal a reading technique by which the translator attempted to anticipate some of these phenomena, likewise resulting in variants through hypercorrections in the course of reading. As a result, the actual act of reading on the part of the translator created a virtual *ad hoc* Hebrew *Vorlage*, which was never part of the material transmission of the Hebrew text, and manifested itself only in the Greek translation.

The reconstruction of the *Vorlage(n)* of LXX Ezek. as well as its reading and translation techniques require consideration of whether or not the Greek translation of the Book of Ezekiel is homogeneous. Pointing to changing patterns of stereotyped renderings between chapters Ezek. 1–25/27 (= α), 26/28–39 (= β), and 40–48 (= γ), previous studies have doubted the latter. In the two most comprehensive studies of this question to date, Leslie J. McGregor (1985, 197–99) proposed a single translator for sections α and γ and a different translator for section β. In contrast, Priscilla D. M. Turner identified four evolving stages of the Greek translation, namely Ezek. 1–15 / 25–30.19 / 40–48, Ezek. 17–20, Ezek. 16 / 21–24, and finally Ezek. 30.19–39, based on the adoption of Greek equivalents from different books of LXX without necessarily assigning the stages to different translators (2001, 290–94). As opposed to these two approaches, Emanuel Tov attributes the discrepancies between sections α, β, and γ to a compilation of an Old Greek version in Ezek. 1–27 with revisional texts in chapters 28–39 and 40–48 (1976, 149–50).[20]

The evidence adduced in this study is distributed across all three sections of the Book of Ezekiel (α:1–25/27; β: 26/28–39; γ: 40–48), for which the existence of different translators has been taken into consideration. The misreadings caused by the paleographic ambiguity of the letters י, ו, ד, and ר, connect *Vorlagen* of Greek variants in sections β and γ (= Turner's first and fourth stage), whereas *Vorlagen* with defective spellings of gutturals can be reconstructed in sections α and γ (= Turner's first and third stage). The variant readings of LXX Ezek. that reflect the established reading technique of virtually reconstructing gutturals are equally discernible in sections α and γ (= Turner's first and third

---

[20] Cf. the discussion and evaluation of the various positions on the question of multiple translators by Johan Lust (2008, 654–57).

stage). The limited number of text examples can certainly not substantiate the assertion of a homogeneity of the Greek translation as a whole. Nevertheless, the distribution of corresponding examples of misreadings argues for the at least partial use of the same *Vorlage* in all sections α, β, and γ (= Turner's first, third, and fourth stage). The reading technique that can be reconstructed from examples in sections α and γ even points to the same translator.

## References

Ben-Ḥayim, Ze'ev, and Avraham Ṭal. 2000. *A Grammar of Samaritan Hebrew: Based on the Recitation of the Law in Comparison with the Tiberian and Other Jewish Traditions, A revised Edition in English.* Winona Lake: Eisenbrauns.

Cornill, Carl H. 1886. *Das Buch des Propheten Ezechiel.* Leipzig: J.C. Hinrichs'sche Buchhandlung.

Cross, Frank M. 'Paleography and the Dead Sea Scroll'. In *The Dead Sea Scrolls after Fifty Years: A Comprehensive Assessment*, edited by by Peter W. Flint and James C. VanderKam, 379–402. Leiden: Brill.

Klein, Michael L. 2011. 'Associative and Complementary Translation in the Targumim'. In *Michael Klein on the Targums Collected Essays*, edited by Avigdor Shinan, Rimon Kasher, Michael Marmur, and Paul V.M. Flesher, 77–88. Studies in the Aramaic Interpretation of Scripture 11. Leiden: Brill.

Kutscher, Edward Y. 1974. *The Language and Linguistic Background of the Isaiah Scroll: (I Q Isa$^a$).* Studies on the Texts of the Desert of Judah 6. Leiden: Brill.

Liddell, Henry G., Robert Scott, and Henry S. Jones, 1996. *A Greek-English Lexicon*. New 9th edition, reprint. Oxford: Clarendon Press.

Lust, Johann. 2008. 'Multiple Translators in LXX-Ezekiel?'. In *Die Septuaginta–Texte, Kontexte, Lebenswelten. Internationale Fachtagung veranstaltet von Septuaginta Deutsch (LXX.D), Wuppertal 20.-23. Juli 2006*, edited by Martin Karrer and Wolfgang Kraus, 654–69. WUNT 219. Tübingen: Mohr Siebeck.

McGregor, Leslie. J. 1985. *The Greek Text of Ezekiel: An Examination of its Homogeneity*. Septuagint and Cognate Studies 18. Atlanta: Georgia Scholars Press.

Mizrahi, Noam. 2012. 'Kings or Messengers?: The Text of 2 Samuel 11:1 in the Light of Hebrew Historical Phonology'. *Zeitschrift Für Althebraistik* 25/28: 57–83.

O'Hare, Daniel M. 2010. *Have You Seen, Son of Man? A Study in the Translation and Vorlage of LXX Ezekiel 40-48*. Septuagint and Cognate Studies 57. Atlanta: Society of Biblical Literature.

Olley, John W. 2009. *Ezekiel, A Commentary Based on Iezekiēl in Codex Vaticanus*. Septuagint Commentary Series. Leiden: Brill.

Patmore, Hector M. 2012. *Adam, Satan, and the King of Tyre: The Interpretation of Ezekiel 28:11–19 in Late Antiquity*. Jewish and Christian Perspectives Series 20. Leiden: Brill.

Qimron, Elisha. 2018. *A Grammar of the Hebrew of the Dead Sea Scrolls*. Between Bible and Mishnah, The David and Jemima Jeselsohn Library. Jerusalem: Yad Yizhak Ben-Zvi.

Reymond, Eric D. 2014. *Qumran Hebrew: An Overview of Orthography, Phonology, and Morphology*. Resources for Biblical Study 67. Atlanta: Society of Biblical Literature.

Seeligmann, Isac L., and Robert Hanhart. 2004. *The Septuagint Version of Isaiah and Cognate Studies*. Forschungen zum Alten Testament 40. Tübingen: Mohr Siebeck.

Schorch, Stefan. 2016. 'Dissimilatory Reading and the Making of Biblical Texts: The Jewish Pentateuch and the Samaritan Pentateuch'. In *Empirical Models Challenging Biblical Criticism*, edited by Raymond F. Person and Robert Rezetko, 109–28. Ancient Israel and its Literature 25. Atlanta: Society of Biblical Literature.

Tov, Emanuel. 1976. *The Septuagint Translation of Jeremiah and Baruch*. Missoula, MT: Scholars Press.

———. 1999. 'The Impact of the LXX Translation of the Pentateuch on the Translation of the Other Books'. In *The Greek and Hebrew Bible—Collected Essays on the Septuagint*. Supplements to Vetus Testamentum 72. Leiden: Brill, 183–94.

Turner, Priscilla D. M. 2001. 'The Translator(s) of Ezekiel Revisited: Idiosyncratic LXX Renderings as a Clue to Inner History'. In *Helsinki Perspectives on the Translation Technique of the Septuagint*, edited by Raija Sollamo and Seppo Sipilä, 279–307. Publications of the Finnish Exegetical Society 82. Göttingen: Vandenhoeck & Ruprecht.

Zimmerli, Walther. 1969. *Ezechiel*. Biblischer Kommentar Altes Testament 13/2. Neukirchen-Vluyn: Neukirchener Verlag.

# READING AND ARTICULATION IN ANCIENT JEWISH TEXTS[1]

*Hindy Najman*

---

This essay reflects on how practices of reading include, but are not reducible to, interpretation or hermeneutics. Reading is a practice that is in-between the oral and the written, and in-between the text and its interpretation (Kivy 2006). Reading does not simply copy what came before but rearticulates it anew each time. Performance, then, is an aspect of reading which articulates and expresses the act of reading and thus captures the space between the oral and the written, as Geoffrey Khan and I have described (Khan and Najman 2022, 259–60):

> By performance of a text we understand the vital and creative act of engagement with an ancient textual tradition that makes the text relevant and meaningful for individuals or for a community at the time of performance. This includes the oral performance of a written tradition and also the written performance of a tradition in the form of innovative texts.

---

[1] Many thanks to Rebekah Van Sant, Ruthanne Brooks, and Tamar Karni for their incisive comments and suggestions. Parts of this essay also appear in Najman (2025).

In this essay I will focus on the example of the *Hodayot* (also referred to as the Thanksgiving Hymns) from the Dead Sea Scrolls because of the way they integrate articulation and reading through the oral expression of prayer. To be sure, the Dead Sea Scrolls irrevocably changed the way we understand interpretation in Jewish antiquity during the Hellenistic period. That is, the Dead Sea Scrolls exhibit the application of a variety of reading practices. There is interpretation, but also political and historical engagement with the present, as well as theological and philosophical transformations for how ideas and concepts from the Hebrew Bible are understood. Thus, in this essay I consider both how the past tradition contributed to and also participated in reading practices, but also how we read our own scholarly presuppositions into ancient texts.

## 1.0. On Reading Practices Past and Present

### 1.1. Reading Practices in Antiquity: Scribal Contributions

We can discern patterns of reading within the Dead Sea Scrolls through the study of scribal comment and correction. By this I mean, tracing these marginal notes reflects the ways in which the scribes worked with texts from earlier periods. Indeed, even as we trace some of these interactions, we can only know of some of the resources these scribes employed beyond the biblical traditions themselves. We can also see parallels and shared traditions between the Hebrew and Greek as well as Aramaic and later Latin traditions that are incorporated and integrated in this scribal tradition.

New texts are composed with an integration and engagement of earlier materials, which are invoked and repurposed in new ways. The earlier reading materials themselves are part of a new composition that takes other textual traditions into account, however, that newness is part of new scriptures that are composed in new contexts. These innovative and creative compositions open up possibilities for reading and for understanding how ancient Jews thought about their own heavenly and terrestrial worlds, and, fundamentally, about how they were thinking about goodness and perfection. This is particularly important when we think about the central ideas in the Scrolls such as reflection on human essence, knowledge (דעת), and perfection (תום). This developmental dimension through reading and performing could be seen to go hand in hand with liturgical readings of Torah as well.[2]

For my case study in this essay, I consider the *Hodayot*. The *Hodayot* are a remarkable collection of songs that reflect a theologically coherent, iterative set of themes across no less than twenty-eight discrete poems; a collection that is notably dynamic. We can trace ongoing growth and variation modes of reading of prior and contemporary traditions of interpretation and of biblical theology across both the Cave 1 and Cave 4 copies of the *Hodayot* (Stegemann et al. 2009). These hymns exhibit ongoing revision and innovation of a series of concepts.

The *Hodayot* as a group of hymns exemplify a collection that reflects an ever-growing commentary of earlier texts as a mode of reading. The *Hodayot* are an assembly of prayers that are

---

[2] Regarding 1QS, please see Arjen Bakker's (2023, 131–8) recent argument on this point from column six of 1QS.

intensely iterative of biblical idioms, themes, and expressions common in the Hebrew Bible (especially Genesis 1–3, Jeremiah, Psalms, and Job). The unity of the *Hodayot* is thematically and lexically iterative, recycling a relatively small number of themes, numerous times, in different orders. The lexical range is consistent, as are the themes. There is also significant clustering together of the *Hodayot* as the collection grows and is curated (Newsom 2021, 1–10).

The collection is contemporaneous with some of the latest editing and writing that is retrospectively part of the biblical canon of the Hebrew Bible, but it also forms a sort of bridge with early Jewish and Christian liturgical developments (see Bakker 2024). The *Hodayot,* as a collection, participate in what we would call both the 'biblical' and 'extra-biblical' as it looks back towards earlier biblical precedent but also paves the way for new pathways for performative and liturgical expression of deity, human essence, and liturgical imagination.[3] The *Hodayot* thus vitalise and revitalise biblical traditions through liturgical idioms that are heavily scripturalised. On this point, Judith Newman (2015, 300) writes:

---

[3] To be sure, 'biblical' and 'extra-biblical' is anachronistic in this period (see Newman 2018). I use this as a kind of shorthand to signal that the practices of which I speak cross the canonical and the non-canonical, albeit these are not the best way to capture these textual collections in the Hellenistic period, at a time when the lines between the canonical and canonical are not compelled. Please note also the discussions around authoritative literature (e.g., Ulrich 2015; see also VanderKam 1998).

In turning to consideration of the renewed covenant in
1QHᵃ, we should observe their general character as heavily
scripturalized, and indeed, given their ongoing use by the
community, they can be characterised as scripturalizing.
That is to say, they both draw on scriptural language in
their composition, but also in their use in ongoing performances, and become authoritative scripts themselves.

It is thus essential for understanding the *Hodayot* to consider the role of inheritance, transformation, and transmission of these liturgical expressions as theological and philological innovations. While interpretative dimensions have been emphasised, many readers of the *Hodayot* have become distracted by a discourse of intertextuality and exegesis.

## 1.2. Contemporary Reading Practices: Scholarly Contributions

I want to problematise the use of intertextuality, which found its legacy—wholly unintended by Julia Kristeva, to be sure—in biblical studies precisely because it fit like hand in glove into what biblicists called exegesis within texts (Kristeva 1980; cf. 1984, 59–60; see also Boyarin 2011). The classical foundations for our field were born in a time when historicism, *prima scriptura* and *sola scriptura* were assumed. But it was also founded on a presupposition that the goal was to get to a place that was ancient Israel, or before Judaism, i.e., to get at the earlier layers of the text. Further, I want to suggest that intertextuality came to be used in conjunction with already established practices of source-critical work the aim of which was both to separate the layers of the text and also to access the earliest layers. This theologically charged practice had embedded within it a complicated and problematic relationship with Judaism in particular. But my problematisation of this practice also speaks to how intertextuality came to be used: not, I want to suggest, as a reading practice that facilitated deep and conceptual understanding, but rather in a way that involved further divisions of the text. The goal continued to be the disassembly of the text into its pre-texts instead of understanding interactions across textual traditions as a source of life.

Intertextuality was a way of naming how ancient Jewish writers composed. Walking backwards, scholars such as James Kugel built on the momentum of the 1960s and 1970s and reopened the world of biblical studies to theory (Kugel 1999). The most current and exciting expression was, for them, through the application of Kristeva's term 'intertextuality'. The term, however, was de-centred from its original meaning and was applied in a variety of inconsistent ways (Hinds 1998; Edmunds 2001). My point is that intertextuality in biblical studies became obsessed with *where* instead of *how* texts interact in conversation across corpora.

For the purposes of our own work, how productive is intertextuality? To what extent does it truly do the hermeneutical work that scholars demand of it? Moreover, it has become a term that is used across a broad array of practices—both our own scholarly practices and ancient practices.

## 2.0. Reading the *Hodayot* as a Unity

### 2.1. Poetic Processes within a Collection

Instead of focusing on the Teacher hymns or the Community hymns, I propose to read the *Hodayot* collection as a unity, consisting of hymns, or even parts of hymns, that generally share features with other hymns, which constitute building blocks that run across the collection (see further on this topic Schuller 1994, 2012; Newsom 2021; Harkins 2018). Those building blocks consist of shared language, concepts, and literary forms, which together form what we now call the *Hodayot* as a collection. This collection can be read as an integrated meditation on the possibility of an emerging self and the ever-aspiring nature of the human towards the creator. This impossibility of ultimate fulfilment does not mitigate the ever-aspiring self within the *Hodayot* to attempt to arrive at the next point of achievement.

The reading of the *Hodayot* does not presuppose an absolute order or singular improvement towards a goal. I do maintain, however, that through the current assembly acknowledged in scholarship, the iterative nature indeed creates a powerful dimension of growth and improvement. I consider the collection as ancient Jewish prayer, which can contribute to our understanding of the history of Jewish prayer and early biblical interpretation of this period in the context of communities that we can identify in sites such as Qumran and Masada.

The *Hodayot* are full of dynamic and creative poetic new readings that betray both the intricate readings of biblical traditions, especially from Genesis 1–3 and Job, but also Isaiah and

Jeremiah, as well as exhibiting philosophical interests. The structure and fluid yet integrated composition suggests developed and sophisticated thinking about creation, acquisition of knowledge, and human essence. The collection points to a philosophically-minded and spiritual practice, which involves repentance, blessing, and paideia.

There is a need for a hermeneutical turn in biblical studies in order to develop a way of reading the Hebrew Bible and the Dead Sea Scrolls that considers the ambiguities that its authors and redactors produced (Schmid and Najman 2022). The emergence and growth of biblical traditions is illuminated by considering collection, hermeneutics, and composition. The work of Peter Szondi is useful for thinking about a dynamic collection, because we find in the *Hodayot* what Peter Szondi called "poetic processes" (Szondi 1986). It is a mode of philology as hermeneutics that both presupposes the rigours of etymology and grammar but moves beyond that mode by applying it to a practice of reading that is intricate and interweaving with respect to the work, or corpus, or even epic. The goal then is to understand an organic whole (not a canonical whole) and thus pave the way to a new mode of critical reading.

Szondi's work can help us appreciate the wholeness of a corpus, but not in such a way that we forget that texts from Jewish antiquity have compositional complexity and history. This is equally relevant to works such as Psalms or Proverbs—as anthologies of prayers or wisdom sayings. To understand the growth of a corpus as generative is to resist the scholarly tendencies to reduce the parts to an original whole (if that is even recoverable).

So, whether the parts are smaller units, historical layers, or intertexts, the work of the reader and the scholar (collector and composer) in antiquity is connected to the creative and incisive work of the scholar (philologist and exegete) in modernity.

Such processes can be studied as a way of understanding textual unity as well as the composition of new authoritative writings in antiquity. Overall, through reflecting on practices of reading and the dynamic and vital form of textual emergence and extension, one can begin to understand how, through interpretation and critical evaluation, new approaches to philology surface. This is an approach that reflects on new composition as performance, as creative and innovative composition, and as the growth of biblical tradition itself, an expansion that redefines this period as a central flashpoint for biblical growth and vitality.

What is essential here is that while the text is replete with biblical language and themes, this collection is not an interpretation or commentary, and neither should it be reduced to intertextual allusion. Rather, the *Hodayot* build up a new theological framework as an expansion of the biblical, which belongs under the framework of vitality.

These texts engage in practices that shed a great deal of light on sapiential and pedagogical modes of thinking in the Second Temple period. While exegesis and history are very much part of the contribution of the *Hodayot*, I want to suggest that they can also teach us a great deal about poetics, liturgy, self-transformation, and theology for the crystallisation of what will come to be canonical and deuterocanonical. In particular, human potential is activated by way of speech and utterance, which both articulates itself in the recognition of deity and is expressed in the form of a blessing. These hymns are particularly illuminating for thinking about vitality in the way that liturgy is articulated and activated for ancient Judaism. This new articulation is expressed through new hymns, interpretations, to be sure, but also creative and innovative accounts of human essence.

## 2.2. Examples of Unity

The ninth column in the *Hodayot* describes the unique task allotted to the human spirit, enabled by God's creation of breath for the tongue and for the lips, according to mysteries and rules analogous to those that govern the paths of the luminaries and other incorporeal spirits in which God who is addressed directly as 'You' is blessed for everlasting ages. And then, ultimately, the 'I' or the protagonist acknowledges God's purification of his or her own human soul, "so that it might recount your wonders before all your creatures."

1QH[a] 9.29–35:

> אתה בראתה רוח בלשון ותדע דבריה ותכן פרי שפתים בטרם היותם
> ותשם דברים על קו ומבע רוח שפתים במדה ותוצא קוים לרזיהם ומֹבֹעֹיْ
> רֹוֹחות לחשבונם להודיע כבודכה ולספר נפלאותיכה בכול מעשי אמתכה
> ומֹ[שֹׁ]פֹּ[ט]יֹ צֹדקכה ולהלל שמכה בפה כול וידעוכה לפי שכלם וברכוכה
> לעולמי עֹ[ולמי]ם
>
> *vacat*
>
> ואתה ברחמיכה וגדול חסדיכה חזקתה רוח אנוש לפני נגע וֹנֹפֹשֹׁ [אביון]
> טהרֹתֹהֹ מרוב עוון לספר נפלאותיכה לנגד כול מעשיכה

'You yourself created breath for the tongue, and you know its words, and you determine the fruit of the lips before they exist. You set the words according to the measuring

line and the utterance of the breath of the lips by measure. And you bring forth the lines according to their mysteries, and the utterances of the breath according to their calculus, in order to make known your glory and to recount your wonders in all your faithful deeds and your righteous jud[gements] and to praise your name with the mouth of all. And they know you according to their wisdom, and they will bless you for everlasting ages.
*vacat*
'And you, in your compassion and your great kindness, you have strengthened the human spirit in the face of affliction and [the poor] soul you have cleansed it from great iniquity, so that it might recount Your wonders before all Your creatures.'[4]

I read the above passage on multiple levels: first, as about a specific 'I' whose human spirit is strengthened in the face of adversity, purified, so that the 'I' can recount (ספר) God's wonders to all humankind. But then within this creation hymn, it speaks about the task of humans at large within God's creation, who are allotted the task of reciting (ספר) God's wonders to all his creation. However, only those humans whom God strengthens and purifies are transformed from mere vessels of clay to those who can speak the right words of praise with their breath, tongue, and lips. Important is the use of the one who responds (מענה לשון), which is used at least seven times in the *Hodayot*.

The first time this phrase appears is in Prov. 16.1:

---

[4] These translations are my own with some consultation to existing editions.

לְאָדָם מַעַרְכֵי־לֵב וּמֵיְהוָה מַעֲנֵה לָשׁוֹן:

'A man may arrange his thoughts, but what he says depends on the Lord.'

Here it is God who provides מענה לשון as the 'final word'. Then in 'I' in 1QH$^a$ 10.9 thanks God with the following words:

ותתן מענה לשון לער[ול] שפתי ותסמוך נפשי בחזוק מותנים

'You have given the proper reply to my uncircum[cised] lips, and you have supported my soul with a potent strength'

One may read and translate מענה לשון as 'responsive tongue', also because the hymn introduces the 'I' as one who teaches those who love discipline and opposes the erring interpreters who still have uncircumcised lips and an alien tongue. Such a reading of מענה לשון may be apt in some other instances, too. However, in other cases, in 4.29–30 and 8.24–5 the 'responsive tongue' (מענה לשון) refers to the 'I''s prayer, 'reciting your righteous acts, and your patience (לספר צדקותיך וארוך אפים), your… and the deed as of your strong right hand (ומעשי ימין עוזך), and confessing the transgressions of my forebears (ולהוֹדוֹת על פשעי ראשונים) and p[rostr]ating myself and begging for mercy (ולהתנפל ולהתחנן)…' (4.29–30), with the התנפל and התחנן repeated with the מענה לשון in 8.24–5 (Newman 2018, 132–7). In all those cases, one might read the מענה לשון as part of a dynamic interaction between the community or between the deity and the protagonist. The role of speech and, in particular, blessing, is particularly important for the transition between the humiliation and glorification of the human.

Columns 19 and 20 of the *Hodayot* are intimately connected to the function of the human tongue from the creation hymn. Thus in col. 19.30–31 we see the language of blessing to God as linked with divine gift.

1QH<sup>a</sup> 19.30–31:

> ברוך אתֹה[ ] אדוני א[שֹ]ר נתתה לעֹבֹדֹכֹה שכל דעה להבין
> בנפלאותיכה וֹ[מ]ע[נ]ה לשון ל[ספר ברוב חסדיכה
>
> 'Blessed are you, O Lord, who has given to your servant insightful knowledge to understand your wondrous works, and a ready answer in order to tell of the abundance of your kindness.'

The addressee of the one to whom the story is retold is still unknown. But a few lines later, another short prayer or blessing, juxtaposes the one 'ready to answer'—מענה לשון—with prayer of praise and supplication.

1QH<sup>a</sup> 19.35–7:

> ברוך אתֹ[ה] אדוני כי אתה פעלתה אלה ותשם בפי עבֹדֹכה הוֹדוֹת
> תֹ[ה]לֹ[ה] ותחנה ומענה לשון
>
> 'Blessed are yo[u,] O Lord, for you have done those things, and you have put into the mouth of your servant hymns of pr[a]is[e] and a prayer of supplication, and a ready answer.'

In this hymn, thanksgiving and prayer for prostrating oneself and supplication are linked with the cycles of the day and night, of the seasons and the festivals. Although I do not accept the traditional division between Teacher and Community hymns made by scholars, it is notable that, following this classification, this 'community hymn' would be considered unrelated to the Creation

Hymn of col. 9. However, with regard to content, it makes explicit the creational task of humankind announced in the Creation Hymn, to pray simultaneously, or in response to, the proper order of the luminaries, in a sense a verbal response, מענה לשון, to the rest of God's deeds. As such, the artificial division inhibits integrated reading of the collection.

The *Hodayot* recount the capability of the human being to overcome humiliation through articulation, breathing out, and expressions of praise (and prayer) towards God. The recognition of God as creator is part of that expression. The recounting of wonders and the celebration of God's compassion is part of the activation of human potential.

One aspect that I did not yet highlight is the language of redeeming or saving. To be sure, the discourse is repetitive of what we have already seen in columns five and nine. But here I wanted also to emphasise the language of purification from sinfulness, which is ultimately a precondition for membership to the community and in turn the passageway from corruption to repair. In that context, there is also celebration and song of praise of God.

1QH$^a$ 11.20–25:

אודכה אדוני כי פדיתה נפשי משחת ומשאול אבדון העליתני לרום עולם
ואתהלכה במישור לאין חקר
ואדעה כיא יש מקוה לאשר יצרתה מעפר לסוד עולם ורוח נעוה טהרתה
מפשע רב להתיצב במעמד עם צבא קדושים ולבוא ביחד עם עדת בני
שמים ותפל לאיש גורל עולם עם רוחות דעת להלל שמכה ביחד רנה ולספר
נפלאותיכה לנגד כול מעשיכה
ואני יצר החמר מה אני מגבל במים ולמי נחשבתי ומה כוח לי

'I thank you Lord that you have redeemed my life from the pit, and that from Sheol-Abaddon you have lifted me up to an eternal height, so that I walk on a limitless plain.

'I know that there is hope for one whom you have formed from the dust for an eternal council. And a perverted spirit you have purified from great sin that it might take its place with the host of the holy ones and enter into community with the congregation of the children of heaven. And you cast for a person an eternal lot with the spirits of knowledge, that he might praise your name in a common rejoicing and recount your wonderful acts before all your works.

'But I, a vessel of clay, what am I? A thing kneaded with water. And by whom am I regarded? What strength do I possess?'

Here we see the emphasis on divine illumination for humanity as part of the grace (חסד) for overcoming the state of birth. Or in other words, another version of the Joban narrative. Thus, human limitation is only mitigated by divine grace and ultimately the human ability to articulate his own lowliness and divine grandeur. Human recollection of sin and compromise is part of the process of growth and transformation.

1QH$^a$ 12.28–31:

ובי האירותה פני רבים ותגבר עד לאין מספר
כי הודעתני ברזי פלאכה ובסוֹד פלאכה הגברתה עמדי והפלא לנגד רבים
בעבור כבודכה ולהודיע לכול החייֹם גבורותיכה מי בשר כזאת ומה יצר
חמר להגדיל פלאות והוא בעוון מרחם ועד שבה באשמת מעל

'Through me you have illumined the faces of many, and you have increased them beyond number.

> 'For you have made me understand your wonderful mysteries, and in your wonderful council you have shown yourself strong to me, doing wondrously before many for the sake of your glory and in order to make known to all the living your mighty deeds. What being of flesh is like this? And what vessel of clay is able to do wondrous great deeds? It (exists) in iniquity from the womb, and until old age in faithless guilt.'

And again, later in col. 12.

1QH$^a$ 12.37–38:

> כי נשענתי בחסדיכה וֹבֹהמון רחמיכה בי תכפר עוון ולטהֹ[ר] [אֹנֹוֹש
> מאשמה בצדקתכה
>
> 'For I rely on your kindness, and according to your abundant compassion to me you pardon iniquity, and thus cleanse a person from guilt through your righteousness.'

The mouth and the function of speech is for goodness and to praise God. Human beings are created for this purpose. The language of planting and growth are part of this discourse of progress and sustenance. The voice of the poet is empowered and inspired. Here are two illuminating illustrations of this from column 15.

1QH$^a$ 15.16–18:

> כי אתה ידעתה כול יצר מעשה וכול מענה לשון הכרתה ותכן לבי
> בֹ[ל]מודיכה וכאמתכה לישר פעמי לנתיבות צדקה להתהלך לפניך בגבול
> [חי]יֹם לשבולי כבוד ושלום לאין הֹ[סר ו]ֹלֹ[ו]אֹ להשבת לנצח.
>
> 'For you yourself know the intention of every deed and scrutinise every verbal response. You make my heart firm according to your teachings and your truth, directing my

steps toward the paths of righteousness, so that I may walk before you in the domain of life on tracks of glory and peace, without turning aside or ceasing forever.'

See also 1QH$^a$ 15.21–23:

ואני נשענתי ברֹוֹב[רחמיכה ולהמון] חסדכה אוחיל להציץ כמֹטע ולגדל נצר להעיז בכוח ולֹ[הפריח פרח כי ב]צֹדקתכה העמדתנֹי לבריתכה ואתמוכה באמתכה.

'But as for me, I rely on your great compassion, and upon your abundant kindness I wait, in order to bloom like a plant, and in order to make a shoot grow, to find security in (your) strength [and in order to make a bud sprout, for by] your righteousness you have stationed me in your covenant, and I have held fast to your truth.'

The *Hodayot* focus on divine grace as sustained by God as the creator and the one who enables articulation and ultimately recognition of the created world through blessing—i.e., articulation—which is itself the singular vehicle for overcoming the state of birth מרחם (from the womb). The *Hodayot* illustrate the ways in which biblical reading and articulation exemplify the development of scripture as a dynamic and ever emerging tradition. This is true through compositional practices, translation across linguistic registers, and the creation of new scriptures. To be sure, reading is at the essence of the life and breath of Judaism from its earliest inception until the present day. The *Hodayot* performs the dynamic between the written tradition and its performance.

## 3.0. Conclusion

In conclusion, I want to problematise some of the central tenets of the field of biblical studies, which has inherited such concepts as intertextuality or citation as the basis for 'reading'. In some of my recent work I have emphasised three dimensions to new trajectories with respect to reading. First, *reading practices*, through which I have intended to think about pretexts that are embedded but not necessarily cited; contexts, which are historically contingent and inform how new texts are read and reading as reception, or as first readers who are inheriting and again transforming. Second, *ethical reading*, which is particularly directed at the way we read as scholars and how we carry with us the traditions of scholarship and violence in our own tradition. This is intended as a way of confronting those presuppositions and redirecting our own modes of teaching and understanding with an eye towards descriptive ethics for the academy. Finally, and thirdly, *scriptural vitality*, which emphasises what I have called a prospective way of thinking about the development of tradition instead of emphasising the past and the reconstructive; this is especially relevant as a way of overcoming a discourse of *Urtext*, closed canon, the end of prophecy, and the Second Temple period as a late Judaism.

These ways of thinking can help us return to texts anew and rethink our own understanding and uncover paths not yet taken in reading texts across the Hebrew Bible, translated biblical traditions such as Targum and LXX, and other scriptures and literatures across Greek, Hebrew and Aramaic literary registers. Our literatures can come to exemplify scribal creativity, interpretive genius, and liturgical and scholarly articulation that always stands in between the oral and the written—if they are read with a renewed openness to the practices of reading and performance.

## References

Bakker, Arjen. 2024. 'Early Configurations of Jewish Prayer: Translating Sacrifice in the Second Temple Period'. *Journal for the Study of Judaism* 55 (4–5): 459–89.

Boyarin, Daniel. 1990. *Intertextuality and the Reading of Midrash*. Bloomington: Indiana University Press.

Edmunds, Lowell. 2001. *Intertextuality and the Reading of Roman Poetry*. Baltimore: John Hopkins University Press.

Harkins, Angela Kim. 2018. *Reading With an I to the Heavens: Looking at the Qumran Hodayot through the Lens of Visionary Traditions*. Boston: De Gruyter.

Hinds, Stephen. 1998. *Allusion and Intertext: Dynamics of Appropriation in Roman Poetry*. Cambridge: Cambridge University Press.

Khan, Geoffrey, and Hindy Najman. 2022. 'Performance in Ancient and Medieval Judaism'. *Dead Sea Discoveries* 29: 259–60.

Kivy, Peter. 2006. *The Performance of Reading: An Essay in the Philosophy of Literature*. London: Blackwell.

Kristeva, Julia. 1980. *Desire in Language: A Semiotic Approach to Literature and Art*. Edited by Leon S. Roudiez. Translated by Thomas Gora, Alice Jardine, and Leon S. Roudiez. New York: Columbia University Press.

———. 1984. *Revolution in Poetic Language*. Translated by Margaret Waller. New York: Columbia University Press.

Kugel, James L. 1999. *The Bible as It Was*. Cambridge, MA: Harvard University Press.

Naeh, Shlomo. 1994. '"Creates the Fruit of Lips": A Phenomenological Study of Prayer According to Mishnah Berakhot 4:3, 5:5'. *Tarbiz* 63 (2): 185–218. [Hebrew]

Najman, Hindy. 2025. *Scriptural Vitality: Rethinking Philology and Hermeneutics*. Oxford: Oxford University Press.

Newman, Judith H. 2018. *Before the Bible: The Liturgical Body and the Formation of Scriptures in Early Judaism*. New York: Oxford University Press.

———. 2015. 'Covenant Renewal and Transformative Scripts in the Performance of the Hodayot and 2 Corinthians'. In *Jesus, Paulus, und die Texte von Qumran*, edited by Jörg Frey and Enno Edzard Popkes. Tübingen: Mohr Siebeck.

———. 2018. 'The Hodayot and the Formative Process of Performing Scripture'. In *Before the Bible: The Liturgical Body and the Formation of Scriptures in Early Judaism*, 132–7. New York: Oxford University Press.

Newsom, Carol A. 2021. 'A Farewell to the Hodayot of the Community'. Dead Sea Discoveries 28 (1): 1–10.

Rosen-Zvi, Ishay. 2005. '"Who will Uncover the Dust from your Eyes?": Mishnah Sotah 5 and R. Akiva's Midrash'. *Tarbiz* 75 (1–2): 95–127. [Hebrew]

Schmid, Konrad, and Hindy Najman. 2022. 'Reading the Blood Plague (Exodus 7:14–25): The Hermeneutics of a Composite Text'. *Journal of Biblical Literature* 141 (1): 23–42.

Schuller, Eileen M. 1994. 'Prayer, Hymnic, and Liturgical Texts from Qumran'. In *The Community of the Renewed Covenant: The Notre Dame Symposium on the Dead Sea Scrolls*, edited by Eugene Ulrich and James C. VanderKam, 153–71. Notre Dame: University of Notre Dame Press.

Schuller, Eileen M., and Carol A. Newsom. 2012. *The Hodayot (Thanksgiving Psalms): A Study Edition of 1QH$^a$*. Atlanta: SBL.

Stegemann, Hartmut, Eileen Schuller, and Carol Newsom (eds). 2009. *1QHodayot$^a$: With Incorporation of 4QHodayot$^{a-f}$ and 1QHodayot$^b$*. Oxford: Clarendon Press.

Szondi, Peter. 1986. *On Textual Understanding and Other Essays*. Translated by Harvey Mendelsohn. Manchester: Manchester University Press.

Ulrich, Eugene. 2015. *The Dead Sea Scrolls and the Developmental Composition of the Bible*. Vetus Testamentum Supplements 169. Leiden: Brill.

VanderKam, James C. 1998. 'Authoritative Literature in the Dead Sea Scrolls'. *Dead Sea Discoveries: A Journal of Current Research on the Scrolls and Related Literature* 5 (3): 382–402.

# READING THE FIFTH SONG OF THE SABBATH SACRIFICE AGAINST THE LOSS OF ITS PERFORMATIVE TRADITION

*Noam Mizrahi*

## 1.0. Introduction

The *Songs of the Sabbath Sacrifice* comprise a liturgical composition, as indicated explicitly in each song's superscription which specifies its designated time and cultic context.[1] One must assume, therefore, that the full significance of the *Songs* was not comprehended merely by reading it as a literary text; rather, it was experienced through ritual performance (Lieber 2004; Newsom 2012; Falk 2015). The surviving manuscripts may be likened to a musical score, which is not quite the same thing as actual

---

[1] The *editio princeps* of the work is Newsom (1985); the official editions were published in DJD 11 (Newsom 1998) and 23 (García Martínez, Tigchelaar and van der Woude 1998). The superscriptions of about half of the songs are preserved, though to varying degrees: Song 1 (4Q400 1i [I] 1), Song 2 (4Q400 3ii + 5 [IV] 8'), Song 4 (4Q401 1 + 2 1), Song 6 (Mas1k i 8 || 4Q406 1 4'), Song 7 (4Q403 1i 30 || 4Q404 3 2'), Song 8 (4Q403 1ii 18 || 4Q405 8–9 [E] 1 || 11Q17 3 1' [II 4]), Song 12 (4Q405 20ii–22 6 [J 16] || 11Q17 16–18 [VII] 9).

music; a score is an abstraction—a simplified, notational representation of music—that can be rendered into a lived experience only by way of performative realisation, which inevitably entails interpretation.

The obvious problem is that much of the information that is essential for a performative rendering is not explicitly encoded in the written score but rather depends on external instructions, often passed orally from one generation of performers to the next. It is only by integrating the written and the oral traditions, for instance, that the Hebrew Bible was recited in synagogues from the Second Temple period down to the Middle Ages (and beyond). Indeed, one's understanding of the biblical text when reading it differs in many respects from one's experience upon performing it, or even upon attending such a performance. All the more so when it comes to liturgical works, composed for performance in the first place. To be sure, reading them is by no means a futile intellectual exercise, but it is only by participating in their actualising performance that one can fully grasp the experiential realisation of their potential.[2]

In the case of the *Songs*, however, the path for a compelling performative interpretation is largely blocked. As far as currently known, the last liturgical performance of the *Songs* took place sometime in the late first century CE. Whether it was done by the refugees who took shelter at Masada—as suggested by the presence of a copy of the work found there (Mas1k)—or maybe even later, in some other part of Judea, remains unknown. But, at least

---

[2] The performance of Jewish sacred textual traditions was recently explored from various vantage points in Najman and Khan (2022).

for the time being, there is no evidence that the tradition of its performance was transmitted by any social group beyond the Roman period.[3] When the last performer of the *Songs* died without teaching it to a disciple, the chain of tradition was broken and all the oral knowledge dictating and regulating its ritual enactment was lost forever.

Nowadays, when even the written text of the work is hopelessly damaged—less than half of it can be reasonably reconstructed—only very faint traces of the performative realisation of the *Songs* are observable. The manuscripts supply little to no data since the scribes copied the text in much the same way as they did with respect to other, non-liturgical works (Schücking-Jungblut 2020, cf. Falk 2014). The surviving copies contain no staging instructions, no poetic layout, and no function-oriented scribal signs encoding performative directives.[4]

---

[3] Admittedly, there are some intriguing parallels between the *Songs* and *Hekhalot* literature, which records the literary output of Jewish mystics of Late Antiquity. However, at least from a philological point of view, the available data does not support the speculation that any of the *Songs* were still available in such a late period. For further discussion, see Mizrahi (2007).

[4] The latter point of scribal signs that might signal performative instructions is not usually taken into account, but it may be worthwhile to mention Werner's (1957, 21–25) observation that some of the scribal marks found in the Qumran scrolls bear graphic similarity to neumes used for Byzantine *Kontakia* (a type of church hymn) preserved in Slavonic sources. Although his comparative method has been severely criticised (e.g., Jeffery 1987), the idea that some of such scribal marks—whose function remains largely unknown (Tov 2004, 178–218, especially 203–8)—functioned as performative instructions may still merit

The textual content of the manuscripts is somewhat more helpful. Literary analysis of Songs 6–8 recovers some hints about their musical realisation: their descriptions of the angelic liturgy—matched by the structural and rhetorical design of such descriptions—point to antiphonal singing as the main mode of musical performance.[5] However, this appears to be restricted mostly to these three songs, which comprise the middle block of the work, whereas the songs comprising the first and last blocks (i.e., Songs 1–5 and 9–13, respectively) generally appear to be differently structured and do not betray comparable clues that could guide a hypothetical reconstruction of any performative feature.[6]

Frustratingly, there is also no directly related extra-textual information that sheds light on this problem. Even if one were to embrace a maximalist view and unequivocally identify the social provenance of the *Songs* as Essene, then the classical sources describing the prayers recited by the Essenes would furnish little to no help.[7] When Josephus and Philo describe their Sabbath

---

further thinking. At any rate, as indicated above, such marks are not employed in manuscripts of the *Songs*, so this particular interpretive crux does not affect our present concern.

[5] For parts of Song 6 (the *Cycle of Praises*) see Mizrahi (2017). For Song 7 (the *Introductory Poem*) see Mizrahi (forthcoming).

[6] Exceptionally, the rhetorical deployment of the best-preserved poetic unit of Song 11 (4Q405 19) could also be reflective of an antiphonal design; see Mizrahi (2019).

[7] See the convenient collection of primary sources by Vermes and Goodman (1989) and the helpful overview by Gusella (2002).

rituals, for instance, they elaborate on their reading, study, and interpretation of scriptural literature; they do supply some information about their daily prayers but make no comment regarding their Sabbath prayers. Similarly, Philo's description of the comparable—and possibly related—group (γένος) of the Therapeutae refers to liturgical practices mainly in the context of a particular festival,[8] which is clearly different from the weekly Sabbath prayers.[9] This generalisation holds true regardless of the scholarly debate about the identity of this festival of the Therapeutae, be it the Festival of Weeks, as some scholars maintain, or a recurring holiday that took place at the end of every seventh week, as others interpret.[10]

How, then, should commentators of the *Songs* proceed? Are they to abandon all hope for understanding the text they seek to interpret, or is there some way to recover something of the work's signification for the ancient community (or communities) that

---

[8] Philo, *On the Contemplative Life* §64–89, esp. 80, 83–88 (Taylor and Hay 2021, 85–89 [translation], 94–96 [textual notes], 264–348 [commentary]). Philo's description of the prosodic and musical performance of the Therapeutae's hymnology is couched in elaborate Greek terminology (Leonhardt 2001, 156–72, §II:2.2; Jeffrey 2004); it is difficult to determine whether—and which—native Jewish practices underlie the Hellenistic picture he portrays.

[9] Philo, *On the Contemplative Life*, §30–33, 36 (Taylor and Hay 2021, 79–81 [translation], 92 [textual notes], 189–204, 209–11 [commentary]).

[10] Leonhardt (2001, 48–50 [§II:1.4.12.2]). For an attempt to use Philo's description of this holiday of the Therapeutae for shedding light on the *Songs* see Lieber (2004, 55–58).

practiced it? A potential way forward along the latter path is suggested by the idea that, regardless of the faith-specific theological meaning of any liturgy, its ritual performance induces an effect comparable to the aesthetic experience of art—taking the adjective "aesthetic" to mean "a type of experience involving the enactment or apprehension of a sense of order or form," thereby communicating "something greater than the sum of its parts" (O'Donnell Polyakov 2020, 32). The notion of performance denotes "an immersion in a deep reality, rather than a construction of illusion. It does not represent reality, but enacts reality," so that "[a] liturgical performance can be understood to be performative when it is seen not merely as an illustration of religious beliefs or narratives, but as an efficacious ritual action" (O'Donnell Polyakov 2020, 33). This approach was demonstrated by analysing scriptural psalms, concluding that "the liturgical performance of the psalms becomes a performance of aesthetic order, in which the aesthetic form of the psalms communicates more than the verbal content" (O'Donnell Polyakov 2020, 37), so that "[t]hrough regular, repeated recitation, the patterns of the psalms can become a pattern for understanding the world" (O'Donnell Polyakov 2020, 38). As a result, "in the interpretation of the liturgical agent or community," "the aesthetic quality of the ritual form becomes transformed... into a performance of the beliefs of the religious community," and "this transformation often takes the shape of the shift from mundane action into transcendent meaning; in other words, it 'does something'" (O'Donnell Polyakov 2020, 38).

Taking a cue from these theoretical observations, I propose that although the liturgical performance of the *Songs* remains beyond our reach, tracing the aesthetic features of the poetic texts that survive nonetheless enables us to capture an echo of its performative effect. The following discussion aims to illustrate this principle by analysing the best-preserved part of Song 5, which contains a poetic unit serving as the song's conclusion. Importantly for the present concern, the theological argument presented by this unit is well-known from other scrolls in terms of content, but its poetic form renders it effective in a very particular way.

## 2.0. Text

Like all other parts of the *Songs*, Song 5 is not preserved intact in any manuscript. It was pieced together and its text was reconstructed in a process that necessarily involved some measure of unavoidable uncertainty. The surviving text of Song 5 is witnessed by three manuscripts: Mas1k (col. i), 4Q402 (frgs. 3ii + 4), and 4Q406 (frg. 1).[11] Two of the manuscripts preserve the scribal demarcation of the end of Song 5, separating it from the beginning of Song 6 by a blank line (Mas1k i 7; 4Q406 1 3′).[12]

---

[11] See Newsom (1985, 152–62 [4Q402 3+4], 168–71 [Mas1k i], 355–56 [4Q406 1]) || Newsom (1998, 226–33 [4Q402 3+4], 240–43 [Mas1k i], 395–96 [4Q406 1]). Cf. Alexander (2006, 23–25).

[12] Following standard Assyriological practice, I distinguish in notation between numbers designating lines of preserved or reconstructed columns (e.g., Mas1k i 7) and numbers of lines as randomly preserved in a given fragment, marked by the prime sign (e.g., 4Q406 1 3′). This

A key material question posed by 4Q402 pertains to the spatial relationship between frg. 3, which preserves a bit of two consecutive columns, and the composite frg. 4. In the latest PAM photograph of 4Q402 (PAM 43.485, from May 1960), John Strugnell ordered the fragments by size, placing the more sizeable frg. 4 before the smaller frg. 3 (Figure 1).[13] Accordingly, in her preliminary edition (1985), Carol Newsom did not consider the possibility that the two fragments are directly related.

Figure 1: 4Q402, frgs. 1–4, detail from PAM 43.485 (May 1960). Photographed by Najib Anton Albina, Palestine Archaeological Museum. Courtesy of the Leon Levy Dead Sea Scrolls Digital Library, Israel Antiquities Authority

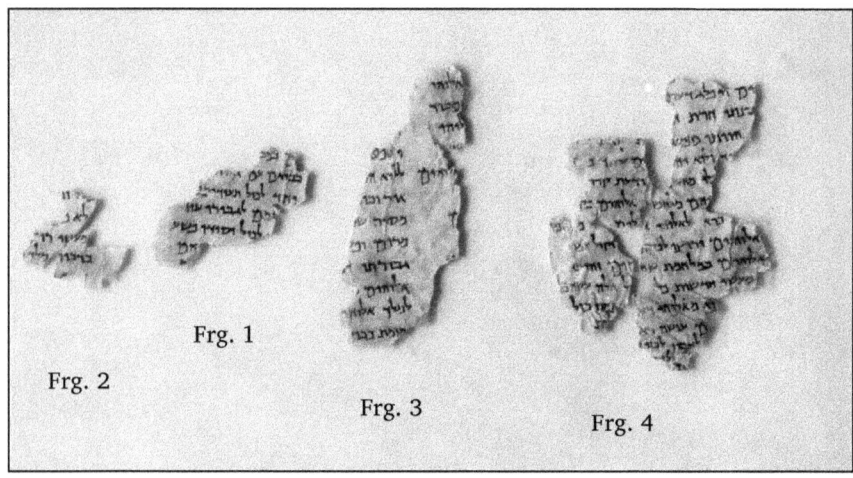

Frg. 1

Frg. 2

Frg. 3

Frg. 4

enables an immediate distinction between the recorded state of a preserved segment of the text and its hypothetical placement within the material reconstruction of a scroll to which it is assigned (e.g., 4Q405 20ii + 21 + 22 6′ [J 16]).

[13] For the full photograph see https://www.deadseascrolls.org.il/explore-the-archive/image/B-284513.

In his review of Newsom's book, however, Elisha Qimron (1986, 360–61, §2.4) proposed a distant join, placing frg. 3 col. ii at the rightmost part of a reconstructed column, and frg. 4 to its left. He may have been inspired by an earlier photograph (PAM 42.631, from July 1958), in which Strugnell similarly aligned the two fragments (Figure 2).[14]

Figure 2: 4Q402, frgs. 1–4, detail from PAM 42.631 (July 1958). Photographed by Najib Anton Albina, Palestine Archaeological Museum. Courtesy of the Leon Levy Dead Sea Scrolls Digital Library, Israel Antiquities Authority.

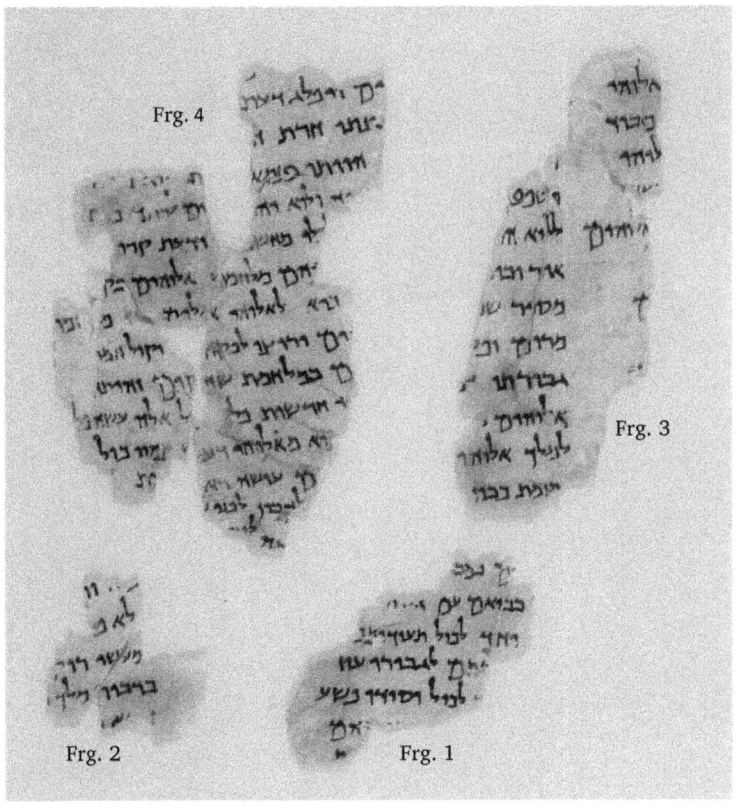

---

[14] For the full photograph see https://www.deadseascrolls.org.il/explore-the-archive/image/B-284042.

In the official publication, Newsom (1998, 222) admitted that the join "appears plausible when 4Q402 4 is used as a base text," yet rejected it on textual grounds: "but the problems with that reconstruction become evident when one uses MasShirShabb as the base text," due to the difference in the amount of preserved or reconstructable text in both witnesses. In his recent edition, Qimron (2010–14 [2023], 2:365) replied that the problem is resolved upon the assumption that the shorter text of the Masada copy results from scribal error (see further below). In my opinion, Qimron is correct, and the following reconstruction adopts his proposal; nonetheless, in order to facilitate easy isolation of each fragment, the text of frg. 3 is marked by half integral signs (⌠ ⌡) in the transcription below (Table 1).[15]

The distant join between frgs. 3 and 4 is important because it produces consecutive text on the bottom part of the reconstructed column. The preceding passage, fragmentarily preserved in lines 7′–11′, apparently described the involvement of angelic

---

[15] I differ slightly from my predecessors only with respect to a few individual readings. For instance, where Newsom (followed by all other commentators, including Qimron) read in Mas1k i 2 דברי דעת 'words of knowledge', I read חברי דעת 'knowledgeable members', as the left vertical stroke of the ḥet is clearly visible in the new, multispectral images produced by the Israel Antiquities Authority, which now allow adjudicating between optional readings that were previously contested. See, e.g., Newsom and Yadin (1984, 80); Puech (1987, 577). See https://www.deadseascrolls.org.il/explore-the-archive/image/B-499067 (infrared), https://www.deadseascrolls.org.il/explore-the-archive/image/B-499066 (full colour).

hosts in an eschatological war, that extends to the heavens.[16] Unfortunately, the rhetorical design of these lines cannot be outlined because too much text is missing from the leftmost part of the column. By contrast, the restoration of text in the concluding passage in lines 11′–15′ is aided by the overlapping text of Mas1k, enabling a nearly complete reconstruction of these lines (highlighted in **bold typeface** in the transcription below).

Table 1: Transcription of 4Q402, frg. 3ii + 4

4Q402 ⌈3ii⌋ + 4 ‖ Mas 1k i 1–7; 4Q406 1 (overlap with both witnesses).

| | | | | |
|---|---|---|---|---|
| 1′ | [ | ] | ]ṃ[ | [ |
| 2′ | [ | ]ים ויפלג דעת[ | | [ |
| 3′ | [ | ]וקי כ[בינתו חרת ח] | | [ |
| 4′ | [ | ]ỵ[ | ]ooo ת וֹלוא [ ] היותו טמאֿ[ | [ |
| 5′ | [ | ]ישפט[ | ]ỵה ולוא יהỵ[ו ]ים ליֿחֿד בֹ[ ]o[ | [ |
| 6′ | [ | ]לֿלוא הֿ[ ] | מכ[לבלי מחשבֿ[תו] ודעת קדוֹשֿ[י] קדושים | [ |
| 7′ | [ | ]אור ובינֿ[ה]    p    [ ]ה̇ם מלחמת אלוהים בכ[ן] | | [ |
| 8′ | [ | ]מסיר שנ[א] | ][ כיא לאלוהי אלֿים [כל]ỵ מֿ[ל]ח̇מון]ת | [ |
| 9′ | [ | ]מרום ופלֿ[ג | ][אלוהי]ם ירוצו לפקוד[תו] וקול המוןֿ] | [ |
| 10′ | [ | ]גבורתו צ[ | ][אלוהי]ם במלחמת שחֿ[קים והיתהֿ ] | [ |
| 11′ | [ | ]אלוהים בֿ[ ] | [מעשי חדשות פל[א] ᵃ**כול אלה עשה פל[א] ᵃ במזמת חֿסדוֿ בֿל** ידמוֿ] |
| 12′ | [ | ]למלך אלוהיֿ[ם̇] **כול חֿברי דעת ᵃ-כיא מאלוהי דעתֿ**-ᵃ **נהיו כול** [**הוֹי עד ומדעתוֿ**] |
| 13′ | [ | ]ᵇ-[ו]**מזמת כבודֿ-**ᵇוֿ] **היו כול תֿעוֿדוֿת עולמֿ**[**יֿם עושה ראיֿ**[**שונ**]**וֿת לעתוֿתֿיהם** **ואֿחֿרונות** |
| 14′ | [**למועדיהם ואין בידעיֿם נגלֿ[**דבר **לֿהֿבין לפני עֿ**[**שותו וֿבֿעשותו לא ישכילו כול**] |
| 15′ | [ | **אלוהיֿם מה יזם כיא ממעשי כבודו ה**[**מֿ**]ᶜ **לֿפֿנֿ**[ **הֿיותם** ] היו בדעֿ[**תוֿ** **vac**   [ |

Variant Readings:

ᵃ⁻ᵃ כֿיא מאלוהי דעתֿ 4Q402 ] > Mas1k (homoioteleuton: דעת⌢דעת)
ᵇ⁻ᵇ [ו]מזמת כבודֿ[ו] 4Q402 ] ומזמוֿ[תֿיוֿ] Mas1k
ᶜ ה[מֿ]ה 4Q402 ] הם Mas1k

---

[16] For this theme see also Davila (1996, especially 262–64).

The text appears to be relatively stable, exhibiting three variant readings: (a) The shorter reading of Mas1k is easily explained as the result of a homoioteleuton: the scribe's eye skipped between the two occurrences of דעת 'knowledge' in lines 2′ and 3′. (b) There is a difference in the grammatical form of the independent pronoun for the third-person masculine plural: while 4Q402 reads the long allomorph הֵמָּה, the Masada copy reads the short variant הֵם. These two forms interchange in Qumran Hebrew;[17] neither the linguistic meaning nor the poetic design is affected by this difference. (c) The most substantial variant concerns the interchange between the construct phrase [ו]מזמת כבוד[ו] 'his glorious plan' (4Q402) and the shorter reading ומזמו[תיו] 'his plans' (Mas1k). The sense of the text is not meaningfully changed, but this variant does affect the rhythmic composition of the poetic text, as discussed below (§4).

## 3.0. Compositional Context and Calendrical Setting

Song 5 concludes the first block of Songs 1–5, which describes various aspects of the angelic priesthood serving at the heavenly temple. It is placed at the point of transition to the middle block of Songs 6–8, which describes the angelic liturgy as performed

---

[17] In Qimron's (2013; 2018, 263–64, §D1.6) view, the independent pronoun for 3mpl was always pronounced as /hemmā/ in Qumran Hebrew so that הם should be regarded as a defective spelling of המה. Reymond (2014, 162–63) cautiously favours the opposite view that these two spellings represent distinct allomorphs as in Biblical Hebrew. This debate does not affect my present concern.

by the Chief and Deputy Princes and by the animate constituent parts of the heavenly temple itself.[18]

Although the superscription of Song 5 is not preserved, its date in the 364-day calendar can be calculated as falling on the second day of the second month (2.II). This date does not coincide with any known festival in the first, third, or fourth quarters of the year. In the second quarter, by contrast, the fifth Sabbath falls on the second day of the fifth month (2.V), immediately followed by the Festival of New Wine (מועד התירוש), the rituals of which are detailed in the Temple Scroll (11Q19 XIX–XXI).[19]

The preserved fragments that can be assigned to Song 5, which all come from its final part, do not include any clear reference to the Festival of New Wine. However, the military theme of the penultimate poetic unit of Song 5 could be indirectly related to this holiday. Although this festival, as prescribed by the Temple Scroll, appears to be a legal innovation of the late Second Temple period, its agricultural nature renders it likely that it was rooted in an older farming tradition, celebrating the production of new wine by offering the first products at the temple.[20] Such a custom may be indirectly reflected in a scriptural source of the

---

[18] For previous surveys of the internal structure of the *Songs* as a whole see, e.g., Newsom (1990, 102–3); Alexander (2006, 15–44); cf. Mizrahi (forthcoming).

[19] For the nature and history of this festival see Werman and Shemesh (2011, 311–15).

[20] This festival may even have a pre-Israelite cultic background, as suggested by the Ugaritic evidence adduced by Reeves (1992).

early Second Temple period: a Trito-Isaianic prophecy, the historical provenance of which is likely the Persian province of Yehud.

Isaiah 62 includes a prophecy addressed to Jerusalem, promising its future deliverance. The concluding two verses illustrate the military salvation from Jerusalem's enemies by asserting that they will no longer take advantage of the Judeans' agricultural produce: "I will not again give your grain to be food for your enemies, and foreigners shall not drink the wine for which you have laboured" (62.8). Rather, the Judeans themselves will be the ones to enjoy their wine and grain, upon offering their first produce at the temple: "those who harvest it shall eat it and praise the Lord, and those who gather it shall drink it in my holy courts" (62.9). Thus, the military triumph over Jerusalem's enemies is linked to the agriculturally-based rituals of presenting the first wine and first grain to the deity.

It is at least possible, therefore, though by no means certain, that this theme—and especially its link to a cult related to offering new wine to the deity—is echoed in the depiction of angelic hosts partaking in the eschatological war as found in Song 5, under the assumption that the performance of the *Songs* was not restricted to the first quarter of the year but rather was rehearsed in the other quarters as well.

## 4.0. Literary Analysis

Although no blank space indicates a paragraph break within line 11′, and the demonstrative אלה 'these' evidently refers backward, to the events recounted in the preceding unit, the clause כול אלה

עשה פלא appears to introduce a new section, which arguably functions as a self-standing poetic unit (cf. Lange 1995, 178, 180).

The internal structure of the poetic units included in the *Songs* is most clearly delineated when the running text is divided into poetic lines, in accordance with their syntactic make-up and thematic development. Obviously, this is an interpretive procedure, and hence subject to debate and potential change (see further below). Nonetheless, it is only by discerning poetic lines that the rhetorical deployment of the text becomes detectable. I propose to identify ten such lines in the text under discussion.[21]

Table 2: Poetical Arrangement of the Concluding Poetic Unit of Song 5

| | |
|---:|:---:|
| כול אלה עשה פלא במזמת חסדו | (i) |
| בל [ידמו] למלך אלוהים כול חברי דעת | (ii) |
| כיא מאלוהי דעת נהיו כול הוי עד | (iii) |
| ומדעתו ומזמת כבודו היו כול תעודות עולמים | (iv) |
| עושה ראישונות [לעתו]תיהם | (v) |
| ואחרונות למועדיהם | (vi) |
| ואין בידעים נגלי [דבר] להבין לפני עשותו | (vii) |
| ובעשותו לא ישכילו כול אלוהים מה יזום | (viii) |
| כיא ממעשי כבודו המה | (ix) |
| לפני היותם [היו בדע]תו | (x) |

---

[21] My lineation matches that of Maier (1995, 387–88); for a different lineation, preferring shorter poetic lines, see Segret (1988, 218). From this point on, the discussion follows a simplified eclectic text of the passage under scrutiny, which is based on the transcription presented in Table 1. Only letters and words restored conjecturally are placed between brackets.

(i) All these, Wonder[22] made by his gracious plan;
(ii) All knowledgeable members cannot [be compared] to the King of divine beings.
(iii) For it is by the God of Knowledge that all everlasting beings came into being,
(iv) And it is by His knowledge and His glorious plan that all eternal designations were (made).
(v) (He) makes the former (i.e., preordained) things [by their tim]es,
(vi) And the latter (i.e., contemporary) things by their dates.
(vii) Whereas among the knowledgeable ones, there are none to whom [a word] was revealed that would enable them to understand (anything) before He makes it,
(viii) And (even) while making, no divine beings are able to fathom what he plans.
(ix) For they are among His glorious deeds,
(x) Before they came into being, [they had been in His think]ing.

In my opinion, a close reading of this poem reveals a unique and complicated relationship between content and form. In terms of content, the passage makes a theological argument well-

---

[22] The term פלא 'wonder' is often used in the *Songs* as a substitute for the Tetragrammaton. This is particularly evident in this poetic line (כל אלה עשה פלא), which is a scriptural allusion to Isa. 45.7, אֲנִי ה' עֹשֶׂה כָל אֵלֶּה (as recognised by Newsom 1985, 159 || 1998, 231). In such cases, I translate 'Wonder' with a capital letter to highlight that the term is used as a proper rather than a common noun.

known from other Qumran scrolls (often categorised as 'sectarian'), most notably the Treatise of Two Spirits included in the best-preserved copy of the Community Rule (1QS, columns 3–4).[23] The core of this argument is a doctrine of predestination: the whole creation follows a preordained plan devised by God, and no created being is able to detract from it nor—being part of the created world—to understand it.[24] However, when cast in its present *poetic* form, the abstract theological argument takes a more complex and evolving concrete shape. If the thematic content of the poem—or the *semantic level* of the verbal utterances it consists of—is its score, then the rhythmic make-up of its lines—or the *prosodic level* of its language—guides the musical realisation, namely, the liturgical performance that sets the lived context in which the text is not only read but also experienced.

Since many aspects of the prosody of ancient Hebrew remain hypothetical or unknown, the present discussion is limited to a rudimentary scan, namely, counting the number of stressed words per line, noting alternations between 'light' lines (consisting of only 2–3 stresses) and 'heavier' ones. This distinction translates into faster vs slower performance time, respectively.[25] Put

---

[23] Newsom (1985, 160 || 1998, 231) calls particular attention to 1QS 3.15; CD$^a$ 2.9–10; 1QH$^a$ 9.21–22 (=1:19–20 in Sukenik's older numbering) and 5.27–28 (=13.11–12 [Suk.]).

[24] For a detailed discussion of the theology of this passage, also in comparison with the rest of the *Songs* and other Qumran texts, see Lange (1995, especially 171–86). Cf. Coulot (2011); Bakker (2014, 372).

[25] My thinking on some aspects of Hebrew prosody was influenced by Harshav (2008); cf. Harshav (2014), especially Chapters 1 and 3. I should underscore that by "*rhythmic* composition," I do not mean to

differently, the shift from a light line to a heavier one means slowing down, whereas the reverse shift from a heavy line to a lighter one means speeding the pace up. As with physical movement, however, these are not absolute renditions, and much depends on the degree of difference in a particular context: adding or subtracting a single beat would have a moderate consequence, whereas a difference that amounts to 2–3 beats or more could have a shocking effect (moving suddenly from 100 to 10 mph does not feel like 'slowing down' but rather like braking to a halt).[26]

Table 3: Rhythmic Composition of the Concluding Poetic Unit

| | | |
|---|---|---|
| – – – – – – | כול אלה עשה פלא במזמת חסדו | (i) |
| – – – – – – – | בל [ידמו] למלך אלוהים כול חברי דעת | (ii) |
| – – – – – – | כיא מאלוהי דעת נהיו כול הוי עד | (iii) |
| – – – – – – – – | ומדעתו ומזמת כבודו היו כול תעודות עולמים | (iv) |
| – – – | עושה ראישונות [לעתו]תיהם | (v) |
| – – | ואחרונות למועדיהם | (vi) |
| – – – – – – | ואין בידעים נגלי [דבר] להבין לפני עשותו | (vii) |
| – – – – – – | ובעשותו לא ישכילו כול אלוהים מה יזום | (viii) |
| – – – – | כיא ממעשי כבודו המה | (ix) |
| – – – – | לפני היותם [היו בדע]תו | (x) |

imply that the *Songs* follow a regulated *metrical* system of the kinds governing contemporaneous Greek and Latin poetry. Rhythm and meter are related yet distinct phenomena, both theoretically and practically.

[26] Following standard practice in the prosodic analyses of poetical texts, stressed units (in this case, whole words) are marked with a horizontal bar (–). Since the following scan focuses on stressed words rather than syllables, there is no need to mark unstressed units (˘).

What emerges immediately from this analysis is that the rhythmic composition of the various poetic lines does not follow a uniform pattern but rather features a dynamic movement, which distinguishes between two 'waves' or parts of the poetic unit: lines i–vi on the one hand, and lines vii–x on the other. This transition is marked by the drastic decrease in the number of stresses from six and seven (in lines i–iv) to three and two (in lines v–vi). Similarly, the move towards the conclusion of the poem—and of Song 5 as a whole—is marked by a somewhat less drastic shift from seven stresses (in lines vii–viii) to four (in lines ix–x).

The matter is slightly complicated by the fact that the transition point between the two parts of the poem can be differently analysed. Above, I have divided the text at this point between two lines (v–vi), because all other lines are arranged in couplets. Syntactically, though, these two lines actually form a single clause. Thus, they can be alternatively analysed as a single poetic line, which would still be noticeably shorter than the previous ones, having only five stresses. In this case, though, the transition between the two parts of the poem would be marked also by the shift from two-lined strophes (or couplets) to a strophe consisting of a single line. Regardless of how one prefers to scan this ambiguous segment of the text, therefore, the prosodic caesura is firmly rooted in the very structure of the poetic unit.

This is not an incidental observation. The structural division that manifests itself in the rhythmic texture correlates to a thematic change of focus. The text as a whole deals with the relationship between God the Creator and the created beings, including the angelic ones; but the first six lines focus on the deity, whereas the last four shift their attention to the created heavenly beings. Accordingly, the first part is framed by statements that refer exclusively to God, while references to whatever He created are presented as the products of His doings. The second part, by contrast, is concerned almost entirely with the heavenly beings, while references to God are only implicit, encoded by the pronominal suffixes (3ms). Thus, the rhythmic break within the poetic structure corresponds to a thematic change of focus from the divine sovereign to His angelic subjects.

The keyword that both connects and separates the two parts is דעת 'knowledge' (and synonymous terms like מזמה, translated here as 'plan'). God is presented as the one holding the ultimate knowledge, namely, the masterplan underlying the universe. The angels have some access to this knowledge, as indicated by their titles, חברי דעת and ידעים.[27] Being part of that plan themselves, however, they cannot decode it in its entirety; their access to the divine knowledge is, by definition, limited and partial.[28] Most saliently, they are unable to predict the future. Unlike God—whom Deutero-Isaiah describes as "declaring the outcome from the beginning and from ancient times things not yet done, saying, 'My purpose shall stand, and I will fulfill my intention'"

---

[27] The latter word can be vocalised as the plural form of either יָדֵעַ or יַדָּע; see Qimron (2018, 309 [§E1.2.6.1]). Licht (1957, 163) seems to have been the first to propose the vocalisation יַדָּעִים (for 1QHᵃ 19.17 [Suk. 11.14]), which reflects a nominal pattern (qattāl) designating a profession or characteristic (nomen opificum).

[28] Lange (1995, 186) highlighted this theme as a point of contrast with earlier conceptions of divine knowledge.

(Isa. 46.10)—the angels are bound to the unidirectional flow of time, and cannot fathom what will unfold.[29]

As this decisive, essential difference between God and the divine beings is outlined, it is also—at the very same time—problematised. Most evidently, the word אלוהים is confusingly employed in this poetic unit for the angelic entities (Mizrahi 2018), whereas God is referred to as פלא 'Wonder,' מלך 'King,' or simply as 'Him', alongside אלוהי דעת 'God of Knowledge' (line iii). But more subtly, the rhythmic configuration of the text highlights the lines that describe such divine beings (lines ii–iv, vii–viii), as these are the longest and heaviest rhythmically, meaning that the most solemn performance is reserved for these lines. And be it incidental or not, one cannot avoid noting that they contain *seven* stresses each, as the number of the highest-ranking Chief Princes. By contrast, the lines that place God at the center are typically shorter and, hence, performed faster. Thus, two independent levels of the text reflect different interests: the semantic level focuses on God, while the prosodic level underscores the angels.[30]

---

[29] The reference to Deutero-Isaiah is not incidental; the poetic unit is replete with allusions to Deutero-Isaianic passages, see Newsom (1985, 159–62; somewhat truncated in Newsom 1998, 231–33); cf. Caquot (1997, 9).

[30] A similar tension drives the composition from Song 5 to the highly intricate poetic constructions that comprise Songs 6–8: formally, the praises and hymns described in these songs are addressed to God and focus on Him; in actuality, though, the poetic imagination is mainly concerned with the angelic liturgy itself, reflecting the speaker's awe upon experiencing it. Cf. Nitzan (1994, 273–318).

## 5.0. Conclusion

Contemporary scholarship can no longer reconstruct the precise liturgical performance of the *Songs of the Sabbath Sacrifice*, as the chain transmitting this tradition was broken over two millennia ago. Nonetheless, close attention to the poetic form of the text, and especially to its rhythmic make-up, enables us to capture an echo of its performative potential. In so doing, one realises that the meaning of the *Songs* is not reducible to the semantic content of its language. Rather, structural permutations—best perceived when reading the text out loud—reshape the content, altering its emphases and transforming its focus. We may no longer be able to hear the angels' original music, but we must compose a tentative tune of our own in its stead if we are to hear anything at all.

## References

Alexander, Philip S. 2006. *The Mystical Texts*. Library of Second Temple Studies 61. London: T&T Clark.

Bakker, Arjen. 2014. 'The God of Knowledge: Qumran Reflections on Divine Prescience Based on 1 Sam 2:3'. *Revue de Qumran* 26 (3) [103]: 361–74.

Coulot, Claude. 2011. 'En quoi est-il unique? La figure de Dieu selon le cantique de l'holocauste du cinquième sabbat (4Q402 4; Mas 1k ShirShabb I)'. In *Le monothéisme biblique: Évolution, contextes et perspectives*, edited by Eberhard Bons et Thierry Legrand, 275–84. Paris: Cerf.

Davila, James R. 1996. 'Melchizedek, Michael and War in Heaven'. *Society of Biblical Literature Seminar Papers* 35: 259–72.

Gusella, Laura. 2002. 'The Therapeutae and Other Community Experiences of the Late Second Temple Period'. *Henoch* 24 (3): 295–329.

Falk, Daniel K. 2014. 'Material Aspects of Prayer Manuscripts at Qumran'. In *Literature or Liturgy? Early Christian Hymns and Prayers in their Literary and Liturgical Context in Antiquity*, edited by Clemens Leonhard and Hermut Löhr, 33–87. Wissenschaftliche Untersuchungen zum Neuen Testament II:363. Tübingen: Mohr Siebeck.

——— 2015. 'Liturgical Progression and the Experience of Transformation in Prayers from Qumran'. *Dead Sea Discoveries* 22 (3): 267–84.

García Martínez, Florentino, Eibert J.C. Tigchelaar, and Adam S. van der Woude et al. 1998. *Qumran Cave 11*. Vol. 2, *11Q2–18, 11Q20–31*. DJD 23. Oxford: Clarendon.

Harshav, Benjamin. 2008. *Metre and Rhythm in Modern Hebrew Poetry*. Jerusalem: Carmel. [Hebrew]

——— 2014. *Three Thousand Years of Hebrew Versification: Essays in Comparative Prosody*. New Haven, NJ: Yale University Press.

Jeffrey, Peter. 1987. 'Werner's *The Sacred Bridge*, Volume 2: A Review Essay'. *The Jewish Quarterly Review* 77 (4): 283–98.

——— 2004. 'Philo's Impact on Christian Psalmody'. In *Psalms in Community: Jewish and Christian Textual, Liturgical, and Artistic Traditions*, edited by Margot Fassler and Harold Attridge, 147–87. SBL Symposium 25. Atlanta: Society of Biblical Literature.

Lange, Armin. 1995. *Weisheit und Prädestination: Weisheitliche Urordnung und Prädestination in den Textfunden von Qumran*. Studies on the Texts of the Desert of Judah 18. Leiden: Brill.

Leonhardt, Jutta. 2001. *Jewish Worship in Philo of Alexandria*. Texts and Studies in Ancient Judaism 84. Tübingen: Mohr Siebeck.

Licht, Jacob. 1957. *The Thanksgiving Scroll*. Jerusalem: Bialik Institute. [Hebrew]

Lieber, Andrea. 2004. 'Voice and Vision: Song as a Vehicle for Ecstatic Experience in *Songs of the Sabbath Sacrifice*'. In *Of Scribes and Sages: Early Jewish Interpretation and Transmission of Scripture*. Vol. 2, *Later Versions and Traditions*, edited by Craig A. Evans, 51–58. London: T&T Clark.

Maier, Johann. 1995. *Die Qumran-Essener: Die Texte vom Toten Meer*. Vol. 2, *Die Texte der Höhle 4*. Munich: Ernst Reinhardt.

Mizrahi, Noam. 2009. 'The Supposed Relationship between the *Songs of the Sabbath Sacrifice* and *Hekhalot* Literature: Linguistic and Stylistic Aspects'. *Meghillot* 7: 263–98. [Hebrew]

——— 2017. 'Earthly Liturgy and Celestial Music: The Poetics of the *Cycle of Praises* of the Sixth Sabbath Song'. In *Gottesdienst und Engel im antiken Judentum und frühen Christentum*, edited by Jörg Frey and Michael R. Jost, 119–39. Wissenschaftliche Untersuchungen zum Neuen Testament II 446. Tübingen: Mohr Siebeck.

——— 2018. 'God, Gods, and Godhead in the Songs of the Sabbath Sacrifice'. In *The Religious Worldviews Reflected in the*

*Dead Sea Scrolls*, edited by Ruth A. Clements, Menahem Kister, and Michael Segal, 161–92. Studies on the Texts of the Desert of Judah 127. Leiden: Brill.

———— 2019. 'The Eleventh Song of the Sabbath Sacrifice: Literary Form and Exegetical Content'. *Tarbiz* 87 (1): 5–35. [Hebrew]

———— Forthcoming. 'The Seventh Song of the Sabbath Sacrifice: From Angelic Liturgy to Architectural Praise'. In *Ritual and Performance in the Dead Sea Scrolls*, edited by Michael Johnson, Jutta Jokiranta and Molly Zahn. Studies on the Texts of the Desert of Judah. Leiden: Brill.

Najman, Hindy, and Geoffrey Khan. 2022. 'Performance in Ancient and Medieval Judaism'. *Dead Sea Discoveries* 29 (3): 259–91.

Newsom, Carol A. 1985. *Songs of the Sabbath Sacrifice: A Critical Edition*. Harvard Semitic Studies 27. Atlanta: Scholars Press.

———— 1990. '"He has established for himself priests": Human and Angelic Priesthood in the Qumran Sabbath *Shirot*'. In *Archaeology and History in the Dead Sea Scrolls: The New York University Conference in Memory of Yigael Yadin*, edited by Lawrence H. Schiffman, 101–120. Journal for the Study of the Pseudepigrapha, Supplement Series 8. Sheffield: JSOT Press.

———— 1998. 'Shirot 'Olat HaShabbat'. In *Qumran Cave 4, VI: Poetical and Liturgical Texts, Part 1*, 173–401 and pls. XVI–XXXI. DJD 11. Oxford: Clarendon.

——— 2012. 'Religious Experience in the Dead Sea Scrolls: Two Case Studies'. In *Experientia*, vol. 2, *Linking Text and Experience*, edited by Colleen Shantz and Rodney A. Werline, 205–21. Atlanta: Society of Biblical Literature.

Newsom, Carol, and Yigael Yadin. 1984. 'The Masada Fragment of the Qumran Songs of the Sabbath Sacrifice'. *Israel Exploration Journal* 34 (2–3): 77–88.

Nitzan, Bilhah. 1994. *Qumran Prayer and Religious Poetry*. Translated by Jonathan Chipman. Studies on the Texts of the Desert of Judah 12. Leiden: Brill.

O'Donnell Polyakov, Emma. 2020. 'Liturgy, Performance Theory, and Aesthetic Experience'. *Journal of Ritual Studies* 34 (2): 31–40.

Puech, Émile. 1987. 'Notes sur le manuscrit des Cantiques du sacrifice du Sabbat trouvé à Masada'. *Revue de Qumran* 12 (4) [48]: 575–83.

Qimron, Elisha. 1986. 'A Review Article of *Songs of the Sabbath Sacrifice: A Critical Edition* by Carol Newsom'. *The Harvard Theological Review* 79 (4): 349–71.

——— 2010–14. *The Dead Sea Scrolls: The Hebrew Writings*. 3 vols. 3rd ed. Jerusalem: Yad Ben-Zvi. Revised digital edition (Tel Aviv 2023). [Hebrew]

——— 2013. 'The Third Person Masculine Plural Pronoun and Pronominal Suffix in Early Hebrew'. In *Hebrew in the Second Temple Period: The Hebrew of the Dead Sea Scrolls and of Other Contemporary Sources*, edited by Steven E. Fassberg, Moshe Bar-Asher, and Ruth A. Clements, 181–88. Studies on the Texts of the Desert of Judah 108. Leiden: Brill.

———. 2018. *A Grammar of the Hebrew of the Dead Sea Scrolls*. Jerusalem: Yad Ben-Zvi.

Reeves, John C. 1992. 'The Feast of the First Fruits of Wine and the Ancient Canaanite Calendar'. *Vetus Testamentum* 42 (3): 350–61.

Reymond, Eric D. 2014. *Qumran Hebrew: An Overview of Orthography, Phonology, and Morphology*. SBL Resources for Biblical Study 76. Atlanta: Society of Biblical Literature.

Schücking-Jungblut, Friederike. 2020. 'Reading the Songs of the Sabbath Sacrifice: Observations on Material, Layout, and Text'. In *Material Aspects of Reading in Ancient and Medieval Cultures: Materiality, Presence and Performance*, edited by Anna Krauß, Jonas Leipziger, and Friederike Schücking-Jungblut, 71–88. Materiale Textkulturen 26. Berlin: De Gruyter.

Segert, Stanislav. 1988. 'Observations on Poetic Structures in the Songs of the Sabbath Sacrifice'. *Revue de Qumran* 13.1–4 [49–52]: 215–23.

Taylor, Joan E., and David M. Hay. 2021. *Philo of Alexandria: On the Contemplative Life—Introduction, Translation, and Commentary*. Philo of Alexandria Commentary Series 7. Leiden: Brill.

Tov, Emanuel. 2004. *Scribal Practices and Approaches Reflected in the Texts Found in the Judean Desert*. Studies on the Texts of the Desert of Judah 54. Leiden: Brill.

Vermes, Geza, and Martin D. Goodman (eds). 1989. *The Essenes: According to the Classical Sources*. Sheffield: JSOT Press.

Werman, Cana, and Aharon Shemesh. 2011. *Revealing the Hidden: Exegesis and Halakha in the Qumran Scrolls*. Jerusalem: Bialik Institute. [Hebrew]

Werner, Eric. 1957. 'Musical Aspects of the Dead Sea Scrolls'. *The Musical Quarterly* 43 (1): 21–37.

# 'TEACHING THE SINNERS': A MOTIF AND ITS APPLICATION IN 4Q372 1

*Amrei Koch*

## 1.0. Motif Analyses as a Topic of 'Reading'—An Example from 4Q372 1

### 1.1. Between Reception and Production—Reading through the Horizons of Tradition

A basic definition of 'reading' is: "to look at and understand the meaning of written or printed words or symbols" (Hornby 2020, 1280). Accordingly, reading is connected to understanding, that is, to making sense out of a given framework of signs. Along these lines, reading means both reception and production: The reader receives the script-bearing artefact (Schücking-Jungblut 2020, 71) and productively constitutes meaning from—and also into—it (Schorch 2007, 120). Consequently, reading unfolds in the tension between a received written account and the paratextual knowledge provided by the reader, based on the intellectual culture of which he or she is part (Leipziger 2021, 3–4, 8–13).

Reading, in this sense, involves an interaction between mainly orally transmitted knowledge and the written artefact.

Thus, reading places a written account within a new and wider context. In this regard, a motif, which is defined as a "minimal thematic unit [of meaning]"[1] (Prince 2020, 71), is a possible textual trigger that can evoke new thematic interrelations (Edenburg 2016, 164–66). By representing the meaning of a particular situation on which it is based, a motif concentrates ideas and expressions and lends itself to adaptation and transformation in different literary settings (Talmon 2013, 4–5, 8). The result is a productive application and re- (or even new) configuration of motifs within the horizons of a tradition (Schorch 2007, 117), which in turn leads the reader to associate texts and contexts within the framework of their intellectual culture (Edenburg 2016, 165–66).

The widespread use and re-combination of textual elements originating from the older Hebrew literature within the Dead Sea Scrolls and further Late Second Temple literature can be described as a distinct form of text production through 'reading' of older texts and textual traditions, and demonstrates that the historical reader of the Late Second Temple period was expected to have access to a wide range of literary motifs.

## 1.2. Motif Analysis as a Path to the Contexts of 4Q372 1

'Teaching the sinners' is a motif that is present in the older Hebrew literature as well as in the Dead Sea Scrolls. Focusing on 'reading' in terms of the reception and production of meaning

---

[1] The supplemented text follows Dupriez (1991, 290). See further Dupriez (1991, 291); Kreuzer et al. (2005, 92).

(see above), the present article offers an analysis of the interaction between mainly orally transmitted knowledge and the written material artefact in the specific case of the motif 'teaching the sinners' and its application in 4Q372 1.

4Q372 1 contains a text about Joseph. It is the largest of the three major fragments of 4Q372, consists of 32 lines—"seven complete or virtually so, and the remaining lines one-third to two-thirds complete" (Schuller 1990, 349)—and is palaeographically dated to the late Hasmonean or early Herodian period (Schuller 1990, 349).

'Teaching the sinners' appears prominently in a short passage in 4Q372 1.27:

...וללמד לפשעים חקיך ולכל עזביך תוֹרֹ[תך–

'...and to teach transgressors your statutes and all who abandon you [your] instru[ction]'[2]

Although the quoted passage appears in a fragmentary context, it can be inferred with a high degree of certainty that Joseph is the one who figures as teacher here.

The fragment contains a narrative and a poetic text. The narrative part contextualises the latter as a prayer of Joseph, who "[was given] into the hands of foreigners" (ll. 14–15; translation: Schuller 1990, 355). As far as the fragmentary context reveals, Joseph's people is scattered among the nations (ll. 4–5, 11) and a "hostile people" (ll. 20; translation: Schuller 1990, 355) dwells in the land, blaspheming and desecrating the sacred in order to make Israel jealous and to enrage Joseph's brothers (ll. 12–14).

---

[2] Translation: author's own.

Schuller (1990, 371) was the first to propose the theory that 4Q372 1 is an anti-Samaritan text. This interpretation has been widely accepted, developed, and modified in research, especially in relation to the figure of Joseph (García Martínez 1991; Knibb 1992; Kartveit 2009). Schuller (1990, 368, 376) argues that the text delegitimises the proto-Samaritans with their sanctuary on Mount Gerizim as the true descendants of Joseph, since Joseph here represents the northern tribes in exile. Kugler, Thiessen, and Mitchell, however, do not share the anti-Samaritan theory: Kugler (2006, 273–4) pays attention to the presupposed reception context of 4Q372 1, identifies Joseph as "an archetype of the [Qumran] community" (Kugler 2006, 267), and places the fragment within the rivalry between the Qumranites and the Jerusalem priesthood. Thiessen (2008, 395) suggests that 4Q372 1 is not necessarily anti-Samaritan, but against those in the southern tribes who claim to be independent from the fate of the northern tribes, whose restoration is yet to come. Mitchell (2009, 192–93) in contrast, distances 4Q372 1 from historical associations and interprets the fragment as a prophetic text promising a Josephite Messiah.

As the discussion shows, the nature of 4Q372 1, including its genre and provenance, as well as the figure of Joseph, remains a contentious topic of research.[3] The present study offers an analysis of the motif 'teaching the sinners' found in 4Q372 1 and fur-

---

[3] For discussion see e.g., Schuller (1990); García Martínez (1991); Knibb (1992); Kugler (2006); Thiessen (2008); Kartveit (2009); Mitchell (2009).

ther ancient Hebrew sources that may have been part of the literary and cultural world in the context of which 4Q372 1 was composed, received, and read. Motif analysis can thus help to reconstruct the intellectual framework of the historical readership and their literary and cultural contexts.

In terms of methodology, this study is concerned with the horizons of understanding, not with the reconstruction of influence. Accordingly, the present paper describes the specific configuration of the motif 'teaching the sinners' and its transformations in textually traceable processes of tradition (Najman 2017, 516–17). In this regard, 'reading' is a means of constituting meaning in the field of tension between material and non-material—mainly oral—contexts.

## 2.0. The Motif of 'Teaching the Sinners' in Ancient Hebrew Texts

### 2.1. Identifying the Motif of 'Teaching the Sinners'

'Teaching the sinners' combines the concepts education and transgression. In the older Hebrew literature, acts of education are mostly referred to by למ"ד *qal/piʿel*, יר"ה₃ *hifʿil*, יס"ר *qal/piʿel* or יכ"ח *hifʿil* (Gesenius 2013, 463), and even יד"ע *hifʿil*—with למ"ד being the most common verb, attested 87 times in the Hebrew Bible (Widder 2014, 215–17). The concept 'transgression' is covered by a broad range of lexemes (Knierim 2001, 365), including especially the verbs פש"ע, חט"א, and רע"ע. According to Knierim, the commonality of these words is that they all point first and foremost to a "violation of values... that God sets and protects for humanity and for Israel" (Knierim 2001, 365; own translation). Education and transgression, thus, represent broad thematic fields with multifarious semantic nuances, which allows for a multitude of configurations and modifications of the motif 'teaching the sinners'. Three questions are guiding the analysis of the motif in its context of use: Who exactly is meant by 'sinners'? Who is the teacher? And what is to be taught?

## 2.2. The Motif of 'Teaching the Sinners' in the Hebrew Bible

### 2.2.1. Deuteronomy

The verb 'to teach' למ״ד *pi"el* is prominently used in Deuteronomy (e.g., Deut. 4.1, 5.31, 20.18). In general, Deuteronomy portrays Moses as the teacher of the people of Israel, teaching them to fulfil the statutes and judgements (חקים and משפטים) of YHWH on His behalf (Deut. 4.1, 5.31).

Deut. 4.1

וְעַתָּה יִשְׂרָאֵל שְׁמַע אֶל־הַחֻקִּים וְאֶל־הַמִּשְׁפָּטִים אֲשֶׁר אָנֹכִי מְלַמֵּד אֶתְכֶם לַעֲשׂוֹת לְמַעַן תִּחְיוּ וּבָאתֶם וִירִשְׁתֶּם אֶת־הָאָרֶץ אֲשֶׁר יְהוָה אֱלֹהֵי אֲבֹתֵיכֶם נֹתֵן לָכֶם:

'And now, O Israel, listen to the statutes and the ordinances I am about to teach you to observe, so that you may live and go in and take possession of the land that the LORD, the God of your fathers, is giving you.'[4]

---

[4] English translations of biblical passages are based on the ESV Bible (2011) and are adapted slightly, whenever necessary, according to my own understanding of the texts.

Although the Israelites are not explicitly referred to as 'sinners', whenever Moses is presented as a teacher, Deuteronomy as a whole repeatedly characterises the Israelites as 'sinners' who violate YHWH's values (e.g., Deut. 1.41; 9.16). Accordingly, the Israelites need to become accustomed to YHWH's laws[5] in order to live and to enter and to dwell in the Promised Land (Deut. 4.1, 5, 10, 14). In this respect, Deuteronomy paints a picture in which people who are unfamiliar with the rules and break them are instructed and rebuked. Such a scene might closely resemble a possible origin of the motif, rooted outside its textual application in an anthropological or historical situation (Talmon 2013, 4–5).

Within the pedagogical concept of Deuteronomy YHWH's statutes are part of a cross-generational learning and teaching process (Eisele 2013, 118; Widder 2014, 110–11), since the Israelites are also called to teach their children (Deut. 4.10; 11.19). In this regard, למ״ד *qal/piʿʿel* aims at the formation of a collective identity in terms of becoming accustomed to a community of tradition (Eisele 2013, 117).

## 2.2.2. Psalms

In several psalms, YHWH himself is frequently referred to as a teacher, giving instructions in his ways and statutes (e.g., Ps. 25.4–5; 94.12; 119.12; 143.10). In Ps. 25.4–5 the psalmist, who

---

[5] Compare also Jenni (1984, 872–75), who emphasises the meaning 'to become accustomed to' for למ״ד.

is identified with David (Ps. 25.1), desires to be instructed by YHWH in his ways (cf. Exod. 33.13).[6]

Ps. 25.4–5

דְּרָכֶיךָ יְהוָה הוֹדִיעֵנִי אֹרְחוֹתֶיךָ לַמְּדֵנִי: ⁵ הַדְרִיכֵנִי בַאֲמִתֶּךָ ׀ וְלַמְּדֵנִי כִּי־אַתָּה אֱלֹהֵי יִשְׁעִי אוֹתְךָ קִוִּיתִי כָּל־הַיּוֹם:

'⁴ Make me know your ways, O LORD; teach me your paths. ⁵ Lead me in your truth and teach me, for you are the God of my salvation; for you I wait all the day long.'

The praying person confesses his sins and hopes for forgiveness (Ps. 25.7, 10). In this context, YHWH is held to be good and righteous because he teaches the sinners in the way.

Ps. 25.8–9

⁸ טוֹב־וְיָשָׁר יְהוָה עַל־כֵּן יוֹרֶה חַטָּאִים בַּדָּרֶךְ: ⁹ יַדְרֵךְ עֲנָוִים בַּמִּשְׁפָּט וִילַמֵּד עֲנָוִים דַּרְכּוֹ:

'⁸ Good and upright is the LORD; therefore he instructs the sinners in the way. ⁹ He leads the humble in what is right, and teaches the humble his way.'

---

[6] Abernethy (2015, 350–51) suggests for Ps. 25.4–5 that instead of the common understanding of the Torah as object of learning, the idea of YHWH teaching his nature and character might be more appropriate, since YHWH makes himself known by acting for his people. In addition, however, it should be noted that in the LXX the focus on the Torah is attested for Ps. 25.4–5 (Böhler 2021, 473). Widder (2014, 208–9), on the other hand, emphasises the dynamics between YHWH, the teacher, and his willing student, as the psalmist wants to be taught what he already knows and only "gains knowledge and insight as YHWH allows it" (Widder 2014, 208).

The sinner is characterised as one who has done wrong, but fears YHWH (v.12).⁷

Ps. 94 refers to 'YHWH's teaching' within rhetorical questions (vv.9–10) in the context of an admonition to the wicked:

Ps. 94.10

הַיֹסֵר גּוֹיִם הֲלֹא יוֹכִיחַ הַמְלַמֵּד אָדָם דָּעַת׃

'He who disciplines the nations, does he not rebuke? He who teaches man knowledge!'

The psalmist reminds the brutish and fool (v.8) of YHWH being the supreme authority, instructing the nations and teaching mankind knowledge (v.10). In the role of the sinners to be taught Ps. 94 introduces the wicked who are proud and arrogant (vv.2–4), harm God's people (vv.5–6), and do not care about YHWH (v.7; Kraus 1978, 827). Consequently, YHWH is called to rise against the wicked, as it is possible for him who teaches nations and mankind (vv.1–2, 10).

Ps. 51 presents the psalmist, identified with David (Ps. 51.1), as teaching. After deeply confessing his sin and praying for

---

⁷ According to Kraus (1978, 353), the reading חַטָּאִים attested in MT seems to be attenuated in the Septuagint: The Greek translator apparently read the particple חטאים*, emphasising the act of sinning rather than a permanent personal inadequacy, to deal with the problem of sinners receiving YHWH's instruction. However, according to Schulz (1969, 12), it could be argued that the use of the participle could express the unity of the perpetrator and his act in an intensifying way, as evident in legal texts (e.g., Exod. 21.12). From this perspective, the Septuagint reading would even emphasise the gap between the sinner and YHWH, which YHWH overcomes through his teaching.

a renewed heart and mind (v.12), the psalmist, like a vow, promises to teach the sinners YHWH's ways (v.15):

Ps. 51.15

אֲלַמְּדָה פֹשְׁעִים דְּרָכֶיךָ וְחַטָּאִים אֵלֶיךָ יָשׁוּבוּ:

'I will teach transgressors your ways, and sinners will return to you.'

According to the structure of parallelism, פשעים is equivalent to חטאים. In the prayer, the psalmist describes himself as a man who has committed transgressions, פשע, and sin, חטאת, (vv.3b, 5). His own experience of transgression and healing in YHWH (vv.8, 14) qualifies him to be a witness, a teacher to sinners who are not yet aware of YHWH's ways (Kraus 1978, 547).[8] In this regard, the sinner is able to recognise his error once he has come to know YHWH's ways (Kraus 1978, 547).

## 2.2.3. Prophetic Texts: Isaiah, Jeremiah, and Ezekiel

The motif of 'teaching the sinners' also relates to the concept of 'knowing YHWH', which is found in many Biblical texts (e.g., Exod. 6.7; Isa. 49.23; Ezek. 20.42). Along these lines, prophetic texts from the books of Isaiah, Jeremiah, and Ezekiel attest to the motif of 'teaching the sinners' (cf. Isa. 45.20–25; Jer. 12.16, 16.21; Ezek. 36.23; 38.23; 39.7). For example, Jer. 16.21 imagines the nations coming to know YHWH (יד״ע *hifʿil*) through his demonstration of power and might:

---

[8] For interpreting the 'ways of YHWH' in Ps. 51.15 also in terms of experiences with YHWH see Widder (2014, 115).

Jer. 16.21

לָכֵן֙ הִנְנִ֣י מֽוֹדִיעָ֔ם בַּפַּ֣עַם הַזֹּ֔את אוֹדִיעֵ֖ם אֶת־יָדִ֣י וְאֶת־גְּבֽוּרָתִ֑י וְיָדְע֖וּ כִּֽי־שְׁמִ֥י יְהוָֽה׃ ס

'Therefore, behold, I will make them know, this once I will make them know my power and my might, and they shall know that my name is the LORD.'

This can be described as a reconfiguration of the motif of 'teaching the sinners', in as far as YHWH makes himself known to people who are not yet accustomed to Him through teaching that is close to revelation (Jer. 16.19–21; Fischer 2005, 536–37).

In particular, texts from the book of Jeremiah seem to express a voice that is critical of human attempts to teach knowledge of God (cf. Jer. 9.4; cf. Fischer 2005a, 173–74).[9] In this respect, the New Covenant proclaimed in Jer. 31.31–34 no longer includes human teaching in knowledge of God.

Jer. 31.34

וְלֹ֣א יְלַמְּד֗וּ ע֜וֹד אִ֤ישׁ אֶת־רֵעֵ֙הוּ֙ וְאִ֣ישׁ אֶת־אָחִ֔יו לֵאמֹ֖ר דְּע֣וּ אֶת־יְהוָ֑ה כִּֽי־כוּלָּם֩ יֵדְע֨וּ אוֹתִ֜י לְמִקְטַנָּ֤ם וְעַד־גְּדוֹלָם֙ נְאֻם־יְהוָ֔ה כִּ֤י אֶסְלַח֙ לַֽעֲוֺנָ֔ם וּלְחַטָּאתָ֖ם לֹ֥א אֶזְכָּר־עֽוֹד׃ ס

'And no longer shall each one teach his neighbour and each his brother, saying, "Know the LORD," for they shall all know me, from the least of them to the greatest, declares the LORD. For I will forgive their iniquity, and I will remember their sin no more.'

---

[9] Widder (2014, 118–19) describes Jeremiah in this respect as an ironic commentary on Deuteronomy.

For the covenant partners, the direct relationship with YHWH replaces and renders superfluous the teaching of a human teacher (Fischer 2005a, 173).

## 2.3. The Motif of 'Teaching the Sinners' in Ancient Hebrew Texts from the Judean Desert

### 2.3.1. 11QPs$^a$ 24

The motif of 'teaching sinners' is attested in 11QPs$^a$ 24 (Syriac Psalm III or Ps. 155; Xeravits and Porzig 2015, 205). In this text, the praying person humbles himself in view of his sins (l. 7, 11: חטאת; l. 11: פשע), as he realises that he cannot stand before YHWH and his judgement because of these sins (ll. 6–7). Consequently, he prays for insight into YHWH's instruction (תורה) and to be taught his laws (משפטים) in 24.8:

הבינני יהוה בתורתכה ואת משפטיכה למדני
'Instruct me, YHWH, in your law, and teach me your precepts.'[10]

The teacher in this psalm is God, who is further characterised as the 'judge of truth' (l. 6: דין האמת). Accordingly, the teaching concerns legal instruction (תורה, משפט). The 'sinner' is a person who turns to YHWH in prayer (l. 3). Thus, he is already aware of YHWH and discerns his dependence on YHWH through introspection (Newsom 2020, 82). In this context, 'sin' is primarily the state of incapability to be righteous before YHWH (l. 7).

---

[10] Translation: García Martínez and Tigchelaar (1999, 1177).

The purpose of teaching also includes a universal perspective in this psalm, l. 9:

וישמעו רבים מעשיכה ועמים יהדרו את כבודכה

'So that many may hear your deeds and nations may honour your glory.'[11]

On the one hand, the teaching is addressed to the praying person, who is characterised as a sinner. On the other hand, it has an effect among the nations (עמים), for YHWH's glory is to be praised among them.

### 2.3.2. Further Modifications of the Motif of 'Teaching the Sinners'

11QPs<sup>a</sup> 18 (Syriac Psalm II or Ps. 154; Xeravits and Porzig 2015, 205), seems to modify the motif of 'teaching the sinners': The focus of the text is not on sinners, but on the wisdom that YHWH gives and teaches to mankind (ll. 3–4). This teaching aims to make known and glorify YHWH and his attributes (ll. 1, 3–7). As a result, 'sin' becomes a characteristic of the wicked (l. 13: רשעים) and has a universal perspective which also addresses 'all simple people' (l. 3: לכול פותאים) and 'those who lack understanding' (l. 5: לחסרי לבב).

Another modification of 'teaching the sinners' is apparently included in 1QH<sup>a</sup> 10.5–21. The text refers to a binary pattern that distinguishes between outsiders and insiders, between sinners and 'those who turn from sin' (Newsom 2004, 304). According to Newsom, the speaker in this concept functions as a horizontal

---

[11] Translation: García Martínez and Tigchelaar (1999, 1177).

and vertical mediator, having a relationship with both groups and with God (2004, 304–5).

1QHª 10.5–21 does not explicitly designate the speaker as teacher. However, the text suggests that the speaker also takes this function: Having received instruction through God himself (l. 19), he is, on the one hand, a מליץ דעת ברזי פלא (l. 15) 'a knowledgeable mediator of secret wonders' (García Martínez and Tigchelaar 1999, 163) for his community of אוהבי מוסר (l. 16) 'those who love moral discipline' (Stegemann et al. 2009, 142). On the other hand, he serves as איש ריב 'an adversary' (Stegemann et al. 2009, 142) for the outsiders, described as מליצי תעות 'mediators of error' (García Martínez and Tigchelaar 1999, 163). Thus, the teaching of the speaker of 1QHª 10.5–21 also affects those who are labelled 'sinners'. In addition, the psalm is usually assigned to the Teacher Hymns, also known as the *Hodayot* of the leader (Newsom 2004, 288; Xeravits and Porzig 2015, 214).[12] The leader as a figure helps "to define clear boundaries for the community" (Newsom 2004, 300), which also implies a pedagogical function.

1QHª 12.6–13.6, also mostly seen as a Teacher Hymn, or *Hodayah* of the leader (Newsom 2004, 288; Xeravits and Porzig 2015, 214), unfolds the binary pattern in the wider horizon of a group of God's people, with the leader standing in contrast to

---

[12] For a discussion of whether the speaking figure is to be identified with the מורה הצדק 'teacher of righteousness' see e.g., Newsom (2004, 287–300); Harkins (2011).

rivals who seduce parts of that people to reject the truth (Newsom 2004, 319). The text portrays the speaker as an agent of the divine:

1QH$^a$ 12.28–29

ובי האירותה פני רבים ותגבר עד לאין מספר כי הודעתני ברזי פלאכה.

'Through me you have illumined the face of many, and you have increased them beyond number. For you have made me understand your wonderful mysteries.'[13]

The ultimate source of enlightenment is God. The speaker has been granted divine insight (ll. 5–6, 28–29) and therefore is able to enlighten others as an intermediary of the divine. Nevertheless, the speaker presents himself in humility:[14] When he realised his sin and guilt and that of his ancestors, he suffered also physically (ll. 34–36) and arose through remembering God's strength and kindness (ll. 36–37). This self-presentation emerges from a general anthropological reflection on sin: Human existence is a lifetime of guilt (ll. 30–31). Only God can atone iniquity (כפ״ר עוון) and purify from guilt (טה״ר מאשמה) through his righteousness (l. 38).

The people who have accepted the speaker's teachings are not called 'sinners' in 1QH$^a$ 12.6–13.6. However, in the light of the considerations given, 'sin' also extends to humanity in general. 'Sin' is therefore both part of the past of each member of the community and remains a common threat.

---

[13] Translation: Stegemann et al. (2009, 166).

[14] On self-negation before God in this context see Newsom (2004, 324–25).

## 2.4. Summary

The selected texts reflect different configurations of the motif of 'teaching the sinners', as it has been taken up, transformed, and adapted to different contexts. In Deuteronomy, Moses is presented as a teacher par excellence. His teaching relates to a particular community and requires intergenerational transmission. In this regard, a fundamental aim of teaching and learning is to fit in with the community order (Eisele 2013, 117, 119). However, in the psalms from the Hebrew Bible that have been analysed, YHWH himself (e.g., Ps. 25, 94, 119), but also a person who has experienced and recognised his own sins (Ps. 51), are presented as the most appropriate teachers for sinners. There is a certain tendency here to suggest that sinners are not necessarily people from one's own community, but may include other nations. The teaching, especially of YHWH, may extend beyond the people of Israel (Ps. 94). This extension can also be seen in prophetic texts (Jer. 16.21; Ezek. 36.23) that connect the motif to the knowledge of God, and even testify to the idea that human teaching of the knowledge of God will be superfluous in the New Covenant (Jer. 31.31–34).[15] Since these texts imply an eschatological dimension, the tendency to include the nations as recipients of teaching seems to be linked to the idea of an eschatological teaching (Widder 2014, 209–10). In this regard, Widder (2014, 204) refutes YHWH's instruction to the nations before the

---

[15] In relation to the knowledge of God, it is noteworthy that the human teaching of the prophet Ezekiel is primarily for the purpose of convicting his listeners of sin (e.g., Ezek. 16.2). The subject of knowing God is beyond his control.

eschatological instruction, but recognises that YHWH generally teaches individuals among Israel and the nations how to use cultural achievements.

The analysed texts also refer to different contents of teaching: In the case of Moses in Deuteronomy, it is YHWH's law, חקים and משפטים (Deut. 4.1). The psalms from the Hebrew Bible also often emphasise YHWH's law and statutes as the subject of instruction (e.g., Ps. 119.12).[16] However, especially in Ps. 25 and 51, the 'ways' (דרכים) of YHWH may also refer to YHWH's nature and character (Abernethy 2015, 350–1), which is close to the idea of knowledge of God. Similarly, the analysed prophetic texts include the knowledge of God in teaching (Jer. 16.21).

'Teaching' also plays an important role in the Dead Sea Scrolls and for the Qumran community. Here, several texts make use of the motif of 'teaching the sinners' in a modified form compared to the older Hebrew literature. Within the analysed texts, God and His mediator, who is construed as the leader of the community, are teachers.[17] The content to be taught refers to legal instruction (11QPs$^a$ 24) and more generally to knowledge of the divine realm (e.g., 1QH$^a$ 10.5–21).

---

[16] See further the LXX reading of Ps. 25.8–10, sharpening the text to an identification of YHWH's 'ways' with his law (Kraus 1978, 353; Bons 2019, 1566–1567).

[17] Furthermore, reference should also be made to the *maśkîl* who functions as a teacher inside the community. For discussion see e.g., Newsom (2004, 165–74); Newman (2015, 249–66); Bakker (2023, 40–49, 127–32).

The people who are taught, however, are for the most part not explicitly called 'sinners' in these texts. Remaining in a generally binary worldview, the examples analysed avoid characterising their own community as sinners across the board and tend to refer to outsiders as 'sinners' (e.g., 1QH$^a$ 10.5–21; 1QH$^a$ 12.6–13.6). However, in an anthropological perspective, the concept of 'sin' can also be applied on mankind in general (1QH$^a$ 12.6–13.6), and the leader and his teachings also have an effect on 'sinners' outside the community (1QH$^a$ 10.5–21), at least in terms of delimitation.

## 3.0. The Motif of 'Teaching the Sinners' in 4Q372 1

4Q372 1 applies the motif 'teaching the sinners' within a prayer put into the mouth of Joseph, who is in captivity, being verbally and probably also physically maltreated (l. 15), crying out to YHWH (ll. 16–32).

The prayer begins with a plea for salvation and justice (ll. 16–17). Joseph then praises God's sovereignty and his mercies that are granted to people who seek him (ll. 18–19). This is followed by a description of the situation, whose text is fragmentarily preserved, but apparently takes up the information of the narrative part (ll. 19–22), including "[Joseph's] complaint that his own land has been taken away from him" (Bernstein 2003, 31). Finally, Joseph announces that he will rise for justice and righteousness, and praise YHWH (ll. 23–32).

The psalm shifts from the plea for salvation through YHWH to the prospect of Joseph's own action, which includes 'teaching the sinners':

4Q372 1.27

...וללמד לפשעים חקיך ולכל עזביך תוֹרֹ[תך–

'...and to teach transgressors your statutes and all who abandon you [your] instru[ction].'[18]

The cotext and context suggest (ll. 24–25) that it is Joseph who teaches the transgressors (פשעים). The parallelism equals פשעים and כל עזביך, suggesting that the 'sinners' once had a relationship with YHWH, but had abandoned him. Therefore, the motif of 'teaching the sinners' in 4Q372 1 most likely does not include the teaching of a foreign nation, as in Ps. 94 or Jer. 16.19–21, but is restricted to Israel. Both this observation as well as the presence of a human teacher, namely Joseph, demonstrates that the motif in 4Q372 1 differs from the prophetic texts in Jer. 16 and Jer. 31.[19] It is therefore unlikely that the historical reader would have inferred that Joseph's 'teaching the sinners' in 4Q372 1 relates to an eschatological event.[20] Moreover, by mentioning a rather specific transgression, namely turning away from YHWH (עזביך), 4Q372 1 does not necessarily induce the reader to apply

---

[18] Translation: author's own.

[19] Schuller (1990, 366) suggests that עזביך refers to Jer. 17.13.

[20] The expression 'time of his (i.e., Joseph's) end' (עת קץ לו) in 4Q372 1.15 does not necessarily imply an eschatological perspective, but could rather refer to a fixed date in the future (Schuller 1990, 362). Similarly, Kartveit (2009, 122–3) interprets עת קץ as referring to Joseph's redemption from the בני נאכר.

the broader anthropological concept of sin as attested in e.g., 1QH$^a$ 12.6–13.6.

The content of Joseph's teaching are YHWH's statutes (חקיך) and his instruction (תֹּו̊רֹ[תך]), the latter being partly based on a very likely reconstruction of the text. In this respect, the configuration of the motif is similar to that in Deuteronomy and 11QPs$^a$ 24.8. Moreover, and unlike e.g., Ps. 94, 119, Jer. 16, and 11QPs$^a$ 18, 24, Deuteronomy and 4Q372 1 refer to a human teacher, as also implied in 1QH$^a$ 10.5–21, 12.6–13.6. However, given the human nature of the teacher in connection with the legal content to be taught, the historical reader is led to associate knowledge primarily from the tradition attested in Deuteronomy, including the idea of a community of tradition and the land, the inheritance of which is tied to legal obedience (Deut. 4.1). However, there are also clear differences to the conceptual world of Deuteronomy:

First, in 4Q372 1 the community is primarily associated with Jacob and Joseph (ll. 13, 19, 21), while in Deuteronomy there is also a strong focus on Moses.

Second, the land is described in a state more reminiscent of the situation in, e.g., Jer. 16.13, 18 (ll. 4–8, 19–20)—once inhabited by themselves, but now lost to people who desecrate it—even though Joseph's brothers have already returned from exile in 4Q372 1.1–10, 14.[21] In this regard, 4Q372 1 also differs from

---

[21] The text apparently applies the Sin–Exile–Return pattern and presupposes "the restoration of the Judean community" (Schuller 1990, 370) after the exile, namely of Levi, Judah, and Benjamin (Schuller 1990,

the narrative situation in Deuteronomy, where the Israelites are about to enter the land, and its loss is merely a future possibility as a punishment for disobedience (Deut. 4.1, 25–27). This punishment has already happened in the conceptual world of Jer. 16.10–11 and probably also 4Q372 1.4, 6.

Finally, the teacher Joseph differs from the human teachers portrayed in the other texts analysed. On the one hand, Joseph is not presented as a sinner. Unlike Ps. 51 and 11QPs$^a$ 24, Joseph's psalm does not contain a confession of sin, which is appropriate here in relation to the teaching. On the other hand, and different from Moses in Deuteronomy and the speaker of 1QH$^a$ 10.5–21, 12.6–13.6, there is no explicit mandate for Joseph to mediate between YHWH and the people in 4Q372 1, at least in the extant text.

However, the mandate to mediate could be associated from the paratextual knowledge of the historical reader, including the prolific Joseph tradition in early Judaism (Kugler 2006, 263–264, 276). Part of that Joseph tradition is also to present him as a wise man, as can be seen in Ps. 105.22 LXX and Aramaic Levi Document 90, where Joseph is characterised as a scholar (Schuller 1990, 366).

Ps. 105.21–22 LXX

> $^{21}$ κατέστησεν αὐτὸν κύριον τοῦ οἴκου αὐτοῦ καὶ ἄρχοντα πάσης τῆς κτήσεως αὐτοῦ $^{22}$ τοῦ παιδεῦσαι τοὺς ἄρχοντας αὐτοῦ ὡς ἑαυτὸν καὶ τοὺς πρεσβυτέρους αὐτοῦ σοφίσαι

---

370). See also Knibb (1992, 165–70); Thiessen (2008, 389–95), focusing more on the fate of the northern tribes.

'²¹ He made him (i.e., Joseph) lord of his house and ruler of all his possessions, ²² to educate his officials to be like himself and to teach his elders wisdom.'²²

AramLev 90

חזו בני ליוסף אחי [ד]מאלפא ספר ומוסר חכמה
'Consider, my sons, Joseph my brother [who] taught scribal craft and the instruction of wisdom.'²³

4Q372 1 seems to take up and further profile this tradition by explicitly mentioning a process of insight in prayer, with Joseph expressing to know and to understand (Kugler 2006, 271):

4Q372 1.31

אני ידעת[י] והתבוננתי
'I know and I understand'²⁴

In this respect, Joseph as described in this psalm is already a wise teacher who is in close relationship with God and gains even deeper insights through prayer, thereby reminding the historical reader of the processes of insight that God himself grants to humans who humble themselves and to human teachers of the divine, as expressed in e.g., Ps. 51, 1QH ͣ 12.28–29. Considering the given textual framework, the mandate to mediate between God and humans can therefore be transferred on the figure of Joseph.

---

[22] Translation: NETS Bible (2000).

[23] Translation: Drawnel (2004, 371).

[24] Translation: author's own.

## 4.0. Conclusion

4Q372 1 presents a combination of elements mainly known from the older Hebrew literature that shape the text, testify to a productive reading and re-assembly of those texts, and determine the reading of 4Q372 1 by associating the different contexts of the applied motif of 'teaching the sinners'. In terms of 'reading', understanding the written artefact involves components that are not contained in the written account. These include knowledge of configurations of this motif in earlier and contemporary traditions as well as the tradition of Joseph.

'Teaching the sinners' is present in the older Hebrew literature of Deuteronomy, Psalms, and prophetic texts. Within the Dead Sea Scrolls, the motif is frequently modified and first and foremost applied in psalmic texts. Remarkably, in the analysed texts of 1QH[a] and 11QPs[a], the characterisation of their own community as 'sinners', as in Deuteronomy or the 'Biblical' prophetic texts, is hardly emphasised in connection with this motif. Moving towards a dualistic worldview (e.g, 1QS 1.1–15; Xeravits and Porzig 2015, 150–52), this motif seems to acquire more significance in prayers that deal with an individual or anthropological dimension of sin (11QPs[a] 24, 1QH[a] 12.6–13.6) as well as with the definition of their own community (1QH[a] 10, 12). In this regard, the use of the motif in 4Q372 1 differs from its application in the analysed texts of 1QH[a] and 11QPs[a].

4Q372 1 most closely resembles the Deuteronomic configuration of this motif, which uses למ״ד and involves a human teacher as subject, the statutes of YHWH as content, and the people of his community as addressees. However, the context of its application is different from that of Deuteronomy, and it is more akin to that referred to, e.g., in the texts of the book of Jeremiah. Nevertheless, 4Q372 1 does not accentuate the eschatological shade of the analysed texts of Jeremiah, but enriches the motif by means of the tradition of Joseph, who is conceived as a wise teacher. Here 4Q372 1 offers an alternative or even counter-tradition to Ps. 51.15 and its attribution to David. Strikingly, the latter forms the closest parallel to the formulation of the motif in 4Q372 1, as if to contrast the figure of Joseph with the figure of David by profiling Joseph beneath David in the tradition of Moses' teaching.

In sum, the various configurations of the motif of 'teaching the sinners' as attested in Deuteronomy, Psalms, and the prophetic texts of the Hebrew Bible, as well as the analysed texts of 1QH$^a$ and 11QPs$^a$, not only help to shed light on its use in 4Q372 1, but are in fact essential for decoding it. Motif analysis, therefore, contributes to the study of this text, and other motifs of 4Q372 1 need to be analysed as well. However, the results of the analysis of 'teaching the sinners' can already be related to the research on 4Q372 1 as follows. The differences between the application of the motif in Jer. 16 and 31 compared to 4Q372 1 suggest that the historical reader would probably not have understood the text as prophecy promising a Josephite Messiah (Mitchell 2009). However, Joseph's profile in that fragment seems to speak in favour of the theory that this is an anti-Samaritan text, as it could be seen as a polemical appropriation of a central figure of Samaritan identification, severely offending the Samaritans and Mount Gerizim. The application of this motif in

4Q372 1 fits with a social group that feels connected to Joseph, holds Deuteronomy in high esteem, and is concerned with 'teaching', a community of tradition, and the land. This could indicate an interest in the fate of the northern tribes (Thiessen 2008), or a connection with the Qumran community (Kugler 2006), even though this explanation has to deal with the problem that any group-specific self-identification as 'sinners' is not emphasised in e.g., 1QH$^a$ and 11QPs$^a$, requiring a transformation of 'sin' into anthropological categories.

## References

Abernethy, Andrew T. 2015. 'God as Teacher in Psalm 25'. *Vetus Testamentum* 65 (3): 339–51.

Bakker, Arjen F. 2023. *The Secret of Time: Reconfiguring Wisdom in the Dead Sea Scrolls*. Studies on the Texts of the Desert of Judah 143. Leiden: Brill.

Bernstein, Moshe J. 2003. 'Poetry and Prose in 4Q371–373 *Narrative and Poetic Composition*$^{a,b,c}$'. In *Liturgical Perspectives: Prayer and Poetry in Light of the Dead Sea Scrolls—Proceedings of the Fifth International Symposium of the Orion Center for the Study of the Dead Sea Scrolls and Associated Literature, 19–23 January, 2000*, edited by Esther G. Chazon, Ruth Clements, and Avital Pinnick, 19–33. Studies on the Texts of the Desert of Judah 48. Leiden: Brill.

Böhler, Dieter. 2021. *Psalmen 1–50*. Herders Theologischer Kommentar zum Alten Testament. Freiburg im Breisgau: Herder.

Bons, Eberhard. 2019. 'Psalm 25[26]'. In *Septuaginta Deutsch: Erläuterungen und Kommentare zum griechischen Alten Testament,* edited by Martin Karrer and Wolfgang Kraus, 1566–7. Stuttgart: Deutsche Bibelgesellschaft.

Drawnel, Henryk. 2004. *An Aramaic Wisdom Text from Qumran: A New Interpretation of the Levi Document.* Supplements to the Journal for the Study of Judaism 86. Leiden: Brill.

Dupriez, Bernard. 1991. *A Dictionary of Literary Devices: Gradus, A–Z.* Translated and adapted by Albert W. Halsall. Toronto: University of Toronto Press.

Edenburg, Cynthia. 2016. *Dismembering the Whole: Composition and Purpose of Judges 19–21.* Ancient Israel and Its Literature 24. Atlanta: SBL Press.

Eisele, Wilfried. 2013. 'Erziehung'. In *Wörterbuch alttestamentlicher Motive,* edited by Michael Fieger, Jutta Krispenz, and Jörg Lanckau, 117–21. Darmstadt: Wissenschaftliche Buchgesellschaft.

Fischer, Georg. 2005. *Jeremia 1–25.* Herders Theologischer Kommentar zum Alten Testament. Freiburg im Breisgau: Herder.

———. 2005a. *Jeremia 26–52.* Herders Theologischer Kommentar zum Alten Testament. Freiburg im Breisgau: Herder.

García Martínez, Florentino. 1991. 'Nuevos Textos no bíblicos procedentes de Qumrán'. *Estudios Bíblicos* 49: 97–134.

García Martínez, Florentino, and Eibert J. C. Tigchelaar (eds). 1999. *The Dead Sea Scrolls Study Edition.* Leiden: Brill.

Gesenius, Wilhelm. 2013. *Hebräisches und Aramäisches Handwörterbuch über das Alte Testament,* edited by Herbert Donner. 18th edition. Berlin: Springer.

Harkins, Angela Kim. 2011. 'Who is the Teacher of the Teacher Hymns?: Re-Examining the Teacher Hymns Hypothesis Fifty Years Later'. In *A Teacher for All Generations: Essays in Honor of James C. VanderKam,* edited by Eric F. Mason, Samuel I. Thomas, Alison Schofield, and Eugene Ulrich, 1:449–67. Supplements to the Journal for the Study of Judaism 153/I. Leiden: Brill.

Hornby, Albert S. 2020. *Oxford Advanced Learner's Dictionary of Current English,* edited by Diana Lea, Jennifer Bradbery, Victoria Bull, Leonie Hey, Stacey Bateman, Kallah Pridgeon, and Gary Leicester. 10th edition. Oxford: Oxford University Press.

Jacob, Benno. 1997. *Das Buch Exodus.* Stuttgart: Calwer Verlag.

Jenni, Ernst. 1984. 'למד lmd lernen'. In *Theologisches Handwörterbuch zum Alten Testament,* edited by Ernst Jenni and Claus Westermann, Vol. 1:872–5. 4th edition. München: Kaiser.

Kartveit, Magnar. 2009. 'Who are the 'Fools' in 4QNarrative and Poetic Composition?' In *Northern Lights on the Dead Sea Scrolls: Proceedings of the Nordic Qumran Network 2003–2006,* edited by Anders Klostergaard Petersen, Torleif Elgvin, Cecilia Wassen, Hanne von Weissenberg, Mikael Winninge, and Martin Ehrensvärd, 119–33. Studies on the Texts of the Desert of Judah 80. Leiden: Brill.

Knibb, Michael A. 1992. 'A Note on 4Q372 and 4Q390'. In *The Scriptures and the Scrolls: Studies in Honour of A. S. van der*

*Woude on the Occassion of his 65th Birthday*, edited by Florentino García Martínez, Anthony Hilhorst, and Casper J. Labuschagne, 164–177. Leiden: Brill.

Knierim, Rolf P. 2001. 'Sünde: II. Altes Testament'. In *Theologische Realenzyklopädie*, vol. 32, edited by Gerhard Müller, 365–72. Berlin: De Gruyter.

Kraus, Hans-Joachim. 1978. *Psalmen. 1. Teilband: Psalmen 1–59*. Biblischer Kommentar. 5th edition. Neukirchen-Vluyn: Neukirchener Verlag.

Kreuzer, Siegfried, Dieter Vieweger, Friedhelm Hartenstein, Jutta Hausmann, and Wilhelm Pratscher. 2005. *Proseminar I: Altes Testament—Ein Arbeitsbuch*. 2nd edition. Stuttgart: Kohlhammer.

Kugler, Robert A. 2006. 'Joseph at Qumran: The Importance of 4Q327 Frg.1 in Extending a Tradition'. In *Studies in the Hebrew Bible, Qumran, and the Septuagint Presented to Eugene Ulrich*, edited by Peter W. Flint, Emanuel Tov, and James C. VanderKam, 261–278. Supplements to Vetus Testamentum 101. Leiden: Brill.

Leipziger, Jonas. 2021. *Lesepraktiken im antiken Judentum: Rezeptionsakte, Materialität und Schriftgebrauch*. Materiale Textkulturen 34. Berlin: De Gruyter.

Mitchell, David C. 2009. 'A Dying and Rising Josephite Messiah in *4Q372*'. *Journal for the Study of the Pseudepigrapha* 18 (3): 181–205.

Najman, Hindy. 2017. 'Ethical Reading: The Transformation of the Text and the Self'. *The Journal of Theological Studies* 68 (2): 507–29.

Newman, Judith H. 2015. 'Embodied Techniques: The Communal Formation of the Maskil's Self'. *Dead Sea Discoveries* 22 (3): 249–66.

Newsom, Carol A. 2020. '"If I had said..." (Ps. 73:15): Retrospective Introspection in Didactic Psalmody of the Second Temple Period'. In *Petitioners, Penitents, and Poets: On Prayer and Praying in Second Temple Judaism*, edited by Timothy J. Sandoval and Ariel Feldman, 69–82. Beihefte zur alttestamentlichen Wissenschaft 524. Berlin: De Gruyter.

———. 2004. *The Self as Symbolic Space: Constructing Identity and Community at Qumran*. Studies on the Texts of the Desert of Juda 52. Leiden: Brill.

Prince, Gerald. 2020. *A Dictionary of Narratology*. Lincoln: Nebraska Paperback.

Schorch, Stefan. 2007. 'Die Rolle des Lesens für die Konstituierung alttestamentlicher Texte'. In *Was ist ein Text?: Ägyptologische, altorientalistische und alttestamentliche Perspektiven*, edited by Ludwig Morenz and Stefan Schorch, 108–22. Beihefte zur alttestamentlichen Wissenschaft 362. Berlin: De Gruyter.

Schücking-Jungblut, Friederike. 2020. 'Reading the Songs of the Sabbath Sacrifice: Observations on Material, Layout, and Text'. In *Material Aspects of Reading in Ancient and Medieval Cultures: Materiality, Presence and Performance*, edited by Anna Krauß, Jonas Leipziger, and Friederike Schücking-Jungblut, 71–88. Materiale Textkulturen 26. Berlin: De Gruyter.

Schuller, Eileen. 1990. '4Q372 1: A Text About Joseph'. *Revue de Qumran* 14 (3): 349–376.

Schulz, Hermann. 1969. *Todesrecht im Alten Testament: Studien zur Rechtsform der Mot-Jumat-Sätze*. Beihefte zur alttestamentlichen Wissenschaft 114. Berlin: Töpelmann.

Stegemann, Hartmut, Eileen Schuller, and Carol Newsom. 2009. *1QHodayot$^a$: With Incorporation of 1QHodayot$^b$ and 4QHodayot$^{a-f}$*. Discoveries in the Judean Desert 40. Oxford: Clarendon Press.

Talmon, Shemaryahu. 2013. *Literary Motifs and Patterns in the Hebrew Bible: Collected Studies*. Winona Lake: Eisenbrauns.

Thiessen, Matthew. 2008. '4Q372 1 and the Continuation of Joseph's Exile'. *Dead Sea Discoveries* 15 (3): 380–95.

Widder, Wendy L. 2014. *'To Teach' in Ancient Israel: A Cognitive Linguistic Study of a Biblical Hebrew Lexical Set*. Beihefte zur alttestamentlichen Wissenschaft 456. Berlin: De Gruyter.

Xeravits, Géza G., and Peter Porzig. 2015. *Einführung in die Qumranliteratur: Die Handschriften vom Toten Meer*. Berlin: De Gruyter.

# PRAISE AS EXORCISM AND EXORCISM AS PRAISE: WRITING FOR SUPERNATURAL AUDIENCES IN THE HYMNS OF THE MASKIL AND LATE-ANTIQUE JEWISH 'MAGIC'[1]

*Dorota Molin*

## 1.0. Introduction

'Reading' is typically framed in terms of communal practices, be they interpretive, scribal, performative or otherwise, and their reception within the performing community. While this model is very useful for a host of ancient Jewish texts, within this same 'library' of texts, we also find compositions that were not intended for human audiences and participants—or at least not

---

[1] I sincerely thank Profs Hindy Najman, Gideon Bohak and Adi Wiener, whose input I benefited from greatly in my research for this paper, and Dr Daniel Waller for our earlier stimulating conversations on Jewish late-antique 'magic'. I also express my sincere gratitude to Prof. Hector Patmore and Dr Johanna van der Schoor for their helpful comments as reviewers.

*only* for these audiences. Such compositions were aimed at supernatural audiences—God, angelic beings, but also evil spirits, such as demons and their dominions. What endowed these compositions and their performance with the power to engage, compel and even co-opt such non-human beings?

In order to show particular examples of these efficacious strategies, this article considers two groups of ancient Jewish texts intended to efficaciously traverse the double permeable boundary between the human and the transmundane. The first is the Hymns of the Maskil (4Q510–511; henceforth 'Hymns'), considered by scholars to be a liturgical-esoteric composition produced within the Qumran community (i.e., 'sectarian'). The second group includes a collection of late-antique apotropaic prayers, traditionally classified as 'magic', 'incantations' or 'amulets',[2] which were either inscribed on metal lamellae (in the Levant and in Egypt), or inside earthenware bowls (in Mesopotamia), and used to perform exorcisms or provide general protection.[3]

---

[2] The word 'magic' is used here as a shorthand and thus in quotation marks. Recent scholarship has highlighted the many intersections of 'magic' with rabbinic discourse and law (e.g., Manekin-Bamberger 2015, 2020; Bhayro 2015; Gross and Manekin-Bamberger 2022), the early Jewish liturgy (e.g., Naveh and Shaked 1993, 22–31; Molin 2023), the transmission of Hebrew (Mishor 2007; Molin 2020; and Frim 2021;) and scribal practices (Waller 2020; Bohak 2024), placing the amulet and bowl production firmly within the Jewish 'mainstream' or 'rabbinic' culture.

[3] The amulets A3 (Naveh and Shaked 1985, 50–54), A25 (Naveh and Shaked 1993, 85–86) and the so-called Amarna amulet (Kotansky, Naveh and Shaked 1992, 9–12), in addition to two bowl texts, bowl 67

Previously, the Qumran Hymns and the late-antique incantations have mostly been studied independently of one another. This seems to have been due to the emphasis on the distinctiveness of the Hymns of the Maskil encountered in the earlier scholarship. This distinctiveness, in turn, was attributed to suggested theological differences between the Hymns on the one hand, and the late-antique Jewish 'magic' plus the 'direct incantations' from Qumran itself on the other (see below).[4] For instance, in her pioneering study on apotropaic prayer, Eshel (2003, 86) suggests that while both the "direct incantations" and the Hymns from Qumran describe God's might, they do so for somewhat different purposes in these two groups of texts. In the case of the Hymns, the reference to God's power constitutes a "part of their thanksgiving to God," while in the incantations, it is "forecasting the doom of the evil forces." Such a dichotomous view of genres is even stronger in the work of Nitzan (1994, esp. 235, 248–49), who believes that the (sectarian) Hymns of the Maskil reflect "a clear limitation upon the magical power under which the Maskil from Qumran acts." Purportedly, the Maskil conducts magic in a more moderate way: he consciously limits himself to "the praise of God over the recitation of Divine Names in an [direct] adjuration" (Nitzan 1994, 248), which is said to be motivated by a reverence towards that name. Lange (1997, 431) also argues for a

---

(republished in Isbell 1975, originally published in Jeruzalmi, 1964) and bowl 69 (Isbell 1976, 32).

[4] E.g., 4Q560, 8Q5, or 11Q11.

limited use of 'magic' by the Maskil, ascribing the power to exorcise demons to God rather than the praying human.[5]

By contrast, in this article, I argue that even the less direct ways of challenging evil forces and the focus on divine praise in the Hymns constitute powerful spiritual 'weapons' in these texts (cf. Angel 2012, 4). Moreover, the Hymns partly parallel certain late-antique spells, in that both combine such the techniques of direct and indirect addresses. Indeed, I suggest that this combination of direct and indirect address is the very key to the efficacy of both of these groups of texts, as unpacked in Section 3.

The integration of the Hymns into the discussion on apotropaic and exorcist prayer is further motivated by research advances which have already begun to show the ways in which the Yaḥad participated in a larger tradition of ancient Jewish 'magic'. For instance, Cohn (2008) has argued for an amuletic origin of the early *tefillin* from Qumran, and several scholars have highlighted the apotropaic features of 11Q11 = 11QApocryphal

---

[5] This interpretation, however, is based on one poorly preserved fragment (4Q511 48–51, l.2), where it is unclear whether the one who 'terrifies' is God or the Maskil. Thus, Lange (1997, 431) transcribes the phrase in question as ובפיﹾ יפחד 'and with my mouth, he terrifies', while Angel (2022, 74) transcribes ובפיﹾ לפחד 'and with my mouth to terrify'. But even with this controversy aside, the power of Maskil's words to terrify remains "a widely distributed theme in the Songs of the Sage" (Angel 2022, 75; 4Q511 35, ll. 6–7 or 4Q510 1, ll. 4–5), so that the Maskil's initiative in the ritual remains undeniable.

Psalms.⁶ Additionally, the very presence of 'direct incantations' such as 4Q516 and 8Q5 at Qumran, despite their apparently non-sectarian origin, suggests their use by the Yaḥad (e.g., Penney and Wise 1994), or at least an interest therein.⁷ Moreover, scholars have identified formulae and interpretive traditions which are shared between Qumran (including possibly sectarian texts) and late-antique 'magic' (e.g., Bohak 2013), such as the (likely) apotropaic use of psalms (esp. 91), the Priestly Blessing (Num. 6.24–26), or the Shema (Deut. 4.6–9).⁸

These research advances invite us to consider texts such as the Hymns of the Maskil in light of other ancient Jewish magic traditions. Indeed, the Hymns can serve as an excellent subject, because they share very concrete philological and broader thematic links with several late-antique amuletic and bowl-inscribed

---

⁶ See, however, Patmore (2022), who offers an alternative reading of 11Q11 v 4–vi 3 ('the Belial psalm'). Patmore suggests that rather than taunting and thus exorcising the demon directly, the 'afflicted' one requests God to do so.

⁷ This cultural permeation may also have occurred in both directions, i.e., towards the Yaḥad, but also from Qumran outwards. For example, a copy of the sectarian Songs of the Sabbath Sacrifice was found outside Qumran, at Masada (see Newsom and Yadin 1999). At least this composition, therefore, was apparently known outside the Yaḥad, raising questions about a wider dissemination of the sectarian literature.

⁸ This practice is found in 11Q11, the Havdala of Rabbi Aqiva, the bowls and amulets, is referred to in the Babylonian Talmud (Shevuot 15b), and eventually becomes 'canonised' in the Jewish prayer book. See e.g., Naveh and Shaked (1993, 22–31), Levene, Marx and Bhayro (2014); see also Shaked (2005), Bohak (2008, esp. 87–119) and Bhayro (2021).

prayers. Bringing these two groups of texts to bear on each other in this paper, I argue that both texts offer us interpretive clues and fresh possibilities for the other family of compositions. These two text groups also exhibit parallels with regard to modes of engaging and leveraging the supernatural, which in turn offers us glimpses of the worldviews which empowered such efficacious rituals.

Specifically, without denying their historical, compositional or performative differences, I show the capacity of both groups of prayers to simultaneously engage multiple transmundane audiences, skilfully recruiting different beings to different aims, often with a single unit of discourse. The specific techniques of multi-audience/participant engagement which stand at the heart of this paper involve the construction of a text as both a 'song of praise' (שיר תשבחות in various orthographies) and as an 'exorcism'. While praise and exorcism can in principle constitute independent modes of engagement with the supernatural, in the Hymns and a group of late-antique compositions, they are brought together to reinforce each other, and to ultimately achieve the same aims. Indeed, the Qumran Hymns testify to a 'conspiracy' of prayer and exorcism, in which both functions are important in their own right, but also interact closely with an eschatological vision. This, in turn, blurs the boundary between 'magic', 'thanksgiving' and '(petitionary) prayer' in the Qumran Hymns. I thus challenge the assumption of 'limited magic' in the Hymns, as well as showing that what may appear an 'indirect exorcism' is still part and parcel of a powerful, apotropaic performance.

These findings, in turn, have broader methodological implications, showing that petitionary prayer, praise and eschatological discourse are non-dichotomous modes of engaging the transmundane. Depending on the specific composition, these modes can either stand alone or converge, and can thus in principle be used to reinforce each other. Their conceptual non-dichotomy also means that these modes may be equally central to the aesthetic and/or efficacy of a single composition. Thus, we need not restrict ourselves to a single 'ultimate' goal of a ritual or a composition (*pace* Eshel 2003).

## 2.0. Overviews of the Compositions: The Hymns and Late-antique 'Magical' 'Songs of Praise'

At the heart of this study are two groups of compositions which feature the language of both praise and exorcism, as shown in Section 2.3. below.

### 2.1. The Hymns of the Maskil from Qumran

The composition labelled as Hymns of the Maskil (or the *Songs of the Sage*) is preserved in two scrolls, 4Q510 and 4Q511;[9] the former in a much more fragmentary state, though the latter is also severely mutilated. The composition consists of several songs, but their exact number remains uncertain, with possible textual differences between the two scrolls obscured by their fragmentary

---

[9] For a text edition based on the material reconstruction of 4Q510–511 with translation, see Angel (2022); the *editio princeps* was produced by Baillet (1982). For other studies, see Nitzan (1994), Lange (1997), Eshel (2003) or Angel (2017).

state. Still, we can establish that the Hymns had at least three songs, likely six, and possibly even more (Angel 2017, 192–93). In her pioneering study on apotropaic texts from Qumran, Nitzan (1994, 243) describes the song as "intertwined thanksgiving, proclamation of frightening, and praise." This "proclamation of frightening" functions here specifically within the dualistic worldview of the Yaḥad, which considered itself especially prone to demonic attacks due to its status as the 'sons of light' within the cosmic battle of light and darkness.[10]

Governed by the heading 'for the Maskil' (see Section 2.3. below), these songs were most likely intended for communal performance. Support for this is provided by the imperative forms in the Hymns (Angel 2022, 31), but we lack clear information concerning their specific liturgical context. Several proposals about the *Sitz im Leben* of these compositions have been offered, including a performance at the annual covenant ceremony alongside the liturgical blessings and curses (Eshel 2003, 83–84), and a regular liturgical performance integrated into the Qumran liturgy (Penner 2014, 190). Others have suggested a performance at times of "danger of supernatural origin" (see Nitzan 1994, 238), as well as initiation into the sect (Kister 1999, 174–76). This obscurity of their original function prevents us from definitely categorising the Hymns as either considered apotropaic (in the strict sense of being preventative) or exorcist. Evidence for the 'sectarian' origin of the Hymns comes from their use of themes such

---

[10] See especially Bohak (2008, 106) and the references therein; also, Kister (1999) and Reimer (2000). For Qumran demonology, see e.g., Tigchelaar (2019).

as earthly-angelic worship, election and participation in divine wisdom, and from the (elevated role of the) Maskil.[11]

## 2.2. Late-antique 'Songs of Praise'

The late-antique texts studied here belong to the corpus of the so-called Palestinian amulets and—more marginally—the Mesopotamian incantation bowls.[12] Most of these amulets and bowl-texts including those studied here are exorcisms of malicious beings. In addition, aggressive magic is also attested in the corpus as a whole, and some texts may have been intended pre-emptively, including for general protection from the evil eye.[13] To achieve their goals, these amulets engage both directly and indirectly with demonic and angelic beings, as well as with God.[14] They use techniques such as adjuration, invocation of names of power, and citation of biblical(-liturgical) formulae in order to achieve protection from evil and to leverage divine power. Some also employ

---

[11] See Angel (2022, e.g., 34 and 39–40) and the references therein for parallels with Hodayot, Community Rule and Songs of the Sabbath Sacrifice, as well as overlaps with the Enochic tradition and Jubilees.

[12] The corpus of the bowls is much larger, with hundreds of inscribed bowls known to date. For a recent overview of the incantation bowls, see the introduction in the volume by Shaked, Ford and Bhayro (2022).

[13] For overviews, see e.g., Naveh and Shaked (1985; 1993) or Bohak (2008, esp. 143–226).

[14] For direct commands to demons, see A3, ll. 4–5, given in Section 2.3 below.

drawings and magical characters to symbolise or seal the exorcism with para-linguistic means, and even narrative and riddles to overpower evil beings (e.g., Waller 2024).

Inscribed on metal sheets ('*lamellae*'), these Jewish[15] amulets come from the Levant, Anatolia and Egypt.[16] There is literary-thematic, lexical and possibly even orthographic/philological evidence to suggest direct contact between the 'magical' practitioners of the Land of Israel and Mesopotamia,[17] pointing to a larger, shared tradition of apotropaic prayer in Jewish Late Antiquity. Such a shared tradition is also suggested by the shared motifs discussed in this paper.

While these amulets show varying levels of scribal acumen and literary complexity, there is little doubt that most of them would have been produced by professionals—scribes, very likely

---

[15] The category of 'Jewish' amulets is used by scholars for texts which feature the Aramaic square script and, typically, Jewish Palestinian Aramaic and sometimes Hebrew. For a discussion on the 'Jewishness' of late-antique 'magic', on cultural convergence and the question of the identity of clients, see e.g., Bohak (2008, 291–350).

[16] See Naveh and Shaked (1985; 1993) for text editions of these amulets. There are some forty amulets found and published to date, though more are known to exist. For an overview of the historical and cultural context of the amulets, see e.g., Bohak (2008, 149–50) and Harari (2017, 216–51).

[17] See, respectively, Naveh and Shaked (1993, e.g., 21), and Molin (2017, e.g., 40–41, 76–77).

acting as medical-spiritual experts in dealing with various supernaturally-caused ailments.[18] On many occasions these practitioners seem to have made use of (tried and tested) 'recipes'. The use of recipes is suggested by the reoccurrence of specific formulae (opening phrases, invocations, biblical-liturgical material). Still, the variation of such formulae within the published corpus suggests a creative process of formulae incorporation, rather than a simple 'copy-paste' method. Such 'variation on a (familiar) motif' is also visible in the amulets which draw from praise phraseology, discussed below.

The composition and inscription of amulets may well have been paired with another ritual, such as their recitation or another performance. Still, the scribal, literary and conceptual acumen visible in many amulets (and in their bowl-inscribed counterparts) strongly suggest that the *material*, i.e., written prayers, were also strongly efficacious, rather than being a mere by-product of a *spoken* incantation.[19] Thus, the very production of these powerful 'text-objects' is treated here as a type or 'performance'. Under this definition, 'performance' refers to the production of the written text, and to its application (on the body, in the case of the amulets, and buried, in the case of the bowls). Like oral performance, such a process would likely have been governed by its own rules of efficacy and aesthetics, and involved communi-

---

[18] See Bohak (2024) on the art of inscribing metal lamellae, and Naveh and Shaked (1993, 22–31) on Jewish/biblical motifs in the amulets.

[19] Waller (2020) and Molin (2023) have emphasised the significance of writing and 'writtenness' in the context of the incantation bowls.

cation through language—significantly, with audiences that despite being non-human, could be reached through the medium of human writing.

## 2.3. The Language of 'Song of Praise' in the Hymns of the Maskil and in Late-antique Apotropaic Texts

The starting point of this paper consists of two striking features of the texts in question. The first is the entanglement of 'praise' with 'exorcism'; the second is that this entanglement occurs in both text groups, despite their separation by time, space and (sectarian) affiliation. The links between these two groups of texts involve not only the general themes, but also the specific lexical constructions conveying these themes.

More specifically, both groups of texts express 'praises' with different variants of the word תשבוחות (תשבאחות, תשבוחות, תושבוחות, etc.), often in combination with שיר 'song'. This praise terminology is especially noteworthy because of its limited presence in the (extant) sectarian Qumran corpus: elsewhere, the Hebrew תשבוחות appears only in the Songs of the Sabbath Sacrifice.[20] In the amulets and bowls where it is attested, this formula always appears in its Hebrew form (i.e., with the Hebrew plural suffix -ות) even while other parts of that same composition are in Aramaic. Such general and specific parallels between the Hymns and the amu-

---

[20] E.g., in 4Q403 1 I 3, 31, 32, 36 (Newsom 1990, 182). Newsom (ibid) points out several other linguistic and thematic parallels between these two Qumranic compositions, implying a strong affinity between these two texts.

lets, in turn, raise questions about the possible liturgical-apotropaic traditions into which the Hymns and the late-antique texts might be tapping, and which may have thrived for centuries.[21] This suspicion concerning a deeper tradition is supported by the choice of Hebrew for this phrase in the amulets in question, rather than (the synchronic) Jewish Palestinian or Babylonian Aramaic.

Within the Hymns of the Maskil, the term תשבוחות 'praises' appears in what was likely the heading of one song, and perhaps even the entire composition.[22] Angel (2022, 82) proposes that the phrase beginning with 'praises' could have been preceded by למשכיל שיר/שירי 'For the Maskil, a song/songs of':

1. [    ]praises, ble[ssings to the k]ing of glory. Words of thanksgiving in psalms of        [    ] תשבוחות בר[כ]ות
  למ[ל]ך הכבוד דברי הודות
  בתהלי

2. [    ]to the God of knowledge, splendour of p[ow]ers, God of gods, Lord of all the holy ones. [His] domini[on]        [ ] לאלוהי דעות תפארת
  ג[בור]ות אל אלים אדון
  לכול קדושים וממש[ל]תו

---

[21] While a broader comparative exploration of such a possible tradition is out of this paper's scope, it remains a possibility. Indeed, scholars have identified specific 'magical' formulae that occur at Qumran as well as in the medieval Cairo Genizah (Bohak 2008, 298–305, and 2013), which also involve the Hekhalot tradition (e.g., Shaked 1995). The broader links between the 'magical' and the liturgical traditions from Qumran to the Middle Ages were already highlighted by Naveh and Shaked (1993, 17–31).

[22] This phrase also appears in also in 4Q511 10.23.

3. is over/against all the power‑ful mighty ones, and by the might of his powe[r] all are terrified and scattered, and they flee in haste from before the majesty of the ab[ode] of     על כול גבורי כוח ומכוח גבור[ת]ו יבהלו ויתפזרו כול ויחפזו מהדר מֹעֹ[ון]

4. his royal glory. *vacat* And I, the Maskil, proclaim his majes‑tic splendor in order to frighten and terr[ify]     כבוד מלכותו ואני משכיל משמיע הוד תפארתו לפחד ולבֹ[הל]

5. all the spirits of the destroying angels and the bastard spirits, demon, hyenas, Lilith, howlers and [desert beasts]     כול רוחי מלאכי חבל ורוחות ממזרים שד אים[23] לילית אחים ו[ציים ]

(4Q510 1 4–5, corresponding to the reconstructed 4Q511 10 1–8)

Comparable designations are found across several late-antique amulets, and in two published bowl texts. For instance, A3 (i.e., 'amulet 3') in Naveh and Shaked (1985, 50–54) is construed entirely as 'a song of praise to the King of the Worlds', paralleling the (reconstructed) song heading from the Hymns:

1. 'A song of praise to the King of the World     שיר תשבחות למלך עלמ[י]ה

2. Yah, Yah, Yah, Yahish of the World, I-am-     [י]ה יה יה יחיש עולמים אהיה

---

[23] On שד אים, see also Mizrahi and Patmore (2019), who argue that these are two demonological terms, based on the conflation of Isa. 13.21–22 and 34.14.

3. who-I-am, the King who speaks with distinct mystery     אשר אהיה מלך ממל<ל> ברוז[24] פרוש
4. To every bad and evil-doing spirit, that you should not     אל כל רוח בישה ומבאשה דלה
5. Cause pain to Rabbi Eleazar the son of Esther…     תיחשין לרבי אלעזר ברה דאסתיר

(A3, Naveh and Shaked 1985, 50–51; bronze amulet, Ḥorvat Kanaf)

In the other late-antique compositions, the expression 'song of praise' is embedded *within* the incantation. In A25, for instance, 'praise' appears in l. 5, following the opening formulae and the request (to angels?) to 'exorcise'. This amulet appears to have been prefabricated, with blank spaces in l. 6 and likely l. 10, where the client's name was later filled (cf. Bohak 2008, 152, n. 19).[25] This, in turn, may suggest that such an exorcist 'song of praise' was a more widely-used template; a formulation considered widely applicable, perhaps transmitted in a spell 'recipe book' (see e.g., Bohak 2011).

---

[24] This *mater lectionis waw* in the word that seems to stand for רז 'mystery' occurs in place where a long *a* is expected (the antecedent of the Tiberian *qameṣ*), and seems to indicate a backed and likely also rounded quality of the vowel. For parallel phenomena and their likely phonetic environments, see e.g., Juusola (1999, 54–68; the Aramaic of the Mesopotamian bowls) and Molin (2017, 17–28; Hebrew in the Mesopotamian bowls).

[25] The space after the name indicates that the name was filled in later; there are no other empty spaces in this amulet; see Naveh and Shaked (1993, 85) for a drawing.

5. Expel the evil spirit from Nona,     גערו רוחה בישתא מן נונ[ה]

6. The daughter of Megale, (*vacat*) in the name of *th wbh yh* (magic symbols)     ברתה דמגלי *vacat* בשם תה ובה יה יה

7. A song of praises to God, to the Highest God, against/over all harm and against     שיר תשבחות לאלהא לאלהא עליה על כל פגע ועל

8. all b(lemish). Da'ot the angel, Sang and Faranges his holy angels...     כל מ(ום) דאות מלאכה סנג ופרנגיס מלאכו[ני קד[ישוי די] [

9. ... evil breathing (?). May they guard [Nona, d]aughter     [ ] [ין נחיר]ין] בישין יטרון ל[נונה ב]רתה

(A25 Naveh and Shaked 1993, 85–86; bronze amulet, unknown provenance)

The so-called Amarna amulet (Kotansky, Naveh and Shaked 1992) also makes use of similar structures, as part of a complex amuletic composition in Greek, Aramaic and Hebrew. Of interest here are especially lines 22–26, which frame its own efficacious discourse as a reiteration of a song performed by David: to exorcise the evil spirits from King Saul (l. 21b).[26] The Amarna amulet's version of this 'Davidic' song begins in l. 22a, with פדני 'save

---

[26] This tradition is also known to us earlier Jewish sources; see for instance the book known as *The Antiquities of the Bible* (Bohak 2008, 98 and the references therein) and the 'apocryphal psalms' of 11Q11 ( = 11QPsalms), which frame Psalm 91 as an apotropaic prayer, possibly also attributing it to David (see Bohak 2008, 108–9).

me'. The amulet seems to become efficacious following the client's performance of this 'save me' formula, since the client is commanded to do so in l. 22b (אמור 'say'). The praiseworthy attributes of the divine addressee of this song are then listed (ll. 22b–23) and the exorcist verse Zech. 3.2 is quoted (l. 23), both of which are likely still part of the 'Davidic' exorcism.[27] These are followed by the exorcism 'proper' in line 25. This whole section is in Hebrew, up to l. 26, at which point Aramaic is resumed.

| | | |
|---|---|---|
| 21b. | These are the words of David, the songs that sing (?), that he used to say over [... Saul] | אלה דברי דויד המנגינות<br>המנגנות שהיה אמר על<br>[ שאול] |
| 22a. | the King: 'Save (O Lord) and rescue me from all the evil [things], the afflictions, and from all the evil spirits | המלך פדיני ---- והצילני<br>מכל הרעים הפגעים ומכל<br>הרוחות הרעות[28] |
| 22b. | that... before the Merci[ful] One (?). Say a song of praise to the honoured king... | ש[ ]ה קדם רחמה אמור<br>שיר תשבחות למלך<br>המכובד... |
| 23. | and mighty, the God that created the spirits... Hallelujah, the Lord rebuke you, who rebukes Satan, ruler of all... | וגיבור האל שברא את<br>הרוחות [ ] אמ]<br>הלליויה יגער— בך הגוער<br>בסטן מושל הכל [ ] |

---

[27] I follow Kotansky, Naveh and Shaked (1992), who mark the end of this exorcist song at the start of line 25, the end being accordingly indicated with ' in the English translation below. L. 24 has angelic invocations and the quotation of Gen. 32.3, it is irrelevant to the present discussion and therefore omitted here.

[28] The four dashes in the amulet may be a way to refer to the divine name.

| | | |
|---|---|---|
| 25. | this God.' I adjure you with (?), (I adjure) you, John son of Benenata... Yah, I adjure,... Yah Yah [ ] Yah [ ] go away from me [ ] | אלוהים זה אשביעית יתכון בא יתכון יואניס בן בנהנאטא בא] [ יה אשבע [ ] יה יה [ ] יה סורה [ ] ממני |
| 26. | from me, do not afflict... God, my God... a song to the king... from all eternity. Yah, Yah, I-am-who-I-am, the king who speaks (?) against/over you said/commanded | ממני אל תגעו ב] [ אל אלהי [ ] שיר למלך [ ] איש [ ] עולמי [ ] (ה)עולמים יה יה אליה אשר אליה[29] מלכה דמלל עליך אמר |
| 27a. | Who has authority over every evil and disease-causing spirit. I adjure you by... | דשליט בכל רוח ביש ומבאש אשבעת {ת} יתכון ב[ ] |

(Kotansky, Naveh and Shaked 1992, 9–12)[30]

Similar 'song of praise' formulae and the description of God's marvellous character are also found in a few published incantation bowls (see Isbell 1975, bowl 67, and Isbell 1976, bowl 69).[31]

---

[29] The end of Hebrew. The Hebrew phrase אשר אליה אליה is most likely a corruption of the divine title אהיה אשר אהיה, reflected in the translation, 'I-am-who-I-am'.

[30] For a discussion of this amulet with further references, see also Wiener (2021, 33–60).

[31] An excerpt from Text 67 is given in Section 3.1. below.

## 3.0. Engaging the Wider Spiritual Realm: Intertwining Participants and Performative Objectives

### 3.1. Who is Reading? The Efficacy of Multiple Addressees

The Qumran Hymns and the late-antique 'praise' amulets introduced above (A3, A25 and the Amarna amulet) invoke and mobilise various supernatural entities, using both direct and indirect invocations. As shown above (Section 1), some earlier studies on the Hymns emphasised the difference between the direct and the indirect invocation types, arguing that reflects theological differences. In this section, however, I argue that the techniques of combined direct and indirect addresses are crucial to the efficacy of both groups of compositions (the Hymns and the amulets) because they enable the simultaneous engagement of the wider spiritual realm, thereby ensuring the ritual's robustness and effectiveness. Thus, even an implicit engagement of a transmundane being can become a powerful way of ensuring this being's participation in the efficacious ritual. Such an engagement of multiple participants, in turn, implies that a single performance could fuse different genres and pursue multiple efficacious goals—a possibility further explored in the subsequent section (3.2).

First, the Hymns of the Maskil self-consciously articulate the intention of affecting demonic entities, doing so throughout the composition. The effects of divine praise on demons are mentioned in at least three different songs, appearing in cols. 3, 5,

10, and 11, as well as in the unplaced frg. 8 (cf. Angel 2022, 34). Col. 11, for example (4Q510 1 4–5, given above in Section 2.3.), seems to have included the beginning of a hymn. There, the Maskil makes explicit the aim of his own praise: to 'scare and terrify all the spirits of the destroying angels' (ll. 4–5). The immediately preceding section of praise (ll. 2–3) is also significant, as it highlights specific divine qualities. Thus, rather than simply praising God in general terms, it specifically gives thanks for God's power over all supernatural beings, including 'the holy ones' (l. 2) and the 'mighty ones', which are to be 'terrified and scattered' (l. 3).

Such specific formulation of praise was thus likely intended to be 'received' by these evil and powerful beings, even though they are not addressed directly (cf. Angel 2012). This impression is reinforced by the Hymns' lexical choices: for instance, in l. 4 above,[32] the Maskil is *making heard* (משמיע) divine attributes which implies a wider audience, rather than just proclaiming them towards God. Even though indirect (and thus in a sense 'limited'), this form of demon intimidation could still have been very powerful; perhaps all the more so for the inclusion of God therein, in this case by means of praise. I elaborate on this in the following section, suggesting that such a multi-participant engagement was intended to trigger a 'chain reaction' and produce an 'efficacious accountability', guaranteeing the success of the performance.

---

[32] See also 4Q511 3.21, 4Q511 15.4, 4Q511 22.3.

The A3 and the Amarna amulet also craft their expressions of praise specifically around God's powerful qualities. In the latter (see Section 2.3. above), God is exalted as the creator of (all) the spirits (l. 22a), and for speaking against or perhaps commanding (evil) beings (l. 26). Intriguingly, God seems to launch a new act of such efficacious speech in the amulet itself; in this instance, to intervene on behalf of the client's: שיר למלך... מלכה דמלל עליך אמר 'a song to the king…, the king who speaks against you; he said/commanded…' (l. 26).[33] The significance of God's efficacious speech is surely especially high in this amulet, which already emphasised the power of the mere divine utterance to create: ובשם מי אמר ונהיה העולם בדברו 'And in the name of [the one] who said and the world came into being by his word' (ll. 8, 16; translation mine), which is reiterated in l. 23 (see Section 2.3. above).[34] Consequently, the statement of God's speech against a demon in l. 26 now rings with an implicit threat, and may even convey an exorcism of God God's self.[35] In either case, if God's words were powerful enough to create spirits, surely they are also capable of punishing or even annihilating them. Such language

---

[33] The pronoun on עליך, rendered as 'against you' or 'over you', is singular and possibly feminine, so that the addressee here may be a specific harmful spirit; likely the רוח(ה) mentioned in ll. 2 or 12. Elsewhere, however, the amulet exorcises multiple demons (e.g., יתכון, l. 25), so that an alternative translation of עליך could be '[the king who speaks] *over* you (i.e., the client)'.

[34] Though this divine epithet is not uncommon in 'magical' texts; see the Cairo Genizah example in Naveh and Shaked (1985, 223).

[35] See footnote 37 below.

of praise, creation and divine speech thus serves to intimidate the spirits being exorcised with the language of God's power, even without a direct command to demons.[36]

God's power to speak efficaciously against demons is apparently also emphasised in A3, which begins as a 'song of praise' (l. 1). In ll. 3–5, God is described as מלך ממ‹ל› ברוז פרוש אל כל רוח בישה ומבאשה דלה תיחשין 'the King who speaks with distinct mystery to every evil spirit that you should not cause pain'.[37] Such a strategy of 'indirect' exorcism (i.e., mediated by God) could be quite parallel to that of the Hymns.[38] In this regard, therefore, it is the Maskil's statement about the exorcist effect of praise that provides a useful interpretive key to these amulets. Indeed, such an effect of praise is stated explicitly—albeit briefly—in A25. Its "song of praises to God, to the Highest God" is performed "*against*" or perhaps "*over* all harm" (l. 7; see Section 2.3. above).[39]

In several amulets, moreover, the method of implicit engagement seems to also work in the entirely opposite direction:

---

[36] Direct exorcisms occur elsewhere in this amulet; see e.g., ll. 9, 18a and 27a.

[37] This interpretation assumes that the preposition אל 'to' in l. 4 is governed by the immediately preceding 'who speaks'. However, in principle, it could also start a new section, specifying to whom the amulet is addressed.

[38] As Angel (2012, 4) put it, "it is precisely the Maskil's vocalization of God's praise that serves as the essential weapon against the malignant forces." See also Lange (1997, esp. 431).

[39] In contrast to A3 and the Amarna amulet, however, this composition does not elaborate further on God's praiseworthy qualities.

towards God. Thus, both A3 and A25 lack a direct request for God to act, but God nevertheless seems to proclaim the banishment of evil. God, it seems, is compelled to act simply by virtue of being praised. Thus, in A3, the praise which immediately follows the identification of the composition as a 'song of praises' and intertwined with an address to evil spirits (ll. 3–4): מלך ממל<ל> ברוז פרוש אל כל רוח בישה ומבאשה דלה תיחשין 'the King who speaks with distinct mystery to every evil and harmful spirit that you should not cause pain' but the source of this anti-demonic commandment is left frustratingly—or perhaps tantalisingly—ambiguous. While it could in principle be the exorcist, it could also be God, since God is the one 'speaking' in the immediately preceding discourse (l. 3).[40] The account of God's qualities in praise in ll. 2–3 thus seems to encourage God to demonstrate these qualities yet again; this time, on behalf of the amulet's client (ll. 4–5). Such a connection of God's general character to its manifestation at this specific instance seems to be cleverly reflected in the language: the two are expressed with one verbal form, the participle ממל<ל> '[one] speaking' (l. 3).

A similar strategy of mobilisation without explicit call seems to be at play also in the Amarna amulet (l. 26) and in Text 67, which is a bowl-inscribed 'song of praises' (Isbell 1975,

---

[40] Note that the command is preceded by the conjunction ד- 'that, so, which' etc., which is compatible with such an explanation ('the king speaks... *so that* you do not...'). Alternatively, if the one commanding is the exorcist, we would translate as follows: 'the king who speaks.... To every evil spirit: *that* you do not...').

147).⁴¹ In the latter, it is God who seems to be the principal agent of the exorcism. Moreover, it is possible that this occurs even without an explicit request to do so:⁴²

| A song of praise to the King, YHWH, YHWH, YHWH, King YHWH | שיר תושבאחות למלך יהוה יהוה יהוה מלך יהוה |
| By the Rock of the World. I-am-who-I-am. King of the kings of the dry land/world | בצור עולם {ס} אהיא אשר אהיא מלך הממללככאא דיבאישתא |
| By the mighty God and warrior, send/[who] sent through Shalmiel, Michael, Raphael, and Qanael to bind him and to close up the house of | ביאל חזק וגיבור שלח ביד {ביד} שלמיאל מיכאל רפאל קנאל למיסרה ולמחד⁴³ ביתה |

(Text 67, bowl)

Admittedly, the identity of the sender and the parsing of the verbal form in the phrase ביאל חזק וגיבור שלח ביד in l. 4 is not entirely

---

⁴¹ In the case of the Amarna amulet, this depends on our translation of the phrase עליך אמר (l. 26). Above, it was taken as 'said/says', but it could also very well mean 'commanded/commands'. If the latter translation is correct, the statement would thus serve as divine exorcism, directed to the demon(s).

⁴² The following transcription is based on Isbell's (1975, 147) reproduction of Jeruzalmi's (1964, 121–23) transcription, but has been corrected in several places.

⁴³ I thank Matthew Morgenstern for correcting the original transcription of Jeruzalmi (1964) as reproduced in Isbell (1975), offering the more comprehensible reading למיסרה ולמחד.

clear. Still, the subject is likely God, since God is mentioned in this very phrase in adjuration. On this account, it is best to understand שלח as a past perfective/perfect form, introducing an asyndetic relative clause (see translation).[44]

Such passages thus seem to provide examples of indirect exorcisms within what is referred to as 'direct magic' from Late Antiquity. This, in turn, problematises the broader division of exorcisms as either 'direct' (i.e., human) and 'indirect' (divine or by consequence).[45] In light of this, we should remain cautious about presupposing such a dichotomy for the Qumran Hymns, also considering their fragmentary nature (see below).

This section has demonstrated that in both the Hymns and the amulets at hand, transmundane beings can be mobilised into action in a subtle manner. Thus, the mere praise of God has the power to expel evil spirits (in the Hymns and most likely also in several amulets), and to encourage or spur God to act against these spirits (likely in A3, the Amarna amulet and bowl text 69). Praise, therefore, triggers an efficacious chain reaction, able to affect more than one being simultaneously, and/or to have more than one simultaneous effect.

---

[44] Alternatively, it could be an imperative, 'send!', which then could also be addressed to God or an angelic being, though no angel has been mentioned so far in this composition.

[45] See the Introduction (Section 1) above.

## 3.2. Praise as Exorcism and Exorcism as Praise in the Hymns and Beyond: Towards the Eschaton

So far, I have shown the capacity of Hymns of the Maskil and the late-antique apotropaic prayers to simultaneously mobilise or affect multiple supernatural entities with a single efficacious performance. These different agents and affectees, in turn, are linked to different efficacious and aesthetic goals of the compositions. Building on this observation, this section returns to the issue of combining different genres within a single composition. I suggest that the multi-participant engagement within these texts enables them to function simultaneously as thanksgiving, praise, exorcism and—in the case of the Hymns—eschatological discourse.

With regard to the Hymns, therefore, I suggest that is best to view exorcism and praise on a par. This also helps us make sense of the other parts of the Hymns, namely the 'historical' and the eschatological ones. Though at first glance "somewhat distant from the realm of magical incantation" (Angel 2022, 35), at a closer look, the eschatological picture of the Hymns is realised by both praise and exorcism, which are therefore both integral for this larger vision of the Hymns.

There are several features which point towards a more equal relationship between praise and exorcism in the Hymns; a relationship in which both function as aims in their own right, as well as reinforcing each other. First, it is likely that the Hymns did include exorcism by direct demonic address. This seems to be attested in at least one unplaced fragment, discussed by Angel

(2017, 189–190; 2022, 108–109). The very existence of this fragment in turn raises questions about the existence of other such exorcist passages, which may have been lost.

| | | |
|---|---|---|
| 1. | ]in etern[i]ty, for[ | [בְּעוֹלָֿמָ֯[י]ֿם כִּ֯יאֿ] |
| 2. | ]your [abom]inations *vac* And aft[er | תוֹעֲ[בֿוֹתיכם וֿאַֿחַֿ]ר |
| 3. | the p]eriods of its wickedness and…[ | קֿ[צִ֯י רשעתה ופ ֯] |
| 4. | ]… the powers, and like a sage[ | [ ֯ הגבורות וכחכום ] |
| 5. | ]… and you have no peace[ | [ ֯כֿ֯ם֯ ואין לכֿם שֿלוֹם] |
| 6. | ]before him, and all…[ ] shall fear[ | מלפֿנוֿ ופחדו כול ֯] |
| 7. | heave]n and earth shall cry out…[ | שמי[ם וארץ ירועו מֿ] |
| 8. | ]… and all[ | [ ֯ בֿוֿ וֿכֿוֿל] |

(Angel 2022, 108–09)

More specifically, the clearly negative phrase 'and you have no peace' in l. 5 is most likely addressed to demons, since it is difficult to see how it would applied to the Yaḥad, angelic hosts or God. This is supported by 1 Enoch (e.g., The Book of Watchers 12.5, 13.1, 16.4), where the phrase אין ל(כם) שלום is uttered against, for instance, the watchers and the fallen angel Asael (Angel 2017, 190). This, in turn, makes 'demons' also the likely referent of the 2nd masculine plural pronoun on תוֹעֲ[בֿוֹתיכם] in l. 2, reconstructed as 'your [abom]inations' by Angel (2017, 190). The proposed noun 'abomination' would fit with terms such as רשעתה 'its wickedness' (l. 3).[46]

The second reason why both praise and exorcism should be considered important to the Hymns' overall efficacious and aesthetic objectives, is that they are both indispensable for the realisation of divine purposes in creation, as outlined in the Hymns themselves. More specifically, both praise and exorcism interact closely with the historical and eschatological vision of the world, which stretches over columns 1–5 of the Hymns.[47] The extant part of the first column (based on 4Q511 2 i; Angel 2022, 44–47) opens with a superscript and then immediately announces (God's?) destruction of the mysterious 'prince of dominions': וזרוש ממשלות השבית לאין (l. 18). This is followed by the recounting of the establishment of the elect community (esp. ll. 20–22 = 4Q511 2 i; Angel 2022, 44–45), and the description of the mirroring hosts of human-angelic worshippers (ll. 23–25). The latter is expressed with the somewhat veiled reference to those who '(will) serve him in/with the lot of the people of his host'; לשרתו בגורל עם

---

[46] A more nuanced understanding of the relationship between praise and exorcism is unfortunately out of our reach, requiring the knowledge of the Hymns' *Sitz im Leben* within the Yaḥad (see Section 2.1 above). For instance, was its performance triggered by specific threats? Or, more likely, was it part of the liturgy, and how was it integrated therein?

[47] The following discussion of the Hymns draws from the material reconstruction proposed by Angel (2022), in turn based is based on an eclectic edition of 4Q510 and 4Q511 to reconstruct the 'original' composition, referred to in Angel's publication as 'Shir'.

צְבָאוּ.⁴⁸ Columns 3–4 and the top of 5 then launch what seems to be an eschatological vision, which includes 'judgement of vengeance to eradicate evil' (e.g., col. 5.1 = 4Q511 35, l. 1; Angel 2022, 54–55). This (future?) punishment notwithstanding, a (partial?) curbing of evil powers is already mentioned in col. 2 (ll. 20–22), where it seems to be described in the past perfective/perfect (*qaṭal*). [א]ל[ו]הים האד[י]ר בכוח '[G]od has acted ma[j]estically with power' (4Q511 2 ii, l. 5; Angel 2022, 48–49).⁴⁹ Moreover, the (apparently) eschatological section in columns 3–5 seems to forecast the worship of the earthly-heavenly temple community, who shall be:

| ... [P]riests, his righteous people, his host, and ministers, the angels of his glory. | כוהנים עם צדקו צבאו ומשרתים מלאכי כבודו |
| They shall praise him for (his) awe-inspiring wonders. | יהללוהו בהפלא נוראות |

(col. 5.5 = 4Q511 35, l. 5; Angel 2022, 56–57)

The salient motifs of these passages, therefore, are the recurrence of God's victory over evil forces,⁵⁰ and the somewhat cryptic reference to the mirroring hosts,⁵¹ whose ultimate, priestly aspiration is the 'uninterrupted blissful praise' in the es-

---

[48] For the interpretation of this phrase, see further Angel (2022, 47).

[49] In principle, however, this phrase could also constitute a generic statement: the form האד[י]ר could also be parsed as a definite adjective, i.e., 'the mighty', which would make it a generic statement.

[50] E.g., cols. 1.18, 2.20–22, and 5.1.

[51] E.g., cols. 1.23–25 and 5.4–5.

chatological age (Angel 2022, 38). All of these are well-established sectarian motifs. The picture which emerges from these combined motifs is an arch of history with its divine plan. Over the first five columns, the Hymns paint the picture 'from Urzeit' (col. 1) 'to Endzeit' (cols. 3–beginning of 5; Angel 2022, 36).[52] This arch is intersected with temporal events, such as God's action in history and the Maskil's present exorcist praise. Thus, this divine plan for creation in its sectarian garb is intimately connected with praise and exorcism.

The reason for this connection is that this ultimate reality begins in the here-and-now,[53] launched by several interacting means. The first of these means is the Maskil's praise. Infused

---

[52] The exact temporal and causal relationship between these different segments of history, however, remains somewhat elusive. The question of whether and how God's power and exultation are already manifest, remains partly unanswered. In fact, the Hymns include both the idea that evil powers can no longer affect the righteous, and that demonic forces still need to be exorcised. This, in turn, prevents us from drawing a sharp dichotomy between the here-and-now and the hereafter. To complicate the picture further, the unplaced fragment 4Q511 11 seems to refer to '[appoi]nted times of distress' מו[עדי צָרוֹת, (l. 2; Angel 2022, 113) which could be consonant with the Enochic idea that 'God has relinquished control of humanity to Belial and his minions' (Angel 2022, 40). This notwithstanding, the Hymns are not resigned to this 'interim rule of evil', as discussed throughout this article. For a discussion on different eschatologies across Qumran's sectarian compositions and beyond, see e.g., Hanneken (2006).

[53] Angel (2022, 38) briefly expresses a similar idea, suggesting that the *topos* of participation with the angels "may be seen as bridging the gap between the future and the present."

with the ability to vanquish evil assailants, it offers the worshipping community a glimpse of God's ultimate victory over evil, and demonstrates God's power, not yet fully manifest (e.g., col. 5.6). Such an interpretation of an incipient eschatology fits with the placement of the Maskil's own, evil-terrifying praise in the Hymns. Appearing in col. 5.6–8,[54] it immediately follows the eschatological vision of cols. 3–5 (see above), and is part of the same song with the preceding:[55]

6. And as for me, I instil the fear of God in the ages of my generations. For the exaltation of the name [I have] spoken, [to frighten]     ואני מירא אל בקצי דורותי לרומם שם לדבר[תי לפחד]

7. by his strength al[l] the spirits of the bastards to subdue them by [his] fear[     בגבורתו כו[ל] רוחי ממזרים להכניעם מ̊י̇רא̊[תו ]

(4Q511 35, l. 6–7; Angel 2022, 56–57)

This suggests a deliberate and intimate connection between the Maskil's exorcisms and the preceding eschatology in the Hymns: the praise of the Sage serves to foreshadow, but also *launch* God's victory over evil. It is even possible to consider the preceding discourse to be the very exorcism which the Maskil performs: the message that instils fear in humans and intimidates demons.

This exorcism enacted by *Maskil's* praise, in turn, stimulates another wave of praise, performed by the community and

---

[54] Lines 8 and 9 are fragmentary, and the following ten or so lines are not preserved, depriving us of more information about this exorcism.

[55] That is, there is no intervening superscript between ll. 5–6 of col. 5.

the natural elements (in 4Q511 1, l. 4). As shown above, col. 3.22–25 (4Q511 1, l. 5–8) contains the call to "rejoice in jubil[ations] of salvation (ברנ]ות ישועות)," "for God's glory has shone forth." The temporality of this praise is somewhat unclear;[56] this call comes in the middle of the so-called 'eschatological vision' of columns 3–5 (see above) and connects praise to the already accomplished vanquishing of evil, so may be either present or envisioned for the future. What seems clear, however, is that this type of praise comes in *response* to God's demonstration of power; which, in turn, is in the Hymns (partly) launched by the Maskil's 'exorcist praise'. Perhaps this exorcism perhaps be seen as the breaking in of the eschaton in history.

But such references to communal praise also enact and foreshadows the mirroring earthly-heavenly worship, which—as the Hymns imply—is to culminate in the eschaton (see col. 5.5, given above). Communal praise, consequently, constitutes the second means of the Hymns' "realized eschatology," to use Angel's (2022, 38) terminology. By calling the community to engage in worship in the here-and-now, it creates a continuity between the present and the hereafter in terms of worship. It also brings human worshippers within the triangular union with angels and God, through praise. Such a union, in turn, doubtless brings further protection to the worshipping community in the present, as well as propelling them to their eschatological, priestly destiny. Doubtless, this all would have also offered spiritual comfort amidst present distress to the performing community. Set in the

---

[56] On this problem, see footnote 56 above.

context of the Hymns, therefore, the well-established sectarian motifs of priestly communion with God and angels and of temple embodiment take on a distinctive function. They are configured to serve the vision of an eschatology realised and foreshadowed by praise and exorcism.[57]

In sum, both praise and exorcism work efficaciously to create continuity between the present age and the period of God's ultimate judgements and revelation of power. They do so in a mutually intertwined way, reinforcing and further stimulating one another. Praise and exorcism, in other words, are the building blocks of the Hymns' vision of the eschaton.

This analysis of the Hymns, in turn, presents us with an invitation to continue to reflect on the configuration of praise and exorcism in the amulets and bowls. On the one hand, the key motivation for the very production of amulets is exorcism and/or protection, suggesting that praise, in the above-studied amulets, functions as a *tool* for exorcism, as highlighted above. But in light of the Hymns, is it also possible to view praise as a tool of proleptic access to an (intuited or hinted at) eschatology as part of the amulet's treatment? At the very least, there could be a proleptic aspect to praise in some amulets in the sense of a response

---

[57] Such a process would be aptly described, with the terminology of folklore studies, as the transformation of a 'motif' into 'motifeme'. This transformation refers to the process whereby a literary feature such as an image, a character, or an action, which is used across a family of compositions, becomes adapted in a specific composition to express and align with a more specific and sometimes even inverted set of values.

to the deliverance expected to follow the efficacious performance. Doubtless, such an expectant glorification of God would have provided spiritual comfort to the client in their present suffering.

## 4.0. Conclusions and Implications

The present study has invited the reader to consider the efficacious mechanics of texts written for non-human audiences. It has compared the techniques of the Qumran Hymns of the Maskil and a few late-antique exorcist texts, all of which are construed as שיר תושבחות, 'a songs of praises'. A deeper look at these texts' efficacious strategies of and their striking philological parallels has problematised the dichotomy of 'direct' and 'indirect' magic, or explicit and moderate forms of exorcism, which were emphasised in some previous studies of the Hymns. Despite their differences in provenance, contents and form, both the Hymns and the amulets at hand are able to mobilise a whole series of transmundane beings into action in a manner that is both subtle, and affects multiple agents simultaneously. This, I argue, is achieved through the construction of exorcism as praise, and of praise as exorcism, in several of the texts. Praise and exorcism thus become intertwined as they mutually reinforce each other. This has been argued for the Hymns, where, I suggested, the mutual interaction between praise and exorcism serves as a tool for bringing about the eschaton, and for bridging the gap between this and the restored world.

I hope that the present model will become a useful heuristic tool for other corpora of ancient Jewish 'magic' and the early liturgy. For instance, the multi-audience orientation of apotropaic performances, emphasised here, seems to have been pivotal for the development of the apotropaic-liturgical use of texts such as Ps. 91, the Priestly Blessing, Zech. 3.2, and perhaps also for the Songs of the Sabbath Sacrifice. For instance, with its language of praise for divine protection, Ps. 91 has become a powerful tool for banishing demons, as well as for mobilising angels for the benefit of the prayerful performer.

# References

Angel, Joseph L. 2012. 'Maskil, Community, and Religious Experience in the Songs of the Sage (4Q510–511)'. *Dead Sea Discoveries* 19 (1): 1–27.

———. 2017. 'Reading the Songs of the Sage in Sequence: Preliminary Observations and Questions'. In *Functions of Psalms and Prayers in the Late Second Temple Period*, edited by Mika S. Pajunen and Jeremy Penner, 185–211. Berlin: De Gruyter.

———. 2022. *The Songs of the Sage*. Leiden, Boston: Brill.

Bhayro, Siam. 2015. 'Divorcing a Demon: Incantation Bowls and BT Gittin 85b'. In *The Archeology and Material Culture of the Babylonian Talmud*, edited by M. J. Geller, 121–31. Leiden: Brill.

———. 2021. 'The Use of Quotations from the Psalms in the Aramaic Magic Bowls'. In *You who Live in the Shelter of the Most High (Ps. 91:1): The Use of Psalms in Jewish and Christian Traditions*, edited by Ida Fröhlich, Nóra Dávid and Gerhard Langer, 69–82. Vienna: V&R Unipress.

Bohak, Gideon. 2008. *Ancient Jewish Magic: A History*. Cambridge: Cambridge University Press.

———. 2011. 'The Charaktêres in Ancient and Medieval Jewish magic'. *Acta Classica Universitatis Scientiarum Debreceniensis* 47: 25–44.

———. 2013. 'From Qumran to Cairo: The Lives and Times of a Jewish Exorcistic Formula'. *Meghillot: Studies in the Dead Sea Scrolls* 10: 163–79. [Hebrew]

———. 2024. 'Scribal Overkill: Textual Density on Ancient Jewish Amulets'. In *Amulets of Protection and Texts for Fears in Antiquity*, edited by Angelika Berlejung and Gideon Bohak, 219–237. Tübingen: Mohr Siebeck.

Cohn, Yehudah. 2008. 'Were Tefillin Phylacteries?'. *Journal of Jewish studies* 59 (1): 39–61.

Eshel, Esther. 2003. 'Apotropaic Prayers in the Second Temple Period'. In *Liturgical Perspectives: Prayer and Poetry in Light of the Dead Sea Scrolls (Proceedings of the Fifth International Symposium of the Orion Center for the Study of the Dead Sea Scrolls and Associated Literature)*, edited by Esther G. Chazon, Ruth Clements and Avital Pinnick, 69–88. Leiden: Brill.

Frim, Daniel J. 2021. 'Hebrew in the Incantation Bowls and in the Babylonian Vocalization Tradition'. *Journal of Semitic Studies* 66 (1): 27–51.

Gross, Simcha, and Avigail Manekin-Bamberger. 2022. 'Babylonian Jewish Society: The Evidence of the Incantation Bowls'. *Jewish Quarterly Review* 112 (1): 1–30.

Hanneken, Todd. 2006. 'Angels and Demons in the Book of Jubilees and Contemporary Apocalypses.' *Henoch* 28 (2): 11–25.

Harari, Yuval. 2017. *Jewish Magic before the Rise of Kabbalah.* Detroit: Wayne State University Press.

Häberl, Charles. 2015. 'Aramaic Incantation Texts between Orality and Textuality.' In *Orality and Textuality in the Iranian World: Patterns of Interaction across the Centuries*, edited by Julia Rubanovich, 365–99. Leiden: Brill.

Isbell, Charles D. 1975. *Corpus of the Aramaic Incantations Bowls.* Society of Biblical Literature Dissertation Series 17. Missoula, MT: Scholars Press.

———. 1976. 'Two New Aramaic Incantation Bowls'. *Bulletin of the American Schools of Oriental Research* 223 (1): 15–23.

Jeruzalmi, Isak. 1964. *Les coupes magiques araméenes de Mésopotamie.* Paris: The Sorbonne.

Juusola, Hannu. 1999. *Linguistic Peculiarities in the Aramaic Magic Bowl Texts.* Helsinki: Finnish Oriental Society.

Kister, Menahem. 1999. 'Demons, Theology and Abraham's Covenant: CD 16:4–6 and Related Texts'. In *The Dead Sea Scrolls at Fifty: Proceedings of the 1997 Society of Biblical Literature Qumran Section Meeting*, edited by Robert A. Kugler and Eileen M. Schuller, 167–84. Atlanta: Scholars Press.

Lange, Armin. 1997. 'The Essene Position on Divination and Magic'. In *Legal Texts and Legal Issues: Proceedings of the Second Meeting of the International Organization for Qumran Studies, Cambridge, 1995, Published in Honour of Joseph M. Baumgarten*, edited by Moshe Bernstein, Florentino Garcia

Martinez, and John Kampen, 377–435. Studies on the Texts of the Desert of Judah 23. Leiden: Brill.

Levene, Dan, Dalia Marx, and Siam Bhayro. 2014. '"Gabriel is on Their Right": Angelic Protection in Jewish Magic and Babylonian Lore'. *Studia Mesopotamica* 1: 185–98.

Manekin-Bamberger, Avigail. 2015. 'Jewish Legal Formulae in the Aramaic Incantation Bowls'. *Aramaic Studies* 13: 69–81.

———. 2020. 'Who Were the Jewish "Magicians" behind the Aramaic Incantation Bowls?'. *Journal of Jewish Studies* 71 (2): 235–54.

Mishor, Mordechai. 2007. 'Hebrew in the Babylonian Incantation Bowls'. In *Shaʿarei Lashon: Studies in Hebrew, Aramaic and Jewish Languages Presented to Moshe Bar-Asher*, vol. 2, edited by Aharon Maman, Steven E. Fassberg, and Yohanan Breuer, 204–27. Jerusalem: Bialik Institute. [Hebrew]

Mizrahi, Noam and Hector M. Patmore. 2019. 'Three Philological Notes on Demonological Terminology in the Songs of the Sage (4Q510 1 4-6)'. *Revue de Qumran* 31 (2): 239–50.

Molin, Dorota. 2017. 'The Language of the Biblical Hebrew Quotations in the Aramaic Incantation Bowls'. MA thesis, University of Cambridge.

———. 2020. 'Biblical Quotations in the Aramaic Incantation Bowls and Their Contribution to the Study of the Babylonian Reading Tradition'. In *Studies in Semitic Vocalisation and Reading Traditions*, edited by Aaron D. Hornkohl and Geoffrey Khan, 147–70. Cambridge: Open Book Publishers.

———. 2023. 'The Bible in the Aramaic Bowls: Between Memorization, Orality, and Writtenness'. *Journal of Biblical Literature* 142 (4): 609–31.

Naveh, Joseph, and Shaul Shaked. 1985. *Amulets and Magic Bowls: Aramaic Incantations of Late Antiquity*. Jerusalem: Magnes Press; Leiden: Brill.

———. 1993. *Magic Spells and Formulae: Aramaic Incantations of Late Antiquity*. Jerusalem: Magnes Press.

Newsom, Carol, and Yigael Yadin. 1999. 'The Masada Fragment of the Qumran Songs of the Sabbath Sacrifice'. In *Hebrew Fragments from Masada*. Vol. 6 of *Masada: The Yigael Yadin Excavations 1963–1965,* edited by Shemaryahu Talmon, 120–32. Jerusalem: Israel Exploration Society.

Nitzan, Bilha, 1994. 'Magical Poetry'. In *Qumran Prayer and Religious Poetry*, 227–72. Studies on the Texts of the Desert of Judah 12. Leiden: Brill.

Penney, Douglas L., and Michael O. Wise. 1994. 'By the Power of Beelzebub: An Aramaic Incantation Formula from Qumran (4Q560)'. *Journal of Biblical Literature* 113 (4): 627–50.

Penner, Jeremy. 2014. *Patterns of Daily Prayer in Second Temple Judaism*. Leiden: Brill.

Reimer, Andy M. 2000. 'Rescuing the Fallen Angels: The Case of the Disappearing Angels at Qumran'. *Dead Sea Discoveries* 7 (3): 334–53.

Shaked, Shaul. 1995. '"Peace be upon You, Exalted Angels": On Hekhalot, Liturgy and Incantation Bowls'. *Jewish Studies Quarterly* 2 (3): 197–219.

———. 2005. 'Form and Purpose in Aramaic Spells: Some Jewish Themes: The Poetics of Magic Texts'. In *Officina Magica: Essays on the Practice of Magic in Antiquity*, edited by Shaul Shaked, 1–30. Leiden: Brill.

Shaked, Shaul, James Nathan Ford, and Siam Bhayro. 2022. *Aramaic Bowl Spells: Jewish Babylonian Aramaic Bowls*, vol. 2. Leiden: Brill.

Tigchelaar, Eibert J. 2019. 'Evil Spirits in the Dead Sea Scrolls: A Brief Survey and Some Perspectives'. In *Dualismus, Dämonologie und diabolische Figuren: Religions-historische Beobachtungen und theologische Reflexionen*, edited by Jörg Frey and Enno Popkes, 125–35. Tübingen: Mohr Siebeck.

Waller, Daniel J. 2019. 'Curious Characters, Invented Scripts, and… Charlatans? "Pseudo-scripts" in the Mesopotamian Magic Bowls'. *Journal of Near Eastern Studies*, 78 (1): 119–139.

———. 2022. *The Bible in the Bowls: A Catalogue of Biblical Quotations in Published Jewish Babylonian Aramaic Magic Bowls*. Cambridge: Open Book Publishers.

———. 2024. 'Fear Transformed: The Use of First-Person Narrative Spells in the Jewish Aramaic Magic Bowls'. In *Amulets of Protection and Texts for Fears in Antiquity*, edited by Angelika Berlejung and Gideon Bohak, 239–256. Tübingen: Mohr Siebeck.

Wiener, Adi. 2021. 'Mobilising God: Biblical Citations in the Amulets of Ancient Jews'. MA dissertation, Tel Aviv University. [Hebrew]

# PHILOLOGY AND THE EVOLUTION OF THE PALESTINIAN TARGUM[1]

*Hector M. Patmore*

We use a range of terminology to refer to individuals who re-used earlier texts: 'editors', 'redactors', 'copyists', or simply 'authors', in cases where these individuals harvest earlier texts for source material. Those classifications are both loaded—as if copyists are 'passive' and editors 'active' re-users of earlier texts; and fuzzy—'editors' copy texts, 'copyists' make editorial changes, and so on. For ease, we will refer in what follows to all types of re-users of earlier texts simply as 'scribes'.

What interests us in this paper is what Khan and Najman have termed "scribal performance." The term 'performance' is liable to misunderstanding, so, for clarity, I understand 'performance' in the way that Khan and Najman (2022, 259–60) have defined it, namely as:

> [T]he vital and creative act of engagement with an ancient textual tradition that makes the text relevant and meaningful for individuals or for a community at the time of

---

[1] This research is part of the TEXTEVOLVE project, which has received funding from the European Research Council (ERC) under the European Union's Horizon 2020 research and innovation programme (grant agreement No. 818702).

> performance. This includes the oral performance of a written tradition and also the written performance of a tradition in the form of innovative texts.

I understand, as they do, each manuscript of a given work to represent a "scribal performance" (Khan and Najman 2022, 285).

Taking that understanding of performance as my starting point, I want to reflect in this paper on the role of innovation in the transmission of ancient Jewish literature in general, and the Palestinian Targum in particular. What I am particularly interested in are forms of 'innovation' that are not apparently accidental, in other words, what we might term *deliberate text change*. I want to focus specifically on writings that re-use earlier works as source material, without the earlier work being an *explicit* object of interest in the newly created work. Compositions that cite or allude to earlier works in order to explicate then, the pesherim for example, are therefore excluded from this analysis.

I hope to shed some light on the liberties and constraints that scribes felt when they re-used earlier works. What did scribes feel they could and could not do with the text in front of them? What constituted an acceptable re-use of a text? What would be an affront to norms, conventions, or expectations? I refer to these liberties and constraints as *philological values*. As such I define philology more narrowly than Khan, Najman, and Rosen-Zvi (2020, 1), who define it as involving

> a broad and variegated range of activities related to texts, their reading and production, codicological and scribal practices, as well as metatextual activities such as commentary, textual development, grammar, and translation.

The question this paper seeks to address can therefore be formulated thus:
> What philological values are reflected in ancient Jewish literature?

One way into this discussion is to begin with modern philology because it seems to me that some of the major shifts in modern philology have come about because modern scholars tried to apply a set of philological values to works that were transmitted by ancient and medieval scribes who held very different sets of philological values. As scholarship became increasingly aware of the incompatibility of these sets of philological values, it was forced to re-think what philology was and how it should be practised.

## 1.0. Modern Philological Values

Since its inception as a modern scientific methodology, philology has served a very practical function, namely to reduce the amount of textual data to a quantity that can be presented in a useable and commercially viable printed edition. While the advent of the digital age may have rendered this basic function of philology redundant, it has not rendered philology redundant, because the aims of philology have never been purely practical. Rather, the modern practice of philology is a value-based exercise, for it seeks to arrive at 'the best possible text'. What constitutes 'the best possible text' involves value judgements.

That modern philology is an enterprise based on value judgements becomes abundantly evident when one reads the contributions of its earliest exponents. The scholar of medieval French literature, Gaston Paris, is normally said to have been the first to have put into practice the principles articulated by Karl Lachmann, by producing a *stemma codicum* that he then used to establish a critical text (the stemma is given in Pannier and Paris 1872, 27). It is curious that so much attention is focussed on Paris—perhaps a reflection of the strength of these theoretical discussions in the francophone world—because Paris himself acknowledged that he was not the first and explicitly assigns this honour to Gustav Gröber (Pannier and Paris 1872, 7–8 n. 1), whose work was published while his own edition was still in preparation (Gröber 1869, on his methodology see 2–38).

Paris's introduction to his critical text is, admittedly, the more interesting read, offering rather more polemical sparkle than Gröber's sober presentation. Paris, for example, bemoans the liberties medieval scribes took—what he terms "renouvellements"—and consciously distinguishes his approach from earlier editors, who he dismissively states relied on instinct—"le goût et le tact"—rather than a properly scientific approach (Pannier and Paris 1872, 8).

These two romance philologists share a common approach, adopting common variant readings as the basis on which to establish the stemma and working back from there by reconstructing the lost intermediaries until they arrive at an archetype. For both Gaston and Gröber, the aim was the recovery of "the original"—a term Gröber is particularly fond of—that is, "the form that the work... had when it left the hands of the author"

(Pannier and Paris 1872, 8).² The *value* of any given reading or textual witness could thus be determined by its proximity to this 'original'.

Figure 1: Gröber's stemma (Gröber 1869, 27)

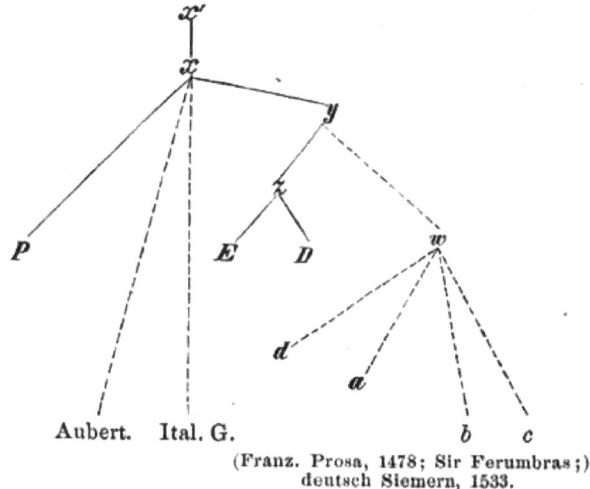

The approach of Gröber, Paris, and others who followed what is broadly referred to as a 'Lachmannian' approach, operated on more or less automatic principles, for "in the case of manuscripts that are not dependent on one another, common variants demonstrate common sources" (Gröber 1869, 9).³ The role of subjective scholarly judgement was therefore minimised, playing a significant role only once the stemma reached a point where there were only two (reconstructed) witnesses.

---

² All the translations in this chapter are the author's own, unless otherwise indicated. Original text: "la forme que l'ouvrage… avait en sortant des mains de l'auteur."

³ Original text: "Bei von einander unabhängigen Handschriften weist Gemeinsamkeit der Abweichungen auf Gemeinsamkeit der Quellen."

## 1.1. Problems with the Genealogical Approach

With the benefit of hindsight, the optimism of scholars like Gröber and Paris, was naïve: numerous problems with the genealogical approach have since been pointed out, not least of which is the recognition that the way in which errors arise is more complicated than they foresaw. Commonly occurring phenomena, such as horizontal transmission (often referred to as 'contamination'; on the terminology see Holmes 2011; Heikkilä 2020) and polygenesis (i.e., two scribes working independently might make the same error or 'improvement'), brought into question the methodology's quasi-automatic nature.

A more fundamental challenge, however, arose from the recognition that scribes often made deliberate and constructive interventions. Such interventions might be confined to mere tweaking and polishing: scribes might correct mistakes, improve the style, and resolve inconsistencies or contradictions (or at least *attempt* to do these things). But equally, they might involve anything from substitutions of a lexeme or a small gloss here and there, through to extensive rephrasing, reordering, or the introduction of new material. An author who produces multiple versions of their own work might also be responsible for such interventions in her/his text, i.e., 'authorial variants' (see the examples given in Beit-Arié 1993, 33–38). A number of factors might drive this kind of deliberate text change: a desire to update the material (most obviously in the case of legal and medical corpora), to save extraneous material from loss, for convenience, simple preference, or in order to adapt it to new audiences as occurred with a range of Jewish texts in Christian transmission (see e.g., Davila 2005, 2–73; Kraft 2009, 3–60; Kulik et al. 2019; for examples of 'active' traditions in Latin and Greek literature, see Reynolds and Wilson 2013, 235–238). Common formats, such as florilegia (i.e., several texts deliberately combined) and epitomes (i.e., a shortened version of longer text), for example, presuppose that the basic structure of a work would be disrupted.

Such 'active' (as opposed to 'quiescent') textual traditions have been seen as problematic for traditional philology because they disrupt the lines of descent in a stemma and make it difficult to 'root' a textual tradition in a single nodal point. But for our present purposes what is more important is the fact that deliberate text change of this kind calls into question traditional philology's value-laden operative model summed up in Gröber's (1869, 64) term "Verkümmerung." Such changes were not 'decline' or 'decay', but improvements. Put simply, it seemed that ancient and medieval scribes simply did not share the philological values on which modern philology was predicated.

## 1.2. Material Philology

It was this cluster of issues that caused the pendulum to swing to the other extreme in the form of what is now usually called 'Material' (or 'New') Philology. The herald of this movement is normally identified as Bernard Cerquiglini, a specialist in medieval vernacular literature, whose book, *Éloge de la variante*, has been widely influential, including outside his own field (see in particular Nichols 1990). The position he sets out in that work can be summed up in one of his own epigrams: "medieval writing does not produce variants, it is variance" (Cerquiglini 1989, 64).[4] In other words, Cerquiglini (1989, 59, 111–12 and *passim*) understood medieval literature to have been the subject of continuous redrafting—"(une) œuvre sans cesse," characterised by "variance," "altérité," and "mobilité." In his view, to fixate on a single form, on a particular nodal point in the history of the text, and on a work's original author, as Cerquiglini claimed Lachmann, Paris and their followers have done, was a "brutal negation" of the intrinsic variability of medieval vernacular literature that reduced scribes to automata (Cerquiglini 1989, 76, 79).

The movement that came in Cerquiglini's wake, has not gone without criticism, not least of which was the observation that many of its desiderata "had been answered by Italian scholars half a century before they were raised" (Roelli 2020, 3). One major issue is that practitioners of this approach are generally less interested—sometimes even uninterested—in the processes by which texts reached the form they did in any given artefact.

These criticisms need not delay us here, because what we are concerned with are the underlying values and on that score Cerquiglini makes the point with considerable panache. What Cerquiglini highlighted is the fact that the scribes of the medieval works that he studied, operated with a set of values that are incompatible with the values with which modern philology often operates. For example, they evidently did not see the text in their *Vorlage* as sacrosanct or immutable, but as plastic, fit to be moulded into their own creative iteration.

---

[4] Original: "[L]'écriture médiévale ne produit pas des variantes, elle est variance."

## 2.0. Philological Values in the Jewish Literature of Antiquity

The swing of the pendulum from archetype to artefact—or rather the debate as to how far that particular pendulum should swing—has not be confined to the study of medieval vernacular literature. In relation to late antique Jewish literature, a category to which most of the Targumim belong, this is exemplified in the series of (somewhat acrimonious) exchanges between Peter Schäfer and Chaim Milikowsky. In 1986, Schäfer published a provocative article arguing that philology "must rid itself of the odium of the whimsical scholar constantly in quest of the 'better' reading." According to Schäfer, the works of late antique Jewish literature to which his comments related, including the rabbinic corpus, elude "fixation," because their manuscript traditions are "dynamic," rather than containing "variants of static texts" (Schäfer 1986, 151–52;[5] 1981, v). This is Cerquiglini *avant la lettre*.

Milikowsky, for his part, dismissed Schäfer's comments about the level of variability in the textual traditions as a gross exaggeration, particularly when applied to many of the midrashim. Reacting against Cerquiglini and passionately advocating a genealogical approach, Milikowsky (2006a, 95, here reacting to Beit-Arié 2000) argued that the call to abandon the quest for the archetype

---

[5] Cf. his comments: "Die Suche nach einem «Urtext» ist jedenfalls hier wie in anderen Bereichen der frühen jüdischen Literatur nicht nur hoffnunglos, sondern auch methodisch verfehlt."

makes sense if our interest is primarily in Jewish medieval cultural history or in the study of medieval scribal practice, but not if we wish to study and to present to our readership rabbinic texts.[6]

In Milikowsky's view, the editor's task is to present readers with "the most original text that it is possible to reconstruct on the basis of textual witnesses that are extant" (2001/02, 24),[7] though more commonly in his publications he speaks simply of reconstructing the "original." One particularly telling point on which Milikowsky and Schäfer disagreed related to terminology: Milikowsky saw variation in the midrashim as "recensional" but not "redactional," whereas Schäfer understands "recension" to imply redactional activity (e.g., Milikowsky 1988, 204; Schäfer 1989; Milikowsky and Schäfer 2010, 80; cf. Milikowsky 2002, 550–53; 2017, 152). This distinction lies at the root of their disagreement about what text-criticism can achieve with rabbinic and related Jewish literature.

Subsequent exchanges between Schäfer and Milikowsky indicated that they were not as opposed as the hostile tone of their initial exchanges implied. On the one hand, Schäfer conceded that his comments were overstated (Milikowsky and Schäfer 2010, 79); and, on the other, Milikowsky (2006a, 90, in reference to Tanhuma-Yelammedenu literature) accepted that stemmatic analysis is not appropriate for traditions in which "each scribe saw himself free to rework the text in whatever manner caught

---

[6] Cf. and similar comments in Milikowsky (2005, 349–65; 2010, 131–32), and in general Milikowsky (2020).

[7] Original: "הטקסט המקורי ביותר שאפשר לשחזר על פי עדי הנוסח ששרדו."

his fancy," as he put it.[8] In his own editorial practice, Milikowsky (2005, 365–67; 2013, I:179–189) applied stemmatic principles where he judged this possible, but otherwise relied on what he called his "considered judgement and critical instinct," in part because the state of the textual witnesses did not allow more (Milikowsky 2006a, 101–2).

I draw attention to this exchange here not to critique one or the other—that is beyond my competence, though I confess that my sympathies lie more with Milikowsky—but simply because, by arguing about what philological values should be applied to the texts they studied, Schäfer and Milikowsky draw attention to differences in the philological values that the scribes who transmitted these texts appear to have held.

In cases such as Genesis Rabbah, Leviticus Rabbah, and Seder Olam—to name works edited or referenced in the debate by Milikowsky (2002; 2017)—the extant textual witnesses suggest that the scribes' aim was to reproduce essentially the same work, albeit in new editions and as far as the exemplars from which they worked allowed (e.g., gaps in exemplars of Lev. Rab. were filled with Pesiq. Rab Kah., for example; Milikowsky 2006b; 2019). In some iterations of the Tanhuma-Yelammedenu (see Bregman 1985; 2003, 173–88; 2007; Stemberger 2011, 336–39) and Hekhalot

---

[8] Cf. Milikowsky (2002, 554; 2005, 360), and his comments on Mishnah and Talmud: "it is unrealistic to separate the study of the text of the work from the study of the reception history of the work, and consequently the primacy of each individual document should not be diluted with variants from different lines of transmission" (Milikowsky 2006a, 100).

literature (see the works of Schäfer cited above and further the overview of Boustan 2007) by contrast, the structure is altered to such an extent that it seems the scribe no longer considered himself to be reproducing essentially the same work, but rather reusing material from existing works to create an essentially new work. In these cases, earlier works were valued primarily as source material that could be manipulated into new structures.[9]

Curiously, in neither case do the scribes abandon *the wording* of the works on which they drew. In the Hekhalot literature, for example, the wording of blocks of texts (what Schäfer referred to as "microforms") have been only lightly modified, even though the scribe has disassembled and reassembled, augmented and truncated the work that lay before him to create new structures ("macroform" in Schäfer's terminology) in which these dislocated blocks of text are relocated (see further e.g., Davila 2017, esp. 327–34; Swartz 2013; cf. Milikowsky's evaluation of the transmission of Pesiq. Rab., Milikowsky 1999). A similar situation pertains in the case of the Tanhuma-Yelammedenu literature, hence Bregman preferred to speak of a "genre" rather then of recensions. At least some of the precursor text was therefore thought worth retaining in the form it was received.

Returning to the question of philological values, we might distil two intersecting axes from the sources we have so far discussed. The first axis, represents the way a scribe considered the

---

[9] According to Milikowsky (2002, 528), the same is true of the parallel material in Pesiq. Rab Kah. and Lev. Rab, e.g., "whichever one used the other [the author] clearly conceived of his activity as creating a new work and reformulating the material."

work he produced in relation to the text(s) from which he worked. We might imagine that at one end of this axis stands scribal performances that understood themselves to be producing a new text of the same work. At the other extreme, stands scribal performances that understood themselves to be producing a new work, albeit on the basis of (an) earlier text(s). In some cases, an author explicitly presents his composition as a new work, in other cases it is plausible to assume that an author regarded his composition as such because he has given it a macroform quite unlike its source material, and so on. The second axis, represents the value a scribe placed on the specific wording of the source text. At one end of the axis are work that have reproduced the wording of their source text with as few changes as possible, while at the other end of the axis, are works in which the wording of the source text was evidently not thought to be worth retaining.

If we zoom right out until we have Jewish literature up to the Gaonic period in view, then we can begin to map out the ways in which these examples differ from, or are similar to, other types of textual re-use. It is perhaps most helpful to begin by mapping out some extremes. The most obvious would be the Masoretic Text from roughly the second century CE onwards (Lange 2016, 158–64), which clearly reflects a scribal intention to reproduce the same work (axis 1) with as few changes as possible to the wording of the source (axis 2). At the opposite extreme on our chart would be a work such as Jubilees: while clearly based on earlier works, the content and wording of which broadly speaking we know (e.g., Genesis), the scribe's aim was clearly to produce a new work (axis 1) without there being any particular intention of retaining the wording of their source text(s) (axis 2).

These cases of the extremes contrast with other examples of textual re-use. For example, roughly half of the books of Chronicles re-use material from Samuel–Kings (the parallels are set out in Endres, Millar, and Burns 1998; see further Kalimi 2014); the same is broadly true of the Gospel of Matthew's re-use of Mark. In each case, the verbatim wording of the source is often substantially retained (axis 2), albeit embedded in the context of a new work (axis 1) by means of reordering, augmentation, and so on. The philological values that appear to have been at play in the composition of these works, are comparable to those reflected in the transmission of, for example, the Hekhalot literature. These works form a cluster that is close to Jubilees but nonetheless distinct from it. Like Jubilees, a new work was produced (axis 1); unlike Jubilees substantial amounts of the wording of the source-text was retained (axis 2).

The transmission of the midrashim that we have discussed belong elsewhere on the chart. Clustered close to these, but from a somewhat earlier period, are works like Ben Sira, which evolved into a number of expanded forms. Whether these were the result of gradual accretion or systematic editorial activity (for a summary of the main scholarly positions see Gile 2011), the result is much the same: relatively small expansions and other minor variants are spread throughout, so that one is left with the impression that scribes tweaked and refined the text(s) from which they worked rather than substantially reworking it.

We might also place at a slightly different point in the same quadrant works like Isaiah, Jeremiah, the War Scroll, and the Community Rule. In each of these cases, scholars have proposed models of textual development in terms of *Fortschreibung* or the closely related idea of a "rolling corpus."[10] By this is understood some (generally limited) re-writing of the original text plus the addition of (a) substantial block(s) of text that has been composed to be in continuity with it. Wilson's (2016, 9) definition of *Fortschreibung* is worth citing:

> ...[A] form of interpretation of an existing text in order to apply that text to the issues, experiences, and perceptions of a later community. During this process the original text is both reread (interpreted) and rewritten in the form of changes made to the original text or in the form of a new text written as a continuation of and supplement to the earlier text.

---

[10] E.g., MacKane (1986, LXXXI) proposed the model of a "rolling corpus" for the textual development of Jeremiah, i.e., the growth of the text over a long period of time through accretion of "exegetical additions of small scope, operating within limited areas of text... triggered by a verse or few verses of pre-existing text." A similar idea was advocated for Isaiah by Albertz (1990, 253), e.g., "[die Trägergruppe] wollte gar nicht ihr eigenes Wort verkünden, sondern die Prophetie Jesajas in dem weltpolitischen Umbruch ihrer Zeit neu zu Gehör bringen," and elaborated by Williamson (1994); for an overview, see Becker (2020, 44–45). Hempel adopted this model for the Community Rule (2013, 119). Schultz (2009) argued that the War Scroll was composed under Hasmonean ascendancy, but expanded (cols 15–19) after 63 BCE, reflecting a pessimistic outlook in the face of a far superior Roman army.

In purely quantitative terms, the textual re-use is similar to, e.g., Chronicles or the Hekhalot literature. Yet the approach to the source text is different, for the structure of the original has been (largely) retained and augmented, rather than disassembled and reassembled. At the same time, the identity of the work was not apparently thought to have been effaced by the reworking of the text: the Book of Isaiah is still the Book of Isaiah, though now in a significantly expanded form that better addressed the concerns of a later community; the Community Rule is still the Community Rule, just *mis à jour*, and so on. In fact, Milikowsky (2002, 526–28 [quote: 527]) has described features of the textual tradition of Genesis Rabbah in similar ways: the received text is largely unaltered, despite the inclusion of "a sizeable amount of additional material."

Visually we might depict this and locate the works we have discussed so far on the graph as follows:

Figure 2: Graph of philological values

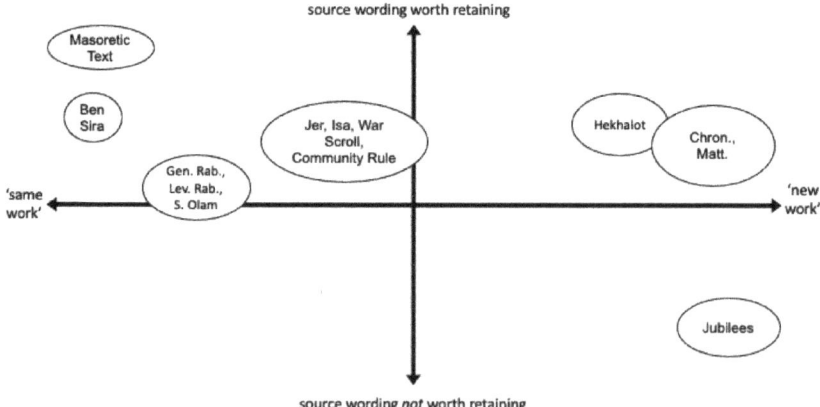

## 3.0. The (Continuous) Palestinian Targum

The analysis just offered is neither exhaustive nor new. That is not my aim. Rather, in bringing works that are not normally compared together in this way I hope to highlight the variety of philological values that scribes of Jewish literature evidently had. Few, it seems, would have shared Paris's view that any real value lay in the form as it "left the hands of the author" (Paris and Pannier 1872, 8). Mapping out the range of philological values in this way has some heuristic value when we approach the textual traditions of less-well-studied works, including the Palestinian Targums to the Pentateuch.

We have only one textual witness, MS Neofiti.1 (*Biblioteca Apostolia Vaticana*), that 1) was written in a consistent 'Palestinian' dialect (as opposed the hybrid text of Targum Pseudo-Jonathan); 2) was transmitted as a continuous text (rather than only as a selection of passages, as we find in the Fragment Targums); *and* 3) is more or less extant for the whole Pentateuch. The Cairo Genizah has furnished us with a number of other manuscripts of what Klein (1986, I:xxii) called "Palestinian Targum proper," that is, manuscripts that originally contained entire books of the Pentateuch or, in some cases, the whole Pentateuch.[11] Like Neofiti.1, these are witness to a continuous Palestinian Targum; the texts contained in these manuscripts are fragmentary by accident, not design. One implication of this is that we are now in a position

---

[11] I.e., Klein's MSS A, B, C, D, E, H, Z. Klein's work expanded on the fragments published by Kahle (1930).

to undertake comparative analysis between these textual witnesses. In theory at least, a genealogical approach to the Palestinian Targum to the Pentateuch—I use the singular here deliberately—on the basis of multiple independent witnesses is now possibile.

My interest in this question was piqued when I found pages of a manuscript of continuous Palestinian Targum that was not included in Klein's collection, namely Bodleian Library, Oxford, MS Heb. b. 17/5 (for image, see cover of this volume; I am currently preparing the text for publication). These pages do not appear in the Neubauer-Cowley catalogue, having been bound only after the completion of the catalogue's second volume. This is presumably why Klein did not include them. These two pages belong to Klein's manuscript D, which dates to c. 1000 CE (according to Beit-Arié in Klein 1986, I:xxxvii), placing it among the earliest extant witnesses to the Palestinian Targum. Manuscript D preserves in a fragmentary state the Targum to Gen. 36.8–Deut. 28.29, alternating verse by verse with the Hebrew (as manuscripts B and C do); these newly identified pages of manuscript D cover Genesis 40.3–14, 41.44–57.

Alongside these 'continuous' witnesses, we also have a number of other 'non-continuous' textual witnesses to Palestinian Targum, namely the Fragment Targums, the text as preserved in liturgical manuscripts, the so-called *Tosefta* Targums, and the marginal notes in Targum Neofiti, which are closely related to the Fragment Targum (see Clarke 1972; Le Déaut 1968; Díez Macho 1970, 23–24). In addition to these *direct* witnesses to Palestinian Targum, we also have two *indirect* witnesses. The first of these is Targum Onkelos. Targum Onkelos and the Palestinian Targum constitute separate works but they share material to such an extent that literary dependence on a common source must be assumed (for an overview see Chilton and Flesher 2011, 109–29). The second of the indirect witnesses is Targum Pseudo-Jonathan. The latest thinking on Targum Pseudo-Jonathan holds it to be an early-medieval composition, the bulk of which is a fusion of material from Targum Onkelos and one or more versions of the Palestinian Targum, enriched with additional material derived from a range of other sources and from the compiler's own creative insights (see Gottlieb 2021; McDowell 2021), though the extent of the latter is difficult to judge (see my comments on Mortensen 2006 in Patmore 2023, 37–38).

## 3.1. Examples from the Text

Only very limited work has been done on the textual affinity between witnesses to Palestinian Targum,[12] with no real work having been done of the textual character and alignment of the Cairo Genizah materials in particular. A full comparative analysis of the continuous Palestinian Targum lies, of course, beyond the scope of this chapter. Nonetheless, in preparation for this chapter a word-by-word synopsis (i.e., a linear-synopsis) of all those verses covered by manuscript D was prepared, on the basis of which the following preliminary impressions might be offered.

---

[12] I.e., Klein (1980, I:37 on the basis of Klein 1975) arranged the FragTg in four textual families, building on the work of Ginsburger (1899, xii–xiii; 1903); Doubles (1965, 17–20); and Díez Macho (1975, 534). See now also Patmore (2023, 27–29).

First, the direct witnesses to the Palestinian Targum offer variant forms of a single work (so we can speak of *the* Palestinian Targum). Secondly, the textual tradition evidenced in the non-continuous witnesses, as well as some textual units in the continuous witnesses (often those verses that are also attested in non-continuous witnesses), may be characterised as 'active', exhibiting (occasionally extensive) expansions, substitutions, and the re-ordering of material. This is perhaps unsurprising, given that the verses covered by non-continuous witnesses such as the Fragment Targum were apparently the object of particular interest (see Patmore 2023, 40–41 and references there). In most other cases, the extent of deliberate textual change is much more limited, so that these sections might be characterised as more 'quiescent'.

Here, I can offer no more than a couple of examples by way of illustration. These I draw from Gen. 40.12 for two reasons: first, we have multiple parallel textual witnesses of this verse (i.e., TgNeof, TgNeof$^{marginalia}$, FragTg$^P$, FragTg$^V$, FragTg$^{StP}$, FragTg$^N$, TgCG$^D$, TgCG$^E$ + TgOnk, and TgPsJ); and secondly, because it is preserved in the newly identified pages of manuscript D (Bodleian MS Heb. b. 17/5, see above).

Across all the witnesses we see the types of errors that one would typically expect, such as:

1) dittography, e.g., TgCG$^D$ ופתר ליה פתר ליה יוסף הווה לא, cf. TgNeof לא הוה יוסף אמר ופתר ליה;
2) parablepsis, e.g., TgCG$^D$ omits ואמר ליה יוסף דין פתרוניה;
3) metathesis, e.g., TgPsJ, FragTg$^P$, FragTg$^{StP}$, TgCG$^E$ עתיד פרעה; TgNeof, TgNeof$^{marginalia}$, FragTg$^V$, FragTg$^N$, TgCG$^D$ דפרעה עתיד; and

4) hebraisms, e.g., FragTg⁽ᴾ⁾ תלתי אבות for תלתי אבהת.

Similarly, we find elements of various sorts that are prone to substitutions and are therefore difficult to classify as likely to be either accidental or deliberate, e.g., FragTg⁽ᴾ⁾ כסיה דפרעה; TgNeof; FragTg⁽ᴺ⁾ כסא דפרעה; FragTg⁽ⱽ⁾; FragTg⁽ˢᵗᴾ⁾; TgCG⁽ᴱ⁾ כסה דפרעה (on the different constructions used to express genitive relationship, see Fassberg 1990, §161).

What really interests us here, though, is evidence of *deliberate* text change. Among these we find minor lexical, grammatical, and orthographic variants that apparently reflect the idiosyncrasies of certain scribes,[13] as well as various types of minor clarifying glosses or improvements to style or flow, and so on. We also find more substantial changes.

## Example 1

Let us begin with a good example from Gen. 40.12 of the 'active' nature of the tradition in the non-continuous witnesses. The earliest recoverable form of the text probably read as follows:[14]

> 'whose [i.e., Abraham, Isaac, and Jacob's] descendants are destined to be enslaved in the land of Egypt and are [also] destined to be liberated by three faithful stewards'

---

[13] E.g., an idiosyncrasy of TgCG⁽ᴱ⁾ is to employ ptc. instead of inf. cst. after adj. עתיד (e.g., משתעבדין and מתפרקין in Gen. 40.12); this is rare in PalTg. to Pentateuch (i.e., TgNeof Gen. 3.19; Frg.Tg.⁽ᴾ⁾ Gen. 40.18; Frg.Tg.⁽ᴾ⁾ Num. 11.26bis; Num. 24.22; Deut. 32.1; Frg.Tg.⁽ⱽ⁾ Num. 24.22; Frg.Tg.⁽ⱽ⁾ Deut. 32.1).

[14] Other orthographies are possible. N.B. TgNeof בשעבודא is probably a dittography.

דמן בני בניהון עתידין למשתעבדא דארעא דמצרים ועתידין למתפרקא על ידי תלתא פרנסין מהמנין

In FragTg^P we find a small expansion:[15]

'whose [i.e., Abraham, Isaac, and Jacob's] descendants are destined to be enslaved in the land of Egypt, by [being forced to work with] mud and bricks, and are [also] destined to be liberated by three faithful stewards'

דמן בני בניהון עתידין למ<שת>עבדא בארעא דמצרים בטינא ובליבנא ועתידין למתפרקא על־ידי תלתא פרנסין <מ>הימנין

In Targum Pseudo-Jonathan, this expansion has become even bigger.

'…by mud and bricks, and by all [kinds of] labour in the open fields…'

בטינא ובליבנא ובכל פולחנא באנפי ברא

We can be confident that these are expansions because this wording originates elsewhere, namely Exodus 1.14:

| | |
|---|---|
| MT | וימררו את־חייהם בעבדה קשה בחמר ובלבנים ובכל־עבדה בשדה |
| TgOnk | ואמרו ית חייהון בפולחנא קשיא בטינא ובלבני ובכל פולחנא בחקלא |
| TgNeof | ומררו ית חייהון בפלחן קשי בטינא ובלבני ובכל פולחן באפי ברא |
| TgPs-J | ואמרירו ית חייהון בפולחנא קשייא בטינא ובליבנין ובכל פולחנא באנפי ברא |

The expansion in FragTg^P and TgPsJ may not, however, come directly from Exodus 1.14, because the wording of Exodus 1.14 can also be found in the TgNeof and the FragTgs in Genesis 40.18. Regardless of its ultimate source, the text of FragTg^P is clearly an expansion of the Palestinian Targum on the basis of another

---

[15] <א> = editorial additions.

verse. TgPsJ in turn is an expansion of a form of the text as we now find it in FragTg$^P$. We might term this 'associative modification', by analogy with the phenomenon that Klein (1982) called 'associative translation'.

## Example 2

The most common way in which the 'active' nature of the textual tradition expresses itself is in the form of substitutions. This may occur in the substitution of single lexemes that are more or less synonymous (e.g., Gen. 40.12, FragTgs$^{V,N}$, and TgPsJ employ יה"ב,[16] whereas TgCG$^E$, FragTgs$^{P,StP}$, and TgNeof employ שו"י), but substitutions of other roughly-synonymous constructions also occur. For example, according to the text of Genesis 40.12 as we find it in TgCG$^D$, FragTg$^{V,N}$, and TgNeof, Joseph explains to the cup-bearer that the cup that he put in Pharaoh's hand in his dream, is the "cup of retribution" (כסא דפורענותה, with variant orthographies) that Pharaoh is destined to drink in the future. According to TgCG$^E$, FragTgs$^{P,StP}$, TgNeof$^{Marginalia}$, and TgPsJ, it will not be a "cup of retribution" that Pharaoh will drink, but a "bowl of wrath" (פיילית דרוגזה, with many variant orthographies; פיילית is the most common form in PalTg). Either one of these readings could be a substitution of the other, or both could be substitutions of some other reading now no longer attested. The evidence on

---

[16] It is possible that the reading of TgPsJ is influenced by the preceding verse, where TgPsJ has יה"ב in the speech of the chief-butler; it is that speech that Joseph is here repeating as indirect speech (there is no Frg. Tg. for Gen. 40.11; CG$^E$ and Tg. Neof. employ שו"י).

this point is ambiguous. The lexeme פיילי (from Gk. φιάλη) is attested early in Targumic Aramaic (e.g., Tg. Judg. 5.25, Isa. 51.17, 22, Amos 6.6, Nah. 2.4; FragTg^P Exod. 25.29, Num. 4.7, 7.13; FragTg^V Num. 4.7) and is found already in Mishnaic Hebrew (e.g., m. Sota 2.2, m. Neg 14.1), but is more common in TgPsJ (e.g., Gen. 40.12, Exod. 25.29, 37.16, Num. 4.7, 7.13, 19, 25, 31, 37, 43, 49, 55, 61, 67, 73, 79, 84–85) and other late Targumim (Tg. 2 Chron. 4.8, 11). In theory, this could be an argument in favour of its posteriority.

Yet, the genitive construction כסא דפורענותה is common in the Targumim (TgOnk Deut. 32.33; TgNeof Deut. 32.34; FragTg^{P,V} Deut. 32.34; Tg. Isa. 27.3, 28.13, Jer 51.7, Ezek. 23.31–33, Obad. 1.16, Lam. 4.21; cf. also TgPsJ Deut. 32.33). The Hebrew Bible knows a number of similar expressions (e.g., כוס חמה Isa. 51.17, 22; כוס שמה ושממה Ezek. 23.33; cf. Jer. 25.15, 49.12; Ps. 75.9; 1QpHab 11.14), and the notion of 'cups' (Hebr. כוס) as an expression of divine punishment is found in the midrashim, e.g. (Genesis Rabbah 88.5, my translation):

> "You will place Pharaoh's cup [in his hand]" (Gen. 40.13 JPS). R. Levi said, "This corresponds to four empires." R. Yehoshua ben Levi said, "This corresponds to four cups of poison that the Holy One—blessed be He—causes those practise idolatry to drink, hence what is written: "For thus said the LORD, the God of Israel, to me: 'Take from My hand this cup of wine—of wrath (כוס היין החמה)'" (Jer. 25.15 JPS); "Babylon was a golden cup in the LORD's hand, etc." (Jer. 51.7 JPS); "He will rain down upon the wicked [a scorching wind shall be their lot (מנת כוסם)]" (Ps. 11.6). Corresponding to them, the Holy One—blessed be He—causes Israel to drink four cups of salvation (כוסות של

ישועה) that are destined to come, hence it is said: "The LORD is my allotted share [and portion (וכוסי)]" (Ps. 16.5).

The (Hebrew) idiom כוס פורענות or כוס של פורענות itself is also relatively widely attested, especially in later literature (e.g., b. Berakhot 51b, in which a second cup of wine is called a כוס של פורענות, because drinking in pairs exposes one to demons; hence no blessing may be spoken over a second cup). Taken together all this might equally favour the posteriority of the reading כסא דפורענותה. In sum, arguments can be advanced in favour of the anteriority of either reading. I will return to this point in my conclusion.

## Example 3

Let me offer one further example from Gen. 40.12 of a similar sort of substitution. According to the text as we find it in TgCG[D], TgNeof, and FragTgs[V,N], the chief cup-bearer is reassured that he will "not lose your reward" (לא מובדין אגרך, reading אגרך for אגרין in TgNeof) on account of his dream. TgCG[E], FragTgs[P,StP], TgNeof[marginalia], and TgPsJ, by contrast, phrase things more positively, having Joseph reassure him "you will receive a good reward" (תקבל אגר טב). Again, from a text-critical perspective the data are ambiguous. The notion of the giving and receiving of 'good rewards' is most commonly associated with rewards for the righteous in the World to Come and is widespread (e.g., PalTg to Gen. 4.8, 15.1, 49.1, etc.), whereas the notion of not 'losing' rewards appears to be encountered mostly in post-Talmudic literature (e.g., Num. Rab. 21.14; Shir haShirim Zutta 1.15; and Bereshit Rabbati on Gen. 40.18).

To these data we might add the observation that when Joseph interprets the chief baker's dream, he informs him that תקבל אגר ביש (FragTg^P מקבל) according to FragTg^P, TgNeof, and TgPsJ (Gen. 40.18; according to FragTg^V he will receive פורענו). Classic text critical principles could be applied here to argue for the priority of either reading. One could, for example, argue on the basis of the lateness of the sources in which the concept is found that לא מובדין אגרך is secondary. Or, one could evoke the principle *lectio difficilior lectio probabilior*, plus the influence of PalTg Gen. 40.18, to argue for the priority of לא מובדין אגרך. I will return to this below, but let me first sum up the preceding discussion.

## 4.0. Conclusion

Significant shifts in modern philology have been the result of the realisation that ancient and medieval scribes did not share the same philological values as modern scholars. Part of the task of the philologist must, therefore, be to try to understand the values with which those scribes operated, and then apply a method of analysis and editorial practice that respects their values. To do that we need to try to understand not just the roots of the tree (i.e., *Urtext* or archetype) or just its leaves (i.e., textual iterations in artefacts), but also the branches in between—how and why the text has changed over time—as many before me have pointed out (most noteably Pasquali 1934; see Macé 2020; cf. the *cri de cœur* in Pollock 2009, especially 951–54). I refer to this approach as 'evolutionary philology'. Not that I imagine it to be new, but rather in order to stress its concern for the whole textual evolution of a work, from archetype to artefact.

Traditional philology may have had a tendency to ignore the creativity of scribes, but material philology equally has a tendency to ignore the fact that many scribes found the wording of the texts from which they worked worth preserving in part or in full. To say "a literary work does not exist independently of its material embodiment" (Lundhaug and Lied 2017, 6, characterising material philology) is only partially true and, as such, risks imposing a different anachronism onto manually transmitted textual traditions. Ancient and medieval scribes evidently *did* think of literary works existing independently of their material embodiments, for they believed they could be taken over from one material embodiment and re-embodied in another. Many of the works of ancient Jewish literature are, in fact, mixtures of innovation and preservation.

What, then, would be a good philological approach for the Palestinian Targum? We can best begin to formulate an answer to this question by locating the Targums on our grid. The direct witnesses to continuous Palestinian Targum appear to aim to reproduce the same work (axis 1), whilst 'improving' its wording (axis 2). By their very nature as epitomes, the Fragment Targums belong slightly further along the first axis; equally the Fragment Targums reflect more active intervention in the wording of the text (axis 2). The Fragment Targums are nonetheless distinct in nature from Targum Pseudo-Jonathan, which freely re-uses both Targum Onkelos and Palestinian Targum to create a new work (axis 1). Visualised, we can represent this as follows:

Figure 3: Graph of philological values with Targums

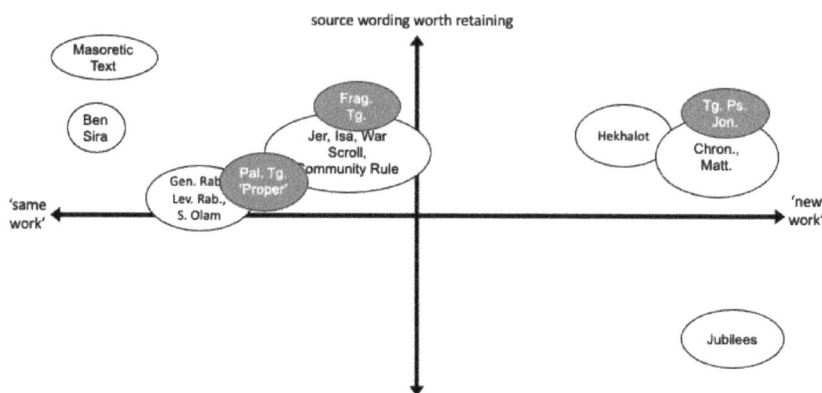

The examples of substitutions given above (examples 2 and 3) provide a clear example of how and why we need to adapt out approach to the philological values reflected in the work's transmission history. In neither case is one reading obviously derived from the other, so priority cannot be established with any degree of certainty; as I have tried to show, the argument in each case could go either way. But more importantly, such examples (which could be multiplied) suggest that the philological values of the scribes who transmitted this material *allowed* substitutions of words or even phrases. Consequently, there is a reasonable chance that neither is the 'original' reading. If in our editorial practice we force ourselves to resolve each point of textual difference to a single reading, what we will create may not be an *arche*-type so much as a *miso*-type—a Frankenstein text. It is, therefore perhaps more realistic (and dare I say better) not to fixate on the *Urtext* or the artefact but to ask instead, "What moments in the life of literary work can the extant witnesses shed light on?"

# References

Albertz, Rainer. 1990. 'Das Deuterojesaja-Buch als Fortschreibung der Jesaja-Prophetie'. In *Die hebräische Bibel und ihre zweifache Nachgeschichte: Festschrift für Rolf Rendtorff zum 65. Geburtstag,* edited by Erhard Blum, Christian Macholz, and Ekkehard W. Stegemann, 241–56. Neukirchen-Vluyn: Neukirchener.

Becker, Uwe. 2020. 'The Book of Isaiah: Its Composition History'. In *The Oxford Handbook of Isaiah,* edited by Lena-Sofia Tiemeyer, 37–56. Oxford: Oxford University Press.

Beit-Arié, Malachi. 1993. 'Transmission of Texts by Scribes and Copyists: Unconscious and Critical Interferences'. *Bulletin of the John Rylands University Library of Manchester* 75 (3): 33–51.

———. 2000. 'Publication and Reproduction of Literary Texts in Medieval Jewish Civilization: Jewish Scribality and Its Impact on the Texts Transmitted'. In *Transmitting Jewish Traditions: Orality, Textuality, and Cultural Diffusion,* edited by Yaakov Elman and Israel Gershoni, 225–47. New Haven: Yale University Press.

Boustan, Ra'anan S. 2007. 'The Study of Heikhalot Literature: Between Mystical Experience and Textual Artifact'. *Currents in Biblical Research* 6 (1): 130–60.

Bregman, Marc. 1985. 'Toward a Textcritical Approach of the Tanhuma-Yelamdenu Midrashim'. *Tarbiz* 54 (2): 289–92. [Hebrew]

———. 2003. *The Tanḥuma-Yelamdenu Literature: Studies in the Evolution of the Versions.* Piscataway: Gorgias. [Hebrew]

———. 2007. 'Tanḥuma Yelammedenu'. In *Encyclopaedia Judaica,* edited by Fred Skolnik, XIX: 503–4. London: Macmillan.

Cerquiglini, Bernard. 1989. *Éloge de la variante*. Paris: Seuil.

Chilton, Bruce, and Paul V. M. Flesher. 2011. *The Targums: A Critical Introduction*. Studies in Aramaic Interpretation of Scripture 12. Leiden: Brill.

Clarke, Ernest G. 1972. 'The Neofiti I Marginal Glosses and the Fragmentary Targum Witnesses to Gen. VI–IX'. *Vetus Testamentum* 22 (3): 257–65.

Davila, James R. 2005. *The Provenance of the Pseudepigrapha*. Supplements to the Journal for the Study of Judaism 105. Leiden: Brill.

———. 2017. 'Translating the Hekhalot Literature: Insights from New Philology'. In *Snapshots of Evolving Traditions: Jewish and Christian Manuscript Culture, Textual Fluidity, and New Philology,* edited by Liv I. Lied and Hugo Lundhaug, 323–46. Texte und Untersuchungen 175. Berlin: De Gruyter.

Díez Macho, Alejandro. 1970. *Neophyti 1: Targum Palestinense Ms de la Biblioteca Vaticana*. Vol. 2. *Exodo*. Madrid: Consejo superior de investigaciones científicas.

———. 1975. 'Un nuevo manuscrito del Targum Fragmentario'. In *Homenaje a Juan Prado: miscelanea de estudios biblicos y hebraicos*, edited by Lorenzo Alvarez Verdes and E. Janvier Alonso Hernandez, 533–51. Madrid: Consejo superior de investigaciones científicas.

Doubles, Malcolm C. 1965. 'Toward the Publication of the Extant Texts of the Palestinian Targums'. *Vetus Testamentum* 15 (1): 16–26.

Endres, John C., William R. Millar, and John Barclay Burns, eds. 1998. *Chronicles and its Synoptic Parallels in Samuel, Kings, and Related Biblical Texts*. Collegeville: Liturgical Press.

Fassberg, Steven E. 1990. *A Grammar of the Palestinian Targum fragments from the Cairo Genizah*. Harvard Semitic Studies 38. Atlanta: Scholars Press.

Gile, Jason. 2011. 'The Additions to Ben Sira and the Book's Multiform Textual Witnesses'. In *The Texts and Versions of the Book of Ben Sira: Transmission and Interpretation*, edited by Jean-Sébastien Rey and Jan Joosten, 237–56. Supplements to the Journal for the Study of Judaism 150. Leiden: Brill.

Ginsburger, Moses. 1899. *Das Fragmententhargum*. Berlin: S. Calvary.

———. 1903. 'Die Fragmente des Thargum jeruschalmi zum Pentateuch'. *Zeitschrift der deutschen morgenländischen Gesellschaft* 57: 67–80.

Gottlieb, Leeor. 2021. 'Towards a More Precise Understanding of Pseudo-Jonathan's Origins'. *Aramaic Studies* 19: 104–20.

Gröber, Gustav. 1869. *Die handschriftlichen Gestaltungen der Chanson de geste "Fierabras" und ihre Vorstufen*. Leipzig: F. C. W. Vogel.

Heikkilä, Tuomas. 2020. 'Dealing with Open Textual Traditions'. In *Handbook of Stemmatology: History, Methodology, Digital Approaches*, edited by Philipp Roelli, 254–72. Berlin: De Gruyter.

Hempel, Charlotte. 2013. *The Qumran Rule Texts in Context: Collected Studies*. Texte und Studien zum antiken Judentum 154. Tübingen: Mohr Siebeck.

Holmes, Michael W. 2011. 'Working with an Open Textual Tradition: Challenges in Theory and Practice'. In *The Textual History of the Greek New Testament: Changing Views in Contemporary Research*, edited by Klaus Wachtel and Michael W. Holmes, 65–78. Atlanta: Society of Biblical Literature.

Kahle, Paul. 1930. *Masoreten des Westens*. Vol. 2. *Das palästinische Pentateuchtargum*. Stuttgart: Kohlhammer.

Kalimi, Isaac. 2014. 'Die Quelle(n) der Textparallelen zwischen Samuel-Könige und Chronik'. In *Rereading the relecture?*, edited by Uwe Becker and Hannes Bezzel, 11–30. Forschungen zum Alten Testament II:66. Tübingen: Mohr Siebeck.

Khan, Geoffrey, and Hindy Najman. 2022. 'Performance in Ancient and Medieval Judaism'. *Dead Sea Discoveries* 29 (3): 259–91.

Khan, Geoffrey, Hindy Najman, and Ishay Rosen-Zvi. 2020. 'Hebrew Philological Practices from Antiquity to the Middle Ages'. *Marginalia Review* (digital commons). Accessed 24 September, 2023. https://themarginaliareview.com/wp-content/uploads/2020/12/Hebrew-Philological-Practices-from-Antiquity-to-The-Middle-Ages.pdf

Klein, Michael L. 1975. 'The Extant Sources of the Fragmentary Targum to the Pentatuech'. *Hebrew Union College Annual* 46: 115–37.

———. 1980. *The Fragment-Targums of the Pentateuch according to their Extant Sources*. 2 vols. Analecta Biblica 76. Rome: Biblical Institute.

———. 1982. 'Associative and Complementary Translation in the Targumim'. In *Harry M. Orlinsky Volume*, edited by Baruch A. Levine and Abraham Malamat, 134–40. Eretz-Israel 16. Jerusalem: Israel Exploration Society.

———. 1986. *Genizah Manuscripts of Palestinian Targum to the Pentateuch*. 2 vols. Cincinnati: Hebrew Union College.

Kraft, Robert A. 2009. *Exploring the Scripturesque: Jewish Texts and their Christian Contexts*. Supplements to the Journal for the Study of Judaism 137. Leiden: Brill.

Kulik, Alexander, Gabriele Boccaccini, Lorenzo DiTommaso, David Hamidoić, and Michael Stone, eds. 2019. *A Guide to Early Jewish Texts and Traditions in Christian Transmission*. Oxford: Oxford University Press.

Lange, Armin. 2016. 'Ancient and Late Ancient Hebrew and Aramaic Jewish Texts'. In *Textual History of the Bible*, volume 1A, *The Hebrew Bible: Overview Articles*, edited by Armin Lange and Emanuel Tov, 112–66. Leiden: Brill.

Le Déaut, Roger. 1968. 'Lévitique XXII 26–XXIII 44 dans la Targum Palestinien'. *Vetus Testamentum* 18 (1–4): 458–71.

Lundhaug, Hugo, and Liv I. Lied. 2017. 'Studying Snapshots: On Manuscript Culture, Textual Fluidity, and New Philology'. In *Snapshots of Evolving Traditions: Jewish and Christian Manuscript Culture, Textual Fluidity, and New Philology*, edited by Liv I. Lied and Hugo Lundhaug, 1–19. Texte und Untersuchungen 175. Berlin: De Gruyter.

Macé, Caroline, 2020. 'The Stemma as a Historical Tool'. In *Handbook of Stemmatology: History, Methodology, Digital Approaches*, edited by Philipp Roelli, 272–91. Berlin: De Gruyter.

MacKane, William. 1986. *A Critical and Exegetical Commentary on Jeremiah I-XXV*. International Critical Commentary. Edinburgh: T&T Clark.

McDowell, Gavin. 2021. 'The Date and Provenance of Targum Pseudo-Jonathan: The Evidence of Pirqe de Rabbi Eliezer and the Chronicles of Moses'. *Aramaic Studies* 19: 121–54.

Milikowsky, Chaim. 1988. 'The Status Quaestionis of Research in Rabbinic Literature'. *Journal of Jewish Studies* 39 (2): 201–11.

———. 1999. 'Further on Editing Rabbinic Texts: A Review-Essay of A Synoptic Edition of Pesiqta Rabbati Based Upon All Extant Manuscripts and the Editio Princeps by Rivka Ulmer'. *Jewish Quarterly Review* 90 (1/2): 137–49.

———. 2001/02. 'Vayyiqra Rabba, Chapter 28, Sections 1-3: Questions of Text, Redaction and Affinity to Pesiqta d'Rav Kahana'. *Tarbiz* 71: 19–65. [Hebrew]

———. 2002. 'On the Formation and Transmission of Bereshit Rabba and the Yerushalmi: Questions of Redaction, Text-Criticism and Literary Relationships'. *Jewish Quarterly Review* 92 (3/4): 521–67.

———. 2005. 'The Search for the 'Original Text': Studies in the Textual History and Editorial Method of Seder Olam and Vayyiqra Rabba'. In *Studies in Talmudic and Midrashic Literature in Memory of Tirzah Lifshitz,* edited by Moshe Bar-

Asher, Joshua Levinson, and Berachyahu Lifshitz, 349–84. Jerusalem: Bialik. [Hebrew]

———. 2006a. 'Reflections on the Practice of Textual Criticism in the Study of Midrash Aggada: The Legitimacy, the Indispensability and the Feasibility of Recovering and Presenting the (Most) Original Text'. In *Current Trends in the Study of Midrash*, edited by Carol Bakhos, 79–109. Supplements to the Journal for the Study of Judaism 106. Leiden: Brill.

———. 2006b. 'Vayyiqra Rabba Chapter 30: Its Transmissional History, Its Publication History and the Presentation of a New Edition (to sections 1 and 2)'. *Bar-Ilan Annual* 30–31: 269–318. [Hebrew]

———. 2010. 'Textual Criticism as a Prerequisite for the Study of Rabbinic Thought: On God Not Giving Recompense for Fulfilling Commandments and on the Immutability of the Created World'. In *Tiferet leYisrael: Jubilee Volume in Honor of Israel Francus*, edited by Joel Roth, Menahem Schmelzer, and Yaacov Francus, 131–51. New York: Jewish Theological Seminary.

———. 2013. *Seder Olam: Critical Edition, Commentary, and Introduction*. Jerusalem: Yad Ben-Zvi. [Hebrew]

———. 2017. 'Scholarly Editions of Three Rabbinic Texts–One Critical and Two Digital'. *Advances in Digital Scholarly Editing: Papers Presented at the DiXiT Conferences in the Hague, Cologne, and Antwerp*, edited by Peter Boot, Anna Cappellotto, Wout Dillen, Franz Fischer, Aodhán Kelly, Andreas Mertgens, Anna-Maria Sichani, Elena Spadini and Dirk van Hulle, 137–46. Leiden: Sidestone.

———. 2019. 'Vayyiqra Rabba Chapter 20: Text, Redaction and Theology'. In *The Wisdom of the Sages: Biblical Commentary in Rabbinic Literature,* edited by in Avigdor Shinan and Israel Jacob Yuval, 231–49. Jerusalem: Carmel. [Hebrew]

———. 2020. 'Philological Practices: Hebrew'. In *Handbook of Stemmatology: History, Methodology, Digital Approaches,* edited by Philipp Roelli, 493–501. Berlin: De Gruyter.

Milikowsky, Chaim, and Peter Schäfer. 2010. 'Current Views on the Editing of the Rabbinic Texts of Late Antiquity: Reflections on a Debate after Twenty Years'. In *Rabbinic Texts and the History of Late-Roman Palestine,* edited by Martin Goodman and Philip Alexander, 79–88. Oxford: Oxford University Press.

Mortensen, Beverly P. 2006. *The Priesthood in Targum Pseudo-Jonathan: Renewing the Profession.* 2 vols. Studies in Aramaic Interpretation of Scripture 4. Leiden: Brill.

Nichols, Stephe G. 1990. 'Introduction: Philology in a Manuscript Culture'. *Speculum* 65: 1–10.

Pannier, Léopold, and Gaston Paris, eds. 1872. *La vie de Saint Alexis, poème du XIe siècle et renouvellements des XIIe, XIIIe et XIVe siècles publiés avec préfaces, variantes, notes et glossaire.* Paris: Franck.

Pasquali, Giorgio. 1934. *Storia della tradizione e critica del testo.* Florence: Felice Le Monnier.

Patmore, Hector M. 2023. 'A Previously Overlooked Manuscript of Fragment Targum (EVR II A 371, National Library of Russia, St. Petersburg)'. *Aramaic Studies* 21: 19–42.

Pollock, Sheldon. 2009. 'Future Philology? The Fate of a Soft Science in a Hard World'. *Critical Inquiry* 35: 931–61.

Reynolds, Leighton Durham, and Nigel Guy Wilson. 2013. *Scribes and Scholars: A Guide to the Transmission of Greek and Latin Literature.* 4th edition. Oxford: Oxford University Press.

Roelli, Philipp, 2020. 'Introduction'. In *Handbook of Stemmatology: History, Methodology, Digital Approaches*, edited by Philipp Roelli, 1–8. Berlin: De Gruyter.

Schäfer, Peter (ed.). 1981. *Synopse zur Hekhalot-Literatur.* Texte und Studien zum antiken Judentum 2. Tübingen: Mohr Siebeck.

———. 1986. 'Research into Rabbinic Literature: An Attempt to Define the Status Quaestionis'. *Journal of Jewish Studies* 37 (2): 139–52.

———. 1989. 'Once again the Status Quaestionis of Research in Rabbinic Literature: An Answer to Chaim Milikowsky'. *Journal of Jewish Studies* 40 (1): 89–94.

Schultz, Brian. 2009. *Conquering the World: The War Scroll (1QM) Reconsidered.* Studies on the Texts of the Desert of Judah 76. Leiden: Brill.

Stemberger, Günter. 2011. *Einleitung in Talmud und Midrasch.* 9th edition. Munich: C.H. Beck.

Swartz, Michael D. 2013. 'Three-Dimensional Philology: Some Implications of the "Synopse zur Hekhalot-Literatur"'. In *Envisioning Judaism: Studies in Honor of Peter Schäfer on the Occasion of his Seventieth Birthday*, edited by Ra'anan S.

Boustan, Klaus Herrmann, Reimund Leicht, Annette Yoshiko Reed, and Giuseppe Veltri, I:529–50. Tübingen: Mohr Siebeck.

Williamson, Hugh G. M. 1994. *The Book Called Isaiah: Deutero-Isaiah's Role in Composition and Redaction*. Oxford: Clarendon.

Wilson, Robert R. 2016. 'Exegesis, Expansion, and Tradition-Making in the Book of Jeremiah'. In *Jeremiah's Scriptures: Production, Reception, Interaction, and Transformation*, edited by Hindy Najman and Konrad Schmid, 3–21. Supplements to the Journal for the Study of Judaism 173. Leiden: Brill.

# THE RABBINIC USE FOR TRANSLATION

*Willem Smelik*

What does a Targum *do* when people switch easily and freely between Hebrew and Aramaic in their daily conversations to the point that such mixing is replicated in letters, deeds and literary works?[1] As would appear from early rabbinic literature, the early rabbis were able to switch freely between these two languages—even allowing for literary stylisation of reported dialogues and traditions and literary functionality of language selection—and there is prima facie no reason to assume that large swaths of the population did not use both languages in tandem, orally at least, even on the admission that the picture must have been varied and language proficiency multifarious in ways we may never fully retrieve.

Besides Hebrew and Aramaic, other languages were used in Roman Palestine, most notably Greek, in different constellations, settings, speakers, places and periods. Even a limited understanding of a language map that varies over time, by person and by

---

[1] This article is based on a paper first given at Stellenbosch, IOSOT 2016, in the joint session on LXX and Targum. I included a brief characterisation of Onkelos at the meeting of the Verband der Judaisten in Deutschland, 'The 72 Languages of the Torah', Universität Düsseldorf, 25–27 February 2019.

place, raises questions about an indiscriminate introduction of a liturgical translation of the Scriptures in the early centuries. Were we to adopt a flexible model that postulates a continuum between different languages and communicative situations, it would facilitate a better understanding of the function of translation, whether Greek or Aramaic, in this period. This model is part of an ongoing research project on language selection in rabbinic literature which includes a study of code-switching (mixed language use) in the two Talmudim.

The question what does a Targum do in a multilingual, shifting world becomes even more acute when we take into account that Jewish societies of the early centuries CE were not yet governed by rabbinic authorities. It is now believed, although perhaps not universally held, that Rabbinic Judaism, once routinely identified as 'mainstream Judaism' and thought to have ruled from 70 CE onward, if not essentially already in Qumran in the shape of a proto-rabbinic movement, only ever so gradually assumed hegemony over religious Jews over the course of the first millennium CE. Following a revised perspective on Rabbinic Judaism which emerged in the last four decades (Alexander 2009),[2] it is clear that in the first half-millennium CE rabbinic

---

[2] Alexander (2009), unpublished: I thank the author for sharing his paper with me. The point I make here does not add up to a collapse of Judaism, as advocated by Schwartz (2001). However, his insistence on a power vacuum still rings true to me and should be taken into account even when allowing for continuous plural Jewish identities. Contrast Schremer (2010, 319–41, 340): "This body of [Tannaitic] literature stands in complete opposition to Schwartz's assertion." For Schwartz, see also Satlow (2005, 151–62).

influence was neither universal in its heartland nor ubiquitous outside its immediate area of influence. How rabbinic Judaism came to rule the roost remains to be fleshed out in far greater detail.

To state the obvious, all this has implications for 'the Jewish view of scriptural translation'—or the 'rabbinic' view, or even just the '*classical* rabbinic' view—yet it is something rarely stated: we cannot assume a single, ideological take on the practice of translation that was coined either during the late Second Temple period or in the early centuries CE, by the rabbinic or proto-rabbinic movement that supposedly remained in force ever since. And even if we could, we should not assume a static, rounded, perfect view on translation, but rather living and therefore evolving views. Regardless of whether our focus is on 'the' Greek or 'the' rabbinic ideology of translation, falling into the trap of social and chronological generalisation is all too easy. We will need to consider the ramifications of these simple observations as regards the mixed language context and the reach of rabbinic power and influence for the uses and the compass of translation, and the concomitant character of translation.

## 1.0. The Case for Translation

The case for translation becomes a different one when we take the multilingual, even multicultural context into account. Translation is not about imposing an authoritative understanding of the Scriptures—or selected Scriptures—upon those that use it, whether by reading or listening, actively or passively, nor necessarily primarily about linguistic deficiencies that must be overcome. The prestige of Greek elicited translations from Hebrew into that language, and likewise translations from Aramaic into Hebrew, may partly follow from the standing of Greek and Hebrew respectively (Crom 2011; Aitken 2020, 203). True, some language deficiencies will have occurred and prompted translations. Multilingualism made the phenomenon of translation inescapable in the court of law, as duly recognised in rabbinic *halakha* (Smelik 2013, 119), at rituals and in the liturgy, and in academic study, but such situations would not be universal in time and place. Moreover, such translations would often aim at understanding both languages (as in the court of law), working bi-directionally. Outside the court houses, translation did not necessarily aim just at those who lacked proficiency in Hebrew, but also at those who wished a deeper understanding of what the texts meant. In contrast to rumours about rabbinic disapproval of various translations, early rabbis held the view that meaning was not *lost* but rather *won in translation* as they embraced multiple languages and translations as the manifold expression of God's language (Smelik 2013, 29–41). The Torah found full expression in the multitude of no less than seventy translations.

This equilibrium of multilingualism, translation, and scriptural interpretation was not to last. As the appreciation of translation changed, we can discern a gradual move away from etymological equivalence and translational irradiation in the interpretation of the Scriptures to inner-Hebrew root-play and Hebrew-only approaches (Smelik 2013, 500–7). This shift does not occur in isolation. At about the same time, an increased emphasis on Hebrew as the Holy Tongue emerged, which would advance the eventual extraction of Aramaic from mixed speech to functionally motivated language choices.

One of the main reasons for a rethink of how translations functioned in Roman Palestine of the first few centuries CE follows from an appreciation of the way Hebrew and Aramaic were used in tandem.[3] Considered from the viewpoint of code-switching, several aspects of language mixing point to Hebrew as a language that was partnered by Aramaic in a highly intimate, intricate fashion: loanwords back and forth, insertions of phrases of one language into the other, and alternating language use between and within sentences. Greek and Latin loanwords are frequently added to the mix, pointing to its reach within the same society.

In the early Amoraic period, the Yerushalmi displays a use of Aramaic in which several things stand out.[4] The use of Hebrew and Aramaic follows established patterns of code-switching between two languages or dialects: borrowing, intra- and inter-sentential code-switching in the shape of alternation and insertion, mid-dialogue and mid-paragraph are the characteristic and predictable fruits of a bilingual culture. Moreover, the use of Hebrew and Aramaic is in large parts strikingly equivalent in terms of use and value (qualitatively), even though the literary use of Hebrew

---

[3] See also Samely (1994). Thanks are due to Philip Alexander for reminding me of this article when we exchanged ideas about the topic of this paper.

[4] See Smelik (forthcoming); as for the Bavli, Smelik (2025).

predominates (quantitatively). This equivalence tends to be overlooked. Characteristically, many direct speech reports involve code-switching between Jewish Palestinian Aramaic and Rabbinic Hebrew.[5] Many anonymous comments switch language as freely as the interlocutors do in speech reports. In the Yerushalmi, the use of Aramaic shows a rather limited tendency to functional differentiation without ever being fully realised (such in contrast to the Bavli[6]). The tendency towards functional differentiation suggests an increasingly applied sociolinguistic attitude towards the pair of languages, retroactively emphasising the distinction, which draws the pattern of code-switching towards alternation rather than a type of congruent lexicalisation with complete equivalence between the two 'codes'.

The type of bi- or multi-lingualism on display in these texts has implications for our understanding of the Hebrew dialect in Roman Palestine. While everyone agrees that the relationship between the two related languages had become ever so close in the Second Temple period, there is disagreement about the time Hebrew ceased to be a language spoken in daily life. The data from code-switching imply that we have placed a premium on the pure species of each language for far too long, and in doing so neglected the unity of a bilingual communication. The question how pure or artificial Hebrew was, has overshadowed the interest in the osmosis between these sister languages, because the focus

---

[5] Scriptural quotations obviously remain in Biblical Hebrew, albeit that some Hebrew rewordings and Aramaic translations occur, too.

[6] The Babylonian Talmud.

always remained on one of the languages as the supposedly dominant one or the source of particular phenomena, not on their interaction. It is obvious that the degree of code-switching and linguistic interference in everyday language went further than we realised it did, because the literary consolidation of speech acts would tend to follow certain conventions and in doing so eclipsed daily patterns of language mixing. Analysis of the Yerushalmi suggests that literary code-switching started as an arbitrary and vernacular phenomenon.

Eventually, the valuation of liturgical and biblical Hebrew resulted in a functional differentiation between the two languages. It is in this very process that I suggest Targum may have been swept up. To assess the function of and use for Greek and Aramaic translations in the evolving multilingual Jewish society of the Tannaitic and Amoraic periods, I will focus on the *scope of translation* as related to the use of languages and the use for translation, and relate the observations to the *character of translation* as evident in Targum Onkelos. The context of translation in a wide sense is the multilingual world, while in a narrower sense it is about the compass of translation in rabbinic eyes.

## 2.0. The Rabbinic Use for Greek Translation

To evaluate the position of the Greek translations in the rabbinic polygon of forces, some broad-brush observations on their origin and development will have to suffice. While it is generally agreed that the Greek Torah originated in Egypt where it was widely used (Aitken 2015, 3–4), the use of Greek translations spread to other areas bordering the Mediterranean Sea, including Palestine, where much of the known editorial and authorial activity of the Septuagint in later times appears to have been located (Tov 2010; more cautiously Aitken 2020, 214). Indeed, the first two centuries CE were bristling with translational activity in Roman Palestine, a tradition with its roots in the Second Temple period (Aitken 2020, 207–15). Many of these translations and revisions display a tendency to mimic the form of the source text to some degree (isomorphism), with some translations now part of the corpus dated to the first century CE, namely Canticles, Ecclesiastes, Lamentations (Dorival, Munnich, and Harl 1988, 97; Aitken 2008; Alexander 2009; Aitken 2009). The Greek translations of Aquila, Symmachus and Theodotion were created a century later,[7] the same century which saw the inception of the so-called Babylonian Targumim.[8] A rich yield for a diverse, yet small society, even considering its diaspora in the West and East. Evidently the Scriptures were the focus of a great deal of Jewish reflection which continued, both in Aramaic (a more scholastic enterprise) and, as Nicholas de Lange (1990; 2006; 2010) has advocated, in Greek among Byzantine Jews.

---

[7] Whether Symmachus is a 'rabbinic' translation remains unclear; see esp. Salvesen (2012). About Theodotion very little is known. That traditions concerning Theodotion were translated into traditions about Jonathan may suggest a perception that the author was indeed Jewish.

[8] The date of Onkelos and Jonathan remains problematic. I am leaving aside the Peshitta, which is sometimes claimed to have Jewish origins; see e.g., Weitzman (1992), van Peursen (2004) and the literature cited there.

The original impetus for translation into Greek has been the subject of speculation and analysis. Whilst the generations for whom the Greek Pentateuch would have been important may not have been as conversant in Hebrew so as to understand the Hebrew Torah, it is clear that the social and cultural status of Greek must have been an important contributing factor in the endeavour to create the translation (Aitken 2015, 3–4). The style of translation of the original Septuagint displays familiarity with the Egyptian Greek translation of Demotic texts—in other words standard practice (Aitken 2020, 202–3).[9] Conversely, the idea that the Septuagint served, like the Targum would, in an interlinear way depending on the Hebrew text has been called into question for good reasons (Law 2013, 41). More specifically, the notion that the Septuagint was used alternatingly with the Hebrew text in the way of the Targum (Levine 2005, 159; Perrot 1984, 118–21), remains a hypothesis that cannot be confirmed at present, and even if it were to ring true as an occasional possibility (certainly not as a broad generalisation), it would only apply to an environment where Hebrew would also be a viable liturgical language. Even so, the dependence of the translation on the original does not necessarily have to be interlinear.[10]

---

[9] Perhaps not a vernacular version (so Lee 1983), but the cultural version of Egyptian Greek.

[10] On the use of Greek in the Diaspora communities, see Schürer (1986, 141–43). I do not like, or agree with, the biased comment on p. 140 that in Palestine itself, "the stream of prophetic religion was not entirely stopped by the strict observances emphasized by the Pharisees."

Things are different, however, in Roman Palestine. The desire for translation in that thoroughly multilingual world surely must have had more dimensions than mere language deficiency (Crom 2011, 80–83; Aitken 2020, 203, 217). Obviously, any Greek-speaking synagogue, such as that reflected by the Theodotus inscription, would have benefitted from a Greek translation in the liturgy (Levine 2005, 626–27; Smelik 2013, 178–79), which, following Diaspora practices, might even have been used in a monolingual recitation of the Scriptures. Mishnah Meg. 1.8 explicitly permits Greek Scriptures. At the same time, we should not overestimate the number of monolingual Greek synagogues in Roman Palestine. Moreover, many translations were probably rarely used in liturgical context but would have made sense at the level of individual or communal study.

Study is the stated purpose of the prologue to the Greek Ben Sira, whose author asks those readers who have access to those texts ("the Law, the Prophets, and others that follow them") to avidly study his grandfather's wisdom, which serves to benefit people "both orally and written" (Sir. 0.1–2, 6; Ziegler 1980, 123; Pietersma and Wright 2007, 719). The oral benefit would follow from publicly declaiming the text, which would be useful to those Greek speakers who could not read, and which envisages a setting of shared study. These are religious and cultural goals that explain the scope of translation, but interestingly, Ben Sira 'translated' the wisdom into *Hebrew*, thus monolingually (also called internal translation), while his grandson seeks to achieve the very same goal in Greek. That the prologue is a construct to validate the authority of the translation makes no difference to this linguistic situation.

The rabbinic presence and the reach of their *halakhic* influence is not unequivocal in Asia Minor, Greece and Egypt in the period under consideration, well into the Amoraic period.[11] It is unwarranted to project the later rabbinic practice of Hebrew recitation on any of these areas in this period, roughly the first half of the first millennium CE. A Greek Torah makes little sense in Babylonia, even among scholars, whereas a Hebrew Torah made little sense outside Palestine and Babylonia where Greek dominated. When the impact of the rabbinic movement made itself felt in various areas remains opaque in detail, but the increasing insistence on using Hebrew in the liturgy, replacing Greek prayers that had been permitted (such as the *Amida* and the *Shema*),[12] and the insistence on the recitation of the Torah, coupled with the premium placed on Hebrew as the holy tongue, ensured that Hebrew and rabbinic notions were on a collision course in the regions where Greek held sway and may have started to make itself present somewhat before the 6th century CE. Eventually, it would become almost unimaginable that the Torah could have been cantillated in a language other than Hebrew.

Rabbinic literature voices opinions which are mutually exclusive, but eventually the Talmud demarcates the proper use of written translations, as both the Yerushalmi and the Bavli play

---

[11] See also the methodological considerations in Alexander (2009).

[12] For Greek prayer, see van der Horst and Newman (2008); for rabbinic rulings withdrawing support for Greek prayers, see Smelik (2025, 67–72).

out two Mishnaic texts against each other, m. Meg. 1.8 and m. Yad. 4.5. In the former, the anonymous voice states that scrolls of Scripture may be written in any language but *tefillin* and *mezuzot* may only be written in [the script called] Ashurit. The Bavli understands the *mishnah* to imply the kosher production of scriptural texts, as it pointedly adds that such translations, once sown with tendons, render the hands unclean (b. Meg. 8b). To render the hands unclean is rabbinic terminology for Holy Writ. Although m. Meg. 1.8 would appear to confirm *de jure* what happened *de facto*, in the later reception this *mishnah* is neutered by aligning the text with another one, m. Yad. 4.5, which stipulates that the Holy Writ must be written in *Ashurit*, or with m. Meg. 2.1, which excludes recitation from a translation in the fulfilment of the halakha on Purim. In medieval times, even the very term בכל לשון would be reinterpreted as 'in any script'.

Although we do hear subdued voices about the use of Greek translation in liturgical contexts, such instances are few and far between and their transmission obscures the fact that sometimes no one was able to deliver a Hebrew recitation. At the same time, we find the statement that recitation in Greek of the Scroll of Esther is permitted, because it is ritually valid for everyone regardless of whether someone is Hellenophone or not (b. Meg. 18a). But these instances do not represent the main interest in Greek translations. The evidence for their use in rabbinic literature concerns stories, lined up for a new purpose, and incidental translations of words. As for real use, the interest in lexemic precision for halakhic purposes is paramount. While it is likely that there was some use of Greek scriptural translations in a liturgical context, the rabbis did not deem it worthy of mention, or more accurately, if they did, they referred to 'translation' without specifying its language. Hence our evidence is very slim and circumstantial at best.

A similar observation pertains to the changes made for King Talmai. Regardless of their putative origin or value for the textual history of the Greek translations, the changes made for Ptolemy's Torah as reflected in rabbinic literature mainly inform us about the rabbinic *perception* of the Greek translation. As Veltri has pointed out, there is a twofold use of the list of changes: their exegetical input is used to make specific points, and along the way the mere fact of changes alter the document's status. It no longer represents the Torah, it has become a *changed* Torah. Obviously, the idea that the changed Torah means that it no longer is the true Torah only works on the assumption that there is a generally acknowledged, single valid version, which we may call authoritative, inspired, or holy. This assumption does not hold water across the centuries, indeed probably was not implied when the list of changes was created, and should therefore be used with caution and awareness of the chronological and social limitations. It is emphasised only in the Babylonian Talmud, which thereby conceals the variety of views both in earlier years and in non-rabbinic milieus.

The quotations of Aquila's translation in rabbinic literature reflect an interest in semantic precision. What is interesting about the rabbinic quotations of Aquila in the Talmud Yerushalmi is not so much the question whether these translations represent a witness to the authentic Greek translation by the man from Pontus, Asia Minor, but the layer of interpretative rewording that the Greek translation received (Smelik 2013, 387–99).[13] They typically involve the Hebrew lemma, "Aquila translated," the translation (usually in Greek), and a Hebrew exposition of said translation. The following example occurs in a list of translated objects (y. Shab. 6.4, 8b, 398, 24–25 [ed. Sussmann 2001]):

> ובתי הנפש תירגם עקילס אסטו־מוכריאה דבר שניתן על בת הנפש
> ובתי הנפש תרגם עק[י]לס אסט[ו] מוכריא דבר שהוא ניתן על בית הנפש
> 'Perfume boxes. Aquila translated "elegant neck ornament", that is an object placed on the neck.'

The first line represents the Leiden manuscript, the second a Cairo Genizah fragment. The biblical noun phrase either denotes 'perfume boxes' or 'amulets' (Baumgartner et al. 1967, I:167; Clines 1993–2011, V:734; Meyer and Donner 2007, 834), a rare expression. Aquila's Greek translation is provided in transliteration which probably did not survive scribal transmission without errors, and transliterations can be hard to interpret as things are. That said, Veltri's suggestion appears spot on, as he reads στόμιον χαρίεν 'elegant neck ornament' (Veltri 1994a, 102). What is most interesting is the structure: biblical lemma (ובתי הנפש), source of interpretation (תירגם עקילס), translation into Greek (אסטו־(ה) מוכריא) and finally a Hebrew exposition of that translation, דבר שהוא ניתן על בית הנפש, 'that is an object placed on the neck'. This

---

[13] For traditions about Aquila not quoting his translation, see Smelik (2013, 434–99). See now also Giambrone (2017).

structure is common to traditions associated with one Aquila, although sometimes some elements may be missing, like the Greek translation in Hebrew characters (Smelik 2013, 387–99, 430–31), and the order of the first two items is reversed here, as it usually is: Aquila interpreted + lemma to be interpreted + Greek translation + Hebrew exposition, sometimes a second exposition. The order had to be reversed, as the co-text is a list of Hebrew lemmata to be interpreted. Of interest is the implication that the translation represents a traditional, veritable and *written* version; no other interpretation is introduced with the past tense of the verb תרגם rather than אמר (Smelik 2013, 395–98 and *passim*).

In the translation and interpretation of Lev. 23.40, Aquila interprets a Hebrew lexeme as if it were Greek—like the rabbis would.[14] The use of Greek homophonous words to explain the Hebrew blends in well with the early rabbinic tradition. The rabbinic formula suggests that a received tradition is drawn upon for exegetical purposes but *not* exploited for its value as a continuing translation within the same rabbinic tradition. Regardless of the question whether these traditions have any bearing on the historical version of Aquila's translation (Labendz 2009; Giambrone 2017), the perception of these quotations suggests a principally exegetical-semantic value. It is not an interest in their possible function as continuous translation of the scriptural text—entirely in keeping with rabbinic interest in translation as displayed in the Talmudim and Midrashim.

---

[14] For the use of such 'etymologies', see Smelik (2013, 11–22, 'The Family of Languages').

In sum, the rabbis take a halakhic interest in the Septuagint mainly for two reasons: first to define the holiness of the Scriptures in translation, then to draw the boundaries of Greek in the liturgical recitation. They do not lay down detailed practical rules for a scriptural recitation in Greek (see, for example, the implicit comments in t. Meg. 3.13), but chip away at the permission to use Greek, and in the process they establish more restrictive rules for non-Greek translations. In terms of the rabbis' use, the interest is lexicographic and semantic, but not as a running translation.

## 3.0. The Rabbinic Use for Aramaic Translation

There is no literary evidence for the existence of any Targum before the same period—sidestepping the Aramaic translations found at Qumran, which represent a different genre of translation (Shepherd 2008).[15] First century sources describe many aspects of the liturgy but a liturgical translation is not among them, nor do any of the Tannaitic writings refer to these Targums as sources. I would not wish to imply, or infer the conclusion, that no translations were used in synagogal liturgy at this point. There is every likelihood that they did in multiple settings, especially since *Tannaitic* sources testify the existence of written translations and designate Scripture in translation as Holy Writ, whether monolingually (against rabbinic preferences) or bilingually (Smelik 2013, 220–70).

---

[15] The picture sketched in Billerbeck (1964, 154–56), is an uncritical retrojection.

The language map of Roman Palestine would have made a whole-sale introduction of a centrally agreed Aramaic translation an inconceivable anomaly before the Amoraic period. What is the point of translating into Aramaic if the intended audience, in all likelihood, by and large were perceived as being able to understand the Hebrew because in ordinary speech people mixed between the supra-regional dialect and the religious language? True, the more complicated Hebrew parts could be daunting, but they would remain so in translation. The tentative solution to this conundrum I will argue today is twofold:

1. to provide a para-lexicon for the Hebrew original, and thereby establish the perceived meaning of the Scriptures as accurately as possible;
2. to astutely steer the reading of the Hebrew text into approved directions (see also Alexander 1988, 239).

The second point implies an audience beyond the elect few of the rabbinic circle. Paradoxically, the rabbis themselves very rarely, if at all, utilise the translations under the second category for their own purposes, as is evident from the relatively sparse occasions on which the early rabbis take recourse to the Targum in rabbinic literature. Even the first category of a para-lexicon must be deemed underused, at least in the explicit references available to us. It seems as if their endeavour for precise equivalents and interpretative notions such as the importance of Torah–obedience was intended for external purposes rather than their own, internal use.

The crucial difference in the rabbinic *use* of translation (rather than use *for*) and the integral interpretative slant of most

Targums is the aspect of cohesion, comprehensive perspective, and aggadic detail. While the character of the Targums reveals a primary interpretative interest, over and above a rewording in another language, it does so in a sustained strategy to represent the Hebrew source text as the original point of reference, illuminated, rendered intelligible, and where necessary, more acceptable or palatable for a public setting. Translation is thus presented as the *dependent* sibling and in that sense the rabbinic reception of Targum steers translation into new waters.

But there is another use and perspective too. The rabbinic regulation for the liturgical recitation of scriptural translation, in practice dealing with Aramaic but in theory including other languages, too, does not reveal the whole story with respect to the place of translation in rabbinic practice. The rabbinic interest in translation, at least as used for their own purposes, was predominantly that of *lexemic* precision, a kind of parallel thesaurus. Strikingly, the rabbis by and large passed up Targum for their *halakhic* considerations, and even in terms of aggadic motifs their use is extremely limited. It is not that they do not know the sources (except that the Palestinian Targum is quoted only in the Yerushalmi, not in the Bavli, whereas Onkelos and Jonathan figure in the Bavli only, while the Midrashim only show an interest in Targum in much later centuries), and occasionally they glitter briefly in the limelight, but on the whole they are little more than extras.

Years ago, Alex Samely (1994) explored the ramifications of an aside by Chaim Rabin about Targum as "monolingual hermeneutics." Samely argues that the primary character of the Targum is a "dedicated exegetical re-wording" of the biblical text: while its language may *look* like it is Aramaic it functions as a rewording in rabbinic Hebrew. Hence his reference to Rabin's notion. There are two languages, but one language does not translate but rather *reword* the other; the differences between source and target text do not follow from incongruities at either the linguistic or cultural level.

It has in fact long been recognised that the Targums have a strong interpretative slant, which renders its character as a translation unique, not just in the often cited interpretative augmentations of the Palestinian Targum, but also in the way the Targums, especially Onkelos and Jonathan, are tied to their Hebrew parent text to the extent that they take part in the combined endeavour as a bilingual text (Alexander 1988, 239). The importance of the element of translation is reduced as it operates within a "monolingual hermeneutics". Samely (1994, 94) points to the Hebraised nature of targumic Aramaic,[16] something grammarians had observed before (Dalman 1905, 13). As a corollary to the nature of translation language, he could have also pointed to the Aramaicised nature of Rabbinic Hebrew as the linguistic background against which Onkelos emerged.

The Targum goes beyond translation in a manner that makes the Aramaic language almost a side-effect: the way Targum goes about its business could have been an inner-Hebrew affair. Yet 'almost' is key here—there is an important distinction

---

[16] He adds the claim that Aramaic hardly has a "cultural-pragmatic aura of its own."

made by extracting meaning in Aramaic. First, the extraction of Aramaic allows Onkelos to serve as a para-lexicon to the Hebrew, and second, the linguistic distance allows Targum, especially but not exclusively of the post-Onkelos variety, to be less than literal, to be presented as a Scriptural text because it remained lined up with the Hebrew, forever its side-kick (Brock 1992, 319–20). At the same time, the alternating use of Hebrew and Aramaic in talmudic literature and culture gradually takes shape in the form of an increased functional differentiation between these two languages. The lexemic equivalence of Hebrew and Aramaic and increasing functional differentiation is as relevant for the scope of translation as it is with regard to the type of code-switching observed in rabbinic literature: two languages kept apart yet tied together.

When rabbinic interest in the form, function and performance of translation arose and resulted in a number of regulations (Alexander 1985),[17] what do these restrictions on translation tell us about the actual function and the rabbinic ideal of translation? Previous research has established that the rabbinic rules for the chanting of the Targum in the synagogue service probably emerged in the (late) Mishnaic period (Safrai 1990). The implications are twofold: first, the rabbis may not have instigated their rules for targumic recitation before the mid-second century CE, and second, these rules may have been devoid of in-

---

[17] For the liturgical Targum as a genre, see Verrijssen (2024).

fluence for quite some time when they did as is suggested by several passages (see the passage in the Yerushalmi discussed below).

The rules for reading and translating were established early on: who may read and translate, how to read and translate, what to read and translate, how many may do so and for how long, and the optional character of translation. Some of the rabbinic pronouncements may have been fleshed out in more detail in Amoraic sources, but they are evident in Tannaitic sources already. Together they keep Scripture and translation apart,[18] yet correlating them so closely that the interpretation may shed light on the original (Alexander 1988, 238). The translation was not to strike out on its own, but dependent on the original text (Alexander 1985, 24), as one half of the oral performance of the Scriptures as a bilingual text (Smelik 2015).

While a child may read and translate[19]—the Talmudim entirely skip this rule, as later tradition would *not* allow children to read—an adult may not translate on behalf of a minor while the minor reads the Scriptures;[20] the difference in standing of the readers presumably reflects the difference in standing of their

---

[18] See t. Meg. 3.20; y. Meg. 4.1, 74d, 768, 32; b. Meg. 21b; b. R. Hash. 27a. In addition, a cantor who reads—something which is discouraged—should be replaced by someone else serving as a cantor (t. Meg. 3.21).

[19] Citing Tannaitic sources here and in the following few notes; m. Meg. 4.6.

[20] So t. Meg. 4(3).21; see the comments by Lieberman (2002, V:1195).

sources. In the same vein, someone who is dressed inappropriately may not read to protect the honour of the Torah, but he may translate.[21] The distinction in standing also applies to the Torah, the Prophets, and the Writings respectively, in order of decreasing importance. Since someone who is blind cannot read the Torah from a written source, he should not read but may translate[22]—that the translation had to be performed *without* such a written source, i.e., from memory, is not attested in Tannaitic sources (Fraade 1992, 256–57),[23] maybe because written translations were still *en vogue* during this period (Alexander 1985, 24; Smelik 2013, 158–68), but the oral mode of delivery by the blind implies the distinction between the written delivery of the Torah and the unaided performance of the translation (Fraade 1992, 256–57).[24]

---

[21] See m. Meg. 4.6. Some of these rules of course relate to the Scroll of Esther specifically.

[22] See m. Meg. 4.6; t. Meg. 2.5.

[23] Note however that t. Suk. 2.10 might seem to imply that the interpreter had no scroll in his hands that forced him to put the *lulav* down, as Fraade suggests, it seems more likely that the reference is not to the *interpreter* (who would then have preceded the reader of the Hebrew in this passage) but to the *spokesman*. For the distinction between the *(me)turgeman* as interpreter and spokesman, see Alexander (1985, 24); Smelik 2013, (158–68).

[24] Note however that t. Suk. 2.10 might seem to imply that the interpreter had no scroll in his hands that forced him to put the *lulav* down, as Fraade suggests, it seems more likely that the reference is not to the *interpreter* (who would then have preceded the reader of the Hebrew in this passage) but to the *spokesman*.

The rules reflect an inclination to put the Hebrew source above its translation, but there is also an impulse to put them in the same bracket. The reader should pitch his voice to that of the interpreter (possibly assuming that the interpreter may be a minor with a less strong voice), the length of what they read and translate is detailed, the exclusion of certain pericopes from the translation,[25] the number of people involved in reading and translating, the exact alternation of reading and translation, and the optional character of translation.

Some of these rules were subject to development during the late Tannaitic and early Amoraic period, such as the pericopes excluded from reading and/or translation, or that interpreters could use a written source. This is not the case for the rule that minors could recite Torah, even though the Tosefta makes clear that it would be unbecoming were a minor to read on behalf of an adult. Still, the rule that a minor could read was carried over well into the Middle Ages only to become properly restricted in the *Shulkhan Arukh*, the 16th century legal code by Joseph Karo (Roth 1988, 45–50).

The question may be raised why the two voices of reader and interpreter had to be so similar, evenly pitched,[26] seamlessly

---

[25] See m. Meg. 4.10; Sot. 7.1–2; t. Meg. 4(3).31–38. and in particular Alexander (1976); Fraade (1992, 256–65). On the development of this notion, Smelik (2013, 173–85).

[26] The pronouncement of equal pitch is only found in b. Ber. 45a, in which a *Baraita* stresses the reciprocal nature of the ruling in contrast to the Amoraic citation that precedes it. Veltri states that the *baraita*

alternating, chanted; why was the voice of the interpreter not more softly sung, just as in some medieval manuscripts the script of the Hebrew was written larger than that of the translation? In modern-day Yemenite chant, the monotonous targumic recitation is very distinct from, and barely contrapuntal to, the Hebrew voice, but that could well reflect a late development in the tradition of Yemenite chant. In these rules the two sources stand at equal grounds, indeed, if the interpreter cannot raise his voice enough (assuming a minor), the reader should lower his to match.

Rules do not reflect reality, prescription is no description (Alexander 1985, 21). Although rules may over time increasingly impact behaviour 'on the ground', this cannot be taken for granted, nor should we take established practice of later times as representative of the variety of earlier reading practices. Among the narrative traditions about the practice of translation, one important passage concerns three statements of R. Shmuel bar Rav Yiṣḥaq which disapprove actual behaviour in the liturgical performance of translation, as recorded in the Yerushalmi.

York (1979, 81–86) has stressed how the Targum merits the same "respect as does the Law itself" in these statements, while the ascription of these statements to R. Shmuel bar Rav Yiṣḥaq indicates how deeply the Targum was embedded in the school system. The last point is dated by now, however, as it depends too much on biography to withstand modern scrutiny.

---

compares the reader to Moses and the interpreter to God, a misunderstanding of the passage; Veltri (1994b, 211 n. 392).

More recently, Fraade (2023, 141–45) points out that the unifying element in these traditions is the perception of the recitation during the synagogue service as a re-enactment of the original revelation at Mt Sinai. I will dwell on these traditions once more to add a few observations on the editorial application of previous tradition, the unfolding of practice and the concept of translation.

y. Meg. 4.1,74d, 768, 6–15

1. ר׳ שמואל בר רב יצחק עאל לכנישתא חד בר נש קאים מתרגם סמיך לעמודא אמ׳ ליה אסור לך כשם שניתנה באימה ויראה כך אנו צריכין לנהוג בה באימה ויראה.
2. ר׳ חגי אמ׳ ר׳ שמואל בר רב יצחק עאל לכנישתא חמא חזנה[27] קאים מתרגם ולא מקים בר נש תחתוי אמ׳ ליה אסיר[28] לך כשם שניתנה על ידי סרסור כך אנו צריכין לנהוג בה על ידי סרסור.
3. עאל ר׳ יודה בר פזי ועבדה שאילה אנכי עומד בין י״י וביניכם בעת ההיא להגיד לכם את דבר י״י.
4. ר׳ חגיי אמ׳ ר׳ שמואל בר רב יצחק עאל לכנישתא חמא חד ספר מושט תרגומא מן גו סיפרא אמ׳ ליה אסיר לך דברים שנאמרו בפה בפה ודברים שנאמרו בכתב בכתב.

1. R. Shmuel bar Rav Yiṣḥaq entered a synagogue. Someone actually translated[29] while resting against a pillar. He said to him, "It is forbidden to you. For just as it was given in awe and fear, so must we deal with it in awe and fear."

---

[27] The Leiden MS actually reads חונה, see below.

[28] The Aramaic אסיר for Hebrew אסור (here and again below) looks like a scribal error, triggered by the preceding Aramaic words and graphic similarity.

[29] In the phrase קאים מתרגם, the first verb is auxiliary.

2. R. Ḥaggay said, R. Shmuel bar Rav Yiṣḥaq entered a synagogue. He saw the sexton actually translating while he had not installed someone in his place. He said to him, "It is forbidden to you, for just as it was given through a go-between so must we deal with it through a go-between."
3. R. Yehuda bar Pazzi entered and turned [the following text] into a question, "…while I stood between the Lord and you at that time, to declare to you the word of the Lord" (Deut. 5.5).[30]
4. R. Ḥaggay said R. Shmuel bar Rav Yiṣḥaq entered a synagogue. He saw some teacher[31] deliver[32] the translation from a book. He said to him, "It is forbidden to you. Things which were said by mouth must be [delivered] by mouth whereas [only] things which were said in writing must be [transmitted] in writing."

A biographical viewpoint would suggest that the Babylonian born and bred R. Shmuel bar Rav Yiṣḥaq would not have attended a Greek-speaking synagogue after he went up to Israel, although he might have witnessed one. But biography is not a good vantage point in rabbinic studies (Samely 2007, 101–2; Strack and Stemberger 1992, 59–62). The historical context of

---

[30] At this point, the preceding clause of Deut. 5.4 may have to be supplemented mentally: "The Lord spoke with you face to face at the mountain." See the discussion below.

[31] A parallel in Yalquṭ reads גבר for ספר; see Schäfer and Becker (2001, 302, 4.1/4).

[32] This is a rather literal translation. Sokoloff (2017, 262) offers a more contextual suggestion: 'declaim'.

rabbinic statements is largely absent beyond the utterances ascribed to persons of the past (Goldberg 1983; Goldberg 1987a). The four traditions brought together in the passage cited above could reflect visits to four different synagogues, brought up in a new halakhic context to articulate points in that new setting. As many rabbinic traditions, these vignettes of liturgical practice have been transmitted together to shed light on an issue in a new alignment of circumstances that brings new possibilities for relevance and regularisation into view (Strohm 2000, 104).[33] They do not reflect a single day in synagogue, nor necessarily a single synagogue: what counts is the abstraction or *distillation of principle* based on reported incidence.

As the traditions cited above do not specify the language of translation on each occasion, they were probably intended as a thematic principle. Whilst later practice in the history of synagogue liturgy makes it difficult to conceive of the bilingual liturgical practice as one in Hebrew and Greek, this is not a valid argument against its very possibility. However, it is commonplace to interpret the translation in these three statements as references to the Aramaic translation, so common that it never seems to require justification. The basis of this prevalent interpretation lies with several instances in rabbinic literature that refer to Targum as 'Aramaic translation' rather than 'translation'. Whereas the *editio princeps* of the Tosefta reads about scrolls at risk during a fire (t. Shab. 13.2): וגונזין אותן היו כותבין תרגום בכל לשון מצילין אותן 'If they are written in *a translation in any language*, they

---

[33] For some examples, see Smelik (2018).

save them [from a fire] and store them away', the manuscripts actually read תרגום ובכל לשון 'Targum and in any language' (edn Lieberman, 57), which appears to distinguish Targum from any language, and fronts Targum separately from a translation in any other language as Aramaic is, on this understanding, apparently more common or more expected in the present context. By contrast, the Mishnah and Yerushalmi support the Tosefta's *editio princeps*, with the former stating אף על פי כתובין בכל לשון טעונין גניזה 'even though they are written in any language, they require storage', a phrasing not even referring to 'translation', and one which is supported by the Yerushalmi's reading.[34] The later phrase with *waw* reflects both a shift in regulation and a semantic shift—the lexeme now is synonymous with 'Aramaic translation', which the Bavli sort of takes for granted, a transformation similar to the semantic shift of the verb תרגם which came to denote the performance of an *oral* translation of the Scriptures. (It is often inaccurately assumed it always had this latter meaning.)

The context of the first tradition is the question whether one should stand while one is before a Torah-scroll. The reader of the Torah should stand, because the Torah was received while standing. The equivalent attitude of awe and fear towards the reading and the translation of the Torah as well as the fact that Moses (the interpreter) stood before God suggests the interpreter should stand as well—and by implication that the translation is accorded the same prestige as the original. It is never stated that the interpreter should sit down for the translation, instead some

---

[34] For y. Shab. 16.1, 15b, 437, 1–2 see Smelik (2013, 287–89). See further Veltri (1994b, 181).

texts indeed suggest that the interpreter stood up to perform the translation.[35] Thus the objection in the first statement does not concern the fact that the interpreter stood, but his *casual* attitude in leaning against a pillar which epitomised a lack of deference towards the Torah *and* its translation.

The second statement, like the third, is cited by R. Ḥaggay. It posits the well-known rule that the roles of reading and interpreting the Torah should be performed by two distinct persons, which the *hazzan*—the cantor or sexton, following variant readings[36]—failed to do on this occasion. The *hazzan* would have been a knowledgeable jack-of-all-trades according to early Palestinian sources, frequently asked to be a teacher, cantor, preacher and more. As he was in charge of the recitation, selecting those who would read, he formed the linchpin of the liturgy. That the cantor is criticised in this tradition for combining two roles the rabbis wanted to keep apart is rather telling. The absence of a formal distinction between reader and interpreter goes against a rule that was probably established early on,[37] yet actual practice was

---

[35] See t. Suk. 2.10. Note that one may sit for both reading and interpreting the *Megilla*, m. Meg. 4.1, but the rules surrounding the recitation of the Megilla differ considerably.

[36] Although the Leiden manuscript followed by the *editio princeps* reads חונה, Yalquṭ Shimʿoni הונה, the commentaries preserve the better reading חזנה , 'sexton'; the manuscript contains a simple graphical mistake. The Rif quotes this passage in its entirety in his הלכות רב אלפס at b. Meg. 14a (חזנא); same reading Tos. b. B. Bat. 15a (s. שמונה). Likewise, the commentaries to the Yerushalmi קרבן העדה, מראה מקום והגהות and ירושלים עמודי.

[37] See fn. 18 above.

apparently varied, so that the rule flew in the face of real-life demands. It is not unlikely that in smaller communities a combination of roles once was a necessity (Levine 2005, 436). Many of the rabbinic traditions about the sexton show a thinly guised desire to keep in check the extent of his role and his importance and to subject him to rabbinic authority; for all his importance, he should not assume any authority of his own ( אינו נוטל שררה לעצמו).[38] But a correct and approved translation was not necessarily an easy thing to accomplish, since the translation was not meant to be spontaneous and free-flowing but bound by tradition and interpretation (York 1979, 82; Alexander 1985, 25).

A question by R. Yehuda bar Pazzi follows as an apparent comment on the distinction between the two roles of reader and interpreter, which he is reported to have raised after entering yet another unspecified place. The comment bears all the hallmarks of an unrelated unit, which editors brought to the same table as it seemed opportune, especially since there is not a real question. R. Yehuda bar Pazzi is reported to have cited a verse which, editorially, is understood to present a challenge. Perhaps the new alignment of this tradition necessitated trimming distracting and irrelevant edges. Deut. 5.5 relates to the agency of Moses, as he stands between God and the people at Mt Sinai. In what capacity he acts as an intermediary for God's word is not univocal. According to most commentators, R. Yehuda bar Pazzi implies that

---

[38] Gen. R. 79, 20; Yalquṭ Shim'oni, Genesis, 133.

Moses served as God's interpreter to the people,[39] a role elsewhere ascribed to Aaron as Moses' spokesman.[40] Why should Moses be the interpreter? As God spoke directly to the people (5.4), Moses' role is marked, thus different, which leads to two distinct roles that are to be observed: reading and interpreting. Since the preceding verse (Deut. 5.4) does *not* feature any go-between, but has God speak directly to the people, it is possible that the distinction is actually based on the phrase פנים בפנים in that verse, which the Targums translate as ממלל לקבל ממלל (TgNeof) or עם ממלל ממלל (TgOnk), 'speech to speech': two voices, i.e., reader *and* interpreter, with Moses confirming the latter role in Deut. 5.5.

That the rabbis may have struggled to bring actual practice under control is corroborated by R. Shmuel bar Rav Yiṣḥaq's third tradition about the delivery of the translation. The phrasing is unusual, מושט תרגומא מן גו סיפרא, but evidently refers to a translation declaimed from what was written in a scroll.[41] The existence of written translations, Greek or Aramaic, is attested in the rabbinic sources.[42] The possible status of Aramaic Targum as Holy Writ was demoted by m. Meg. 1.8 even before the translation

---

[39] See, e.g., Qorban HaEdah; Fraade (2023, 144).

[40] TgOnk Exod. 7.1 (translating נביאך with מתורגמנך, TgNeof תרגמנך); t. Meg. 3.21 (by analogy with TgOnk); Mekh. SbY וארא 6.2 (Moses speaks Hebrew, Aaron translates it into Egyptian); Tan. וארא 10.

[41] It is theoretically possible that the translation referred to here was based on the Hebrew text in said scroll, therefore performed extemporaneously.

[42] For a full discussion, see 'Between Holy Writ and Oral Torah', in Smelik (2013, 220–270). See further York (1979, 78).

could have become a full-fledged part of the synagogue service. The LXX on the other hand had already been established to the point that it could not simply be cancelled without undermining the venerability of tradition. Even traditions about saving a Targum from a fire on a Shabbat suggest that the Targum still partook in the holiness of the Scriptures to some extent, while also betraying signs of a conceptual development that would eventually result in the relegation of Targum as a subordinate, optional text (Smelik 2013, 240–58). In the final tradition, the distinction between the two voices is articulated as one of format. The articulation of what is proper in liturgical cantillation based on case observations inadvertently displays the *aberrant* nature of some of the described practices, indicating that things did and could not always go to plan yet, and above all that the concept of Targum as Oral Torah was still in flux, both in reality and in notion.

## 4.0. The Character of Onkelos

The rabbinic use for Aramaic translations can be augmented by a brief example of the style of TgOnk—the style of Greek translations such as Aquila has been the topic of ample previous research. Of course, this example works only on the assumption that Onkelos, as we now have it, reflects rabbinic goals and an early provenance, later editorial touches notwithstanding. Here is a very brief but generally representative passage from Gen. 14.15–18:[43]

---

[43] For a rigorous description of Targum Onkelos, see Samely (2011a). A comparison with other Targums can be found in Fraade (2023, 147–155).

## The Rabbinic Use for Translation

Heb 15 ויחלק עליהם לילה הוא ועבדיו ויכם וירדפם עד חובה אשר משמאל לדמשק :

Ara 15 ואתפלג עליהון בליליא הוא ועבדוהי ומחנון ורדפינון עד חובה דמציפונא לדמשק :

Heb 16 וישב את כל הרכש וגם את לוט אחיו ורכשו השיב וגם את הנשים ואת העם :

Ara 16 ואתיב ית כל קניניא ואף ית לוט אחוהי וקנייניה אתיב ואף ית נשיא וית עמא :

Heb 17 ויצא מלך סדם לקראתו אחרי שובו מהכות את כדר לעמר ואת המלכים

Ara 17 ונפק מלכא דסדם לקדמותיה בתר דתב מלממחי ית כדר לעמר וית מלכיא

Heb אשר אתו אל עמק שוה הוא עמק המלך : 18 ומלכי צדק מלך שלם

Ara דעימיה למישר מפנא הוא בית ריסא דמלכא : 18 ומלכי צדק מלכא דירושלם

Heb הוציא לחם ויין והוא כהן לאל עליון :

Ara אפיק לחים וחמר והוא משמיש קדם אל עילאה :

|     | MT | TgOnk |
| --- | --- | --- |
| 15 | Then he divided [his forces] against them by night, he and his servants, and beat them and pursued them as far as Hobah, which is north of Damascus. | Then they *divided themselves*[44] against them at night, he and his servants, and beat them and pursued them as far as Hobah, which is north[45] of Damascus. |
| 16 | Then he brought back all the goods, and also brought back his brother Lot with his goods, and also the women and the people. | Then he brought back all the goods, and also brought back his brother Lot with his goods, and also the women and the people. |
| 17 | Then the king of Sodom went out to meet him, after he had re- | Then the king of Sodom went out to meet him, after he had re- |

---

[44] The Hebrew expression, lit. 'he divided himself', but here translated with its plural subject, refers to the deployment of forces. The Targum is literal to the point of changing the meaning.

[45] Hebrew שמאל can denote 'left side', or 'north'; the translators identified the latter meaning as correct. GenAp 22.10 identifies the place with חלבון, which is modern day Halbūn, indeed north of Damascus.

| | |
|---|---|
| turned from smiting Chedorlaomer and the kings who were with him, at the Valley of Shaveh (that is, the King's Valley). | turned from smiting Chedarlaomer and the kings who were with him, at the *cleared* plain (that is, the King's *Hippodrome*). |
| 18 Then Melchizedek, the King of Salem, brought out bread and wine; he was priest of God Most High. | Then Melchizedek, the king of *Jerusalem*, brought out bread and wine, and he *ministered* before God Most High. |

As the table shows, the Targum follows the Hebrew very closely, in no small part facilitated by the similarity between the two languages. Every single lexeme in the Hebrew has been represented in Aramaic, in exactly the same word order. Most Aramaic equivalents, moreover, can be dubbed literal, even when the differences between the two languages necessitate change.[46]

There are changes the Targum does *not* make, although they might have been expected. Hebrew ויחלק עליהם refers to the deployment of separate forces in battle,[47] a military expression, which has a connotation not apparent in Aramaic.[48] The literal interpretation still denotes a mode of operation which is approximately the same to the Hebrew's military deployment, but being literal and non-committal, this translation *does* lend itself to new interpretations—as will become apparent below—even when not realised in the translation itself.

---

[46] Hebrew *wayyiqtol* forms become *waw-perfects*, the definite article elicits the emphatic noun state, the genitive construct state the ד-particle.

[47] See 1QM 18.4 (and further 1QM 2.13–14; 9.6).

[48] The same Aramaic expression is used for Hebrew קרע מעל in 2 Kgs 17.21 (cited as a motif in TgJon Isa. 7.17, 8.14 and Zech. 11.7, as well as Tg 2 Chron. 15.3, without a literal parallel in the Hebrew).

In one version of Onkelos, supported by a large number of Ashkenazi manuscripts, the text reads ליליא instead of בליליא,[49] which in one sense might be taken as a closer alignment with MT, were it not that Biblical Hebrew does not require the preposition here, but TgOnk's dialect does, and indeed routinely supplies one. Without the preposition, Onkelos can be read as if 'the night was divided against them', a literal interpretation of the Hebrew which occurs in multiple Midrashim.[50] With the preposition, as in the Genesis Apocryphon (22.8; Lehmann 1958, 261), Abraham is the verb's subject; without, it is either the night itself or God—thereby implying that the attack took place at midnight exactly. The variant reading of Onkelos facilitates an interpretation without elaborating upon it.

Another example of a variant reading concerns Lot, who is called Abraham's brother, seemingly in conflict with Gen. 11.27 and 12.5, where he is the son of Haran, Abraham's brother, hence Abraham's nephew. TgOnk maintains the aspect of brother, perhaps understood more widely as brotherhood, i.e., kinsman. Some later copyist rectified this: Codex Solger, and the first two Bomberg Bibles that depend on it, read בר אחוהי 'his nephew', in

---

[49] Following Sperber's edn (Sperber 1959, 19): three early editions (the first two Bomberg Bibles and the 1490 Ixar edn), as well as t225 (Cod. Hebr. 4, Halle), which is an 18th c. Yemenite copy (which, of this date, may well display Western influences) and t90 (Or. 9400 of the British Library). Sperber does not record that in t1 (Codex Solger, Nürnberg) a later hand crossed out the preposition. The Babylonian witness L152 (t339), not included in Sperber, attests the preposition.

[50] Gen. R. 43.3; PesK 7.5; PRE 27; Tan. לך לך 9. Cf. Mek. Exod. 12.29.

agreement with Targum Neofiti—and a whole lot of modern Bible translations. Onkelos does not provide an implicit comment or harmonisation.

Some obvious differences between Genesis and Onkelos are found in the last verses. To begin with, the Hebrew reference to the Plain of Shaweh, or the King's plain, which the targumist identified as a reference to the Royal Hippodrome—a levelled ground, based on the Hebrew toponym עמק taken literally, while drawing on popular folklore about Solomon's שוה racecourse (Milik 1961; McNamara 2000; Newman 2005). In a sense, the equivalent for Shaweh can be understood as a literal equivalent, were it not that the targumic rendition is more particular than the Hebrew is. Another toponym, Salem, in v. 18 is equated with Jerusalem, which is routine in early Jewish literature (Jacob 1934, 378).

Finally, in 14.18, Melchizedek is named king as well as priest in the Hebrew text. Rabbinic and early Christian literature identify Melchizedek with Shem, the son of Noah,[51] who, according to rabbinic traditions,[52] lost the priesthood due to the disrespect he had shown to God, and who could therefore no longer be considered a proper priest even though he acted like one. Onkelos captures his traditional appraisal by translating 'priest of God' as one who 'ministered before God'—avoiding the term 'priest' although admitting that he did what a priest would do. It

---

[51] So explicitly TgNeof Gen. 14.18. See Aberbach and Grossfeld (1982, 89–90 n. 25); Horton (1976, 114); Ginzberg (1899, 103–5).

[52] See b. Ned. 32b; Lev. R. 25.6, and the references cited in the previous footnote.

is a subtle semantic shift reflecting associations not made explicit in Onkelos itself. Interestingly, TgNeof and FragTP have him 'minister in the high priesthood',[53] a rare description, yet reminiscent of Christian traditions naming Melchizedek a high priest (McNamara 2000, 22–26).

The character of Onkelos as a translation can be summarily described as follows:

1. By and large Onkelos is a one-to-one translation, with a precise (not necessarily literal) equivalence of the Hebrew source and Aramaic target text.
2. Within this one-to-one equivalence, Onkelos may subtly steer the meaning of the base text into new directions by using equivalents that represent a subtle shift or a substitution in semantic terms, and by employing occasional pluses vis-à-vis the Hebrew, but it tends to do this without breaking the pre-extant mould of the narrative, usually even keeping its mirror of the lexemic sequence of the Hebrew intact.
3. Some of the translations can serve as a springboard for more extensive interpretations which are facilitated by Targum Onkelos yet not included.
4. When the translation includes elements of aggadic expansion, as it sometimes does, the pluses are always neatly integrated into the running text.

---

[53] The avoidance of his priestly status does not occur in the Genesis Apocryphon (Fitzmyer 2004, 45).

5. The semantic differences with the Hebrew text are generally found to agree with rabbinic exegesis.

What distinguishes Onkelos from, say, the King James version? Both will share a lot of features that they inherit from the source text, the Hebrew Bible: the narratives in their given sequences, with their protagonists and places, the laws, and so on. They also share a tendency to bend the grammar of their respective languages to that of the source text and to account for the vast majority of morphemes in Hebrew. That is not unusual: we observe similar tendencies in the isomorphic Greek versions of the Hebrew Bible. They also share the common translational aspect of interpreting parts of the source text within their own current horizon: the hippodromes of Onkelos, and the virgin mothers of King James.[54]

Where does Onkelos differ? First of all, Onkelos differs in the historical way its text has been *presented*, namely as a text alternating verse by verse with its source. Even manuscripts without the complete text of the Hebrew Bible still tend to refer to it by opening each and every verse of the Targum with one or two Hebrew lemmata (Smelik 2003, 71–73; Attia 2014).[55] In later centuries, Onkelos could be displayed as a marginal text, in a smaller column besides the source text, when it had come to be seen as more of a commentary than a translation. This co-textual

---

[54] See LXX Isa. 7.14. As Judah Goldin (1973–1974, 94) stated, "God be with you if you introduce a *parthenos* where it isn't too safe even for an *almah*."

[55] This characteristic is one of the sub-categories of Targum in Samely (2011b, 17).

positioning points to an important conception of translation as a text that depends on another text, to the point that it is never circulated independently from that other text.[56] By contrast, the Hebrew Bible was not restricted to such a bilingual format. This conceptual framework of the Targum reflects rabbinic opinion about the position of the translation.

Onkelos differs to the extent that the entirety of Scripture influences the choice of Aramaic equivalents for Hebrew lexemes. With certain words, the translation is stereotypical, whereas the King James is not. The preface to the King James in fact states, "We have not tied ourselves to an uniformity of phrasing, or to an identity of words, as some peradventure would wish that we had done." Onkelos, by contrast, has a number of translations that unify the original text in a way few translations do and which deflect from a strictly isomorphic translation (Alexander 1988, 226–29; Klein 2011). It may simplify the text by using the same equivalent for a number of different Hebrew lexemes. It may draw on more texts to translate a verse, by associative or complementary translation. It may harmonise two apparently contradictory verses (although not always). It stresses the importance of Torah-obedience, the coherence of God's interventions, the majesty of God, and the dichotomy between worship and idolatry, sanctity and the profane (Churgin 1907 [=1927]; Samet 2005). Onkelos and Jonathan to the Prophets also share the tendency to replace אלהים by the Tetragrammaton (never the other way around), which does not represent a variant reading

---

[56] That is, until a millennium later.

in the targumists' exemplar, but translational precision to avoid any possible implication of polytheism: the plural Hebrew form is translated literally wherever the co-text defines it sufficiently as a reference to Israel's God, and where it might, just might be open to heretical interpretation, it is replaced by the Tetragrammaton (Drazin 1982, 38; Chester 1986, 347–51; Smelik 1995, 318–21).

In a similar vein, Onkelos shares with Greek Bible translations a measured tendency towards isomorphism, but also breaks with it, not so much in its one-to-one aspect but in its explicit interpretative slant. Onkelos further differs in its occasional, albeit rare, inclusions of extra-biblical materials.

Finally, there are overlaps between rabbinic literature and Onkelos, so frequent that the label 'rabbinic' is justified for this Targum, but there are occasional instances that would suggest an origin in an extra-rabbinic milieu. A conspicuous feature of Onkelos (and Jonathan) is the phenomenon of the *memra of Hashem* as a translation for the Tetragrammaton. On the one hand, it parallels rabbinic Hebrew references to God's presence, *Shekhinta*, or Glory, *Yeqara*, but the word *memra* does not occur in rabbinic literature other than as a reference to Amoraic statements, mostly post-talmudic. Convincing explanations for the ubiquitous targumic motif of the *memra* are still lacking, but Churgin's intuition that the motif must be old (Churgin 1907 [=1927], 21–22; Bovarin 2001), strikes me as correct, including the notion that the term acquired additional meaning which explains the fact that the rabbis dropped the term with this semantic meaning altogether, unlike the Glory and the Presence.

## 5.0. Conclusions

What then is the function of Greek and Aramaic translations in rabbinic eyes during the first few centuries CE when multilingualism set the stage and the rabbinic movement was yet to impose itself as the dominant Jewish force? The answer depends on setting, timing, and location. At about the end of the second century CE and beyond, in Roman Palestine, the answer will be different from the Islamic period, the 'high' medieval period in Europe, and the subsequent centuries loosely named pre-modern and modern. The Western Diaspora differed from the Eastern one, and in both, society was unlike that of Roman Palestine. All these are trite considerations, but given common generalisations about scriptural translation still necessary to insist on.

Early on, a single model, let alone a wholesale imposition of a bilingual reading practice would have been an ideal rather than a reality. The multilingual situation implies a variety of reading practices, which, it must be said, were accommodated in early rabbinic sources and thus acknowledged. Therefore, the suggestion that the regularisation of reading and interpreting dates to the second half of the second century CE, without a chance of full implementation yet, fits both the linguistic developments and the gradual emergence of the rabbinic movement. The translation *en vogue* in the rules may not have been specifically Aramaic, for ultimately the encompassing principle for translation was of more concern.

The scopes of translation vary from the liturgy, individual, or joint study, to concerns of appropriate interpretation together with an interest in a thesaurus. Translations served study purposes from well before the common era. The multifarious Greek translations of the few centuries before and after the beginning of the common era testify to a lively and sustained interest in the Scriptures. When translations did find their way into the liturgy in ways the rabbis could approve of, their function and performance took on a specific form. The Greek versions could not easily be denied a place, until rabbinic circles garnered influence, but even then, its limitation would be initiated from Babylonia where Greek could not sway the practice anyway. Conversely, Aramaic had never enjoyed a privileged position, even as a scriptural language.[57] In a society code-switching between Hebrew and Aramaic, Targum separates the source from the exposition, the bare original from its semantic side-kick, but as Targum extracts the Aramaic from its vernacular embrace it simultaneously ties both Hebrew and Aramaic together, as the Targum always functions in a bilingual context. Regardless of the extent at which people understood the intricacies of Classical Hebrew or their degree of literacy, they would understand some Hebrew as it continued to be used in Jewish society. Making the commentary an Aramaic one is signalling the different status and function of each text. The Targum is half the text, in its inception bilingual to the core.

---

[57] R. Shmuel bar Nahman in the name of R. Yohanan defends Aramaic as a Scriptural language (y. Sot. 7.2, 21c, 933, 35–37), but not from a position of strength.

The phenomenon of such a Targum also disentangles Aramaic from the Hebrew. What used to be a shared vernacular lexicon becomes a parallel literary lexicon. Yes, separating Hebrew from Aramaic may have been the corollary of the decline of Hebrew among the masses, or some of them, and yet it also represents a deliberate move to steer the use of translation into safe waters. In point of fact, this functional differentiation may be the prelude to an ever-starker functional divide between the two languages over the course of time. While we see in the Talmud Yerushalmi signs that the languages were code-switched on equal terms, in the Bavli we notice a tendency to a far more consistent, even if never completely achieved functional differentiation.

It is significant that Hebrew and Aramaic were commonly confused in the literary references of the first century CE. Both Flavius Josephus and John identify Aramaic words as Hebrew while Philo of Alexandria designates the language of the Torah as Aramaic (Dalman 1905, 1). Such confusion on the part of Greek speakers may lend credibility to the idea of a colloquial speech that is composed of two entwined local languages, which is not only perfectly possible but also much more likely than usually given credit for. If this is indeed the case, its original speakers were probably fluent in both languages, albeit to varying degrees. The practice of bilingual communication becomes easily intelligible when we take into account the religious and literary prestige of Hebrew and the undeniable ubiquity of Aramaic. That is, Aramaic may have been the substrate of the colloquial as the dominant vernacular with Hebrew as the token language that imparts esteem to the language used. It is far from unusual that one language blends with another if the latter enjoys a higher status.

A second development concerns the status of Greek and the practice of Aramaic. In the rabbinic tradition both Aquila and LXX are antiquarian, received tradition, with the LXX unassailable until the very end of the Amoraic period: in the minor tractates and Geonic responses, Greek was finally demoted, although it took someone of the stature of Maimonides to kill its legal status off. As argued above, that is not to say bilingual Greek–Hebrew recitation never occurred. Even without positive evidence for a bilingual Greek–Hebrew recitation in Roman Palestine, it would not come as a surprise, especially if we curb any retrojective instincts. Indeed, Pierre Nautin once argued that the first 3 or 4 columns of the Hexapla reflect a Jewish work which paved the way for Greek speakers to first pronounce and then read the Hebrew text (Nautin 1977). The evidence is just so slim to suggest that the rabbis did not really take an interest—unless they did, and their rulings are commonly mistaken for interference with Aramaic translations rather than Greek. Take for example the two translations of Job hidden away by Rabban Gamaliel the elder and son.[58] It is routinely assumed that these translations were written in Aramaic, although there is no proof for this other than the term 'targum', which in this period simply meant 'translation'. On the whole, however, it seems that Greek was out on its own while Aramaic and Hebrew were paired. The fact that

---

[58] See t. Shab. 13.1–3.

Hebrew was grafted onto Aramaic made the Semitic pair a logical combination, which did not apply in quite the same way to the prestige cultural and imperial tongue, Greek. The Aramaic translation is cited in rabbinic literature and in occasional traditions even pivotal to hermeneutic proceedings, but even in those cases Targum served as a lexemic source, never as a running translation in spite of official consent within the well-known restrictions. And this essential rather than auxiliary function faded over the course of time. Was Targum originally such a shadowing exercise? If it was a true translation co-opted by the rabbinic movement and altered into a counterpoint voice, we no longer have the evidence for the change, only for the eventual result. The extraction of Aramaic from the colloquial embrace of Hebrew coincides with what Nicholas de Lange has termed the revival of Hebrew in the Amoraic period. It also shows that the targumic model is not interlinear but contrapuntal, the very compass for translation the rabbis endorsed.

## References

Aberbach, Moses, and Bernard Grossfeld. 1982. *Targum Onkelos to Genesis: A Critical Analysis together with an English Translation of the Text (Based on A. Sperber's Edition)*. New York: Ktav.

Aitken, James K. 2020. 'The Septuagint and Jewish Translation Traditions'. In *Septuagint, Targum and Beyond: Comparing Aramaic and Greek Versions from Jewish Antiquity*, edited by Jan Joosten, David James Shepherd, and Michaël van der

Meer, 197–227. Supplements to the Journal for the Study of Judaism, 193. Leiden: Brill.

———. 2008. 'Phonological Phenomena in Greek Papyri and Inscriptions and their Significance for the Septuagint'. In *Studies in the Greek Bible: Essays in Honour of Francis T. Gignac*, edited by Jeremy Corley and Vincent Skemp, 256–77. Catholic Biblical Quarterly Monograph Series 44. Washington: CBA.

———. 2009. 'The Jewish Use of Greek Proverbs'. In *The Jewish Reception of Greek Bible Versions*, edited by Julia G. Krivoruchko, Nicholas de Lange, and Cameron Boyd-Taylor, 53–77. Tübingen: Mohr Siebeck.

———. 2015. 'Introduction'. In *T&T Clark Companion to the Septuagint*, edited by James K. Aitken, 1–12. London: Bloomsbury Publishing.

Alexander, Philip S. 1976. 'The Rabbinic Lists of Forbidden Targumim'. *Journal of Jewish Studies* 27 (1): 177–91.

———. 1985. 'The Targumim and the Rabbinic Rules for the Delivery of the Targum'. In *Congress Volume Salamanca 1983*, edited by John Adney Emerton, 14–28. Supplements to Vetus Testamentum 36. Leiden: Brill.

———. 1988. 'Jewish Aramaic Translations of Hebrew Scriptures'. In *Mikra: Text, Translation, Reading and Interpretation of the Hebrew Bible in Ancient Judaism and Early Christianity*, edited by Martin Jan Mulder, 217–53. Assen: Van Gorcum; Minneapolis: Fortress.

———. 2009. 'The Cultural History of the Ancient Bible Versions: The Case of Lamentations'. In *The Jewish Reception of Greek*

*Bible Versions*, edited by Julia G. Krivoruchko, Nicholas de Lange, and Cameron Boyd Taylor, 80–90. Tübingen: Mohr Siebeck.

———. 2009. 'Did the Rabbinic Movement Lose the West? Reflections on the Fate of Greek-speaking Judaism after 70'. Unpublished manuscript. PDF file.

Attia, Elodie. 2014. 'Targum Layouts in Ashkenazi Manuscripts: Preliminary Methodological Observations'. In *A Jewish Targum in a Christian World*, edited by Eveline van Staalduine-Sulman, Alberdina Houtman, and Hans-Martin Kirn, 99–122. Jewish and Christian Perspectives 27. Leiden: Brill.

Baumgartner, Walter, Ludwig Koehler, and Johann Jakob Stamm. 1967–1995. *Hebräisches und Aramäisches Lexikon zum Alten Testament.* 5 Vols. Leiden: Brill.

Billerbeck, Paul. 1964. 'Ein Synagogengottesdienst in Jesu Tagen'. In *Zeitschrift für die neutestamentliche Wissenschaft* 55 (2): 143–61.

Boyarin, Daniel. 2001. 'The Gospel of the Memra: Jewish Binitarianism and the Prologue to John'. *Harvard Theological Review* 94 (1): 243–84.

Brock, Sebastian. 1992. 'To Revise or Not to Revise: Attitudes to Jewish Biblical Translation'. In *Septuagint, Scrolls and Cognate Writings: Papers Presented to the International Symposium on the Septuagint and Its Relations to the Dead Sea Scrolls and Other Writings (Manchester, 1990)*, edited by Barnabas Lindars and George J. Brooke, 301–38. Atlanta: Scholars Press.

Chester, Andrew. 1986. *Divine Revelation and Divine Titles in the Pentateuchal Targumim*. TSAJ 14. Tübingen: J.C.B. Mohr [Paul Siebeck].

Churgin, Pinkhos. 1907 [=1927]. *Targum Jonathan to the Prophets*. New Haven: Yale University Press.

Clines, David J.A. 1993–2011. *The Dictionary of Classical Hebrew*. 8 vols. Sheffield: Sheffield Academic Press and Sheffield Phoenix Press.

Dalman, Gustaf. 1905. *Grammatik des Jüdisch-Palästinischen Aramäisch nach den Idiomen des palästinischen Talmud und Midrasch, des Onkelostargum und der Jerusalemischen Targume*. 2nd edition. Leipzig: J.C. Hinrichs'sche Buchhandlung.

de Crom, Dries. 2011. 'Translation and Directionality in the Hebrew–Greek Tradition'. In *Complicating the History of Western Translation: The Ancient Mediterranean in Perspective*, edited by Siobhán McElduff and Enrica Sciarrino, 77–87. London: Routledge.

de Lange, Nicholas. 1990. 'Sem et Japhet: Les Juifs et la langue grecque'. *Pardes* 12: 90–105.

———. 2006. 'Jewish Use of Greek in the Middle Ages: Evidence from Passover Haggadoth'. *Jewish Quarterly Review* 96 (4): 490–97.

———. 2010. 'The Greek Bible Translations of the Byzantine Jews'. In *The Old Testament in Byzantium*, edited by Paul Magdalino and Robert Nelson, 39–54. Washington, DC: Dumbarton Oaks Research Library and Collection.

Dorival, Gilles, Olivier Munnich, and Marguerite Harl. 1988. *La Bible grecque des septante: Du judaïsme hellénistique au christianisme ancien*. Paris: Editions du CERF (CNRS).

Drazin, Israel. 1982. *Targum Onkelos to Deuteronomy: An English translation of the text with analysis and commentary*. Hoboken: Ktav.

Fitzmyer, Joseph A. 2004. *The Genesis Apocryphon of Qumran Cave 1 (1Q20): A Commentary*. 3rd ed. Biblica et Orientalia 18/B. Roma: Pontificio Istituto Biblico.

Fraade, Steven. 1992. 'Rabbinic Views on the Practice of Targum'. In *The Galilee in Late Antiquity*, edited by L. I. Levine, 253–86. New York: The Jewish Theological Seminary of America.

———. 2023. *Multilingualism and Translation in Ancient Judaism: Before and After Babel*. Cambridge: Cambridge University Press.

Giambrone, Anthony. 2017. 'Aquila's Greek Targum: Reconsidering the Rabbinical Setting of an Ancient Translation'. *Harvard Theological Review* 110 (1): 24–45.

Ginzberg, Louis. 1899. *Die Haggada bei den Kirchenvätern: Erster Theil*. Amsterdam.

Goldberg, Arnold. 1983. 'Der verschriftete Sprechakt als rabbinische Literatur'. In *Schrift und Gedächtnis*, edited by Jan Assmann, Aleida Assmann, and Christof Hardmeier, 123–40. Munich: Wilhem Fink Verlag.

Goldin, Judah. 1973–1974. 'Reflections on Translation and Midrash'. *Proceedings of the American Academy for Jewish Research* 41 (1): 87–104.

Horton, Fred L., Jr. 1976. *The Melchizedek Tradition: A Critical Examination of the Sources to the Fifth Century A.D. and in the Epistle to the Hebrews*. Cambridge: Cambridge University Press.

Jacob, Benno. 1934. *Das erste Buch der Tora: Genesis, übersetzt und erklärt*. Berlin: Schocken Verlag.

Klein, Michael. 2011. *Michael Klein on the Targums: Collected Essays 1972–2002*, edited by Avigdor Shinan and Rimon Kasher. Leiden: Brill.

Labendz, Jenny R. 2009. 'Aquila's Bible Translation in Late Antiquity: Jewish and Christian Perspectives'. *Harvard Theological Review* 102: 353–88.

Law, Timothy Michael. 2013. *When God Spoke Greek: The Septuagint and the Making of the Christian Bible*. Oxford: Oxford University Press.

Lehmann, Manfred R. 1958. '1 Q Genesis Apocryphon in the Light of the Targumim and Midrashim'. *Revue de Qumrân* 1 (2): 249–63.

Levine, Lee I. 2005. *The Ancient Synagogue: The First Thousand Years*. 2nd ed. New Haven: Yale University Press.

Lieberman, Saul. 2002. תוספתא כפשוטה: באור ארוך לתוספתא. New York: The Jewish Theological Seminary of America.

McNamara, Martin. 2000. 'Melchizedek: Gen 14,17–20 in the Targums, in Rabbinic and Early Christian Literature'. *Biblica* 81 (1): 1–31.

Meyer, D. Rudolf and Herbert Donner. 2007. *Wilhelm Gesenius Hebräisches und Aramäisches Handwörterbuch über das Alte Testament*. Vol. 4. 18th ed. Berlin: Springer.

Milik, Józef T. 1961. 'Saint–Thomas de Phordêsa et Gen. 14,17'. *Biblica* 42 (1): 77–84.

Nautin, Pierre. 1977. *Origène: sa vie et son œuvre*. Paris: Beauchesne.

Newman, Hillel I. 2005. 'A Hippodrome on the Road to Ephrath'. *Biblica* 86 (2): 213–28.

Perrot, Charles. 1984. 'La lecture de la Bible dans la diaspora hellénistique'. In *Études sur le Judaïsme Hellénistique, Congrès de Strassbourg (1983)*, edited by Raymond Kuntzmann and Jacques Schlosser, 109–134. Paris: Cerf.

Piertersma, Albert, and Benjamin G. Wright. 2007. *A New English Translation of the Septuagint and the Other Greek Translations Traditionally Included under That Title*. Oxford: Oxford University Press.

Safrai, Ze'ev. 1990. 'The Origins of Reading the Aramaic Targum in Synagogue'. *Immanuel* 24/25 (1): 187–93.

Salvesen, Alison. 2012. 'Did Aquila and Symmachus Shelter under the Rabbinic Umbrella?' In *Greek Scripture and the Rabbis*, edited by Timothy M. Law and Alison Salvesen, 107–125. CBET 66. Leuven: Peeters.

Samely, Alexander. 1994. 'Is Targumic Aramaic Rabbinic Hebrew? A Reflection on Midrashic and Targumic Rewording of Scripture'. *Journal of Jewish Studies* 45: 92–100.

———. 2007. *Forms of Rabbinic Literature and Thought: An Introduction*. Oxford: Oxford University Press.

———. 2011a. 'Profile Targum Genesis Onqelos'. In *Aramaic Studies* 9: 39–45.

———. 2011b. 'The Targums within a New Description of Jewish Text Structures in Antiquity'. In *Aramaic Studies* 9: 5–38.

Samet, Nili. 2005. 'The Distinction between Holy and Profane in Targum Onkelos'. *Megadim* 43 (1): 73–86.

Satlow, Michael L. 2005. 'A History of the Jews or Judaism? On Seth Schwartz's Imperialism and Jewish Society, 200 B.C.E. to 640 C.E.'. *Jewish Quarterly Review* 95 (1): 151–62.

Schäfer, Peter, and Hans-Jürgen Becker. 2001. *Synopse zum Talmud Yerushalmi.* Band II/5–12. *Ordnung Mo'ed.* Tübingen: Mohr Siebeck.

Schremer, Adiel. 2010. 'The Religious Orientation of Non-Rabbis in Second-Century Palestine: A Rabbinic Perspective'. In *"Follow the Wise": Studies in Jewish History and Culture in Honor of Lee I. Levine,* edited by Ze'ev Weiss et al., 319–41. Winona Lake: Eisenbrauns.

Schürer, Emil. 1986. *The History of the Jewish People in the Age of Jesus Christ (175 B.C.–A.D. 135).* Vol. 3.i. Edited by Geza Vermes, Fergus Millar, and Martin Goodman. Edinburgh: T&T Clark.

Schwartz, Seth R. 2001. *Imperialism and Jewish Society, 200 B.C.E. to 640 C.E.* Princeton: Princeton University Press.

Shepherd, David. 2008. 'What's in a Name? Targum and Taxonomy in Cave 4 at Qumran'. *Journal for the Study of the Pseudepigrapha* 17(3): 189–206.

Smelik, Willem F. 1995. *The Targum of Judges.* Oudtestamentische Studiën 35. Leiden: Brill.

———. 2003. 'Orality, the Targums, and Manuscript Reproduction'. In *Paratext and Megatext as Channels of Jewish and*

*Christian Traditions*, edited by Ulrich Schmidt, August den Hollander and Willem F. Smelik, 49–81. Leiden: Brill.

———. 2013. *Rabbis, Language and Translation in Late Antiquity*. Cambridge: Cambridge University Press.

———. 2015. 'The Translation as a Bilingual Text: The Curious Case of the Targum'. *AJS Perspectives*, The Translation Issue: 8–10.

———. 2018. 'A Single, Huge, Aramaic Spoken Heretic: Sequences of Adam's Creation in Early Rabbinic Literature'. In *Ancient Readers and their Scriptures*, edited by Garrick Allen and John Anthony Dunne, 175–209. Ancient Judaism and Early Christianity. Leiden: Brill.

———. 2025. 'Bilingualism: Hebrew and Aramaic as Literary Strata'. In *What is the Talmud?*, edited by Christine Hayes. Cambridge, MA: Harvard University Press (in press).

———. Forthcoming. *Bilingual Voices: Code-Switching in the Yerushalmi*.

Sperber, Alexander. 1959. *The Bible in Aramaic Based on Old Manuscripts and Printed Texts: The Pentateuch According to Targum Onkelos*. Vol. 1. Leiden: Brill.

Stemberger, Günter. 2011. *Einleitung in Talmud und Midrasch*. 9th ed. München: C. H. Beck.

Strack, Herman L., and Gunter Stemberger. 1992. *Introduction to the Talmud and Midrash*. Minneapolis: Fortress Press.

Strohm, Paul. 2000. *Theory and the Premodern Text*. Medieval Cultures 26. Minneapolis: University of Minneapolis Press.

Sussmann, Yaaqov. 2001. *Talmud Yerushalmi: According to Ms. Or. 4720 (Scal. 3) of the Leiden University Library with Restorations and Corrections*. Jerusalem: The Academy of the Hebrew Language.

Tov, Emmanuel. 2008. 'Reflections on the Septuagint with Special Attention Paid to the Post-Pentateuchal Translations'. In *Die Septuaginta—Texte, Theologien, Einflüsse: 2. Internationale Fachtagung veranstaltet von Septuaginta Deutsch. Wuppertal 23.–27. 7 2008*, edited by Martin Karrer, Wolfgang Kraus, and Martin Meiser, 3–22. Wissenschaftliche Untersuchungen zum Neuen Testament 252. Tübingen: Mohr Siebeck.

van der Horst, Pieter W., and Judith H. Newman. 2008. *Early Jewish Prayers in Greek*. Commentaries on Early Jewish Literature. Berlin: Walter de Gruyter.

van Peursen, Willem. 2004. 'The Peshitta of Ben Sira: Jewish and/or Christian?' In *Aramaic Studies* 2: 243–62.

Veltri, Guiseppe. 1994a. *Eine Tora für den König Talmai: Untersuchungen zum Übersetzungsverständnis in der jüdisch–hellenistischen und rabbinischen Literatur*. Texte und Studien zum Antiken Judentum 41. Tübingen: J.C.B. Mohr.

———. 1994b. 'Der griechische Targum Aquilas: Ein beitrag zum rabbinischen übersetzungsverständnis'. In *Die Septuaginta zwischen Judentum und Christentum*, edited by Anna Maria Schwemer and Martin Hengel, 92–115. Wissenschaftliche Untersuchungen zum Neuen Testament 72. Tübingen: Mohr Siebeck.

Verrijssen, Jeroen. 2024. 'The Medieval European Liturgical Targum: A Text-Critical Study of Targum in Mahzorim'. PhD dissertation, Katholieke Universiteit Leuven.

Weitzman, Michael. 1992. 'From Judaism to Christianity: The Syriac Version of the Hebrew Bible'. In *The Jews among Pagans and Christians*, edited by John North, Judith Lieu, and Tessa Rajak, 147–73. London: Routledge.

York, Anthony D. 1979. 'The Targum in the Synagogue and in the School'. *Journal for the Study of Judaism* 10 (1): 74–86.

Ziegler, Joseph. 1980. *Septuaginta: Vetus Testamentum Graecum Auctoritate Academiae Scientiarum Gottingensis editum*. Vol. XII, 2: *Sapientia Iesu Filii Sirach*. 2nd ed. Vandenhoeck & Ruprecht.

# TO READ OR NOT TO READ: PRACTISING (NON-)READING TARGUM IN MEDIEVAL EUROPE[1]

*Shlomi Efrati*

## 1.0. Introduction

That targums—or better: Aramaic translations of the Hebrew Bible—were composed, preserved, studied, and regularly recited by Aramaic-speaking Jewish communities before and during the Talmudic period, appears natural, if not trivial.[2] In contrast, dur-

---

[1] This research is part of the TEXTEVOLVE project, which has received funding from the European Research Council (ERC) under the European Union's Horizon 2020 research and innovation programme (grant agreement No. 818702). I would like to thank the participants in the conference "Reading: Performance and Materiality in Hebrew and Aramaic Traditions" (Oriel College, Oxford, 30 October–1 November, 2023) for their thoughtful comments and questions, which helped me refine some of my arguments. I am also grateful to Eveline van Staalduine-Sulman and Simcha Emanuel, who read and commented on an earlier version of this article.

[2] That being said, some of the main characteristics of the Targums are not trivial at all: their tendency to interpret and expand, their status as

ing the early Middle Ages the use and knowledge of Aramaic rapidly declined, both as a spoken language and a literary tool. What use could an Aramaic translation have in such circumstances? Or better: what uses did medieval communities make of the Targums?

While Targum remained an important source for exegetical, narrative, moral, and other traditions, its liturgical function is usually depicted solely in terms of decline and negligence (e.g., Alexander 1988, 241). In this article I would like to offer a more nuanced view on this aspect of Targum through a re-examination of a peculiar medieval custom relating to the Targum for the Haftarah (a reading portion from the Prophets; pl. Haftarot), which has no clear precedence in Talmudic literature. Scholars have noted this practice and its reflection in some Targum manuscripts (Smelik 2003, 57–58; Houtman 2012, 9), yet neither its extent nor its broader implications for the significance of Targum reading in Medieval Europe were fully appreciated. On the basis of a new systematic collation of medieval European manuscripts containing Haftarot Targum, I hope to shed light on this particular practice and, more generally, on medieval Targum-related practices.

---

accompanying rather than replacing the Hebrew Bible, and their particular liturgical usage—to be discussed below—all set them apart from most other biblical translations (and may be interrelated; cf. Lehnardt 2014, 32–35). On the bilingual aspects of the Targum see further Tal (2001); Smelik (2015); Fraade (2023, 125–61). For general introductions to Targum see, e.g., Flesher and Chilton (2011); Shinan (2016–17); Tal (2018); McDowell (2022), with previous bibliography.

In the first part of this article, I will highlight the liturgical function of Targum in Talmudic sources (part 2.0), followed by a brief survey of its decline during the early medieval period (part 3.0). I will draw attention to both the actual practices reflected in medieval sources and the attitudes of their authors to the situations they were describing. Against this background, I will examine the medieval reading of the Haftarah Targum, on the basis of both the testimonies of medieval authors (part 4.1) and medieval European manuscripts (part 4.2). I will evaluate these findings in light of broader tendencies and practices concerning medieval Targum reading (part 4.3). This, I hope, will lead to a better understanding of the place and significance of Targum in medieval Europe, not merely as a text copied and studied but also as a living liturgical experience. Furthermore, I hope to demonstrate the value—and limitations—of studying Targum manuscripts in order to assess contemporaneous reading practices.

## 2.0. Targum as a Liturgical Act

Aramaic (and other) translations of the Hebrew Bible were regularly discussed throughout rabbinic literature both as textual objects and as a liturgical practice (Kalmin 2013; Smelik 2013, 232–58; Fraade 2023, 102–24). In some cases, Aramaic (and other) translations were brought into discussion for their interpretative value, to elucidate difficult or debated phrases. Yet most rabbinic discussions regarding Targum concern its religious status vis-à-vis other (written) forms of Scripture (e.g., t. Shabbat 13.1–2; m. Yadayim 4.5; Furstenberg 2022, 144–45) and the proper way for translating Scripture—or reciting its Targum—as part of the liturgical service (e.g., m. Megillah 4.4, 6, 10).

The liturgical function of Targum, rather than its exegetical or didactic significance, may be illustrated with the following regulations concerning its public reading (t. Megillah 3.20):

> [A] One person reads the Torah and one translates. Neither should one read and two translate,[3] nor two read and one translate, nor two read and two translate.
>
> [B] One person reads the Prophets and one translates, [or] one reads and two translate. But neither should two read and one translate, neither two read and two translate.
>
> [C] One person reads the Megillah and one translates, [or] one reads and two translate, [or] two read and one translates, [or] two read and two translate.

These regulations establish a hierarchy between the different sections of the Hebrew Bible (Torah, Prophets, Writings) as well as between the Hebrew text and its translation: the less important texts and practices may be read or recited by more than one person (arguably, while in the Torah *not even two* may read, in the Prophets and the Megillah *two or more* may read or translate, cf. the prescription quoted below from the Babylonian Tal-

---

[3] The possibility that two or more persons may 'translate' simultaneously (see below) strongly suggests that the 'translators' were actually reciting a more or less fixed text. This is further corroborated by the stipulation that a child may 'translate,' i.e., recite the translation (m. Megillah 4.6; Alexander 1985, 24–25). An explicit distinction between live translation and recitation of Targum appears in b. Qidushin 49a, though this passage reflects the situation in a later Babylonian milieu.

mud). This multiplicity of readers probably concerns the simultaneous reading of a given text-unit by multiple people, rather than successive reading by different readers. For if the latter were the case, the requirement that one person only should read in the Torah would stand in stark contradiction to the normal practice (according to rabbinic literature) of dividing the Torah reading among three readers at least (m. Megillah 4.1–2), with special regulations devised for cases where only one reader is found (t. Megillah 3.12).

While the regulations from Tosefta Megillah quoted above do not explain why simultaneous (public) reading is problematic, both Talmuds conclude that two people should not read or translate because "two voices cannot enter one ear" (y. Megillah 4.1, 70d), that is, "two voices cannot be heard" (b. Rosh Hashanah 27a). Thus, at least according to the interpretation in the Talmuds, these regulations secure the comprehensibility of Scripture (and its translation). But as these regulations do allow the simultaneous reading or recitation of some texts, they also highlight and affirm the non-informative aspect, so to speak, of the public reading of Scripture. Reading or translating by more than one person does not contribute to communicating the words of Scripture and their appropriate interpretation, but rather enhances the impressive or aesthetic aspect of the performance itself.

This aspect is even more apparent in the version of regulation C as it appears in the Babylonian Talmud: "In the Hallel (Ps. 114–18)[4] and the Megillah, even ten [people] may read and ten

---

[4] Some manuscripts of b. Megillah omit "the Hallel."

may translate"[5] (b. Rosh Hashanah 27a; b. Megillah 21b). Such an excess of readers seems to reflect the wish to create an impressive reading event, regardless of the comprehensibility of the text itself—though the Talmud asserts that such a (hypothetical?) practice was only permitted "since they like it (the Megillah, and therefore) they pay attention and hear (i.e., comprehend)."

## 3.0. The Decline of Targum Reading

The decline of Aramaic as a spoken language in most Jewish communities also affected the liturgical practice of Targum. After all, if Aramaic is no longer spoken or understood, there seems to be little reason to use it as a means to interpret and make accessible the Hebrew Bible. Some authorities vehemently opposed the abandonment of Targum (Berliner 1884, 2:167–75; Elbogen 1993, 153–55; McDowell 2022, 299–301), and by so doing expressed quite a different understanding of its religious function and significance. A lucid expression of both attitudes is found in a response by R. Natronai b. Hilai Gaon (Babylonia, 9th c.; Brody 2011, 153–54):

---

[5] The clause "and ten may translate" is missing in the printed edition of b. Rosh Hashanah (but appears in all manuscripts) and in almost all manuscripts of b. Megillah (but appears in the printed edition). However, it is supported by early authorities such as R. Hananel, R. Isaac Alfasi, and Rashi, the latter declaring it to be erroneous since there is no Targum for the Writings (see b. Megillah 3a). It is likely that Rashi's authority contributed to the elimination of the clause from some Talmud witnesses (but cf. Tosafot ad loc.).

[A] Those who do not read the Targum, saying: "we do not need to translate with the Targum but rather in our own tongue, a tongue the public understands"—

[B] they do not fulfil their (religious) duty. Why? Because our rabbis found support from biblical verses for the Targum of the rabbis... therefore one cannot translate except with this Targum of the rabbis...

[C] But if they avoid translating (i.e., reading the Targum) as a provocation (להכעיס), they deserve excommunication; and if (they avoid it) because they do not know to translate, they should learn and translate and thus fulfil their (religious) duty.

[D] And if in a certain place they wish to have (Scripture) interpreted for them, then someone besides the translator (i.e., reader of Targum) should stand and interpret for them in their own language.

While those whose practice Natronai opposes (section A) seem to regard Targum mainly from a pragmatic point of view, as a means to elucidate the Hebrew Scripture (within the framework of liturgy), Natronai completely detaches the religious and liturgical function of Targum from any interpretative value it may have: the proper recitation of the Targum has to be studied on its own right (section C), and the one 'interpreting' Scripture (i.e., translating it into the vernacular) is distinguished from the one reading the Targum (section D).

Natronai's view of the Targum as a self-standing religious act, which does not derive from any pragmatic considerations, goes hand in hand with his definition of Targum as a religious duty (section B). Yet, although Natronai quotes various Talmudic regulations to prove that the rabbis considered the Targum obligatory, the sources he refers to never say so explicitly. In fact, several sources not quoted by Natronai explicitly present the reading of Targum as voluntary (see immediately below). Thus, Natronai's insistence that "Those who do not read the Targum... do not fulfil their (religious) duty" signifies an important development in the religious status of Targum.

Another, and probably related development is reflected in Natronai's demand to read "the Targum of the rabbis" ( תרגומא דרבנן), that is, Onkelos and Jonathan (to the Pentateuch and the Prophets, respectively). In all likelihood, these Targums were prevalent in Babylonia already in the time of the Talmud (Berliner 1884, 2:112–114; Müller-Kessler 2001; Kalmin 2013; Smelik 2013, 325–433, esp. 364–87). Yet the Talmudic sources never specify *which* Targum should be recited (cf. b. Qidushin 49a).[6] While Natronai does not refer here to other Aramaic Targums, authors of roughly the same period did express some doubts concerning their status and authority.[7]

A similar approach, in response to a similar situation, finds expression a couple of centuries later in the writings of Yehudah b. Barzillai of Barcelona (ca 11th–12th c.; Sefer HaItim §179; Shor 1903, 268):

> In our humble opinion, we think that currently, in most places, (the people) are altogether sinning by not reading

---

[6] On 'translating' as 'reciting the Targum', see n. 3 above.

[7] See, e.g., Rav Hai's response in Harkavi (1887, 7 [§15] = 124 [§248]); Ginsburger (1901, 235–36); cf. Yehudah b. Barzilai, Sefer HaItim §175 (Shor 1903, 258).

the Targum in public at all, to the extent that most people, including the simpletons among them, forgot the commandment of Targum.

It is fitting to rebuke them concerning this... For the commandment of Targum on its proper time is far weightier than studying Torah, and Targum must not be disparaged at our time. Whoever acts stringently concerning this, removing Israel from an aberrant practice and restoring it to how it used to be, his reward is kept by God.

R. Yehudah forcefully declares Targum a "commandment," whose proper liturgical performance is even more important than public Torah study. Yet the urgency of R. Yehudah's call to "remove the aberrant practice," and his insistence that "Targum must not be disparaged at our time," underscore the actual negligence of public Targum reading. In fact, it is noteworthy that Targum was still read at all, even if only in few communities—if R. Yehudah's reference to the negligence of this practice in 'most places' (רוב מקומות) should be taken literally.

Other authorities, however, while upholding the principal obligation of reading Targum, expressed a more realistic approach on this matter. For instance, R. Hai, the 'last' and one of the most influential Babylonian Geonim (late 10th–early 11th c.), affirms that the liturgical reading of Targum מצוה היא תחלה "is, *in principle*, a meritorious practice," implying that nevertheless it is not an absolute obligation (Ginzberg 1929, 87).[8] R. Shmuel

---

[8] Later quotations of Rav Hai's response, including by R. Yehudah b. Barzilai mentioned above, omitted the crucial term כתחלה 'in principle' (Ginzberg 1929, 75). To be sure, Rav Hai himself declared the negligence of Targum 'an improper custom' (לא יפה מנהג זה) which needs to

HaNagid, who was active slightly later in Spain (11th c.), emphatically denied that the Jews living in Spain have ever abandoned the Targum, but in fact affirmed that Targum was not regularly read in public. This, HaNagid insisted, was not due to 'heresy' (מינות) but a special measure taken due to practical considerations, and because (Sefer HaItim §179; Shor 1903, 268):

> As time went by, they disburdened themselves of the Targum of the Torah and the Prophets, for it is said (b. Megillah 23b): "(this ruling refers to) a place where they do not read the Targum"…
>
> And in the Yerushalmi, it is written (y. Bikkurim 3.8[5], 65d = Megillah 4.1, 74d): "Is the Targum indispensable? R. Yose said: "From the fact that we see our rabbis going forth to a fast and reading (the Torah in public) without translating, we infer that the Targum is not indispensable."

Thus, HaNagid effectively finds a legal justification for the "aberrant practice" which R. Yehudah b. Barzilai so emphatically condemned. The collective French commentary on the Talmud, known as the Tosafot, comments on the same statement from b. Megillah with even less reservation: "On this we rely for not reading the Targum of the Haftarah throughout the entire year, as well as the Targum of the Torah" (Tosafot, Megillah 23b, s.v. לא שנו. Cf. Lehnardt 2014, 44 n. 19).[9]

---

be addressed (Emanuel 2018, 63 §55; cf. Sefer HaItim §179). I am grateful to Simcha Emanuel for drawing my attention to this source.

[9] On the relatively late character of the Tosafot for Megillah see Aharonov 2016; cf. Urbach 1986, 617–18.

## 4.0. Reading the Targum in Medieval Europe: The Festival Haftarot

### 4.1. Medieval Authors on the Festival Haftarot Targum

Against the background of the preceding statements, it may come as a surprise that Targum was, nevertheless, still read and practised among some medieval European communities, on certain special occasions.[10] Thus R. Shmuel HaNagid, who justified the cessation of public Targum reading in Spain, nevertheless insisted on the Spanish Jews' principal commitment to this practice (Sefer HaItim §179; Shor 1903, 268):

> Whenever a bridegroom is present, and in the (reading from the) Prophet on a festival, and on the day of completion (of the yearly cycle of Torah reading), many stand up and read the Targum[11] for the sake of adorning (the religious act).
>
> Hence, how can anyone claim they have abandoned the Targum? Rather, the fact they do not regularly read the Targum was due to a (particular) measure, as we have said.

---

[10] Targum was still regularly read in some Mediterranean communities in the high Middle Ages (Goitein 1962, 37–38 n. 9; 1971, 158; 175–77), and the practice survived among Yemenite communities almost until the present day (see, e.g., Van der Heide 1981, 11–14; Shinan 1983, 41).

[11] Whether these 'many' read the Targum simultaneously or successively is not clear; the latter appears more probable.

His apologetic overtones notwithstanding, HaNagid attests here to the actual practices in (some) contemporary communities. These not only demonstrate that public Targum reading was still, to some extent, significant (as HaNagid emphatically insists), but also suggest the reason for its persistence: on these special occasions, Targum was recited 'for the sake of adorning' (משום הידור) the liturgy and, by extension, the festival or celebration of the day. This 'adorning' had nothing to do with the *content* of the Targum. Rather it seems that its reading, even by multiple participants (cf. section 2.0 above), was perceived as an important religious *act* on its own right.

Similarly, the Tosafot (Megillah 24a, s.v. ואם היו) commented that Targum is only (publicly) read on festivals, specifically on Pesach and Shavuot, 'to publicise the miracle' (כדי לפרסם הנס).[12] But even this reading is not done according to the Talmudic requirements (Tosafot, Megillah 24a, s.v. ובנביא שלשה):

> We do not currently read (anything more than) one (Hebrew) verse (at a time) even for the translator of the Prophets, lest he makes a mistake. Only at the beginning of the Haftarah do we read three (verses) for the translator, to make known that such is the ruling (we should have followed) if we were not concerned he would make a mistake.

In regard to m. Megillah 4.4, which requires that the Haftarah reader should read for the translator three verses at a time, the Tosafot commented that 'currently'—in their own time and

---

[12] See also the liturgical instruction from Mahzor Vitry and the responsum quoted below next to n. 26. Cf. Elbogen (1993, 154–55); Lehnardt (2014, 44–46).

place—the reading from the Prophets is done on a verse-by-verse basis, except for "the beginning of the Haftarah." The Tosafot further claim that this change reflects the decline in Aramaic literacy, an argument which I will reconsider further below (section 4.3).

Further details concerning the practice of the Haftarah Targum and its development appear in an earlier halakhic compilation, Sefer HaItur, composed by R. Yitzhak b. Abba Mari (Marseille, 1179; Sefer HaItur, Ten Words: Hallel [end]; Kneset 2019, 2:220 §932):

> [A1] We read (in m. Megillah 4.4): "The one reading the Torah… should not read for the translator more than one verse (at a time), but in the Prophets—three (at a time)."
> [A2] But they sent from the Academy:[13] "One, or two, or three."
>
> [B] It was the custom of the earlier ones to read the first three verses and translate (them), and from there they would read one verse at a time and translate (it).
>
> [C] But now it is customary to read the entire Haftarah one verse at a time (and translate one at a time).

Both the Tosafot and HaItur thus attest to an important shift in the actual practice of reading the Haftarah Targum: Rather than reading three verses at a time, first from the Hebrew text and then from the Targum, as the Mishnah requires (section A1 in HaItur), some communities switched to reading one verse

---

[13] 'Academy' (מתיבתא) probably refers here to one of the centres of the Babylonian Geonim.

at a time (section C; henceforth the 'one–one' practice), or combined both practices and read the first three verses together and the rest verse-by-verse (section B; henceforth the 'three–one' practice). HaItur states that this hybrid practice was actually the earlier one, while the 'one–one' practice is the result of further change (or decline). Yet the testimony of the Tosafot suggests that the 'three–one' practice was still known, and apparently still in use, also in later periods (see n. 9).

The 'one–one' practice simply equates the Haftarah reading with that of the Torah. This does not necessarily contradict the Mishnah, which can reasonably be understood as *allowing* the reading of *up to* three verses at a time—but also less than that. This is exactly how HaItur interpreted it, on the authority of what seems to be a Geonic responsum (section A2). Still, the change from 'three–three' to 'one–one' alternation probably reflects practical consideration and, as a result, suggests that the public reading of Targum (on certain occasions) was an actual practice.[14] The 'three–one' practice is even more telling in this regard. There is nothing natural or obvious in the decision to combine the 'three–three' and 'one–one' practices in this particular manner. The 'three–one' practice may thus reflect not only practical needs but also ideological or aesthetic tendencies concerning Targum reading in medieval Europe.

---

[14] But cf. n. 21 below.

## 4.2. The Haftarot Targum in Medieval European Manuscripts

In order to better evaluate the importance and the broader implications of the reading practices just described, it is necessary to corroborate the testimonies of the Tosafot and HaItur with further evidence concerning the actual practices in contemporary synagogues. Important clues concerning these practices can be provided through an examination of the manuscripts which were produced and used by these medieval communities.[15]

The first observation arising from such an examination is negative: While there are over a hundred European manuscripts with Targum for the *festival* Haftarot alone, either in a 'biblical' context (i.e., accompanying the Pentateuch) or included in dedicated prayer books (Mahzorim), European manuscripts containing the Targum for *all* the Haftarot are extremely rare:[16] I am aware of only two such codices.[17] This is not at all surprising,

---

[15] To date there is no exhaustive catalogue of manuscripts containing Targum. I compiled an initial inventory of European manuscripts containing Haftarot Targum on the basis of the Targum Institute online database (http://targum.nl). Unfortunately, this website is no longer active. This I supplemented with additional information based on my research on Onkelos manuscripts. I am grateful to Eveline van Staalduine-Sulman for her help on this matter.

[16] By contrast, manuscripts with Targum for all Haftarot are common in the Yemenite tradition—where the Targum for both the Torah and the Haftarah was indeed regularly read until quite recently.

[17] (1) London, Valmadonna trust 3 (currently in a private collection; Institute of Microfilmed Hebrew Manuscripts [IMHM] film n. F 49189), Pentateuch and Haftarot (Ashkenazi script, 13th–14th c.); (2) Turin,

since by the time these manuscripts were produced, mainly from the thirteenth century onwards, the Targum was no longer regularly read in any European community. Yet the fact that the Targum for the festival Haftarot *was* copied is a strong indication that it was still publicly read in some communities.

An examination of the layout of the Targum for the festival Haftarot is also revealing, but here a short explanation is required. In general, one of the most common ways of presenting the Targum (for the Pentateuch and Prophets, at least) in Medieval manuscripts was alternating with the Hebrew text verse-by-verse. This inter-verse layout, as Stern (2017, 106) aptly designated it, may originally derive from the practice of (publicly) reading the Targum alternating with the Hebrew text, verse-by-verse.[18] Its persistence in medieval manuscripts certainly owes

---

National University Library 28 (A.II.8), Pentateuch, Haftarot, Scrolls, and Job, all with Targum (Ashkenazi script, 14th c.?). The latter was severely damaged in the fire that erupted in the library on 25–26 January 1904, and has not yet been fully restored. I consulted its remains at the Turin library in April 2024 and could verify it contains Targum for each and every Haftarah (which was preserved). I wish to thank Fabio Uliana, Director of the Library special collections, for granting me permission to consult the manuscript, and for the special collections reading room staff for their kind assistance during my visit.

[18] Targum (Onkelos) in this layout appears on an incantation bowl from Sassanian-period Babylonia (Kaufman 1973; Fraade 2023, 146–47). On the layouts of Targum manuscripts see Smelik (2003, 71–73); Houtman (2012); Attia (2014); Van Staalduine-Sulman (2014); Stern (2017, 88–157); Del Barco (2023). See also the following note.

something to scribal conservatism, but may also reflect the practice of *private* reading of the Targum alongside the weekly reading from the Torah.[19]

Scholars have noted that some manuscripts which contain Haftarot Targum employ a peculiar variation of the inter-verse layout: In each Haftarah, the first three verses are grouped together, both for the Hebrew text and the Targum, followed by the rest of the Haftarah verses, Hebrew and Targum, alternating verse–by–verse (Smelik 2003, 57–58; Houtman 2012, 9). This, of course, is simply the typographic reflection of the 'three–one' reading practice described above. However, what has not been noticed is the pervasiveness of the 'three–one' layout in certain textual traditions.

Table 1: Inter-verse layout[a] of Haftarah Targum in European 'Liturgical Pentateuchs'

|  | 3 / 3 | 3 / 1 | 1 / 1 | N/A | Total |
| --- | --- | --- | --- | --- | --- |
| Ashkenazi / French | 0 | 19 | 3 | 19 | 40[c] |
| Italian | 0 | 1[b] | 2 | 0 | 3 |
| Sefardi | 0 | 1 | 6 | 1 | 7[d] |
| Total | 0 | 21 | 11 | 20 | 50[e] |

[19] This practice was recommended in the Babylonian Talmud: "One should always complete (reading) his Torah portions at the same time as the public—twice the scripture and once the Targum" (b. Berakhot 8a–b). It seems to have gained some popularity but also gave rise to considerable debates in medieval communities. See further Peretz (2008); Weber (2015, 10–15); Stern (2017, 106–9).

Notes to Table 1

(a) For the sake of simplicity I count as 'inter-verse' also two manuscripts which present a continuous Targum text with Hebrew lemmata: Parma, Pal. 3218 (see note (b) below) and Vienna, ÖNB hebr. 11 (Ashkenazi script, 1302). In the latter the lemmata are given for each verse from the fourth verse onwards, so that the first three verses appear as a single unit.

(b) The sole Italian representative (thus far) of the 'three–one' layout is Parma, Pal. 3218 (De Rossi 7; IMHM film n. F 13924), an exquisitely executed Pentateuch with Haftarot and Scrolls (Italy, 1475). However, the Targum layout here is somewhat unusual: The Targum was copied in a separate column beside the Hebrew text, supplied with Hebrew lemmata (as in the Pentateuch). The lemma for the fourth verse in each Haftarah is markedly larger, thus clearly distinguishing the first three verses from the following ones. This 'hybrid' layout likely reflects scribal creativity rather than a living practice, though it also attests to some familiarity with the 'three–one' practice.

(c) The sum is lower than its parts because one manuscript presents both the 'one–one' and 'three–one' layout: London, British Library, MS Add 26878 (IMHM film n. F 5063), Pentateuch, Haftarot, and Scrolls (Ashkenazi script, 14th–15th c.). The Targum for the Haftarah of the first day of Pesach was copied in 'one–one' layout, while those for the other Pesach Haftarot are in 'three–one' layout. The beginning of the Targum for the first day of

Shavuot was copied in the margins, and the scribe stopped copying it after one page.

(d) Again, one manuscript presents both the 'one–one' and 'three–one' layouts: Parma, Palatina 2539 (De Rossi 1317; IMHM film n. F 14296), Haftarot according to the Sefardi rite (Sefardi script, 15th c.). The Targum for most of the Pesach Haftarot is in 'one–one' layout, but for the last day of Pesach and first day of Shavuot it is in 'three–one' layout.

(e) A couple of 'Liturgical Pentateuchs' reportedly containing Targum for the festival Haftarot could not currently be checked: (1) Fulda, University and State Library, MS fol. A 1, Pentateuch, Scrolls, and Haftarot (Ashkenazi script, 14th c.?); (2) Regensburg, City Archive, MS B a 1 (IMHM film n. F 19179), Pentateuch and Haftarot (Ashkenazi script, 15th–16th c.).[20]

Table 1 presents the different inter-verse layouts of the festival Haftarot Targum attested in 'Liturgical Pentateuchs'—manuscripts containing those biblical books and chapters which were read in the liturgy: the Pentateuch, Haftarot, five Scrolls, and sometimes additional books as well (Stern 2017, 89–90). I also include in this category few manuscripts which contain a self-standing collection of Haftarot.

---

[20] The consultation of MS Cambridge, St. John's College A 1, was made possible thanks to the kind assistance of my colleague Dr. Estara Arrant and Dr. Adam Crothers from the Special Collections team at St John's College library.

In addition to the fact that inclusion of Targum is characteristic of Ashkenazi–French 'Liturgical Pentateuchs' rather than of Italian and Spanish ones (Stern 2017, 106), table 1 also demonstrates the prevalence of the 'three–one' layout: it is found in about two thirds (21 out of 30) of all manuscripts which employ the inter-verse pattern. Furthermore, this pattern is characteristic of the Ashkenazi–French tradition: almost all manuscripts which present it are Ashkenazi–French, and almost all Ashkenazi–French manuscripts which employ the inter-verse pattern are in the 'three–one' layout (19 out of 21).

Beside the 'three–one' layout also the 'one–one' pattern is well documented, but, perhaps surprisingly, the 'three–three' layout—the one corresponding with the Mishnah's ruling—is not attested at all among European manuscripts.[21]

As mentioned above, Targum portions for the festival readings are also found in prayer books and similar liturgical compilations. My study of this corpus is still far from complete,[22] but some preliminary observations can be suggested here. Thus far I have examined ca. 30 liturgical compilations which contain Targum for the festival Haftarot. Among these the 'three–one' practice is attested mainly in Ashkenazi manuscripts, but it is far less

---

[21] Non-European witnesses of Haftarot Targum, particularly Yemenite, also seem to prefer the 'one–one' layout. Whether this reflects actual practice or scribal convention is difficult to ascertain, but it should be noted that the Yemenite reading practice is 'one–one' both for the Torah and the Haftarot Targum (Goitein 1962, 54 n. 22; Van der Heide 1981, 12).

[22] For this reason, I will not present my findings in a table form.

common than in the 'Liturgical Pentateuchs': only four manuscripts thus far reflect this practice in one way or another. The 'one–one' practice is reflected in 15 manuscripts, and 17 others do not employ an inter-verse layout. The 'three–three' pattern is not attested at all.

To sum up: European manuscripts with Haftarot Targum attest *only* the festival Targums (with very few exceptions). These appear in layout patterns which correspond remarkably with the testimony of medieval authors such as the Tosafot and HaItur—and not with Talmudic regulations. In particular, Ashkenazi-French manuscripts attest to the prevalence of the 'three–one' practice, which represents a significant innovation in comparison to the Talmudic sources. The cumulative evidence of such a large body of manuscripts is a strong indication for the actual reading of the festival Targum, as well as for the modes of its reading.

Certainly, in some manuscripts the Targum layout, and even the inclusion of Targum, was conventional rather than practical (Wasserman 2023, 112 n. 41). This is all the more likely in those cases where one manuscript employs different layout patterns in different Haftarot, or when a scribe did not bother to complete the Targum for every Haftarah.[23] Moreover, the relative scarcity of the 'three–one' layout in mahzorim may be compared to the testimony of HaItur concerning the decline of this practice

---

[23] See notes (b)–(d) to table 1. Fleischer (1985, 43–44) describes in detail a particularly confused and incomplete copying of Haftarah Targum in the Worms Mahzor (MS Jerusalem, National Library Heb. 4°781/1). The use of different layouts for different Haftarot seems to be more common in mahzorim than among 'Liturgical Pentateuchs'.

(see p. 359 above), while its prevalence among 'Liturgical Pentateuchs' may represent a scribal convention. Yet the fact that the 'three–one' pattern became a convention is illuminating in itself, as it shows to what extent this innovative practice became common.

## 4.3. Haftarot, *Reshuyot*, and the Aesthetics of Targum Reading

The prevalence and commonality of the 'three–one' practice calls for explanation. This practice has no clear precedent in the Talmudic sources, and its particular manner of combining the two distinct Talmudic practices ('three–three' and 'one–one') is not obvious. An early attempt to answer these questions was offered by the Tosafot commentary quoted above (p. 358): lack of competence in Aramaic. Presumably, as readers of Targum hardly understood the texts they were reading, they found the handling of long text-units too difficult. Hence the 'one–one' alternation practice was adopted for the Haftarah Targum—except for the first three verses, which were still read together as a reminder of the formally required practice.

The difficulty described here would have been particularly acute if Targums were recited by heart, as some Talmudic sources presumably require (see y. Megillah 4.1, 74d; Furstenberg 2022, 140–41). It should be noted, however, that medieval instructions concerning the festival Targum do not require its oral performance, or ban the use of written Targum. The relative abundance of manuscripts containing festival Targum also suggests it was usually read from a book. In this situation the difficulty of alternating between long Hebrew and Aramaic reading sections might have been less severe, though not completely resolved.

The Tosafot's explanation is thus reasonable, and similar reasoning can be found among modern scholars as well (e.g., Houtman 2012, 9). However, it does not explain the great popularity of the 'three–one' alternation over against the 'one–one' practice. Moreover, the assumption that the decline in Aramaic literacy led to preference of shorter reading units is not as obvious as it may seem. In fact, the medieval festival Targum texts tend rather to increase—sometimes dramatically so—through the additions of prose and verse segments.[24] It appears that some medieval readers and hearers of the festival Targum were willing to recite, even compose, long and complex Targum sections, much longer than three prophetic verses in a row.

This observation not only renders the Tosafot's reasoning questionable, but may also help explain the popularity of the 'three–one' practice itself. Examine, for instance, the following liturgical instruction from Mahzor Vitry (France, early 12th c.; Hurwitz 1893, I:158, §§166–67; Goldschmidt 2009, 2:584, Torah Readings and Haftarot §9):

---

[24] See the material assembled in Zunz (1865, 74–80); Bacher (1873); Ginsburger (1900; 1921); Klein (1993); Fraenkel (1993, 608–61; 2000, 385–593); Kasher (1996). Discussions in Kasher (1996, 16–18); Lehnardt (2014, 46–51); Wasserman (2023, 108–23). On the text of the medieval festival Targum see further Klein (1980, 21–23); Kaufman and Maori (1991, esp. 16–23); Lehnardt (2014, 51–57); Verrijssen (2023); and Jeroen Verrijssen's article in this volume.

On a festival when it is customary to read the Targum of the Haftarah, the one reading the Haftarah reads three verses. Then the translator says *reshuyot* (introductory poems)… and translates those three verses which were read. From there on the reader reads one (verse) and the translator translates one.

A similar practice in relation to the festival Torah Targum is reported in an anonymous responsum, perhaps of the Geonic period (Goldschmidt 1989, 27–28):[25]

It is customary in our place that, both on the last day of Pesach and on Shavuot, when the reader of the concluding portion (of the Torah) has read the first verse (of this portion), the translator stands up and recites poems while the Torah scroll is open, and after the poems he translates the Scripture. Thus for each verse, until he completes (the reading section). Is this custom allowed or forbidden?[26]

According to these descriptions, the first segment of the festival Targum consists, in addition to the translated scriptural verse(s), of one or more Aramaic *reshut*-poem (plural *reshuyot*). This is an ancient and popular poetic genre, through which the prayer leader asks the formal permission of the congregation to recite the following liturgical 'station' (Fleischer 1977; Granat 2020). Some of the *reshuyot* for the festival Targum (for both the

---

[25] It was included in a collection of responsa by R. Isaac Alfasi (North Africa, 11th century) but apparently is not from him. The editor attributed the response to R. Hai Gaon, though without firm evidence. However, the response provides a detailed description of festival Targum reading in Babylonia and refers to the (Geonic) Academy (ישיבה).

[26] I wish to thank Joseph Glantz for drawing my attention to this source.

Torah and the Haftarah) may originate from Late Antique Palestine, when Aramaic was still actually spoken; many others are medieval compositions, some by known authors (Zunz 1865, 74–80; Lehnardt 2014, 46–51). Importantly, these *reshuyot* were not recited before the Torah or Haftarah reading but within it, after the first Hebrew verse(s) was (were) read.[27] The recitation of *reshuyot* thus served as a kind of proem, an impressive and elaborate opening for the Targum reading.

Here, I would like to suggest, is found another possible reason for the spread of the 'three–one' reading practice. This composite and unusual alternating format allowed for a distinct opening for the Haftarah Targum. While the three-verse opening is not nearly as elaborate and impressive as a *reshut*, it still fulfils a similar aesthetic expectation. The 'three–one' practice may indeed reflect a compromise between the Talmudic regulations and pragmatic considerations, as the Tosafot argued, but its pervasiveness and popularity attest also to the relevance and importance of Targum reading for some medieval communities, who creatively adapted the ancient practice according to their aesthetic preferences.

## 5.0. Concluding Remarks

In this article I attempted to provide a different perspective on the function and significance of Targum in the religious life and practice of medieval European communities. I demonstrated the commonality of the 'three–one' reading practice of the festival

---

[27] The question cited above indeed calls this practice into question, and the respondent approved it.

Haftarah Targum among Ashkenazi–French communities, compared it to the popularity of *reshuyot* for the festival Targum, and suggested that both of these developments reflect the ongoing significance and relevance of Targum as a liturgical practice.

Of course, the subtle changes in the exact performance of the festival Haftarah Targum are fundamentally different from the impressive and highly sophisticated Aramaic *reshuyot* which were added to the Targum. Yet precisely because the adoption of the 'three–one' practice has nothing to do with the content of Targum, it reveals something concerning the needs and preferences of those who experienced its reading first and foremost as an act, as a religious performance, regardless of its instructive or communicative value.

The persistence of the festival Targum reading shows the value and relevance of this act. The shifts and developments which this Targum underwent, both in terms of its content and its actual practice, suggest that even at a time and place when Aramaic was no longer spoken and only rarely used as a literary language, and when the practice of regular Aramaic 'translation' of Scripture had long ceased, still the liturgical function of Targum was retained, in some aspect even enhanced. The evidence gathered in this study, along with recent re-evaluations of the place of Aramaic in medieval liturgy (Wasserman 2023), call for a more nuanced approach towards Targum, and Aramaic more generally, in the Middle Ages (Gottlieb 2014; Bar-Asher Siegal 2020). They offer a story not only of decline, negligence, and obsoleteness, but also of creativity, innovation, and vitality.

## Appendix

The following tables present the inventory of European 'Liturgical Pentateuchs' containing the Haftarah Targum according to their script-type (Ashkenazi–French, Italian, and Sefardi). The entries are arranged by inter-verse pattern (first 3/1, then 1/1, then other layouts), then by date. The palaeographical data is based on existing catalogues and particularly on KTIV: The International Collection of Digitized Hebrew Manuscripts (https://www.nli.org.il/en/discover/manuscripts/hebrew-manuscripts).

Table 2: Ashkenazi-French 'Liturgical Pentateuchs' containing the Haftarah Targum

| | Shelfmark | Date | Haftarot Targum | Inter-verse pattern |
|---|---|---|---|---|
| 1 | London, Valmadonna 1 (Sassoon 282; Richler 1) | 1189 | Pesach, Shavuot | 3/1 |
| 2 | Parma, Pal. 1854 (De-Rossi 555) | 1200 | Pesach, Shavuot, Tosefta to Hanukkah | 3/1 |
| 3 | Oxford, Bodl. Jesus College 95–97 (Neubauer 2436) | 1296 | Pesach, Shavuot | 3/1 |
| 4 | Oxford, Bodl. Kenn. 3 (Neubauer 2325) | 1299 | Pesach, Shavuot | 3/1 |
| 5 | Leipzig 1 | 13th c. | Pesach, Shavuot | 3/1 |
| 6 | Oxford, Bodl. Opp. Add. Qu. 47 (Neubauer 21) | 13th c. | Pesach, Shavuot | 3/1 (Targum Pesach following Haftarah) |
| 7 | Parma, Pal. 2168 (De-Rossi 614) | late 13th–early 14th c. | Pesach, Shavuot | 3/1 |
| 8 | Parma, Pal. 3111 (De-Rossi 30) | late 13th–early 14th c. | Pesach, Shavuot | 3/1 |
| 9 | London, BL Add. 21160 (Margoliouth 75) | 13th–14th c. | Pesach, Shavuot | 3/1 |
| 10 | Vienna, ÖNB hebr. 11 | 1302 | Pesach, Shavuot | 3/1 (Targum in separate column, lemmatized) |
| 11 | Hamburg, SUB Levy 19 | 1309 | Pesach, Shavuot | 3/1 |
| 12 | Parma, Pal. 2003–2004, 2046 (De-Rossi 12, 722) | 1311 | Pesach, Shavuot | 3/1 |
| 13 | Paris, BnF hébr. 40 | 1335 | Pesach, Shavuot | 3/1 |

| # | Manuscript | Date | Holidays | Notes |
|---|---|---|---|---|
| 14 | Oxford, Bodl. Opp. 14 (Neubauer 20) | 1340 | Pesach, Shavuot | 3/1 |
| 15 | Hamburg, SUB Cod. hebr. 2 | 14th c. | Pesach, Shavuot | 3/1 |
| 16 | Stuttgart, WLB Cod. bibl. fol. 1 | 14th c. | Pesach, Shavuot | 3/1 |
| 17 | London, BL Add. 26878 (Margoliouth 177) | 14th–15th c. | Pesach, (Shavuot-only 1 page copied) | 3/1, 1/1 (Pesach 1st) |
| 18 | Parma, Pal. 2867 (De-Rossi 345) | 15th c. | Pesach, Shavuot | 3/1 |
| 19 | Hamburg, SUB Cod. hebr. 20 | ? | Pesach, Shavuot | 3/1 |
| 20 | London, Valmadonna 3 (Richler 3) | 13th–14th c. | All | 1/1 |
| 21 | Berlin, SB Or. Qu. 1 | 14th–15th c. | Pesach, Shavuot | 1/1 |
| 22 | Cambridge, St. John College A 1 | 1260 | Pesach, Shavuot | Targum following Haftarah (Pesach 1st lemmatized 1/1) |
| 23 | London, BL Add. 11639 (Margoliouth 1056) | 1280 | Pesach, Shavuot | Only Targum |
| 24 | Nüremberg, SB Cent. V app. 1-2 | 1297 | Pesach, Shavuot | Targum following Haftarah |
| 25 | Parma, Pal. 3081 (De-Rossi 924) | late 13th c. | Pesach, Shavuot | Targum following Haftarah |
| 26 | Vatican, Urbinati Ebr. 3 | late 13th c. | Pesach, Shavuot | Targum following Haftarah |
| 27 | London, BL Add. 09403 (Margoliouth 73) | 13th c. | Shabbat haGadol, Pesach, Shavuot | Targum in separate column |
| 28 | Oxford, Bodl. Oriel Coll. 73 (Neubauer 2437) | 13th c. | Pesach, Shavuot | Targum following Haftarah |
| 29 | Parma, Pal. 2523 (De-Rossi 266) | late 13th–early 14th c. | Pesach, Shavuot | Targum following Haftarah |
| 30 | London, BL Harley 1861 (Margoliouth 169) | 13th–14th c. | Pesach, Shavuot | Targum in separate column |

| 31 | London, BL Harley 5709 (Margoliouth 170) | 13th–14th c. | Pesach, Shavuot | Targum in separate column |
| 32 | Paris, BnF hébr. 44 | 1303 | Pesach, Shavuot | Only Targum |
| 33 | Vatican Ebr. 480 | early 14th c. | Pesach, Shavuot | Targum in separate column |
| 34 | Parma, Pal. 2338–2339 (De-Rossi 11) | late 14th c. | Pesach, Shavuot | Targum in separate column |
| 35 | Parma, Pal. 3080 (De-Rossi 948) | 14th c. | Pesach, Shavuot | Targum in separate column |
| 36 | Uppsala, UB O. Cod. Hebr.1 | 14th c. | Pesach, Shavuot | Targum in separate column |
| 37 | Vienna, ÖNB Hebr. 28 | 14th c. | Pesach, Shavuot | Targum in separate column |
| 38 | Sydney, UL Nicholson 33 | 14th c. | Pesach, Shavuot | Targum in separate column |
| 39 | Turin, BNU 28 (A.II.8) | 14th c. | All | Targum in separate column |
| 40 | St. Petersburg, Ebr. II B 105 | ? | Pesach, Shavuot | Only Targum |

Table 3: Italian 'Liturgical Pentateuchs' containing the Haftarah Targum

| | Shelfmark | Date | Haftarot Targum | Inter-verse pattern |
|---|---|---|---|---|
| 1 | Parma, Pal. 3218 (De-Rossi 7) | 1475 | Pesach, Shavuot | 1/1 (3/1) (Targum in separate column, lemmatized, 4th lemma enlarged) |
| 2 | Parma, Pal. 2818 (De-Rossi 562) | 1411 | Pesach, Shavuot | 1/1 |
| 3 | Dublin, Chester-Beatty 772 | 15th c. | Shabbat haGadol, Pesach, Shavuot | 1/1 |

Table 4: Sefardi 'Liturgical Pentateuchs' containing the Haftarah Targum

| | Shelfmark | Date | Haftarot Targum | Inter-verse pattern |
|---|---|---|---|---|
| 1 | Parma, Pal. 2539 (De-Rossi 1317) | 15th c. | Pesach (ex. 7th), Shavuot (ex. 1st) | 1/1, 3/1 (Pesach 8th, Shavuot 2nd) |
| 2 | Parma, Pal. 2522 (De-Rossi 951) | 14th c. | Pesach (1st, 8th) | 1/1 |
| 3 | Vatican, Ebr. 21 | 14th c. | Shabbat haGadol, Pesach | 1/1 |
| 4 | Parma, Pal. 2678 (De-Rossi 989) | 14th–15th c. | Pesach | 1/1 |
| 5 | Parma, Pal. 2520 (De-Rossi 688) | 15th c. | Shabbat haGadol, Pesach, Shavuot | 1/1 |
| 6 | Parma, Pal. 2 (Perreau 9) | Late 15th c. | Pesach (ex. 7th), Shavuot (ex. 1st) | 1/1 |
| 7 | Parma, Pal. 2817 (De-Rossi 476) | 15th c. | Shabbat haGadol, Pesach, Shavuot | Targum in separate column |

## References

Aharonov, Ariel Efraim. 2016. 'An Examination of the Attribution of the Tosafot for Megillah to R. Juda Messer Leon'. *Qovetz Hitzei Giborim Plaitas Sofrim* 9: 522–39. [Hebrew]

Alexander, Philip S. 1985. 'The Targumim and the Rabbinic Rules for the Delivery of the Targum'. In *Congress Volume: Salamanca 1983*, edited by John A. Emerton, 14–28. Supplements to Vetus Testamentum 36. Leiden: Brill.

———. 1988. 'Jewish Aramaic Translations of Hebrew Scriptures'. In *Mikra: Text, Translation, Reading and Interpretation of the Hebrew Bible in Ancient Judaism and Early Christianity*, edited by Martin-Jan Mulder, 217–54. Assen: Van Gorcum.

Attia, Élodie. 2014. 'Targum Layouts in Ashkenazi Manuscripts: Preliminary Methodological Observations'. In *A Jewish Targum in a Christian world*, edited by Alberdina Houtman, Eveline van Staalduine-Sulman, and Hans-Martin Kirn, 99–122. Jewish and Christian Perspectives Series 27. Leiden: Brill.

Bacher, Wilhelm. 1873. 'Alte aramaische Poesien zum Vortrage des Haphtara-Targum'. *Monatsschrift für Geschichte und Wissenschaft des Judentums* 22 (N.F. 5): 220–28.

Bar-Asher Siegal, Elitzur. 2020. 'Medieval Jewish Literary Languages: The Aramaic of the Zohar as a Test Case'. In *Medieval Hebrew and Aramaic: Studies in Language and Grammatical Thought*, edited by Elitzur Bar-Asher Siegal and Doron Ya'akov, 19–63. Jerusalem: The Academy of The Hebrew Language. [Hebrew]

Berliner, Abraham. 1884. *Targum Onkelos*. 2 vols. Berlin: Gorzelanczyk & Co.

Del Barco, Javier. 2023. 'The Layout of the Glossed Hebrew Bible from Manuscript to Print'. In *From the Thames to the Euphrates: Intersecting Perspectives on Greek, Latin and Hebrew Bibles*, edited by Patrick Andrist, Élodie Attia, and Marilena Maniaci, 128–40. Manuscripta Biblica 9. Berlin and Boston: De Gruyter.

Elbogen, Ismar. 1993. *Jewish Liturgy: A Comprehensive History*. Translated by Raymond P. Scheindlin. Philadelphia: Jewish Publication Society; New York and Jerusalem: Jewish Theological Seminary of America.

Emanuel, Simcha. 2018. *Newly Discovered Geonic Responsa and Writings of Early Provençal Sages*. Jerusalem: Ofeq Institute.

Fleischer, Ezra. 1977. 'The Emergence and Development of the Reshuiot'. *Proceedings of the World Congress of Jewish Studies* 3.C: 359–62. [Hebrew]

———. 1985. 'Prayer and Piyyuṭ in the Worms Mahzor'. In *Worms Mahzor: MS Jewish National and University Library Heb 4°781/1. Introductory Volume*, edited by Malachi Beit-Arié, 36–78. Jerusalem: National and University Library; Vaduz: Cyelar Establishment.

Flesher, Paul V.M., and Bruce Chilton. 2011. *The Targums: A Critical Introduction*. Studies in the Aramaic Interpretation of Scripture 12. Leiden: Brill.

Fraade, Steven D. 2023. *Multilingualism and Translation in Ancient Judaism: Before and After Babel*. Cambridge: Cambridge University Press.

Fraenkel, Jonah. 1993. *Maḥzor for Passover, in Accordance with the Ashkenazic Rite in All Its Branches*. Jerusalem: Koren. [Hebrew]

———. 2000. *Maḥzor for Shavu'oth, in Accordance with the Ashkenazic Rite in All Its Branches*. Jerusalem: Koren. [Hebrew]

Furstenberg, Yair. 2022. 'The Invention of the Ban against Writing Oral Torah in the Babylonian Talmud'. *AJS Review* 46 (1): 131–50.

Ginsburger, Moses. 1900. 'Aramäische Introduktionen zum Thargumvortrag an Festtagen'. *Zeitschrift der Deutschen Morgenländischen Gesellschaft* 54 (1): 113–24.

———. 1901. 'La traduction de la Bible d'après Haï Gaon'. *Revue des Etudes Juives* 42 [84]: 232–36.

———. 1921. 'Les introductions araméennes à la lecture du Targoum'. *Revue des Etudes Juives* 73 (145): 14–26, (146): 186–94.

Goitein, Shelomo Dov. 1962. *Jewish Education in Muslim Countries: Based on Records from the Cairo Geniza*. Jerusalem: Ben-Zvi Institute—The Hebrew University. [Hebrew]

———. 1971. *A Mediterranean Society: The Jewish Communities of the Arab World as Portrayed in the Documents of the Cairo Geniza*. Vol. 2, *The Community*. Berkeley: University of California Press.

Goldschmidt, Aryeh. 1989. 'Responsa by Rav Hay Gaon'. In *Esh Tamid: A Memorial Book for Eliezer Schlesinger*, 23–30. Jerusalem. [Hebrew]

———. 2009. *Mahzor Vitry*. Jerusalem: Mekon Otzar HaPoskim. [Hebrew]

Gottlieb, Leeor. 2014. 'Composition of Targums after the Decline of Aramaic as a Spoken Language'. *Aramaic Studies* 12: 1–8.

Granat, Yehoshua. 2020. '"Let Me Have Your Permission": Hebrew and Aramaic in the Early *Reshut* Poems, from Late Antiquity to the Middle Ages'. In *Medieval Hebrew and Aramaic: Studies in Language and Grammatical Thought*, edited by Elitzur Bar-Asher Siegal and Doron Ya'akov, 121–52. Jerusalem: The Academy of The Hebrew Language. [Hebrew]

Harkavi, Avraham. 1887. *Studien und Mittheilungen aus der Kaiserlichen Oeffentlichen Bibliothek zu St. Petersburg. Vierter Theil: Responsen der Geonim (zumeist aus dem X.–XI. Jahrhundert)*. Berlin: H. Itzkowski.

Houtman, Alberdina. 2012. 'The Use of Paratextual Elements in Targum Research'. *Aramaic Studies* 10: 7–21.

Hurwitz, Simon. 1893. *Machsor Vitry*. Berlin: Itzkowski. [Hebrew]

Kalmin, Richard. 2013. 'Targum in the Babylonian Talmud'. In *Envisioning Judaism: Studies in Honor of Peter Schäfer on the Occasion of His Seventieth Birthday*, edited by Ra'anan S. Boustan, Klaus Herrmann, Reimund Leicht, Annette Yoshiko Reed, and Giuseppe Veltri, I:501–28. Tübingen: Mohr Siebeck.

Kasher, Rimon. 1996. *Targum Toseftot to the Prophets*. Jerusalem: Magnes. [Hebrew]

Kaufman, Stephen A. 1973. 'A Unique Magic Bowl from Nippur'. *Journal of Near Eastern Studies* 32 (1/2): 170–74.

Kaufman, Stephen A., and Yeshayahu Maori. 1991. 'The Targumim to Exodus 20: Reconstructing the Palestinian Targum'. *Textus* 16 (1): 13–78.

Klein, Michael L. 1980. *The Fragment-Targums of the Pentateuch according to their Extant Sources*. Analecta Biblica 76. Rome: Biblical Institute Press.

———. 1993. 'Introductory Poems (*R'shyuot*) to the Targum of the Hafṭarah in Praise of Jonathan Ben Uzziel'. In *Bits of Honey: Essays for Samson H. Levey*, edited by Stanley F. Chyet and David H. Ellenson, 43–56. South Florida Studies in the History of Judaism 74. Atlanta: Scholars Press.

Kneset. 2019. *Sefer HaItur HaMugah*. 2 vols. Jerusalem: Makhon Kneset. [Hebrew]

Lehnardt, Peter Sh. 2014. 'The Role of Targum Samuel in European Jewish Liturgy'. In *A Jewish Targum in a Christian world*, edited by Alberdina Houtman, Eveline van Staalduine-Sulman, and Hans-Martin Kirn, 32–62. Jewish and Christian Perspectives Series 27. Leiden: Brill.

McDowell, Gavin. 2022. 'Aramaic Texts'. In *Textual History of the Bible*, vol. 3A, *The History of Research*, edited by Armin Lange, 292–335. Leiden: Brill.

Müller-Kessler, Christa. 2001. 'The Earliest Evidence for Targum Onqelos from Babylonia and the Question of Its Dialect and Origin'. *Journal of the Aramaic Bible* 3: 181–98.

Peretz, Yosi. 2008. '"Twice the Scripture and Once the Targum": In Light of the Findings in Medieval Ashkenazi Torah Manuscripts'. *Taleley Orot* 14: 53–61. [Hebrew]

Shinan, Avigdor. 1983. 'Live Translation: On the Nature of the Aramaic Targums to the Pentateuch'. *Prooftexts* 3.1: 41–49.

———. 2016–17. 'Targumim'. In *Textual History of the Bible*, vol. 1B, *Pentateuch, Former and Latter Prophets*, edited by Armin Lange, 152–67. Leiden: Brill.

Shor, Yaakov (ed.). 1903. *Sefer Haltim*. Krakow: Fischer. [Hebrew]

Smelik, Willem F. 2003. 'Orality, Manuscript Reproduction, and the Targums'. In *Paratext and Megatext as Channels of Jewish and Christian Tradition: The Textual Markers of Contextualization*, edited by August den Hollander, Ulrich Schmid, and Willem F. Smelik, 49–81. Jewish and Christian Perspectives Series 6. Leiden: Brill.

———. 2013. *Rabbis, Language and Translation in Late Antiquity*. Cambridge: Cambridge University Press.

———. 2015. 'The Translation as a Bilingual Text: The Curious Case of the Targum'. *AJS Perspectives*, The Translation Issue: 8–10.

Stern, David. 2017. *The Jewish Bible: A Material History*. Seattle: University of Washington Press.

Tal, Abraham. 2001. 'Is there a Raison d'Être for an Aramaic Targum in a Hebrew-Speaking Society?'. *Revue des Études juives* 160 (3–4): 357–78.

———. 2018. 'Aramaic Translations of the Bible'. In *The Classic Rabbinic Literature of Eretz Israel: Introductions and Studies*, edited by Menahem Kahana, Vered Noam, Menahem Kister, and David Rosenthal, I:403–52. Jerusalem: Yad Ben-Zvi. [Hebrew]

Urbach, Efraim Elimelech. 1986. *The Tosaphots: Their History, Writings and Methods*. 5th enlarged edition. Jerusalem: Bialik Institute. [Hebrew]

Van der Heide, Albert. 1981. *The Yemenite Tradition of the Targum of Lamentations: Critical Text and Analysis of the Variant Readings*. Studia Post Biblica 32. Leiden: Brill.

Van Staalduine-Sulman, Eveline. 2014. 'A Variety of Targum Texts'. In *A Jewish Targum in a Christian world*, edited by Alberdina Houtman, Eveline van Staalduine-Sulman, and Hans-Martin Kirn, 9–31. Jewish and Christian Perspectives Series 27. Leiden: Brill.

Verrijssen, Jeroen. 2023. 'The Liturgical Targum to Pesach'. *Aramaic Studies* 21: 166–84.

Wasserman, Gabriel. 2023. 'Aramaic–between Heaven and Earth: On the Use of Aramaic in the Liturgical Life of Medieval European Jewry'. In *Hebrew between Jews and Christians*, edited by Daniel Stein Kokin, 95–124. Berlin: De Gruyter.

Weber, Annette. 2015. '"The *Masorah* Is a Fence to the Torah": Monumental Letters and Micrography in Medieval Ashkenazi Bibles'. *Ars Judaica* 11: 7–30.

Zunz, Leopold. 1865. *Literaturgeschichte der synagogalen Poesie*. Berlin: L. Gerschel.

# ON THE SHORES OF THE RED SEA: A MEDIEVAL RECONSTRUCTION OF PALESTINIAN TARGUM?[1]

*Jeroen Verrijssen*

## 1.0. Background

The expansion of the ארבע כיתין, or 'four groups', appears in all the different recensions of Palestinian Targum (PalTg): the 'running text' Targums such as Targum Neofiti (TgNeof) and some manuscripts from the Cairo Genizah (TgCG) as well as the consciously collected units of Targum found in the Fragment Targums (FragTgs). It is also found in Targum Pseudo-Jonathan (TgPsJ). To this list we can now add the Targum units preserved in medieval *mahzorim* (festival prayerbooks), also known as the

---

[1] This research is part of the TEXTEVOLVE project, which has received funding from the European Research Council (ERC) under the European Union's Horizon 2020 research and innovation programme (grant agreement No. 818702).

Liturgical Targum.[2] These manuscripts contain the Targum portions that were traditionally read for the major festivals. The *mahzorim* still extant, however, only contain the readings for the seventh day of Pesach for the crossing of the Red Sea (Exod. 13.17–15.26) and the first day of Shavuot for the Decalogue (Exod. 19.1–20.26).

This expansion has received only scant scholarly attention: Zunz (1867, 21) mentions it, though he only provides the opening words; Epstein (1895, 48–49) published the version he found in *Mahzor Vitry*; Klein (1980, 21–22) mentions this expansion in his discussion of the Fragment Targums; and Díez-Macho (1981, 248–49) published the expansion as he found it in Parma, Palatina, MS 3089 and discusses some of the rabbinic and midrashic parallels.

The story of the four groups of Israelites standing on the shores of the Red Sea knew a history outside of its attestations within the various Palestinian Targums. A Hebrew version is attested in early sources such as the Palestinian Talmud (y. Taʿanit 5.2) and the *Mekhilta de R. Shimon ben Yochai*. It remained popular throughout the Middle Ages, appearing in various midrashic collections such as *Leqach tov* (Exod. 14.14), *Sekhel tov* (Exod. 14.14), and an expanded version in *Sefer haYashar* (Book of Exodus 51). Exactly how and when the Aramaic version(s) of the expansion originated is unclear, however their attestations in

---

[2] A text-critical study of the Liturgical Targum was the focus of my dissertation, titled 'The Medieval European Liturgical Targum' (KU Leuven, 2024). For a survey of previous scholarship concerning this tradition, consult Verrijssen (2023, 166–184; 2024, 30–38).

various redactions of the Palestinian Targum as well as their continued transmission within liturgical manuscripts signify their popularity alongside their Hebrew counterparts.

The version that we find in the Palestinian Targums is structured as a dialogue between the four groups of Israelites and Moses. With Pharaoh's troops in pursuit, the Israelites plead with Moses and suggest four different routes of action. To each of these suggestions, Moses provides an answer in the form of (part of) a biblical verse. The verses in question are Exod. 14.13–14, which is also where the expansion is found in all but one of the Palestinian Targum witnesses.

In FragTg<sup>P</sup> (Paris, Nationale, MS hébreu 110), and in many *mahzorim*, we find the expansion at Exod. 15.3. In its transposition, the text underwent a fundamental change which reveals important clues about the transmission of this expansion and the Palestinian Targum in general.

## 2.0. Text

I present below two versions of the ארבע כיתין expansion. One is preserved in Parma, Biblioteca Palatina, MS 2894 (a French *mahzor*) and another in London, British Library, MS Add. 19944–19945 (an Italian *mahzor*). I have added the letters in parentheses (a–d; א–ד) to present the structure of the expansion more clearly.

Legend

   (x) deletion by scribe
  <x> insertion by scribe
   {x} completion of an abbreviation

## 2.1. Parm. 2894, Biblioteca Palatina (13th century)

Exod. 15.3:

ארבע כיתין איתעבידו בני ישר{אל} כד הוה קיימין על ימא דסוף

(a) חדא הוה אמרה ניפול בימא

(b) וחדא הוה אמרה <נחזור למצראי>

(c) וחדא הוה אמרה נימני[3] לקיבליהון סידרא קרבא

(d) וחדא הוה אמרה נימני ליקיבליהון ונערבב יתהון

(א) כתא דהוה אמרה ניפול בימא אמר להון משה לא תדחלון איתעתדו וחמון לפורקנא דייי דיעביד לכון יומא דין[4]

(ב) כתא דהוה אמרה נחזור למצראי אמר להון משה לא תידחלון ארום כמא דחמיתון ית מיצראי יומא דין לא תוספון למיחמיהון בשיעבוד עוד עד עלמא

(ג) כתא דהוה אמרה נסדר לקיבליהון סדרי קרבא אמר להון משה לא תידחלון <ייי> ביקר שכינתיה הוא דעביד לכון נחצני קרביכון

(ד) כתא דהוה אמרה נמני לקיבליהון ונערבב יתהון אמר להון משה לא תידחלון קומו ושתוקו והבו יקר ותשבחן ורוממן לאלהכון

ייי גברא עביד ניצחני קרבכון ייי שמיה כשמיה כן גבורתיה כן תוקפיה כן מלכותיה יהא שמיה מברך ומשבח לעלם ולעלמי עלמין:

Translation:

The Isra{elites} formed four groups when they were standing by the Sea of Reeds.

  (a) One said: "Let us fall to into the sea."

  (b) And one said: < "Let us return to Egypt." >

  (c) And one said: "Let us form battle-ranks before them."

---

[3] The form נימני here is a scribal corruption, a conflation with the following line. The appropriate form attested in other witnesses is נסדר. We have translated נסדר for clarity.

[4] ייי is the convention in these texts to refer to the Tetragrammaton.

(d) And one said: "Let us chant before them and confuse them."

(א) [Regarding] the group that said: "Let us fall into the sea," Moses said to them: "You should not fear! Stand firm and see the salvation of the Lord, that he has performed for you this day."

(ב) [Regarding] the group that said: "Let us return to Egypt," Moses said to them: "You should not fear! Because just as you saw the Egyptians this day, you will never see them in enslavement (= as enslaved people) ever again."

(ג) [Regarding] the group that said: "Let us form battle-ranks before them," Moses said to them: "You should not fear! <The Lord>, by the glory of his Shekinah, is he that will make the victories of your battles for you."

(ד) [Regarding] the group that said: "Let us chant before them and confuse them," Moses said to them: "You should not fear! Stand, be silent, and give glory, praise, and exultation to your God."

(Exod. 15.3) The Lord is a warrior, (who) makes the victories of your battles. *Adonai* is his name! As is his name, so is his might! So is his strength! So is his kingdom! May his name be blessed and praised forever and ever.

Each of the four suggestions, (a) 'Let us fall into the sea', (b) 'Let us return to Egypt', (c) 'Let us form battle ranks before them', and (d) 'Let us shout before them and confuse them', have a suitable response from Moses that incorporates part of a biblical verse. To the group that suggests (a) *falling* into the sea, Moses answers (א) '*stand firm* and see the salvation of the Lord' (first half of Exod. 14.13); to the group that suggests (b) returning to *Egypt*, Moses answers 'you will never see them [the *Egyptians*]... again' (second half of Exod. 14.13); to the group that suggests (c) forming *battle*-ranks, Moses answers (ג) 'the Lord... will make the victories of your *battles* for you' (first half of Exod. 14.14); and lastly, to the group that suggests (d) *chanting* before them and confusing them, Moses answers (ד) 'stand and *be silent*...' (second half of Exod. 14.14). At the end of the expansion, we find Exod. 15.3, the verse to which it is attached in this manuscript.

The version of the expansion preserved in this manuscript has a logical sequence of suggestions and answers, and largely reflects the versions preserved in other witnesses of the Palestinian Targum, which strongly suggests that this is the original version.

Below I present the text according to an Italian *mahzor*, where an interesting change has occurred within the text.

## 2.2. Add. 19944–19945, British Library (14th/15th century)

Exod. 15.3:

ארבע כתין אתעבידו בני ישראל כד הוו קיימין על ימא דסוף

(a) כיתא חדא הות אמרה נפול לימא

(b) וחדא הות אמרה נחזור למצרים

(c) וחדא הות אמרה נסדר לקבליהון סדרי קרבא

(d) וחדא הות אמרה נלבלב לקבליהון ונערבב יתהון

(א) כיתא חדא דהות אמרה נפול לימא אמר להון משה לא תדחלון אתעתדו וחמון לפורקניה דייי דהוא עביד לכון יומא דין

(ב) וכיתא דהות אמרה נחזור למצרים אמר להון משה לא תדחלון היך מה דחמייתון למצראי יומא דין לא תוספון למחזיהון תוב עד עלמא

(ד) וכיתא דהות אמרה נסדר לקבליהון סדרי קרבא אמר להון משה לא
תדחלון קומו ושתוקו והבו יקר ותושבחתא ורממו לאלהכון

(*ג) וכיתא דהות אמרה נלבלב[5] לקבליהון ונערבב יתהון אמר להון משה
לא תדחלון ייי גברא עביד לכון סדרי נצחני קרביכון ייי שמיה
כשמיה כן גבורתיה כן תוקפיה כן מלכותיה יהא שמיה מברך לעלם
ולעלמי עלמין:

Translation:

The Israelites formed four groups when they were standing by the Sea of Reeds.

(a) One group said: "Let us fall into the sea."

(b) And one said: "Let us return to Egypt."

(c) And one said: "Let us form battle-ranks before them."

(d) And one said: "Let us shout before them and confuse them."

(א) [Regarding] the group that said: "Let us fall into the sea," Moses said to them: "You should not fear! Stand firm and see the salvation of the Lord, that he has performed for you this day."

(ב) [Regarding] the group that said: "Let us return to Egypt," Moses said to them: "You should not fear! As you saw the Egyptians this day, you will never see them ever again."

(ד) [Regarding] the group that said: "Let us form battle-ranks before them," Moses said to them: "You should not fear! Stand, be silent, and give glory and praise; and exult your God."

---

[5] The form נלבלב is likely a corruption of the forms נלולי (as preserved in TgCG^J, see Klein 1986, 225) and נבלבל, both meaning 'to confuse'.

(ג*) [Regarding] the group that said: "Let us shout before them and confuse them," Moses said to them: "You should not fear! The Lord is a warrior who forms the ranks of the victories of your battles for you. *Adonai* is his name! As is his name, so is his might! So is his power! So is his kingdom! May his name be blessed forever and ever."

If we compare the previous example (i.e., Parma, MS 2894) to what we find in London, MS Add. 19944–19945, we find that Moses' responses (ג) and (ד) have switched places. Furthermore, Exod. 15.3 has been incorporated into (ג).

As mentioned previously, most known witnesses of the PalTg tradition (TgNeof, FragTg[V], FragTg[StP], TgCG[J], TgCG[FF]) as well as TgPsJ and Parma, MS 2894 (above) follow the original version. In MS Add. 19944–19945, however, the expansion has been transposed and adapted to accommodate its new place at Exod. 15.3. This transposition was possible due to the similarity between the first half of Exod. 14.14 and the first half of Exod. 15.3, which is conflated to (ג) ייי גברא עביד לכון סדרי נצחני קרביכון 'the Lord is a warrior ($\approx$ Exod. 15.3), (who) forms the ranks of the victories of your battles' ($\approx$ Exod. 14.14).

## 3.0. Klein's Explanation

This paper is not the first to address the peculiarities of this expansion, as the late Michael Klein (1980, 21–22) noticed the ארבע כיתין expansion in his work on the Fragment Targums. In this brief section, Klein made two key observations that laid the foundation for this present work. He noted:

(1) Festival-liturgical targums[6] frequently transfer expansions from their original places to verses within the Song of the Sea. Since most targumic expansions end with the verse they are expanding, when ארבע כיתין was transposed, the ending was changed to accommodate its new place at Exod. 15.3. Klein noticed that in some liturgical manuscripts, answers (ג) and (ד) were sometimes switched so that the expansion would end with Exod. 15.3, but suggestions (c) and (d) remained in their original positions, resulting in incorrect sequencing. To the group that suggests forming battle-ranks (c), Moses answers (ד) 'stand and be silent'; and to the group that suggests shouting before them and confuse them, Moses answers (ג) 'the Lord makes the ranks of the victories of your battles for you' (as in MS Add. 19944-19945 above).

(2) FragTg[P] also transposes ארבע כיתין from Exod. 14.13–14 to Exod. 15.3, and contains the alternative sequencing, which, in Klein's eyes, contributed to his suspicion that some of the material in FragTg[P] belonged to the "festival-liturgical" genre.

This paper seeks 1) to confirm Klein's preliminary observations on the expansion with a larger text corpus and 2) to explore a case of Targum reconstruction (or 'recycling') related to the expansion and the version found in FragTg[P].

---

[6] It is important to note that Klein's designation of 'festival-liturgical collections' includes more than simply the Targum units in *mahzorim*; he includes some (parts of) the Fragment Targums and manuscripts from the Cairo Genizah (some of which may actually be *mahzorim*) under this category.

## 3.1. Expanding the Data Set

Klein only had a few *mahzorim* at his disposal, and therefore his initial observations about the ארבע כיתין expansion within the festival-liturgical manuscripts were not sufficiently substantiated.

This present work is part of my doctoral research on the Liturgical Targum (the Targum contained in medieval European liturgical manuscripts). I transcribed the Targum text of 32 *mahzorim* (from the 13th–16th centuries) from various European liturgical rites (Italian, Ashkenazi, French, Romanian, Carpentras, Sephardi) and compared them with the 'known' Targums (i.e., TgOnk, TgNeof, TgPsJ, the FragTgs, and TgsCG).[7]

Out of our corpus of *mahzorim*, 28 manuscripts contain the ארבע כיתין expansion. Using a larger corpus of textual data, it is possible to evaluate Klein's initial observations and substantiate them with more evidence.

## 3.2. Transposition and Alternative Sequencing

Klein's first observation was that liturgical manuscripts transfer expansions from their original places to the Song of the Sea, though he gave no motivation as to why this happened.[8] He noticed that all of the festival-liturgical collections with the exception of TgCG<sup>J</sup> end ארבע כיתין with Exod. 15.3, and that this was the result of the transposition of the expansion from Exod. 14.13–

---

[7] The full list of manuscripts can be found in Verrijssen 2024, 44–63.

[8] This not only applies to ארבע כיתין, but also for other expansions such as ארבע לילוון 'the Four Nights', whose original place was Exod. 12.42 but appears in Ashkenazi *mahzorim* at Exod. 15.18 (Klein 1980, 23).

14 to Exod. 15.3. While this is true for most *mahzorim*, there are a few exceptions in our corpus. Parma, Palatina, MS 2894 and Parma, Palatina, MS 3000, both thirteenth-century French *mahzorim*, contain the entirety of the text in the original order (i.e., ending with (d) → (ד); Exod. 14.14) and add Exod. 15.3 at the end, separate from the expansion, instead of conflated in (ג). A fourteenth-century Romanian *mahzor* (Oxford, Bodleian, MS Oppenheim Add. 4° 171) also contains the correct order of suggestions and answers.

Furthermore, as Klein noticed in a few manuscripts, the transposition of the expansion led to the adaptation of the text and the alternative sequencing of suggestions (c) and (d), and their corresponding answers (ג) and (ד). This sequencing is present in 16 of the 28 *mahzorim* in the corpus: all 11 Italian *mahzorim* exhibit this feature, alongside three of the 13 French/Ashkenazi *mahzorim*, and two Sephardi *mahzorim*. Even more striking is the fact that, though the Italian *mahzorim* end the expansion with Exod. 15.3, the text is found at Exod. 14:13–14 (i.e., introduced by the lemma ייי ילחם לכם). In other words, the version of the expansion that was adapted to Exod. 15.3 has been 'returned' to its original position at Exod. 14.13–14. Therefore, the ארבע כיתין expansion must have entered Italian liturgical collections after it had already been transposed and adapted to Exod. 15.3.

## 3.3. Reading Traditions and Textual Adaptation

The question remains why the expansion was transposed in the first place. This is likely due to the diminishing tradition of reading the Targum in the synagogue—the direct effect of which is already visible in the fact that, by the Middle Ages, only the readings for the seventh day of Pesach and the first day of Shavuot have stood the test of time. These readings, it would seem, were further reduced.

This shortening of the reading (see also, Mikva 2011, 319–42) is most clearly evident in the Italian *mahzorim*, which preserve only select expansions (e.g., ארבע כיתין, והוה כד שלח פרעה, or the *piyyut* איזל משה) and the Song of the Sea (Exod. 14.30–15.18) instead of the entire reading (Exod. 13.17–15.26). In Ashkenazi *mahzorim*, the manuscripts that contain the verses before and after the Song of the Sea contain TgOnk. In the reduction of the reading, expansions that were attached to verses before the Song of the Sea were at risk of being lost. ארבע כיתין, which was originally attached to Exod. 14.13–14, was therefore transposed as an act of conscious preservation by scribes. The expansion was moved to a verse that was conveniently similar so that it would not seem out of place, namely Exod. 15.3.

## 4.0. Palestinian Targum Recycling

Apart from the liturgical manuscripts and FragTg$^P$,[9] which place ארבע כיתין at Exod. 15.3, all other PalTg witnesses have the expansion at Exod. 14.13–14. When something is moved from one

---

[9] The similarity between FragTg$^P$ and the Liturgical Targum tradition has been argued in Verrijssen (2023, 179–82), and in more detail in Verrijssen (2024, 145–201). To summarise, we believe that FragTg$^P$ copied some of its material from a Sephardi liturgical manuscript. See also, Gleßmer (1988, 204–40); Kaufman and Maori (1991); and Campbell (2002, 105–14).

place to another, an empty space is left behind. How did scribes deal with the lacuna left at Exod. 14.13–14 in the witnesses that transposed ארבע כיתין to Exod. 15.3? The following tables compare Exod. 14.13–14 as it is found in TgOnk, FragTg[P], Parma, MS 2894 (a French *mahzor*), and Parma, Palatina, MS 2411 (a Sephardi *mahzor*).

Exodus 14.13

TgOnk    ואמר משה לעמא לא תדחלון אתעתדו וחזו ית פורקנא דייי דעביד לכון יומא דין ארי דחזיתון ית מצראי יומא דין לא תוספון למחזיהון עוד עד עלמא :

Moses said to the people: "You should not fear! Stand firm and see the salvation that the Lord has performed for you this day, for (as) you saw the Egyptians this day, you will never see them ever again."

Parm. 2894    ואמר משה לעמא לא תידחלון איתעתדו וחזו ית פרקנא דייי דיעביד לכון יומא דין ארי כמא דחזיתון ית מצראי יומא דין לא תוספון למיחזיהון עוד עד עלמא :

Moses said to the people: "You should not fear! Stand firm and see the salvation of the Lord, that he has performed for you this day, for as you saw the Egyptians this day, you will never see them ever again."

Parm. 2411    ואמר משה לעמא לא תדחלון אתעתדו וחמון ית פורקנא דייי דיעביד לכון יומא דין ארום היך מה דחמיתון ית מצראי יומא דין לא תוספון למחמי יתהון בשעבוד תוב עד עלם :

Moses said to the people: "You should not fear! Stand firm and see the salvation of the Lord, that he has performed for you this day, for as you saw the Egyptians this day, you will never see them in enslavement (= as enslaved people) ever again."

| | |
|---|---|
| Frag-TgP | ואמר משה לעמא בני ישראל לא תדחלון אתעתדו וחמון ית פורקנא דייי דיעביד לכון יומא דין ארום כמא דחמיתון ית מצראי יומא דין לא תוספון למחמיהון תוב עד עלמא : |

Moses said to the people, the Israelites: "You should not fear! Stand firm and see the salvation of the Lord, that he has performed for you this day, for as you saw the Egyptians this day, you will never see them ever again."

Exodus 14.14

| | |
|---|---|
| TgOnk | ויוי יגיח לכון קרב ואתון תשתקון : |

The Lord will wage war for you and you will be silent.

| | |
|---|---|
| Parm. 2894 | ייי יגיח לכון קרב ואתון תשתקון : |

The Lord will wage war for you and you will be silent.

| | |
|---|---|
| Parm. 2411 | אמר משה לישראל לא תדחלון דמימרא דייי יגיח לכון קרבא קומו שתוקו והבו יקר ותושבחתא ורוממו לאלהכון : |

Moses said to Israel: "You should not fear! For the Memrah of the Lord will wage the war for you. Stand, be silent, and give glory and praise; and exult your God."

| | |
|---|---|
| FragTgP | מימרא דייי יגיח לכון קרבא קומו שתוקו והבו יקר ותושבחתא לאלהכון : |

The Memrah of the Lord will wage the war for you. Stand, be silent, and give glory and praise to your God.

For Exod. 14.13, Parma, MS 2894 simply has the text of TgOnk, like the vast majority of French/Ashkenazi *mahzorim*.[10] Parma, MS 2411 and FragTg$^P$ however, have a Palestinised version of the text of TgOnk. In other words, their versions are identical in meaning but contain dialectal differences (i.e., ארום vs. ארי, דחמיתון vs. דחזיתון).[11]

It is possible that, in the case of these two latter manuscripts, the text of TgOnk was adopted and Palestinised in order to fill the gap left by the transposition of ארבע כיתין from Exod. 14.13–14 to Exod. 15.3.

Another possibility, which becomes quite evident in Exod. 14.14, is that scribes recycled or reconstructed material from the ארבע כיתין expansion in order fabricate a PalTg version of Exod. 14.13–14. Where Parma, MS 2894 has a version of Exod. 14.14 identical to TgOnk, Parma, MS 2411 contains a direct quote of (ג) from ארבע כיתין, including the addition ואמר משה לישראל לא תדחלון 'Moses said to Israel: 'You should not fear!'. As we know from our presentation of the expansion above, the phrase 'You should not fear!' is repeated four times in ארבע כיתין, introducing each of Moses' answers.

---

[10] Some of the French/Ashkenazi *mahzorim* contain some Palestinian Aramaic variants, e.g., London, British Library, MS Or. 2735 which contains דחמיתון instead of דחזיתון. In another French/Ashkenazi *mahzor*, London, British Library, MS Add. 19664, a scribe has even corrected the form found in TgOnk למיחזיהון to the Palestinian form למיחמיהון.

[11] Parma, MS 2411 contains a minor addition of בשעבוד 'in enslavement', which was added as clarification, i.e., as you saw the Egyptians today, *being an enslaved people*, you will never see them again.

In our opinion, it is very likely that the scribe recycled (ג) from ארבע כיתין and placed it at Exod. 14.14. The same applies to the second half of the verse, קומו שתוקו והבו יקר ותושבחתא לאלהכון 'stand, be silent, and give glory and praise to your God'; this expanded version of the second half of Exod. 14.14 is otherwise only attested in ארבע כיתין.

## 5.0. Adaptation as Preservation

Due to the diminishing of the Targum tradition in Medieval Europe, the reading for the seventh day of Pesach was shortened to only the most 'interesting' part, namely the Song of the Sea (Exod. 14.30–15.18). Expansions attached to verses before or after the Song of the Sea were at risk of being lost, and as such, were moved to verses within the Song of the Sea. These expansions were then adapted to their new location at Exod. 15.3. In some manuscripts, the adaptation led to an alternative sequencing of the expansion. It was thus the result of a conscious act of preservation that these expansions were moved and adapted.

In the manuscripts where this transposition had taken place (i.e., French/Ashkenazi and Sephardi *mahzorim*, as well as Frag-Tg[P]), scribes were creative in filling the lacuna that was left at Exod. 14.13–14; some opted to simply provide the text of TgOnk, while others recycled PalTg from the ארבע כיתין expansion.

## References

Alexander, Philip. 1988. 'Jewish Aramaic Translations of Hebrew Scriptures'. In *Mikra: Text, Translation, Reading and Interpre-*

*tation of the Hebrew Bible in Ancient Judaism and Early Christianity*, edited by Martijn J. Mulder, 217–53. Assen: Van Gorcum.

Beit-Arié, Malachi, and Benjamin Richler. 2001. *Hebrew Manuscripts in the Biblioteca Palatina in Parma: Catalogue*. Jerusalem: Jewish National and University Library.

Campbell, Ronald. 2002. 'Parashiyyot and Their Implications for Dating the Fragment-Targums'. In *Targum and Scripture*, edited by Paul Flesher, 105–14. Studies in the Aramaic Interpretation of Scripture. Leiden: Brill.

Dalman, Gustaf. 1894. *Grammatik des jüdisch-palästinischen Aramäisch nach den Idiomen des palästinischen Talmud und Midrasch, des Onkelostargum (Cod. Socini 84) und der jerusalemischen Targume zum Pentateuch*. Leipzig: Hinrichs.

Díez-Macho, Alejandro. 1960. 'The Recently Discovered Palestinian Targum: Its Antiquity and Relationship with Other Targumim'. *Vetus Testamentum, Supplements* (1): 222–45.

———. 1981. 'Nueva fuente para el Targum Palestino del dia septimo de Pascua y primero de Pentecostes'. *Salmanticensis* 28 (1/2): 233–57.

Elbogen, Ismar. 1993. *Jewish Liturgy: A Comprehensive History*. Translated by Raymond Scheindlin. Philadelphia: Jewish Publication Society; New York: Jewish Theological Seminary of America.

Epstein, Abraham. 1895. 'Tosefta du Targoum Yerouschalmi'. *Revue des études Juives* (1): 44–51.

Fassberg, Steven. 1990. *A Grammar of the Palestinian Targum Fragments from the Cairo Genizah*. Harvard Semitic Studies 38. Atlanta: Scholars Press.

Flesher, Paul, and Bruce Chilton. 2011. *The Targums: A Critical Introduction*. Waco, TX: Baylor University Press.

Frenkel, Yona. 1993. מחזור פסח לפי מנהגי בני אשכנז לכל ענפיהם. Jerusalem: Koren.

———.2000. מחזור שבועות לפי מנהגי בני אשכנז לכל ענפיהם. Jerusalem: Koren.

Ginsburger, Moshe. 1895. 'Die Thargumim zur Thorahlection am 7. Pesach-und 1. Schabuoth-Tage'. *Monatsschrift für Geschichte und Wissenschaft des Judentums* 39 (3): 97–105.

———. 1899. *Das Fragmententhargum*. Berlin: Calvary.

———. 1900. 'Aramäische Introduktionen zum Thargumvortrag an Festtagen'. *Zeitschrift der Deutschen morgenländischen Gesellschaft* 54 (1): 113–24.

———. 1921. 'Les introductions araméennes à la lecture du Targoum (suite et fin)'. *Revue des études Juives* 73 (145): 14–26.

———.1966. 'Die Fragmente des Thargum jeruschalmi zum Pentateuch'. *Zeitschrift der Deutschen Morgenländischen Gesellschaft* 57 (1): 67–80.

Ginzberg, Louis. 1947. *The Legends of the Jews*. Philadelphia: The Jewish Publication Society of America.

Gleßmer, Uwe. 1988. 'Entstehung und Entwicklung der Targume zum Pentateuch als literarkritisches Problem, dargestellt am Beispiel der ZusatzTargume'. PhD dissertation, University of Hamburg.

Houtman, Alberdina, and Harry Sysling. 2009. *Alternative Targum Traditions: The Use of Variant Readings for the Study in Origin and History of Targum Jonathan*. Studies in the Aramaic Interpretation of Scripture 9. Leiden, Boston: Brill.

Kasher, Rimon. 1985. 'The Aramaic Targumim and Their "Sitz Im Leben"'. *Proceedings of the World Congress of Jewish Studies* 75–85.

———. 1996. *Targumic Toseftot to the Prophets*. Jerusalem: World Union of Jewish Studies. [Hebrew]

Kaufman, Stephen, and Yeshayahu Maori. 1991. 'The Targumim to Exodus 20: Reconstructing the Palestinian Targum'. *Textus* 16 (1): 13–78.

Klein, Michael L. 1980. *The Fragment-Targums of the Pentateuch: According to their Extant Sources*. Analecta Biblica 76. Rome: Biblical Institute Press.

———. 1986. *Genizah Manuscripts of Palestinian Targum to the Pentateuch*. Cincinnati, OH; Hoboken, NJ: Hebrew Union College Press.

Lehnardt, Peter. 2010. 'Redactions of the Prayer Book according to the Italian Rite: First Reconsiderations on the Basis of Different Outlines of the Liturgical Poetry'. *Italia* 20 (1): 31–66.

Mikva, Rachel. 2011. 'Midrash in the Synagogue and the Attenuation of Targum'. *Jewish Studies Quarterly* 18 (4): 319–42.

Patmore, Hector, Shlomi Efrati, and Jeroen Verrijssen. 2024. 'Aramaic from Antiquity to the Middle Ages'. In *Jewish Languages and Book Culture*, edited by Judith Olszowy-

Schlanger and César Merchán-Hamann, 30–47. Oxford: Bodleian Library Publishing.

Sperber, Alexander (ed.). 2013. *The Bible in Aramaic: Based on Old Manuscripts and Printed Texts*, 3rd ed. Leiden, Boston: Brill.

Tal, Abraham. 1975. לשון התרגום לנביאים ראשונים ומעמדה בכלל ניבי הארמית. Tel Aviv: University of Tel Aviv.

———. 1986. 'The Dialects of Jewish Palestinian Aramaic and the Palestinian Targum of the Pentateuch'. *Consejo superior de investigaciones científicas* 46 (1): 441–48.

———. 2001. 'Is There a Raison d'être for an Aramaic Targum in a Hebrew-Speaking Society?'. *Revue des études Juives* 160 (3–4): 357–78.

———. 2008. 'The Role of Targum Onqelos in Literary Activity during the Middle Ages'. In *Aramaic in Its Historical and Linguistic Setting*, edited by Holger Gzella and Margaretha Folmer, 135–47. Wiesbaden: Harrassowitz Verlag.

Ta-Shma, Israel. 2006. 'Ashkenazi Jewry in the Eleventh Century'. In *Creativity and Tradition: Studies in Medieval Rabbinic Scholarship, Literature and Thought*, edited by Israel Ta-Shma, 1–5. Cambridge, MA: Harvard University Press.

Verrijssen, Jeroen. 2023. 'The Liturgical Targum to Pesach'. *Aramaic Studies* 21 (2): 166–84.

———. 2024. 'The Medieval European Liturgical Targum'. PhD dissertation, KU Leuven.

Zunz, Leopold. 1867. *Literaturgeschichte der synagogalen Poesie*. Berlin: Adolf Cohn Verlag und Antiquariat.

# PSEUDO-JONATHAN AS A EUROPEAN TARGUM: CLUES FROM *PIRQE DE-RABBI ELIEZER*[1]

*Gavin McDowell*

Despite recent research, the exact date and provenance of Targum Pseudo-Jonathan (TgPsJ) remains a mystery. A few years ago, Gottlieb (2021) and I (McDowell 2021)—following separate lines of reasoning—arrived at a similar conclusion: Targum Pseudo-Jonathan could not have been written before the twelfth century. Furthermore, we both postulated a European provenance. My own method relied heavily on the sources used by the Targumist, particularly *Pirqe de-Rabbi Eliezer* (PRE) and the 'Minor Midrash' known as the Chronicles of Moses (CM). The article showed that the Targumist could have used PRE and CM as sources (and, indeed, probably did), given the close verbal parallels between them. The reverse, however, could not be the case: PRE is unaware of the Palestinian Targum traditions found throughout TgPsJ, while the Targum uses a secondary, expanded

---

[1] This chapter is part of the TEXTEVOLVE project, which has received funding from the European Research Council (ERC) under the European Union's Horizon 2020 research and innovation programme (grant agreement No. 818702).

version of CM. This form of CM is only attested from the twelfth century onward, hence the proposed date for the Targum.

The provenance of the Targum remains an open question. The proposed European (specifically, Italian) provenance is based on the fact that only Italian authors (e.g., Menahem Recanati, Elias Levita, Azariah dei Rossi) seem to have known about the work prior to the *editio princeps* in 1590. I have since become aware of additional potential witnesses to the Targum (Patmore 2015, 59–60).[2] Not all of them are equally convincing, but all of them are European. Whether the Targum is specifically Italian is perhaps immaterial. What is more important is whether the Targum is European, written in a milieu where Aramaic never was a living language.

The most substantial support for TgPsJ's European provenance comes from a familiar yet unexpected source: *Pirqe de-Rabbi Eliezer* (PRE). According to the work of Eliezer Treitl (2012), the manuscripts of PRE can be divided into three families: European (א), Yemenite (ת), and the printed edition (ד), which is closely related to the European branch. There are also some isolated manuscripts (sigla ס and צ) which are of European provenance and are related to families א and ד. I have included a

---

[2] Patmore refers to 1) the Italian Isaiah ben Mall di Trani the Elder (d. 1260), who cites a text similar to TgPsJ to Num. 6.1; 2) the thirteenth-century Frenchman Jacob of Marvège, who alludes to TgPsJ's rendition of Deut. 22.5 without citing it; and 3) Jacob b. Moses Moellin of Mainz (d. 1427), who brings up a Targum text in a discussion about whether Iyyar should be written with one *yod* or two (TgPsJ writes it with two).

description of Treitl's manuscripts and their sigla in an appendix to the present article.

Targum Pseudo-Jonathan shares upwards of fifty verbal or thematic parallels with PRE (McDowell 2025). In the ten cases where there is a discernible difference between the European and Yemenite readings of these parallels, TgPsJ favors the European reading in seven. In the remaining three cases, at least one European witness (Families א or ד) attests TgPsJ's reading. These examples require more explanation, so I have labeled them 'Difficult Cases'.

The modest goal of this article is to present the data pertaining to these ten cases in an organised and easily digestible format. This requires firstly citing the relevant portion of the solitary manuscript of TgPsJ (British Library Add. 27031)[3] and then the evidence from PRE, that is, the readings from all the available manuscripts. For these, I have relied on Eliezer Treitl's online synopsis of PRE manuscripts.[4] I have confirmed all readings from the original manuscripts and indicated their folio number, except in two cases where the manuscripts were held by private owners (2ת and 4ת).

The data shows that the Targumist's *Vorlage* was from the European tradition, an ancestor of Treitl's families א and ד. Unfortunately, this manuscript no longer exists.

---

[3] I have also checked the *editio princeps* (Venice, 1590), but I only found one textual variant of note (in 1.3).

[4] Available online as part of the Friedberg Genizah Project (https://fjms.genizah.org), under the rubric 'Mahadura'.

## 1.0. Clear Cases

### 1.1. Tequfot

Targum Pseudo-Jonathan's rendition of Gen. 1.14 (BL Add. 27031, f. 4a) adds many technical details to the Hebrew original, including references to intercalations (עיבורין) and seasons (תקופות).

> ואמר אלקים יהון נהורין ברקיעא דשמייא לאפרשא ביני יממא וביני לילייא ויהון לסימנין ולזמני מועדין ולממני בהון חושבן יומין ולמקדשא רישי ירחין ורישי שנין עיבורי ירחין ועיבורי שנין ותקופות שמשא ומולד סיהרא ומחזורין
>
> 'God said, "Let there be lights in the firmament of heaven, to divide between the day and between the night, and let there be signs and appointed times, and to count through them the calculation of days, and to sanctify the new moons and new years, the intercalations of months (עיבורי ירחין) and the intercalations of years (עיבורי שנין), the seasons of the sun (תקופות שמשא), and the new moon (מולד סיהרא), and the cycles (מחזורין)."'[5]

The Targumist derives this vocabulary from the astronomical chapters of PRE 6–8. In the European tradition, the very first line of PRE 8 (or PRE 7 in some manuscripts, such as 4א and 5א) adds the redundant word תקופות ('seasons') after קצים (which also means 'seasons'). These manuscripts also use the plural form עיבורים rather than עבורות, which is found in a couple of Yemenite

---

[5] All translations are my own.

manuscripts. The word תקופות is not found in ד2 or ס. These are the only exceptions. Every member of family א has this reading.

ד1 (f. 5b): בעשרים ושמונה באלול נבראו חמה ולבנה ומניין שהוא שנים וחדשים וימים ולילות שעות וקצים **ותקופות** ומחזורות **ועבורין** היו לפני הקבה

ד2 (f. 6b): בעשרים ושמונה באלול נבראו חמה ולבנה ומניין שנים וחדשים וימים ולילות שעות וקצים ומחזורות **ועיבורין** היו לפני הב'ה

א1 (f. 87b): בכ"ח באלול נבראו חמה ולבנה ומניין שנים וחדשים ימים ולילות שעות קיצים ומחזורות **תקופות ועיבורים** היו לפני הק'ב'ה

א2 (f. 22a): בעשרים ושמנה באלול נבראו חמה ולבנה ומניין שנים וחדשי' וימים ולילות וקיצים ומחזורים **ותקופות** ומחזורים **ועבורים** היו לפני הק'ב'ה

א3 (ff. 9b–10a): בכ"ח באלול נבראו חמה ולבנה ומניין שנים וחדשים וימים ולילות וקצים **ותקופות** ומחזורות **ועבורים** היו לפני הק'ב'ה

א4 (f. 8a): בשמנה ועשרים באלול נבראו חמה ולבנה ומניין שנים וחדשים וימים ולילות וקצים **ותקופות** ומחזורות **ועבורים** היו לפני הק'ב'ה

א5 (f. 9a): בכ"ח באלול נבראו חמה ולבנה ומניין שנים וחדשים וימים ולילות וקיצים **ותקופות** ומחזורות **ועיבורים** היו לפני הב'ה

א7 (f. 61b): בכ"ח באלול נבראו חמה ולבנה ומניין שנים וחדשי' וימים ולילות וקצים **ותקופי'** ומחזורות **ועיבורי'** היו לפני הק'ב'ה

א8 (f. 12a): בעשרים ושמונה באלול נבראו חמה ולבנה מנין שהם שנים חדשים וימים ולילות וקיצים **ותקופות** ומחזורות **ועיבורים** היה לפני הב'ה

א9 (f. 148a): בעשרים ושמונה באלול נבראו חמה ולבנה מיניין שנים וחודשים ימים ולילות שעות וקיצים **תקופות** ומחזורות **ועיבורים** היו לפני הק'ב'ה

\*

**ס: (f. 10b)** בעשרים ושמונה באלול נבראו חמה ולבנה למניין שנים וחדשים ימים ולילות ושעות ומחזורות **ועיבורים** היו לפני הק'ב'ה'

By contrast, תקופות is universally missing in the available Yemenite manuscripts, and עיבור sometimes takes a feminine rather than a masculine plural ending.

**ת1 (f. 88a):** בעשרים ושמונה באלול נבראו חמה ולבנה מניין שנים וחדשים ימים ולילות ושעות וקצים ומחזורים **ועבורות** היה תחלה לפני הק'ב'ה'

**ת2:** בעשרים ושמונה באלול נבראו חמה ולבנה מנין שנים וחדשים ימים ולילות ושעות וקצין ומחזורות ועבורין היו תחלה לפני ה'ק'ב'ה'

**ת3 (f. 2a):** בעשרים ושמונה באלול נבראו חמה ולבנה מנין שנים היו לפני הב'ה'

**ת4:** בעשרים ושמונה באלול נבראו חמה ולבנה מניין שנים וחדשים ימים ולילות [שעות] ק[צ]ים ומחזורות **ועיבורות** היה תחלה [לפני] הק'ב'ה

**ת8 (f. 13b):** בעשרים ושמונה באלול נבראו חמה ולבנה מנין שנים וחדשים ימים ולילות ושעות וקצין ומחזורות ועיבורין היו תחלה לפני הק'ב'ה'

Of note is that the reading עיבורין, which agrees with the European family, is found only in manuscripts ת2 and ת8, which, along with ת7 are related, as we will see in examples below.

## 1.2. Noah's Altar

The next example comes from TgPsJ to Gen. 8.20 (BL Add. 27031, ff. 10b–11a), the description of Noah's altar after the Flood.

> ובנא נח מדבחא קדם ה' הוא מדבחא דבנא אדם בעידן דאיטרד מן גינתא
> דעדן ואקריב עילוי קרבנא ועילוי אקריבו קין והבל ית קרבנהון וכד נחתו
> מוי דטובענא איתצד ובנייה נח ונסב מכל בעירא דכיא ומן כל עוף דכי
> ואסיק ארבע עלוון על ההוא מדבחא

'Noah built an altar before the Lord, the very altar that Adam built in the time when he was driven from the Garden of Eden, and he offered upon it a sacrifice, and Cain and Abel offered their sacrifice, and when the waters of the Flood descended it was destroyed. Noah rebuilt it, and he took from every clean animal and from every clean bird, and he offered four burnt offerings on that altar.'

Every manuscript of PRE 21 mentions that Cain and Abel, on Adam's instruction, offered a Passover sacrifice (see also TgPsJ to Gen. 4.2–4). The Targum recalls this event in its translation of Gen. 8.20, as does PRE 23 where it describes Noah's sacrifice after the Flood. This parenthetical note is found in every single member of Family א as well as the *editio princeps* (but not ד2).

(f. 16a) **ד1: ובנה את המזבח הראשון שהקריב עליו עולות קין והבל**
והקריב עולות ארבע שנאמר ויבן נח מזבח ליי'

(f. 19b) ד2: בנה את המזבח והקריב עליו עולות

(f. 97b) **א1: ובנה את המזבח הראשון שהקריבו קין והבל** והקריב עולות
ארבע

(f. 54b) **א2: ובנה את המזבח הראשון שהקריב קין והבל** והקריב עולות
ארבע

**א3**: (f. 30a) ובנה את המזבח הראשון שהקריבו עליו קין והבל והקריב עולות ארבע

**א4**: (f. 21b) ובנה את המזבח הראשון שהקריבו עליו קין והבל והקריב ארבעה עולות

**א5**: (f. 28a) ובנה את המזבח הראשון שהקריבו עליו קין והבל והקריב עולות ארבע

**א6**: (ff. 15b–16a) ובנה את מזבח הראשון שהקריבו עליו קין והבל והקריב עולות ארבע

**א7**: (f. 78a) ובנה מזבח הראשון שהקריבו עליו הבל וקין והקריב עולות ד'

**א8**: (f. 37b) ובנה את המזבח הראשון שהקריבו עליו קין והבל והקריב עולות ארבע

In manuscript ס, the adjective 'first' is transferred from 'the first altar' to 'the first Adam'. This change is of special interest because it comes closest to reflecting the *Vorlage* of the Targum. On the other hand, manuscript צ hews closer to the Yemenite tradition, which omits any reference to the earlier patriarchs.

**ס**: (f. 33a) ובנה מזבח הוא המזבח שהקריב בו אדם הראשון והוא המזבח שהקריבו בו קין והבל והקריב עליו עולות במזבח

**צ**: (f. 4a) ובנה מזבח והקריב עליו ארבע עולות

The Yemenite manuscripts do not mention Cain and Abel, with the sole exception of ת3, a manuscript of the seventeenth century. It differs from the above in that it is shorter, omitting any mention of the 'first altar' (or even the 'first Adam'). The reference to Cain and Abel is most likely a gloss added just to this manuscript. It would be more difficult to explain why someone would remove it.

**ת1** (f. 109a): ובנה מזבח והקריב עולות ארבע

**ת2**: בנה מזבח ולקח מכל בהמה טהורה שור וכבש עולה ושעיר לחטאת ומכל עוף טהור תור ובן יונה והקריב עליו עולות ארבע

**ת3** (f. 32a): ובנה המזבח **שהקריבו קין והבל** והקריב עליו עולות ארבע

**ת4**: ובנה מזבח והקריב עולות ארבע

**ת5** (f. 16b): ובנה מזבח והקריב עולות ארבע

**ת6** (f. 31b): ובנה מזבח והקריב עולות ארבע

**ת7** (f. 27a): בנה מזבח ולקח מן הבהמה הטהורה שור וכשב עולה ושעיר לחטאת ומן העוף הטהור תור ובן יונה והקריבן עלה

**ת8** (f. 51a): בנה מזבח ולקח מכל הבהמה טהורה שור וכשב ומכל עוף טהור תור ובן יונה והקריב עליו עולות ארבע

**ת9** (f. 24b): ובנה מזבח והקריב עולות ארבע

Note that manuscripts ת2, ת7, and ת8, while omitting Cain and Abel, also have a much longer reading about the animals sacrificed on the altar. This is the second indication of the three manuscripts being related.

## 1.3. Every Nation, Its Writing and Language

TgPsJ's rendering of Gen. 11.8 (BL Add. 27031, ff. 12b–13a) adds that God descended to the Tower of Babel with a retinue of seventy angels, each one taking responsibility for the seventy nations and their respective languages.

ואיתגליאת מימרא דה' עילוי קרתא ועימיה שובעין מלאכיא כל קבל שומעין (שובעין :read) עממיא וכל חד וחד לישן עממיה ורושם (משם :*ed. pr.*) כתביה בידיה ובדרינון מתמן על אנפי כל ארעא לשיבעין לישנין

'The Word of the Lord appeared above the city, and with him seventy angels, each corresponding to the seventy nations and each one having the language of his people and script of his writing in his hand, and he scattered them from there over the face of the earth into seventy languages.'

The passage is parallel to PRE 24, which cites both Gen. 11.8 and Deut. 32.8. The Targum has broken up the tradition in PRE and assigned the different portions to the appropriate prooftexts. Thus, TgPsJ to Gen. 11.8 has the creation of the seventy languages, while the Targum's rendition of Deut. 32.8 mentions the casting of lots among the nations.

The targumic phrase "each one having the language of his people and script of his writing in his hand" (וכל חד וחד לישון עממיה ורושם כתביה בידיה) is an approximate translation of the Hebrew phrase "each one a nation according to its script and its language" (כל אחד ואחד גוי ככתבו ולשונו). The variant from the *editio princeps*, where רושם becomes משם, leaves all the parallel words intact. The phrase is attested in both members of the ד family.

**(f. 16b) ד1:** וירד הקבה ושבעים המלאכים הסובבי' כסא כבודו ובלבל את לשונם לשבעי' גוים ולשבעים לשון **כל אחד ואחד גוי ככתבו ולשו'**

**(f. 20a) ד2:** וירד הב'ה' ושבעים המלאכים הסובבים כסא כבודו ובלבל את לשונם לשבעים גוים ולשבעים לשון **כל אחד ואחד גוי כתבו ולשונו**

However, the phrase has fallen out of the א family, except for 2א. It is also in a different place in the text. Instead of following God's descent to Babel, it occurs earlier, when God and the angels are casting lots for the nations.

**(f. 56a) א2:** והפילו גורלות ביניהם **כל אחד ואחד גוי וכתבו ולשונו** ומנין שהפילו גורלות ביניהם

The two isolated manuscripts both have the phrase, although in different places. Manuscript ס places it at the beginning of the pericope, when God and the angels are first introduced. Manuscript צ, however, situates the phrase in the same place as the ד family, which is the approximate place in the story where the Targumist has placed it, between verses 7 and 8.

(f. 34a) **ס**: ר' יהושע אומ' אמ' הק'ב'ה' לשבעים מלאכים הסובבים את כסאו בואו ונרד ונבלבל את לשונם לשבעים גוים ולשבעים לשונות **כל אחד ואחד גוי כתבו ולשונו**

(f. 2a) **צ**: וירד הק'ב'ה' ושבעים מלאכים הסובבים את כסא כבודו ובלבלו את לשונם לשבעים גוים ולשבעים לשונות **כל אחד ואחד גוי כתבו לשונו**

Meanwhile, the Yemenite manuscripts know the tradition, but the exact text (איש בכתבו ובלושנו) is different. It less closely resembles the targumic version, and, like manuscript א2, occurs at the moment the angels cast lots for the nations.

(f. 109b) **ת1**: והפילו גורלות עליהן **איש בכתבו ובלשונו** מניין שהפילו עליהן גורלות

**ת2**: והפילו גורלות עליהם **איש בלשונו** ומניין שהפילו גורלות עליהם

(f. 33b) **ת3**: ואפילו גורלות עליהן **איש בכתב לשונו** מניין שהפילו גורלות עליהן

**ת4**: והפילו גורלות עליהם **איש בכתבו ולשונו** מניין שהפילו עליהם גורלות

(f. 17b) **ת5**: והפילו גורלות עליהן **שאיש בכתבו ובלשונו** מנין שהפילו עליהן גורלות

(ff. 32b–33a) **ת6**: והפילו גורלות עליהן **איש בכתבו ולשונו** מניין שהפילו עליהן גורלות

(f. 27b) ת7: והפילו גורלות עליהן **איש בכתבו איש בלשונו** ומנין שהפילו גורלות עליהן

(f. 53a) ת8: והפילו גורלות עליהם **איש בכתבו איש בלשונו** ומנין שהפיל גורלות עליהם

(f. 25a) ת9: והפילו גורלות עליהן **איש בכתבו ולשונו** מניין שהפילו עליהן גורלות

The data suggests that the placement of the tradition in א2 and Family ת (that is, at the casting of the lots) is the original. As PRE entered Europe, the wording changed and, eventually, the placement changed as well. The Targum reflects both changes, as found already in the ד family.

## 1.4. Peletith

The next example is TgPsJ to Gen. 18.21 (BL Add. 27031, f. 19a).

> אתגלי כדון ואחמי הא כקבילתא דריבא פליטית דעלתא קומוי עבדו גמירא הינון חייבין ואם עבדין תתובא הלא הינון קדמיי
> 
> '[God said:] "It will be revealed now, and I will see whether they have done according to the outcry of the young woman Peletith (פליטית) that has gone up before me."'

The oldest source for the story of Peletith, the daughter of Lot, is PRE 25. The Targum only alludes to a story that PRE tells in full. Of interest here is the spelling of the girl's name, which differs across the various manuscript traditions of PRE. For example, Family ד has 'Pelutith' (פלוטית).

(f. 17a) ד1: פלוטית     (f. 21a) ד2: פלוטית

The spelling favored by Family א is 'Pelitath' (פליטת). There are some exceptions. In א1, she is 'Peliti', while in א7 she is

'Pelitah'. Manuscript 2א doesn't have the girl's name at all. She is merely 'the daughter of Lot'. The variants are explicable as scribal errors.

| | |
|---|---|
| א1: (f. 98b) פליטי | א5: (f. 30a) פליטת |
| א2: (f. 58a) בתו של לוט | א6: (f. 17b) פליטת |
| א3: (f. 32a) פליטת | א7: (f. 79b) פליטה |
| א4: (f. 22b) פליטת | א8: (f. 40a) פליטת |

The isolated manuscripts reflect the readings of both the א and ד families.

| | |
|---|---|
| ס: (f. 35b) פליטת | צ: (f. 5a) פלוטית |

The Yemenite tradition, however, has a third alternative: 'Paltiyah' (פלטיא or פלטיה).

| | |
|---|---|
| ת1: (f. 111a) פליטה | ת6: (f. 34b) פלטיא |
| ת2: פליטה | ת7: (f. 28b) פליטה |
| ת3: (f. 35a) פלטיא | ת8: (f. 55a) פליטה |
| ת5: (f. 18b) פליטה | ת9: (f. 26a) פליטה |

None of these are identical to the spelling in the Targum (פליטית). However, the targumic spelling could be a deformation of the name as found in the ד family (פלוטית). The confusion of *yod* for *waw* and vice-versa is extremely common in Hebrew manuscripts. It would be harder to explain the Targum's particular form of the name from the Yemenite tradition.

## 1.5. The Death of Nimrod

The beginning of TgPsJ to Gen. 25.27 (BL Add. 27031, f. 27b) has an offhand reference to the death of Nimrod and his son at the hands of Esau.

> ורביאו טליא והוה עשו גבר נחשירכן למיצוד עופן וחיוון גבר נפיק חקל
> קטיל נפשן דהוא קטל ית נמרוד וית חנוך בריה

'The boys grew, and Esau became a powerful hunter, hunting birds and beasts, a man who went out into the field and killed the living (this is the one who killed Nimrod and his son Enoch).'

Although it is not apparent from the quoted passage, the tradition is tied to the garments of Adam and Eve, which Jacob eventually inherited. In the Palestinian Targums (Neofiti and the Fragment Targums) this tradition is attached to Gen. 48.22. In TgPsJ, it is attached to a different verse, Gen. 27.15.

Genesis 27.15 is cited at the end of every manuscript of PRE 24, which explains that Nimrod had obtained Adam and Eve's garments, but Esau coveted them and killed him. Rebekah then gave the garments to Jacob, which is how he obtained them. The tradition in PRE, which contradicts the Palestinian Targum tradition (that Abraham inherited the garments and gave them to Isaac, who gave them to Jacob), presumably influenced the placement of the tradition in TgPsJ

Every member of the א and ד families (as well as ס and צ) adds that Nimrod's garments were the source of Esau's prowess as a hunter, citing Gen. 25.27 as a prooftext. This is the exact verse where TgPsJ has decided to mention the manner of Nimrod's death. Even though Nimrod's death at the hands of Esau is found in every manuscript of PRE, Gen. 25.27 is only cited in the European tradition. Due to the length of the passage and the consistency of this tradition, I have only cited one example each from families ד and א.

**ד1: (f. 16b)** ר' אומ' עשו אחיו של יעקב ראה את הכתונת שעשה הקבה לאדם ולחוה על נמרוד וחמד אותם בלבו והרגו ולקח אותה ממנו ומנין שהיו חמודות בעיניו שנמ' *ותקח רבקה את בגדי עשו בנה הגדול החמודות* (Gen. 27.15) **וכשלבש אותם נעשה בם גם הוא גבור שנמ' *ויהי עשו איש יודע ציד*** (Gen. 25.27) וכשבא יעקב מאת פני יצחק אביו אמ' אין עשו הרשע ראוי ללבוש את הכתנת הללו וחפר וטמנם שם שנמ' *טמון בארץ חבלו* (Job 18.10)

**א1: (f. 98a)** ר' מאיר אומ' עשו אחיו של יעקב ראה הכתונת על נמרוד וחמד אותה בלבו והרגו ולקחו ממנו ומניין שהיו חמודות בעיניין שנ' *ותקח רבקה את בגדי החמודות וג'* (Gen. 27.15) **וכשלבש אותם נעשה גם הוא גיבור ציד שנ' *ויהי עשו איש וג'*** (Gen. 25.27) ויצא יעקב מאת פני יצחק אביו אמ' אין עשו ראוי ללבוש הכותנות הללו מה עשה חפר וטמנם בקרקע שנ' *טמון בארץ חבלו* (Job 18.10)

However, the phrase and its prooftext are found in none of the Yemenite manuscripts, even though the relevant passage is preserved in all of them. Again, I have only cited one example.

**ת1: (f. 110a)** ר' מאיר אומ' עשו אחי יעקב ראה את הכתנת שהיתה על נמרוד חמד אותה בלבו והרגו ולקחן ממנו מניין שהיתה חמודה בעיניו שנ' *ותקח רבקה את בגדי עשו בנה הגדול החמודות* (Gen. 27.15) וכשיצא יעקב מאת פני יצחק אביו אמ' הכתונות הללו אין עשו הרשע ראויות לו כדי ללבוש אותם וחפר בארץ וטמנם שנ' *טמון בארץ חבלו ומלכדתו עלי נתיב* (Job 18.10)

Enoch, the son of Nimrod, comes from a different part of PRE. Chapter 32, which only alludes to Gen. 25:27 without quoting the verse, mentions that Esau killed Nimrod and his son, variously named as חור, חויר, חוור, and similar variants. It would not have been hard for a careless copyist to misread חויר as the more common name Enoch (חנוך). There is once again a geographical distinction here. The form חויר is only found in European manuscripts (א3, א5, and א6; cf. א4, חזיר), while Yemenite manuscripts favour חור (ת1, ת3, ת4, and ת5; cf. ת9, חוור) with חיור as the only alternative (the related manuscripts ת2, ת7, and ת8). All told, an error like חנוך is more likely to have resulted from a four-letter word than a three-letter one, and from חויר rather than חיור.

## 1.6. The Angels' Praise

According to TgPsJ, Rebekah gave Jacob the garments originally belonging to Adam and Eve to fool his father. She also taught her son why this night—the night of Passover—is different from other nights, repeating something Isaac had already told Esau in TgPsJ to Gen. 27.1. Her statement is found in TgPsJ to Gen. 27.6 (BL Add. 27031, f. 29a).

> ורבקה אמרת ליעקב ברה למימר הא ליליא הדין עילאי משבחין למרי עלמא ואוצרי טלין מתפתחין ביה
> 
> 'Rebekah said to Jacob, her son, "Behold, this night the ones on high praise the Lord of the World, and the treasuries of dew are opened."'

Both TgPsJ Gen. 27.1 and 27.6 are directly parallel to statements of Isaac and Rebekah in PRE 32. In Families ד and א (along with, again, ס and צ) she proclaims that "on this night" (הלילה הזה) the treasuries of dew are opened and the angels (literally, 'the ones on high') "sing a song" (אומרים שירה), repeating that such an event transpires "on this night."

(f. 23a) ת1: אמרה רבקה ליעקב בני **הלילה הזה** אוצרות טללים נפתחים בו העליונים אומ' שירה הלילה הזה

(f. 26b) ת2: אמ' רבקה ליעקב בני **הלילה הזה** אוצרות ברכה נפתחים בו העליונים אומ' בו שירה הלילה הזה

(f. 75b) א2: אמרה רבקה ליעקב בני **הלילה הזה** בו אוצרות טללים נפתחים הלילה הזה בו העליונים אומרים שירה

(f. 43a) א3: אמרה רבקה ליעקב בני **הלילה הזה** אוצרות טללים נפתחים הלילה הזה בו העליונים אומרי' שירה

(f. 30a) א4: אמרה רבקה ליעקב בני **הלילה הזה** אוצרות טללים נפתחים הלילה הזה העליונים אומרין שירה

(f. 40b) א5: אמרה רבקה ליעקב בני **הלילה הזה** בו אוצרות טללים נפתחים הלילה הזה בו העליונים אומרי' שירה

(f. 29b) א6: אמרה רבקה ליעקב בני **הלילה הזה** אוצרות טללים נפתחים הלילה הזה בו העליונים אומ' שירה

(f. 88b) א7: אמרה רבקה ליעקב בנה **הלילה הזה** בו אוצרות טללים נפתחים הלילה הזה בו העליוני' אומ' שירה

(f. 47b) ס: אמרה רבקה ליעקב בנה **הלילה הזה** בו עליונים יורדים **אומרים שירה הלילה הזה בו** אוצרות טללים יורדים

(f. 17a) צ: אמרה רבקה ליעקב בנה בני **הלילה הזה** אוצרות ברכות נפתחין בו **הלילה הזה** העליונים אומרין בו שירה והלל

In the Yemenite tradition, something curious has occurred. A reduplication crept into the manuscripts, where the treasuries of dew are mentioned twice and the angels' song not at all. Three manuscripts (ת2, ת7, and ת8) retained the angels' speech, but the text is slightly different. Instead of "singing a song" (אומרים שירה), the ones on high "sing praise" (אומרים הלל), which is arguably closer to the targumic rendering, "praise" (משבחים). Uniquely, צ has both readings.

However, there is another difference between the European and Yemenite traditions. The European manuscripts, with TgPsJ, say that the angels' praise occurs "on this *night*," but every Yemenite manuscript, without exception, reads "on this *day*" (ביום הזה).

(f. 120a)　ת1: אמרה רבקה ליעקב בנה בני **היום הזה** בו אוצרות ברכות טללים נפתחין

ת2: אמרה רבקה ליעקב בני **היום הזה** בו אוצרות טללים נפתחים **היום הזה בו העליונים אומרים הלל**

(f. 46b)　ת3: אמרה רבקה ליעקב הנה בני **היום הזה** בו אוצרות טללים נפתחין **היום הזה** בו ברכות טללים

ת4: אמרה רבקה ליעקב בנה בני **היום הזה** הזה בו אוצרות ברכות טללים נפתחים **היום הזה** בו ברכות וטללים

(f. 25a)　ת5: אמרה רבקה ליעקב בני **היום הזה** בו אוצרות טללים וברכות נפתחים **היום הזה** בו ברכות טללים

(f. 38b)　ת7: אמ' רבקה ליעקב בני **היום הזה** אוצרות טללים נפתחים בו היום הזה עליונים אומ' הלל

(f. 73b)　ת8: אמרה רבקה ליעקב בני **היום הזה** בו אוצרות טללים נפתחים **היום הזה בו העליונים אומרים הלל**

(f. 34b)　ת9: אמרה רבקה ליעקב בני **היום הזה** בו אוצרות ברכות טללים נפתחים **היום הזה** בו ברכות טללים

## 1.7. The Baby in the Brick

The last of the clear examples involves the gruesome tale of the Israelite newborn who became mixed into the mortar for the bricks during the slavery in Egypt. The Targum tells this tale in its rendering of Exod. 24.10 (BL Add. 27031, f. 85a), a description of the throne of God.

ותחות אפיפודין דריגלוי דמייצע תחות כורסייה הי כעובד אבן ספירינון מידכר שיעבודא דשעבידו מצראי ית בני ישראל בטינא ובליבנין והוואן נשיא בטשן ית טינא עם גובריהון הות תמן ריבא מפנקתא מעברתא ואפילת ית עוברא ואתבטש עם טינא נחת גבריאל ועבד מיניה לבינתא ואסקיה לשמי מרומא ואתקניה גלוגדק תחות אפיפודין דמרי עלמא

'Under the footstool of his feet that was spread out under his throne there was something like a work of sapphire stone, recalling the slavery with which the Egyptians subjected the children of Israel by clay and by bricks. While the women were treading the clay with their husbands, there was a delicate young woman there who was pregnant. She miscarried the fetus, and it was trampled with the clay. Gabriel descended, made a brick from it, and brought it to the high heavens. He affixed it as a stool in the place of the footstool of the Lord of the World.'

The placement of the story is strange. It is attached to this verse because it describes the throne of God, and the brick has become part of the throne as a permanent reminder of the cruelty of the Egyptians. Originally, however, the story explained God's impetus to finally act against the Egyptians. In PRE 48, it is placed immediately before God strikes down the Egyptian firstborn on Passover.

The European manuscripts that feature this chapter mention, with the Targum, that an angel descended and brought the brick before God's throne. The main difference is that the angel is Michael rather than Gabriel, as in the Targum. Every member of Family א has this sentence. It is missing, however, in ד2 and צ (ס does not have this chapter).

(f. 39b) ד1: ועלתה צעקתה לפני כסא הכבוד **וירד מיכאל המלאך ולקח את המלבן בסיס שלו והעלהו לפני כסא הכבוד** ובאותו הלילה נגלה הקבה והכה כל בכורי מצרים

(f. 46a) ד2: ועלתה צעקתה לפני כסא הכבוד ובאותו הלילה נגלה הב"ה והכה כל בכורי מצרים

(f. 127a) א2: ועלת צעקתה לפני כסא כבוד **וירד מיכאל המלאך ולקח את המלבן בטיט והעלהו לפני כסא הכבוד** ואותו הלילה רד הקב"ה והכה את בכורי מצרים

(f. 73b) א3: ועלת צעקתה לפני כסא הכבוד ובאותה הלילה **ירד מיכאל המלאך והעלהו לפני כסא הכבוד** ואותו הלילה ירד הב'ה' והכה בכורי מצרים

(f. 50b) א4: ועלת צעקתה לפני כסא הכבוד ובאותה הלילה **ירד מיכאל המלאך והעלהו לפני כסא הכבוד** ואותו הלילה ירד הק'ב'ה' והכה בכורי מצרים

(f. 69a) א5: ועלת צעקתה לפני כסא הכבוד **וירד מיכאל המלאך ולקח את המלבן בטיט והעלהו לפני כסא הכבוד** ואותו הלילה ירד הב'ה' והכה את בכורי מצרים

(f. 51b) צ: ועלתה צעקתה לפני כסא הכבוד ובאותה הלילה נגלה הק'ב'ה' והרג כל בכורי מצרים

While the change of angel might be an important difference, the European manuscripts are still closer to the Targum than the Yemenite family, which does not have this sentence at all.

(f. 146a) ת1: ועלתה צעקתה לפני כסא הכבוד באותה הלילה נגלה הק'ב'ה' והכה כל בכורי מצר'

ת2: ועלתה צעקתה לפני כסא כבוד ובאותו הלילה נגלה
הק׳ב׳ה׳ והכה כל בכורי מצר׳

ת6 (f. 87b): ועלת צעקתה לפני כסא הכבוד באותו הלילה נגלה
ה׳ק׳ב׳ה׳ והכה כל בכורי מצרים

ת7 (f. 64a): ועלתה צעקתה לפני כסא כבודו ובאותו הלילה נגלה
הק׳ב׳ה׳ והרג כל בכורי מצרים

ת8: ועלתה צעקתה לפני כסא כבוד ובאותו הלילה נגלה
הק׳ב׳ה׳ והכה כל בכורי מצר׳ (ff. 128b–129a)

ת9 (f. 59a): ועלתה צעקתה לפני כסא הכבוד באותו הלילה נגלה
הק׳ב׳ה׳ והכה כל בכורי מצ׳

## 2.0. Difficult Cases

### 2.1. Eliezer b. Nimrod

Thus far, we have looked at cases where TgPsJ displayed a clear preference for European readings of PRE over their Yemenite counterparts. We now turn to three examples that complicate this picture, where the traditions in PRE are poorly attested in European manuscripts but found in Yemenite ones. This evidence does not contradict the hypothesis of the Targumist's use of a European *Vorlage* of PRE, but it does require explanation.

The first example pertains to an offhand comment in TgPsJ to Gen. 14.14 (BL Add. 27031, f. 15b) that Eliezer, the servant of Abraham, was the son of the tyrant Nimrod.

וכד שמע אברם ארום אשתבי אחוי וזיין ית עולמויי דחניך לקרבא מרבייני
ביתיה ולא צבו למהלכא עמיה ובחר מינהון ית אליעזר בר נמרוד דהוה
מתיל בגבורתא ככולהון תלת מאה ותמניסר

'When Abram heard that his brother was taken captive, he armed his servants whom he had trained for war, the young men of his house, but they did not want to go with him. He chose from them Eliezer the son of Nimrod, who was comparable in strength to all of them, 318 men.'

The same identification is found in PRE 16, though primarily in the Yemenite manuscripts. Of the European manuscripts, only א5 identifies Eliezer as Nimrod's 'firstborn' (בכורו). All other manuscripts in Family א, as well as Family ד and ס, call Eliezer Nimrod's 'servant' (עבדו).

**ד1** (f. 11a): ועמד נמרוד וכתב את **עבדו** אליעזר לאברהם

**ד2** (f. 13b): עמד נמרוד המלך וכתב **עבדו** אליעזר עבד לעולם

**א1** (f. 92b): זקן ביתו של אברהם היה **עבדו** אליע' וכתבו לעבד עולם

**א2** (f. 39a): ולקח נמרוד את **עבדו** אליעזר וכתבו לו עבד עולם

**א3** (f. 20a): ולקח נמרוד **עבדו** אליעזר וכתבו לו עבד עולם

**א4** (f. 15a): ולקח נמרוד **עבדו** אליעזר ונתנו לו עבד עולם

**א5** (f. 18b): ולקח נמרוד את **בכורו** אליעזר וכתבו לו לעבד עולם

**א6** (f. 7b): ולקח נמרוד **עבדו** אליעזר וכתבו לו עבד לעולם

**א7** (f. 70a): לקח נמרוד את **עבדו** אליעזר וכתב לו לעבד עולם

**א8** (f. 25b): ולקח נמרוד את **עבדו** אליעזר וכתבו לו כתב עולם

**א9** (f. 155a): זקן ביתו של אברהם היה אליעזר **עבדו** וכתבו לו עבד עולם

**ס** (ff. 21b–22a): ולקח נמרוד את **עבדו** אליעזר וכתבו עבד עולם

The same reading is found in most Yemenite manuscripts. Three, however, state that Eliezer was Nimrod's 'son' (בנו): 2ת, 7ת, and 8ת. We have previously seen (in examples 1.1, 1.2, and 1.6) that these three manuscripts tend to agree with each other against the rest of the Yemenite tradition.

**ת1** (f. 100b): ועמד נמרוד וכתב לו את אליעזר **עבדו** עבד לעולם

**ת2**: ועמד נמרוד המלך וכתב לו את **בנו** אליעזר עבד לעולם

(f. 17b) ת3: ועמד נמרוד וכתב לו את **עבדו** אליעזר עבד עולם במכתב עולם

(f. 9b) ת5: ועמד נמרוד וכתב לו את אליעזר **עבדו** עבד לעולם

(f. 18a) ת7: ועמד נמרוד המלך וכתב לו את אליעזר **בנו** עבד עולם

(f. 33a) ת8: ועמד נמרוד המלך וכתב לו את **בנו** אליעזר עבד לעו'

(f. 16a) ת9: ועמד נמרוד וכתב לו את אליעזר **עבדו** עבד לעולם

The difference in the readings is easy to explain. Immediately after this line, near the end of PRE 16, Eliezer is further identified with Og, king of Bashan. This is found in every manuscript of PRE, but it contradicts PRE 23, which states that Og lived before the Flood and hitched a ride with Noah. Nimrod, a descendant of Ham via Cush, was born long after the Flood. The reading 'his servant' is a transparent attempt to correct this mistake. The original reading must have stated Eliezer was a son of Nimrod. This is also dictated by the sense of the passage. It is not much of a gift for a king to offer only one of his servants!

I believe that the original reading is the one in א5, 'his first-born' (בכורו). A clever scribe could massage this word into the vaguely similar 'his servant' (עבדו), while one branch of the Yemenite tradition preserved the sense of the passage but not the wording. Thus, only a European manuscript preserves the original reading. Furthermore, the Targum had access to one of these rare manuscripts that called Eliezer a son of Nimrod (the Targumist, however, does not confuse Og and Eliezer).[6]

---

[6] It has been pointed out to me that *Midrash Aggadah,* a twelfth-century Midrash loosely associated with the mysterious R. Moshe ha-Darshan, also calls Eliezer the son of Nimrod. This obscure work, of uncertain provenance (Moses ha-Darshan lived in Provence; the sole manuscript

## 2.2. Abraham's Altar

The next example is similar to 1.2 above. The passage once again concerns the altar used by the patriarchs, in this case Abraham. The tradition is attached to Gen. 22.9 (BL Add. 27031, f. 23a).

> ובנא תמן אברהם ית מדבחא דבנא אדם ואיתפכר במוי דטובענא ותב נח
> ובנייה ואיתפכר בדרא דפלוגתא

'Abraham rebuilt there the altar which Adam had built, which was destroyed in the waters of the Flood. Noah returned and rebuilt it, but it was destroyed again in the generation of the division.'

The Targum names the main patriarchs who had used the altar prior to Abraham: Adam and Noah. PRE 21 mentions the use of the altar by Cain and Abel, while European manuscripts of PRE 23 mention that Noah rebuilt and used the same altar. In PRE 31—the *Aqedah*—the altar appears once more.

In both witnesses of Family ד, the list of worthies who had used the altar include 'Adam ha-Rishon' (אדם הראשון), literally 'the first Adam', Cain and Abel, Noah and his sons, and other 'Rishonim' (ראשונים) or 'predecessors'. I have eliminated the prooftexts from the citations below.

---

of *Midrash Aggadah* is from Aleppo), uses PRE and even names the book as a source (see Buber 1894, I:vii). It is immaterial whether TgPsJ knew PRE traditions directly or from intermediary sources. For this tradition in the Midrash, see Buber (1894, I:35). For more information about this Midrash (but not much more), see Mack (2010, 195–97).

ד1: הוא המזבח שהיה **אדם הראשון** מקריב בו מקודם הוא
(ff. 21b–22a) המזבח שהקריבו בו **קין והבל** הוא המזבח שהקריבו בו **נח
ובניו**... הקריבו בו **ראשונים**
ד2: הוא המזבח שהיה **אדם הראשון** מקריב מקדם הוא המזבח
(ff. 25a–25b) שהקריבו **קין והבל** הוא המזבח שהקריבו נח ובניו... הקריבו
בו **ראשונים**

This reading is a doublet. The original text of PRE started with Cain and Abel then continued with Noah and his sons. These are the two groups who explicitly sacrificed on the altar according to PRE. The list ended with a vague reference to the 'Rishonim'. This original reading is found in all of Family א as well as ס and צ. Again, I have omitted the prooftexts.

א1 (f. 103a): הוא המזבח שהקריבו בו **בני נח ונח**... הוא המזבח שהקריבו
בו את **הראשונים**

א2 (f. 72a): הוא המזבח שהיה. מקדם הוא המזבח שהקריבו בו **קין והבל**
הוא המזבח שהקריבו בו **נח ובניו**... הוא המזבח שהקריבו בו
**הראשונים**

א3 (f. 40b): והוא היה המזבח שהקריבו בו **קין והבל** הוא המזבח שהקריבו
בו **נח ובניו**... הוא המזבח שהקריבו בו **הראשונים**

א4 (f. 27b): והוא היה המזבח שהקריבו **קין והבל** והוא המזבח שהקריבו
**נח ובניו**... הוא המזבח שהקריבו בו **הראשונים**

א5 (f. 38b): והוא היה המזבח שהקריבו בו **קין והבל** הוא המזבח שהקריבו
בו **נח ובניו**... הוא המזבח שהקריבו בו **הראשונים**

א6 (f. 27b): הוא היה המזבח שהקריבו בו **קין והבל** הוא המזבח שהקריבו
בו **נח ובניו** הוא המזבח שהקריבו בו אברהם... הוא המזבח
שהקריבו בו **הראשונים**

א7 (f. 86b): הוא המזבח שהקריבו בו **קין והבל** הוא המזבח שהקריבו בו
**נח ובניו**... הוא המזבח שהקריבו בו **הראשוני'**

(f. 45b) ס: מזבח שהקריבו בו **קין והבל** הוא המזבח שהקריבו בו **נח**
ובניו... הוא המזבח שהקריבו בו **הראשונים**

(f. 15a) צ: בזה המזבח הקריב בו **נח ובניו**... המזבח שהקריבו **ראשונים**

The Yemenite manuscripts do something different. The vague reference to the 'Rishonim' has been changed to the specific 'Adam ha-Rishon' and placed at the beginning of the list. This happens in most Yemenite manuscripts, with the exceptions of the related manuscripts 2ת, 7ת, and 8ת, which reflect something closer to the original reading.

(f. 118b) ת1: הוא המזבח שהקריב בו **אדם הראשון** הוא המזבח שהקריב בו
**קין והבל** הוא המזבח שהקריב בו **נח**

ת2: הקריבו בו **הראשונים**

(f. 62a) ת3: הוא המזבח שהקריב בו **אדם הראשון** הוא המזבח שהקריבו
בו **קין והבל** הוא המזבח שהקריב בו **נח**

ת4: הוא המזבח שהקריב בו **אדם הראשון** והוא המזבח שהקריב
בו **קין** והוא המזבח שהקריב בו **נח**

(f. 24b) ת5: הוא המזביח שהקריב בו **אדם הראשון** הוא המזביח שהקריב
בו **קין והבל** הוא המזביח שהקריב בו **נוח**

(f. 35a) ת7: הקריבו בו **הראשונים**

(f. 70a) ת8: הוא המזבח שהקריבו בו **קין והבל** הוא המזבח שהקריבו בו
**הראשונים**

(f. 33a) ת9: ההוא המזבח שהקריב בו **אדם הראשון** הוא המזבח שהקריבו
בו **קין והבל** הוא המזבח שהקריב בו **נח**

Which manuscript did the Targumist see? One from the ד family is the only response consonant with the evidence of the preceding examples. That is, since the reference to Adam ha-Rishon appears in both European (Family ד) and Yemenite witnesses, it does not contradict the hypothesis that the

Targumist used a European manuscript. In almost all cases, TgPsJ reflects the readings of Family ד. The only exceptions are the previous example (2.1) and the next one, which is also the last.

## 2.3. Joseph's Silver and Gold

The final example involves the wealth of Korah, the rebel who challenged Moses' authority during the years of wandering in the desert. His wealth, says the Targum, came from the treasuries of Joseph, which were filled with both silver and gold. The relevant passage comes from Num. 16.19 (BL Add. 27031, f. 160a), in the midst of the story of his rebellion.

> וכנש עליהון קרח ית כל כנישתא לתרע משכן זימנא ואתנטיל בעותריה
> דאשכח תרין אוצרין מן אוצרוי דיוסף מליין כסף ודהב
>
> 'Korah assembled against them the entire congregation at the entrance of the tent of meeting. He carried himself high because of his wealth, for he had found two treasuries of the treasuries of Joseph, full of silver and gold.'

Korah's wealth was proverbial and already appears in the Talmud (b. *Pesahim* 119a; b. *Sanhedrin* 110a). The tradition, as it is formulated in both passages, reads: "R. Hama b. R. Hanina said: Joseph buried three treasures in Egypt (ג' מטמוניות המטין יוסף במצרים). One was revealed to Korah, one was revealed to Antoninus b. Severus, and one is reserved for the righteous in the future to come."[7] While the tradition is well-known, PRE 50 and TgPsJ phrase it in a manner that is wholly distinct from the

---

[7] Translated from the Vilna Shas.

talmudic tradition. This seemingly minor aside nevertheless reveals a clear geographical divide in the manuscript tradition. In Family ד, for instance, Korah only has access to Joseph's gold.

(f. 41a) ד1: ר' פנחס אומ' שני עשירים היו בעולם **קרח בישראל שמצא אוצרות זהב של יוסף** והמן באומות העולם

(f. 47b) ד2: ר' פינחס אומ' שני עשירים עמדו בעולם **קרח בישראל שמצא אוצרות זהב של יוסף** המן באומות העולם

In Family א, manuscripts do not even mention the source of Korah's wealth. There are exceptions. Manuscript 1א mentions both silver and gold—the only European manuscript to do so. Manuscripts 3א and 4א, like Family ד, only mention the gold.

(f. 113a) א1: ר' פינחס אומ' שני עשירים עמדו בעולם אחד מישר' ואחד מאומות העולם **קורח מבני ישר' שמצא אוצרות של זהב ושל כסף של יוסף** והמן מאומות העולם

(f. 131a) א2: ר' פנחס אומ' שני עשירים עמדו בעולם אחד בישראל ואחד באומות העולם קרח בישראל והמן באומות העולם

(f. 76b) א3: ר' פנחס אומ' שני עשירים עמדו בעולם אחד בישר' ואחד באומות העולם קרח בישר' והמן באומות העולם **קרח שמצא אוצרות של זהב של יוסף** והמן שלקח כל אוצרו' של מלכי יהודה

(f. 52a) א4: ר' פנחס אומר שני עשירים עמדו בעולם אחד בישראל ואחד באומות העולם קרח בישראל והמן באומות העולם **קרח שמצא אוצרות של זהב של יוסף** והמן שלקח כל אוצרות של מלכי יהודה

(f. 71a) א5: ר' פנחס אומ' שני עשירים עמדו בעולם אחד בישראל ואחד באומות העולם קרח בישראל והמן באומות העולם

The Yemenite manuscripts, on the other hand, more consistently mention both the silver and gold, the exceptions being (as one might expect by now) ת2, ת7, and ת8, which only have gold.

ת1: (f. 148a) ר' פינחס אומ' שני עשירים עמדו בעולם אחד בישר' ואחד באומות העולם **קרח בישראל שמצא אוצרות שלזהב ושלכסף שליוסף** והמן באמות העולם

ת2: ר' פינחס אומ' שני עשירים עמדו בעולם הזה אחד בישר' ואחד באומות העולם **קרח בישראל שמצא אוצרות זהב שליוסף** והמן באומות העולם

ת6: (ff. 85b–86a) ר' פנחס או' שני עשירים עמדו בעו' אחד מישראל ואחד באומות העו' **קרח ביישר' שמצא אוצרות שלזהב ושלכסף שליוסף** והמן באומות העו'

ת7: (f. 66a) ר' פנחס אומ' שני עשירים עמדו בעולם הזה אחד מישראל ואחד מאומות העולם **קרח מישראל שמצא אוצרות זהב שליוסף** והמן באומות העולם

ת8: (f. 132b) ר' פנחס אומר שני עשירים עמדו בעו' הזה אחד בישר' ואחד באומות העו' **קרח בישר' שמצא אוצרות זהב שליוסף** והמן באומות העו'

ת9: (f. 61a) ר' פינחס אומ' שני עשירים עמדו בעו' אחד ביש' ואחד באמות העו' **קרח ביש' שמצא אוצרות שלזהב ושלכסף שליוסף** והמן באמות העו'

The only comment I have to offer is that א1 at least shows the Targum's reading was known in Europe, even if it appears to have dropped out in transmission.

## 3.0. Conclusions

With these examples, I have endeavoured to show that Targum Pseudo-Jonathan reflects knowledge of a specifically European version of *Pirqe de-Rabbi Eliezer*. The first seven examples show that the Targum knows readings from the א and ד families but not Family ת. The final three examples are readings that are found in the א or ד families as well as in Family ת. In no case does the Targum reflect a reading from PRE exclusive to Family ת.

The first conclusion to be drawn from this evidence is that the manuscript used by the Targumist no longer exists. No extant manuscript or manuscript family accounts for all the readings found in the Targum. The witness that comes closest is not a manuscript at all but the *editio princeps* (ד1), which shares eight of the ten readings with TgPsJ (the exceptions being 2.1 and 2.3). It might be tempting to simply label the Targumist's manuscript as a member of Family ד. After all, the two extant witnesses disagree with each other more often than ד1 disagrees with TgPsJ (see examples 1.1, 1.2 and 1.7). It might be more prudent to state that the Targumist's *Vorlage* was an ancestor of the ד and א families.

The course of this study has also revealed some aspects of the original version of PRE and its manuscript stemma, which Treitl did not elucidate in his study. The difficult cases can only be untangled by deducing the original readings. The Targum is sometimes a witness to these original readings, as in 2.1 and 2.3. As for the stemma, the Yemenite manuscripts ת2, ת7, and ת8 stand out as belonging to the same subgroup (see examples 1.1, 1.2, 1.6, 2.1, 2.2, and 2.3). In fact, they appear to be a missing link between the European and Yemenite manuscripts. This information will prove useful should anyone wish to attempt a critical edition of PRE.

Finally, this study has shed some light on how the Targumist engaged with his sources. He was not only a translator of the Torah but a translator of other works that he incorporated into the Targum. He has stayed close enough to his *Vorlage* that one can deduce when he is using PRE (and which version), but he has not merely transcribed the text. There are enough examples above where he has rearranged the text, offered slightly different wording, or added new traditions. The Torah may have been a sacred text for the Targumist, but PRE clearly was not.

## 4.0. Appendix: Eliezer Treitl's Sigla for PRE Manuscripts

The following is a summary of the major manuscripts of PRE, based on the work of Eliezer Treitl (2012, 278–88).

### 4.1. The Printed Edition (ד)

- 1ד: *Editio princeps* of Constantinople, 1514. Basis for Venice, 1544 (the 'vulgate'; see Börner-Klein 2004). Complete.
- 2ד: St. Petersburg, The National Library of Russia, MS EVR I 249, 15th or 16th c., 47 pages (NLI F 51144). Sephardi. Covers PRE 1–50.

### 4.2. The European Family (א)

- 1א: Warsaw, The Library of the Emanuel Ringelblum Jewish Historical Institute, MS 240, 13th or 14th c., ff. 84b–115b (NLI F 11607). Ashkenazi. Many scribal omissions between PRE 36–50. Covers 85% of the text.
- 2א: Rome, The Casanatense Library MS 3158, 15th or 16th c., ff. 2a–143b (NLI F 98). Sephardi. Complete.

**3א**: Moscow, The Russian State Library, MS Guenzburg 111, 1468, ff. 2a–85b (NLI F 6791). Sephardi. Complete.

**4א**: Rome, The Casanatense Library, MS 2858, 15th or 16th c., ff. 1a–58 10484a (NLI F 735). Sephardi. Complete.

**5א**: New York, The Jewish Theological Seminary of America, MS 10484, 1509, ff. 1b–79a (NLI F 72979). Sephardi. Written in Thessalonica. This is the manuscript translated by Gerald Friedlander (1916, repr. 1970). Complete.

**6א**: St Petersburg, The National Library of Russia, MS EVR II A 374, 14th c., 58 pages (NLI F 64672). Sephardi. PRE 9–45.

**7א**: Parma, The Palatina Library, MS 2454 (De Rossi 1203), 14th c., ff. 56a–92b (NLI F 13459). Byzantine script. PRE 2–33.

**8א**: Rome, The Casanatense Library, MS 3061, 14th c., 67 pages (NLI F 57). Sephardi. Covers approximately 38 chapters. Lacuna between PRE 29 and 35.

**9א**: Parma, The Palatina Library, MS 2295 (De Rossi 563), 13th or 14th c., ff. 142a–159a (NLI F 13202). Ashkenazi. PRE 1–20.

## 4.3. Isolated Manuscripts Related to ד and א

**ס**: Cincinnati, Hebrew Union College, MS 75, 14th or 15th c., 76 pages (NLI F 17358). Oriental script. PRE 3–41.

**צ**: Moscow, Russian State Library, MS Guenzburg 1455, 15th c., 53 pages (NLI F 48514). Italian script. PRE 23–49.

## 4.4. The Yemenite Family (ת)

1ת: New York, The Jewish Theological Seminary of America, MS 3847, 1653, ff. 79b–155a (NLI F 29652). Yemenite. Complete.

2ת: New York, The Manfred and Anne Lehmann Foundation, MS 300, 1596, 1a–86a (NLI F 24645). Yemenite. Complete.

3ת: New York, The Jewish Theological Seminary of America, MS 8874, 17th c., 80 pages (NLI F 49383). Yemenite. PRE 7–39.

4ת: London, David Solomon Sassoon, MS 944, 14th c., 234 pages (NLI F 9056). Yemenite script. The text is a mixture of the Yemenite tradition and the printed edition. Yemenite: PRE 7–10; 11–16; 17–19; 21–42; 43–48. Printed edition: PRE 1–7; 10–11; 16–17; 19–21; 42–43; 48–51; 52–54.

5ת: Cincinnati, Hebrew Union College, MS 2043, 18th or 19th c., 37 pages (NLI F 41694). Yemenite. Two different manuscripts bound together: MS A covers PRE 1–10 (printed edition); MS B covers PRE 13–17; 18–42; 43–46. Chapters 17 and 42 have been completed from the printed edition.

6ת: Oxford, The Bodleian Libraries, MS Opp. Add. Qu. 167 (Neubauer 2495), 15th c., 87 pages (NLI F 22207). Yemenite. Damaged manuscript covering PRE 6–50 (about 50% of the text).

7ת: New York, The Jewish Theological Seminary of America, MS 4925, 1643, 73 pages (NLI F 73112). Yemenite script.

The text is a mixture of the Yemenite tradition and the printed edition. Yemenite: PRE 15–19; end of 20–45; 45–54. Printed edition: PRE 1–first line of 15; 19–20; 46–48 (midway).

**8ח**: New York, The Jewish Theological Seminary of America, MS 4927, 15th c., 141 pages (NLI F 73114). Yemenite script. The text, though largely Yemenite, is a mixture of the Yemenite tradition and the printed edition. Yemenite: Middle of PRE 6–beginning of 53. Printed edition: PRE 1–6.

**9ח**: Jerusalem, The National Library of Israel, MS Heb. 28°1270, 1576, 44 pages (NLI B 121 28°1270). Yemenite. PRE 11–54.

## References

Börner-Klein, Dagmar (ed.). 2004. *Pirke de-Rabbi Elieser: nach der Edition Venedig 1544 unter Berücksichtigung der Edition Warschau 1852.* Studia Judaica 26. Berlin: De Gruyter.

Buber, Salomon (ed.). 1894. *Agadischer Commentar zum Pentateuch nach einer Handschrift aus Aleppo.* 2 vols. Vienna: A. Fanto.

Friedlander, Gerald (trans.). 1970. *Pirkê de Rabbi Eliezer (The Chapters of Rabbi Eliezer the Great) According to the Text of the Manuscript Belonging to Abraham Epstein of Vienna.* Reprint. New York: Hermon Press.

Gottlieb, Leeor. 2021. 'Towards a More Precise Understanding of Pseudo-Jonathan's Origins'. *Aramaic Studies* 19: 104–20.

Mack, Hananel. 2010. *The Mystery of Rabbi Moshe Hadarshan*. Jerusalem: Bialik Institute. [Hebrew]

McDowell, Gavin. 2021. 'The Date and Provenance of Targum Pseudo-Jonathan: The Evidence of Pirqe deRabbi Eliezer and the Chronicles of Moses'. *Aramaic Studies* 19: 121–54.

———. 2025. *The Rewritten Bible in Late Antiquity: Pirqe de-Rabbi Eliezer, Jubilees, and the Cave of Treasures*. Studia Judaica. Berlin: De Gruyter.

Parenzo, Asher (ed.). 1590. *Ḥamišah Ḥumše Torah… Targum Onqelos We-Targum Yerušalmi… 'im Targum Yonatan Ben 'Uzzi'el*. 3 vols. Venice: Giovanni di Gara.

Patmore, Hector M. 2015. *The Transmission of Targum Jonathan in the West: A Study of Italian and Ashkenazi Manuscripts of the Targum to Samuel*. Journal of Semitic Studies Supplement 35. Oxford: Oxford University Press.

Treitl, Eliezer. 2012. *Pirke de-Rabbi Eliezer: Text, Redaction and a Sample Synopsis*. Jerusalem: Yad Izhak Ben Zvi. [Hebrew]

Treitl, Eliezer. 2020. 'Pirke de-Rabbi Eliezer: Transcription and Synopsis'. Accessed 10 June 2024. https://fjms.genizah.org/ (under "Mahadura").

Vilna Shas = Talmud Bavli. Vilna: Widow and Brothers Romm. 37 vols. 1880–1886.

# FROM פשוטו של מקרא TO פשטיה דקרא: THE ORIGINS OF PESHAT COMMENTARY IN ELEVENTH AND TWELFTH CENTURY RABBINIC EXEGESIS

*Robert Harris*

From the time that Sarah Kamin began to investigate the significance of the term פשוטו של מקרא and the implications for methodology in the biblical commentaries of Rashi, she had determined that it would be worthwhile to preface that investigation with research into the formulaic expression פשטיה דקרא in ancient rabbinic literature before arriving in the Middle Ages. Kamin proceeded in this way to more explicitly clarify the ways in which Rashi innovated in his approach to reading Scripture beyond his predecessors in northern Europe and, in particular, to clarify the distinction between Rashi's eschewing reliance on the ancient Rabbinic Aramaic formula פשטיה דקרא in favour of the Hebrew term מקרא של פשוטו (Kamin 1986, 23). And as is well known by now, Kamin concluded that one ought not to treat the two similarly sounding terms as equivalent semantically in any way. The goal of the present study is to examine the subject in the hopes of clarifying the circumstances through which Rashi and the northern French exegetes who followed him chose the פשוטו של

מקרא terminology to express their understanding of 'the plain sense of Scripture'.

Two caveats before I proceed: in this study I will not treat the development of Arabic expressions of what would later be identified as *peshat* methodology in the context of Judeo–Islamic cultural and intellectual interaction. Even though both rabbinic and Karaite exegetes in the Mediterranean/Islamic world adopted some of the fundamental principles and methodologies of plain sense exegesis that were current in Islamic intellectual circles well before any such development took place in northern Europe, the vast preponderance of this scholarship was expressed in Arabic—and this language was all but unknown in Europe, among both churchmen and rabbis, until well into the twelfth-century and beyond. As it happened, the principal fruits of this scholarship were first made known among the rabbis of northern France only in the mid twelfth-century via the biblical commentaries of R. Abraham ibn Ezra, whose principled understanding of the 'rule of *peshat*' differed significantly from that which had developed by that time in northern France (see Cohen 2020).

My second caveat: I do not intend to offer any 'smoking gun' of evidence for Christian influence on the origins of *peshat* among the rabbis of northern France: contrary to Mordechai Cohen's musings about the parallels between Bruno the Carthusian and Rashi (see Cohen 2020, 111–23; see also Cohen 2017, 2021; and in response Harris 2023), I do not believe he has made a strong case. Moreover, I doubt that evidence of such contact between Rashi and specific Christian scholars is ever likely to turn up. Although here and there one may discover evidence of rabbis' knowledge of Christian exegesis or culture in their own biblical commentaries, in the main there was simply too much animus between them to make much of that possible. And while we have plenty of evidence for Jewish–Christian intellectual and social exchange with respect to biblical interpretation in the twelfth-century and beyond, there is previous little that is concrete for the eleventh-century and earlier. Rather, my hope is always to provide a likely scenario for such influence, and building upon the research of certain key scholars,[1] seek to find within the supremely dominant intellectual world of Christian Europe a plausible argument for the ways in which *peshat* interpretive methodologies developed among the rabbis who lived there, in a Christian environment in which a new emphasis on *sensus litteralis* emerged in virtually the same time and place.

## 1.0. Rashi's Turn towards the Plain Sense

As I stated earlier, since a scholar like Rashi could not read most of the classic works of grammar and lexicography, which were composed almost exclusively in Arabic, we would do well to search for the answers to questions surrounding the origin of *peshat* both in the circumstances of Rashi's own rabbinic education, as well as setting that within the context of contemporary Christian scholarship. Put differently, my claim is that the dramatic developments in the methodologies of biblical interpretation in northern Europe during the mid-eleventh-

---

[1] In particular, I have been greatly influenced by the scholarship of Sarah Kamin, Elazar Touitou, Sara Japhet, Avraham Grossman, and Brian Stock.

century, represented initially by the exegesis of Rashi, grew out of both ancient, and especially more immediately, prior rabbinic scholarship that he had studied and incorporated, as well as trends of which Rashi may have been aware in the surrounding Christian environment and that he applied (whether consciously or unconsciously) to his own program of scholarship.

The overall contours of Rashi's rabbinic knowledge are well known and have been sketched well by Avraham Grossman (1988, 233–96; 1995, 121–253). Under the guidance of R. Jacob b. Yakar in Mainz and R. Isaac Halevi in Worms, as well as other teachers, Rashi mastered the entire legacy of rabbinic Judaism, law and lore, much of which 'Oral Torah' already existed in written format when he studied in Germany.[2] In the context of this essay, the most important written work that helped guide him away from the purely midrashic exegesis that was dominant in rabbinic circles and towards a consideration of plain sense exegesis was the *Mahberet* by Menahem ibn Saruk, a biblical Hebrew lexicon written in tenth-century Muslim Spain that was one of the few major (albeit early) works of grammar and linguistics composed in Hebrew. Rashi's high estimation of Menahem is well-known.[3] Moreover, as I have demonstrated elsewhere,

---

[2] Grossman attests to the great number of manuscripts Rashi was able to consult in the German yeshivot.

[3] For the investigation of Rashi's reliance on Menahem, I am grateful for the help of Hillel Novetzky and the search engines at www.alhatorah.org. Rashi cites Menahem some nine times in his Genesis commentary (at Gen. 11.28, 15.2, 30.8, 30.41, 30.42, 32.25, 35.16, 49.19, 49.26), six times in Exodus (at Exod. 2.10, 3.22, 9.33, 13.16, 21.13, 28.22) and twice each in Leviticus (Lev. 19.19, 26.21), Numbers (Num.

beyond pure philology, Rashi relied on Menahem to develop an understanding of a variety of dimensions of biblical composition. But most importantly for our purposes, Rashi adopted Menahem's pithy adage about context as the most important determinant of meaning, פתרונו לפי ענינו, 'its explanation follows its context'.[4]

---

10.36, 2.8), and Deuteronomy (Deut. 7.13, 32.26). In most of these, Rashi refers to Menachem with variations of "Menahem composed/interpreted/explained" ("מנחם פירש", "חברו מנחם", or "מנחם פתר"). In a couple of these cases, Rashi cites the fuller name, "מנחם בן סרוק". This was already noted by Abraham Berliner (1866; 1905) in his editions of Rashi, and Zvi Filipowski (1854) in his edition of the *Mahberet*. More recently, Aaron Mirsky (1987) also attempted to demonstrate that there are cases where Rashi is relying on the *Mahberet* even though he does not cite it. He notes that there are several instances where Rashi brings the same explanation as Menachem, with the same proof texts, in the same order, even when that order does not match that of Bible. See, for example, Rashi on Gen. 31.36 (compared to the *Mahberet* s.v. דלק); Rashi on Lev. 1.15 (compared to the *Mahberet* s.v. מץ); and Rashi on Gen. 24.20 (compared to the *Mahberet* s.v. ער). In his commentary on the rest of the Bible, Rashi cites Menahem another 200 or so times (see Novetsky, n.d., nn. 67–68). The superb, recently published critical edition of the *Mahberet* (Maman and Mirsky 2023) arrived too late to be included in this study.

[4] On Menahem's development of this adage, see Harris (1997, 282–86 and nn. 7–15). Rashi cites the phrase only in his commentaries on the prophetic books, which leads one to assume that he only read Menahem later in life, having long left the German academies of his youth. See Rashi on 2 Sam. 17.20; 2 Kgs 17.9; Ezek. 21.20; Hos. 13.5; Joel 2.7; Mic. 1.10. Elsewhere I have demonstrated that Rashi relied on Menahem for his understanding of interrogative parallelism, and adopted Menahem's כפל terminology to describe it (see Harris 2004, 35–47).

Nonetheless, Menahem's status as a source of Rashi's methodological approach to interpreting Scripture pales in comparison to the role played by ancient rabbinic literature: it is to Rashi's deep knowledge of rabbinic texts gained through his study in the German *yeshivot* that we must turn to begin assessing the roots of his exegetical methodology, and it is through this that we look to see the role the root פש״ט played in expressing his interpretation of Scripture.

## 2.0. The Root פש״ט in Early Rabbinic Exegesis

Let us turn first to what had often (though erroneously) been thought of as a forerunner to medieval rabbinic *peshat*. The ancient rabbinic sages employed two terms that employ the same root of פש״ט in the context of biblical exegesis.[5] These are rabbinic Hebrew פשוטו של מקרא and the Aramaic formulation, פשטיה

---

[5] The sages also used other terms to express what is generally construed as 'plain sense', most prominently the word משמע, *sense*; see, e.g., Mekhilta de Rabbi Ishmael, *Nezikin* 21:6: מה תלמוד לומר ועבדו לעולם – עד היובל. או ועבדו לעולם כמשמעו, תלמוד לומר ושבתם איש אל אחוזתו, "What does Scripture mean by stating and *he shall serve him forever*? (Exod. 21.6). It means: Until the Jubilee. Or perhaps it means 'forever' according to (the word's common) sense (meaning)? Scripture (elsewhere) states: *each person shall return to his (family) holding* (Lev. 25.10)" (See Horowitz and Rabin 1960, 254). But an examination of that technical term throughout ancient rabbinic interpretation requires its own investigation.

דקרא.⁶ While the root פש״ט exists in Biblical Hebrew, most frequently in the sense of 'removing clothing',⁷ the sages do not define either term when the root is found ostensibly in the context of biblical exegesis. In general, Kamin understood both phrases in their ancient contexts not as methodological formulas akin to the way they were employed by medieval exegetes, but as a term equivalent to "the biblical text itself" (Kamin 1986, 27–31).⁸ The former (Hebrew) term appears only three times in the Talmud, and even there, is stated only with respect to the lack of importance the idea held for the ancient rabbinic sages. We see this most clearly in one of the three attestations of the phrase in rabbinic literature:

א"ר כהנא כד הוינא בר תמני סרי שנין והוה גמירנא ליה לכוליה תלמודא
ולא הוה ידענא דאין מקרא יוצא מידי פשוטו עד השתא.

'R. Kahana stated: I was eighteen years old and had studied already the entirety of the Talmud,⁹ and I did not know that

---

⁶ Arguably, the term פשט, 'peshat', which functions as a medieval rabbinic Hebrew noun, is itself Aramaic (see Japhet 2013).

⁷ See, e.g., Gen. 37.23; Lev. 6.4; 16.23, etc. Other uses include: to flay an animal offering (Lev. 1.6); and to deploy as a military formation (Judg. 9.44).

⁸ Moreover, Kamin echoes Bacher's nineteenth-century observation that, paradoxically, even most of the contexts in which the ancient sages employ the expression פשטיה דקרא generally appear with reference to midrashic explanations of the biblical text (see Kamin 1986, 29, n. 32).

⁹ Since R. Kahana lived in the third century, the reference to 'Talmud' must mean the Mishnah.

"a Scriptural-verse never leaves the hands of the text, itself."[10]

In contradistinction to the Hebrew formula פשוטו של מקרא, however, the ancient rabbis also employ the Aramaic expression פשטיה דקרא several times. One example must suffice to demonstrate how a formula like פשטיה דקרא in ancient rabbinic literature does not mean what the root פש״ט came to mean in medieval exegesis, despite the apparent closeness of the term might otherwise indicate. In b. *Ketubot* 111b, the sages consider various matters with respect to the World to Come and who might merit such an eternal reward. A variety of rabbinic voices come to the fore, as well as the anonymous voice of the Talmudic narrator. Deep into this discussion, the narrator adduces elements of Genesis 49:11–12 as a prooftext. At this point, the Talmud records:

> פשטיה דקרא במאי כתיב? כי אתא רב דימי אמר: אמרה כנסת ישראל לפני הקב״ה: רבונו של עולם, רמוז בעיניך דבסים מחמרא, ואחוי לי שיניך דבסים מחלבא.
>
> 'The text itself—with respect to what is it written? When Rav Dimi came [from the Land of Israel] to Babylonia, he said: The congregation of Israel said before the Holy One, Praised be God: Master of the Universe: Hint with Your eyes that which is sweeter than wine, and show me Your teeth through that which is sweeter than milk.'

It is patently obvious that when the anonymous narrator asks what the פשטיה דקרא might be, the answer that Rav Dimi gives is

---

[10] This is the formulation found in b. Shabb. 63a; the rule is also cited in b. Yeb. 11b, 24a.

nothing close to what a medieval *pashtan* might construe as the plain meaning of the verse, but rather he offers a beautiful midrashic interpretation about the love God holds for the entire congregation of Israel.[11] And as some of our medieval exegetes might say, as they point out what they consider to be a general feature of biblical composition, "I will share this one example, and let it teach about all of the others:"[12] the overwhelming majority of ancient rabbinic biblical interpretations are pure midrash, they fill both Talmuds and absolutely every work of rabbinic interpretive 'literature', and while on occasion the ancient rabbis do

---

[11] In addition to Ketubot 111b, the phrase פשטיה דקרא במאי כתיב occurs six additional times in ancient rabbinic literature (Kiddushin 80b; Eruvin 23b; Hulin 6a, 133b; Arakhin 8b, 32a); see Kamin (1986, 28, n. 29). The phrase does experience a revival in a variety of medieval rabbinic literature, including both biblical and talmudic commentaries, late midrashim, and legal literature. This may be due primarily to the strength of Aramaic as a language of discourse in medieval rabbinic literature, but the matter deserves its own study.

[12] I employ here an expression that several rabbinic exegetes use when they want to reference a ubiquitous rule or phenomenon: the exegete will cite one occurrence and "let that one stand for all of the others." See, e.g., R. Yosef Kara's observation in his commentary at Isa. 3.1, as is a representative example of his tendency to cite only an example or two and let these stand for the rest of Scripture: "You must apply this principle whenever you read: every place in which you find two words in close proximity, whose (meaning) is not made explicit; or two brief phrases side-by-side and they, being brief, are opaque, do not weary yourself in search of their explanation (i.e., do not turn to a midrashic explanation) for you will always find their explanations within their contexts (lit. 'by their sides'). And I will explain a few of them, and these few will be instructive about the rest of them."

evince interest in what the 'plain meaning' of a biblical text might mean, they do not do so through a consistent formula involving the root פש״ט, nor do they ever develop a consistent approach to interpreting the Bible that is not purely midrashic in character.

To be clear, when most of us think of the noun *peshat* or the methodology of biblical exegesis that the word conveys, the historical context in which we meet the word is typically medieval. In searching for a way to describe the plain sense exegesis in which they were occupied, the medieval commentators drew on the Talmud's five–word 'rule': אין מקרא יוצא מידי פשוטו, 'A scriptural verse never exits from the hands of its... *peshat*(!).'[13] And as is well known, neither ancient or medieval rabbis ever defined that key last word, *peshat* or *peshuto*.[14] To that end, Sarah Kamin (1986, 14) offered a working definition that has been more or less accepted by modern scholars:

> [Peshat is] an explanation (of a biblical passage) according to its language; its syntactic structure; its (immediate) literary context; its literary type, within a dynamic interaction among all of these components. Put differently, an interpretation according to peshat is an interpretation that considers all of the linguistic foundations in its literary

---

[13] Again, the rule is found in antiquity only in b. Shabb. 63a; b. Yeb. 11b, 24a.

[14] For the root פש״ט as found in the Bible, see above. Again, while most often it is found in the context of 'stripping off clothing', it is also found in military contexts; however, unless one wishes to consider the possibility of 'attacking' or 'assaying' a text, it seems the first types of usages are more relevant. For the use of the root in ancient rabbinic literature (פשטיה דקרא and the like), see Kamin (1986, 25–56).

composition, and assigns to each of them an understanding within a complete reading.[15]

However, what may be considered as 'universally accepted' in contemporary scholarship was by no means the case in the Middle Ages; moreover, even then the methodology and its contours developed differently in the Mediterranean world of the Judeo–Islamic intellectual world and that of the Jews in Christian Europe. But neither of these particularly adhered to the way in which the rabbinic Sages employed the root פש״ט in the service of biblical interpretation.

For Rashi, in any case, the preferred terminology through which he expressed his awareness of the Bible for plain–sense exegesis was the Hebrew expression פשוטו של מקרא, most famously expressed in his celebrated comment on Genesis 3:8 (MS Leipzig 1):

יש מדרשי אגדה רבים, וכבר סדרום רבותינו על מכונם בבראשית רבה ובשאר מדרשים. ואני לא באתי אלא לפשוטו של מקרא, לאגדה המיישבת דברי המקרא, ופשוטו ושמועתו, דבר דבור על אפניו.

'There are many homiletical midrashim (on these verses), and the Rabbis have long ago arranged them in their proper place in Genesis Rabba and the other midrashim. Whereas I have only come to explain Scripture according to its plain

---

[15] See also Japhet (2000, 55): "[peshat is an exegetical method] through which the text is explained in its context and understood as a linguistic expression which is subject to all the rules of language and methods of literary expression and in which the understanding of the text is based on common sense and accepted customs [מנהגו של עולם; lit., the custom of the world]" (my translation).

meaning [*peshuto*], [and] according to the aggadah that settles matters of Scriptures and [both] its plain meaning and its sense (will be) "a matter understood according to its character" (lit. 'a word fitly spoken'; see Prov. 25.11).'[16]

While this is not the place to fully consider the ramifications and details of this passage, nor the precise version we should attribute to Rashi (the manuscript tradition being quite muddled in many particulars), the main point of this passage is clear enough for our present purposes: Rashi has chosen the Hebrew expression he found in the Talmud, פשוטו של מקרא, to express his incipient understanding of the plain sense of biblical literature. And even if Rashi's Torah commentary is in the main a midrashic anthology and not primarily a 'plain sense' enterprise—the ratio of *derash* to *peshat* in Rashi's Torah commentary is approximately 75% to 25% (Grossman 1995, 194)—it is important for us to appreciate his choice of terminology within the context of his truly innovative project.

Thus, given the utter dominance of midrash in ancient rabbinic biblical exegesis, and possibility of at least some variety in 'available' terminology to express what would come to be considered *peshat* by the twelfth-century, it is important for us to ask: What led an exegete like Rashi to choose the path of incorporating the goal of explicating the 'plain meaning' of the Bible in his exegesis? And in particular for our purposes: what led him to

---

[16] This key statement is famously difficult, and has been transmitted in the best manuscripts and early editions in a variety of versions. See Harris (2023, 5 n. 13).

choose the term פשוטו של מקרא to describe the 'plain sense exegesis' that his commentary occasionally featured?[17]

I believe the most plausible explanation for Rashi's decision to incorporate plain sense exegesis in his commentary, even if infrequently, and specifically to adopt the formula פשוטו של מקרא to describe plain sense, was due to the turn towards *ad litteram* exegesis that the Christian world saw particularly in the post-Carolingian period. In fact, we might even go so far as to suggest that Rashi's decision to incorporate the phrase פשוטו של מקרא as representative of this new turn in exegesis was precisely because it seemed like a Hebrew expression of the Latin term *sensus litteralis (scriptoris)*.

---

[17] Of course, were we to consider the full exegetical program that Rashi's commentary represented, we would be duty bound to ask similar questions with respect to the terminology Rashi developed to express the terms through which he channeled the midrashim he incorporated, adapted and/or combined and rewrote in his commentary. I am thinking of the term האגדה המיישבת, 'aggadah [rabbinic narrative] that settles matters of Scriptures', or any exegetical observation he made employing the root יש״ב in the *piʿel* and other related Hebrew conjugations. Whatever Rashi precisely intended by this elusive term, he employs it to signal some sub-category of midrashic texts from the larger corpus of midrashic literature that had reached the European Jewish academies of his day. Moreover, applying the root Hebrew root יש״ב in the *piʿel* conjugation, in contexts of biblical exegesis, is a strategy that he essentially invented whole cloth: the root in the *piʿel* conjugation is exceedingly rare in all forms of Hebrew literature that preceded him. The root occurs precisely one time in the Hebrew Bible (Ezek. 25.4). See Greenberg (1997, 518); there, Greenberg cites the usage in rabbinic Hebrew, j.Shabbat 13c.

## 3.0. Charlemagne's Educational Reforms and the Origins of *Peshat*

Analogous to the way in which any examination of the origin of Judeo–Arabic plain sense biblical exegesis (among both Rabbanites and Karaites) must begin with the Muslim conquest of the remnants of the Roman empire from the Middle East to North Africa and Spain, and the subsequent inheritance of ancient Greek wisdom by learned Muslim scholars, so, too, we ought to look for the origins of *peshat* in northern Europe in the conquests of Charlemagne in the late eighth-century. For I believe that one can only understand the twelfth-century 'renaissance' in Christian scholarship, with its emphasis on *ad litteram* biblical studies, in light of the re-introduction of the curriculum of the *trivium*—and in particular grammar and rhetoric—by key players in Charlemagne's government.[18]

It is well documented that Charlemagne (and his father and sons), in an effort to establish and legitimise their new dynasty

---

[18] Whether or not we can really call this period a 'renaissance' is still much debated, but there can be no question that these centuries saw a great upswing in cultural and intellectual productivity. This can be illustrated most simply in terms of book production, that is, by the number of manuscript books that were copied in the Carolingian period. The total number of surviving Latin manuscript books that were produced in Europe before the year 800 is less than two thousand, whereas for the period c. 800–900 we have more than four times as many, perhaps nine thousand (see Pollard n.d.). This represents an enormous growth, and it is worthwhile to remember this when we consider the impact of the study of ancient Roman rhetoric in the ninth–through–eleventh centuries.

following their removal of the Merovingians, engaged the Roman Church and its institutions and endeavoured to co-opt them in the maintenance of the kingdom. This engagement had political, social, and cultural, as well as religious, ramifications in the Carolingian revival. Our concern lies principally in the effects of Carolingian innovations on the development of new strategies for reading, in general, and in interpreting the Bible, in particular.

To be sure, Charles was not only concerned with increasing Christian doctrinal and exegetical knowledge and religious commitment, but also and equally with the creation of a learned and literary caste.[19] In general, Charlemagne's approach was to co-opt ancient secular learning in the service of the Church. To accomplish this on the most rudimentary level, of course, he needed to institute schools that would teach far greater numbers of people how to read.[20] Moreover, the interests of Charlemagne and his advisors were by no means limited to Christian liturgy and

---

[19] Charlemagne's *Epistola de Litteris Colendis,* 'the Epistle on the Cultivating of Letters' (786) already demonstrates this interest: "Since it is our concern that the condition of our churches should always advance towards better things, we strive with vigilant zeal to repair the manufactory of learning… [and] to master the studies of the liberal arts" (Translation from King 1987, 208).

[20] See the *Admonitio Generalis* (paragraph 72), which states: "And let schools for teaching boys the psalms, musical notation, singing, computation and grammar be created in every monastery and episcopal residence. And correct catholic books properly, for often, while people want to pray to God in the proper fashion, they yet pray improperly because of uncorrected books. And do not allow your boys to corrupt them, either in reading or in copying" (King 1987, 217).

the recitation of Psalms. Rather, they directed steps to be taken that would open up the ancient cultural heritage of Greco–Roman antiquity to the scholars whom they sponsored at various centres of learning throughout the Carolingian empire. Charlemagne's interest led to a revival of the ancient *triivium*, the first three of the so-called liberal arts including rhetoric, logic and, first and foremost, grammar.[21] In general, Charlemagne's efforts to cultivate study and learning in his kingdom encompassed a serious and long-term policy to establish the study of 'literature' (or letters) as the foundation of the learned Christian society to which he aspired.[22] And while Charlemagne's decrees encompass a clear

---

[21] As Martin Irvine states, Charlemagne's famous *Admonitio Generalis* and other legislative acts "effectively made grammatical culture the law of the land... *Grammatica* supplied special technologies of authority—literacy, normative latinity, knowledge of a literary canon, the scribal arts, book production—which became part of a larger ideology. Without *grammatica* laws and charters could not be written, the Scriptures could not be read, copied, or interpreted..." (Irvine 1994, 305–6; see also 521, n. 112).

[22] Charlemagne's *Epistola de Litteris Colendis*, 'the Epistle on the Cultivating of Letters', is an important witness to his aspiration for the creation of a literary culture. In it, he requires that the clergy should "devote their efforts to the study of literature and to the teaching of it, each according to his ability, to those on whom God has bestowed the capacity to learn; that, just as the observance of a rule gives soundness to their conduct, so also an attention to teaching and learning may give order and adornment to their words" (cited from Loyn and Percival 1975, 63–64; for a different translation, see King 1987, 232–233). As we shall see, noting "order and adornment" in biblical literature are key components of twelfth-century commentaries.

doctrinal agenda for the establishment and practice of orthodox Christianity, nonetheless the directive to incorporate ancient Roman, pre-Christian tracts in the effort to understand holy scripture will, as we shall see, unleash in the twelfth-century a 'truthful' understanding of biblical literature that would be seen (both in Christianity and in Judaism) was at variance with established and authoritative traditions of interpretation.[23]

## 4.0. The Eleventh Century

In two brilliant studies, Brian Stock (1983; 1996) has demonstrated the significance of the movement away from oral culture and towards literacy that took place in northwest Europe during the eleventh and twelfth centuries. To take but a single case that exemplifies this shift, in his discussion of the eleventh-century scholarship of Anselm of Canterbury, Stock (1983, 333) concluded that "in composing the Monologion, Anselm effectively replaced a living audience... with a reading public." He continues (Stock 1983, 334):

---

[23] See the continuation of Charlemagne's Epistle: "Wherefore we urge you, not merely to avoid the neglect of the study of literature, but with a devotion that is humble and pleasing to God to strive to learn it, so that you may be able more easily and more rightly to penetrate the mysteries of the holy scriptures. For since there are figures of speech, metaphors and the like to be found on the sacred pages, there can be no doubt. that each man who reads them will understand their spiritual meaning more quickly if he is first of all given full instruction in the study of literature" (Loyn and Percival 1975, 64).

> When [Anselm] states… that he intends to support his position not at all through scriptural authority… we must understand, not a rejection of the Bible, but an attempt to move beyond simple reading and discussion to a more logical, abstract consideration of biblical texts…. His intention is not to improve on the ancients, but to discuss matters which had not sufficiently attracted their attention…[24]
> In other words, the text is the bridge between *ratio* and *auctoritas*… Anselm, therefore, plays the role…of someone in conversation with himself who both internalizes a textual methodology and anticipates a written product.

In that example, Stock pointed to philosophical discourse; my concern here is exegesis, and the hermeneutical perspective that drove it. But Stock is insightful about the way in which his observation may also encompass the semantic autonomy of exegesis: "When writing replaces speaking, the result is 'literature'…. In the interplay of text and audience, the work helps to create… [a] very segmented public" (Stock 1996, 102–3).

Essentially, my claim herein is that twelfth-century *pashtanim* and *ad litteram* exegetes were one such "very segmented public." Rabbinic and Victorine biblical exegetes were the משכילים, *maskilim*, literally, the *illuminati*,[25] who reimagined what it meant to 'access' biblical texts, and who chose to express their principles and observations by means of glossed commentaries. Moreover,

---

[24] See Rashbam's claim that in pursuing *peshat* exclusively, he is 'merely' concentrating on matters that the ancients ignored (commentary on Gen. 37.2).

[25] This is the group of rabbinic intellectuals to whom Rashbam repeatedly appeals throughout his commentaries; see, e.g., his comment on Gen. 1.1 and his introduction to Exod. 21.

while glossing in this way was not a new technology of reading for Christians, it marked for Jews the incorporation of a completely new genre in Jewish intellectual output. In fact, it became the mode, par excellence, of Jewish intellectual expression precisely during the era in which rabbinic Judaism transitioned from a predominantly oral culture to a literary culture.[26] Moreover, the modality of the glossed commentaries that both the French rabbis and Christian schoolmen produced during the twelfth-century Renaissance were predominantly rhetorical in character, that is, they followed, either consciously or unconsciously, the rhetorical programs set forth in the ancient Roman works of Cicero and Quintilian for their interrogation of biblical literature.

In a 1995 study entitled *Rhetoric, Hermeneutics, and Translation in the Middle Ages*, Rita Copeland (1995, 63) perspicaciously states, "Medieval exegesis replicates rhetoric's productive application to discourse."[27] She suggests that to truly understand the work of the medieval Christian exegete, one must learn how they have appropriated models of classical rhetoric such as are found in Quintilian's *Institutio* (Copeland 1995, 64):

---

[26] In a series of past studies, I have stressed the significance of northern French rabbinic adoption of the commentary genre to express the new plain sense exegesis, a process that I have described as "two–fingered exegesis," with one finger, so to speak, in the core text while a second finger followed an *ad locum* gloss to be guided towards the meaning of the passage in context (see e.g., Harris 2019, 62–63). For an insightful study of the movement 'from oral to literary' in rabbinic Judaism, see Fishman (2011).

[27] I am grateful to Kathy Eden for first directing me to Copeland's important study.

> [C]ommentators use rhetorical systems and techniques as modi interpretandi... First there is the analysis of rhetorical devices of style, structure, and argument in the text.... But there is also a second level at which textual commentary appropriates rhetorical principles. Commentaries use rhetorical categories of argumentation or, more generally, heuristic strategies, to define and organize the exposition itself. In this respect then, commentaries do not simply discover and describe rhetorical elements in the texts they treat. Rather, the commentaries themselves are governed by rhetorical assumptions.

What is striking is that this definition is equally characteristic of the rabbinic *peshat* commentaries of the twelfth-century Renaissance. While not perhaps presented in as sophisticated terminological or philosophical construct as found in typical Christian exegesis, the transition from eleventh-century rabbinic exegetes such as Rashi to exclusively plain-sense twelfth-century commentaries such as Rashbam or R. Eliezer of Beaugency demonstrates an increased attention to strictly literary matters and rhetorical concerns.

As it is increasingly understood that the Jewish community of twelfth-century France was not isolated as was once thought but was completely immersed in and an essential part of Christian society (see Chazan 2010), it is difficult to believe that this integration was social and economic only and not also touched at least to some important degree by the intellectual changes that were sweeping through Europe. We know of a certainty that Jews and Christians, both learned and unlearned, discussed Scriptures with each other, not only in overtly polemical constructs (which were more characteristic of the thirteenth-century and later), but in a wide variety of social and economic circumstances (see Van Engen 2001, 153; and in response to this, Harris 2011). It is true that one cannot cite a twelfth-century rabbinic source that explicitly cites an ancient Roman work of rhetoric; indeed, it is highly unlikely that any ever did. But I think that holding an argument to that level of prooftext is unfair and counter-productive, as it effectively blinds the eye to the possibility of Jewish scholars being exposed in one manner of speaking or another to Christian intellectual currents. While it is, of course, not sufficient to rely entirely on an argument of *Zeitgeist,* one ought not ignore the implications of northwest European rabbinic culture developing a particular type of literary expression that had virtually no Jewish precedent (and certainly none in Europe) but which was precisely the type of expression increasingly employed by the surrounding and dominating Christian culture (see Touitou 2003, 11–33).

## 5.0. Conclusion

The present study has suggested that the innovative nature of eleventh- and twelfth-century rabbinic culture be understood in three distinct ways: (a) the fundamental idea of a individually-intuited and consistent plain sense exegesis that represents a remarkable shift away from the traditional, authoritative exegesis represented by ancient rabbinic midrash and Christian *allegoria*; (b) the adoption of the formula פשוטו של מקרא as an eleventh-twelfth-century rabbinic concomitant to contemporary Christian *sensus litteralis*, with the attendant emphasis on a rhetorical understanding of the biblical literature in question; and (c) the commentary genre through which Rashi and all subsequent rabbinic exegetes expressed themselves (a written genre that while typical of Christian scholars from its foundational period but all but completely unknown in rabbinic culture expressed in Hebrew)—all these are hallmarks of contemporary Christian intellectual thought and practice that were hitherto unknown in northern European rabbinic culture.

## References

Berliner, Abraham. 1866. *Rashi on the Torah: The Commentary of Solomon B. Isaac*. Berlin: Levant Publishers.

———. 1905. *Rashi: The Commentary of Solomon B. Isaac on the Torah*. Frankfurt: J. Kauffmann

Chazan, Robert. 2010. *Reassessing Jewish Life in Medieval Europe*. New York: Cambridge University Press.

Cohen, Mordechai Z. 2017. 'A New Perspective of Rashi of Troyes in Light of Bruno the Carthusian: Exploring Jewish and Christian Bible Interpretation in Eleventh Century Northern France'. *Viator* 48 (1): 39–86.

———. 2020. *The Rule of Peshat: Jewish Constructions of the Plain Sense of Scripture and Their Christian and Muslim Contexts, 900–1270*. Philadelphia: University of Pennsylvania Press.

———. 2021. *Rashi, Biblical Interpretation, and Latin Learning in Medieval Europe: A New Perspective on an Exegetical Revolution*. Cambridge: Cambridge University Press.

Copeland, Rita. 1995. *Rhetoric, Hermeneutics, and Translation in the Middle Ages: Academic Traditions and Vernacular Text*. Cambridge: Cambridge University Press.

Filipowski, Zvi. 1854. *Mahberet Menahem*. London: Hebrew Antiquarian Society.

Fishman, Talya. 2011. *Becoming the People of the Talmud: Oral Torah as Written Tradition in Medieval Jewish Cultures*. Philadelphia: University of Pennsylvania Press.

Greenberg, Moshe. 1997. *Ezekiel 21–37: A New Translation, With Introduction and Commentary*. New York: Doubleday.

Grossman, Avraham. 1988. *The Early Sages of Ashkenaz*. Jerusalem: The Magnes Press, The Hebrew University. [Hebrew]

———. 1995. *The Early Sages of France: Their Lives, Leadership and Works*. Jerusalem: The Hebrew University Magnes Press. [Hebrew]

Harris, Robert A. 1997. 'The Literary Hermeneutic of Rabbi Eliezer of Beaugency'. PhD dissertation, Jewish Theological Seminary.

———. 2004. *Discerning Parallelism: A Study in Northern French Medieval Jewish Biblical Exegesis*. Providence, RI: Brown Judaic Studies.

———. 2011. 'The Book of Leviticus Interpreted as Jewish Community'. *Studies in Christian–Jewish Relations* 6: 1–15.

———. 2019. 'From "Religious Truth–Seeking" to Reading: The Twelfth Century Renaissance and the Emergence of Peshat and Ad Litteram as Methods of Accessing the Bible'. In *The Oral and the Textual in Jewish Tradition and Jewish Education*, edited by Jonathan Cohen, Matt Goldish, and Barry Holtz, 54–89. Jerusalem: The Hebrew University Magnes Press.

———. 2023. 'Peshat Rules: Two Recent Publications By Mordechai Cohen'. *JSIJ: Jewish Studies, an Internet Journal* 23: 1–15.

Horowitz, Haim S., and Israel A. Rabin. 1960. *Mekhilta De-Rabbi Yishmael*. Jerusalem: Bamberger & Wahrman.

Irvine, Martin. 1994. *The Making of Textual Culture: 'Grammatica' and Literary Theory, 350–1100*. Cambridge: Cambridge University Press.

Japhet, Sara. 2000. *The Commentary of Rabbi Samuel Ben Meir (Rashbam) on the Book of Job*. Jerusalem: The Hebrew University Magnes Press.

Kamin, Sarah. 1986. *Rashi's Exegetical Categorization in Respect to the Distinction Between Peshat and Derash*. Jerusalem: The Hebrew University Magnes Press. [Hebrew]

King, P. D. 1987. *Charlemagne: Translated Sources*. Lambrigg, Kendal, Cumbria: P. D. King.

Loyn, H. R., and John Percival. 1975. *The Reign of Charlemagne: Documents on Carolingian Government and Administration*. New York: St. Martin's Press.

Maman, Aaron, and Hananel Mirsky. 2023. *The Maḥberet of Menaḥem Ben Saruq: Annotated Critical Edition*. Jerusalem: Academy of Hebrew Language.

Mirsky, Aaron. 1987. 'Rashi and the Mahberet Menahem'. *Sinai* 100: 579–86.

Novetsky, Hillel, et al. n.d. 'R. Shelomo Yitzchaki (Rashi)'. Accessed 25 April 2024. https://alhatorah.org/Commentators: R._Shelomo_Yitzchaki_(Rashi)/0

Pollard, Richard Matthew. n.d. 'Carolingian Literature at Reichenau and St. Gall'. In *Carolingian Culture at Reichenau & St. Gall: The Carolingian Libraries of St. Gall and Reichenau,* edited by Patrick J. Geary et al. Accessed 25 April 2024. https://web.archive.org/web/20210427014057/http://www.stgallplan.org/en/tours_carol_literature.html

Stock, Brian. 1983. *The Implications of Literacy: Written Language and Models of Interpretation in the 11th and 12th Centuries.* Princeton: Princeton University Press.

———. 1996. *Listening for the Text: On the Uses of the Past.* Philadelphia: University of Pennsylvania Press.

Touitou, Elazar. 2003. *Exegesis in Perpetual Motion: Studies in the Pentateuchal Commentary of Rabbi Samuel Ben Meir.* Ramat Gan: Bar Ilan University Press. [Hebrew]

Van Engen, John. 2001. 'Ralph of Flaix: The Book of Leviticus Interpreted as Christian Community'. In *Jews and Christians in Twelfth-Century Europe,* edited by Michael A Signer and John Van Engen, 150–70. Notre Dame, IN: University of Notre Dame Press.

# INDEX OF TEXTS

## Hebrew Bible

### Genesis

265, 320 n. 38, 326, 444 n. 3

1–3: 136, 139
1.1: 458 n. 25
1.14: 408
1.29: 19
3.8: 451
3.9: 273 n. 13
3.15: 59
4.2–4: 411
4.8: 277
6.2: 110 n. 11
8.20: 411
11.8: 413–14
11.27: 325
11.28: 444 n. 3
14.14: 425
14.15–18: 322
14.18: 326 n. 51
15.1: 277
15.2: 444 n. 3
15.4: 60
18.21: 416
19.19: 59
22.9: 428
24.20: 445 n. 3
24.48: 54
25.27: 418–19
27.1: 420
27.6: 420
27.15: 418–19
27.19, 31: 59 n. 31
30.8, 41, 42: 444 n. 3
31.29: 95 n. 18
31.36: 445 n. 3
32.3: 229 n. 27
32.25: 444 n. 3
35.16: 444 n. 3
36.8: 270
37.2: 458 n. 24
37.7: 28
37.20: 58 n. 29, 66 n. 45
37.23: 447 n. 7
37.33: 66 n. 45
37.37: 58 n. 29
38.9: 31
40.3–14: 270
40.11: 275 n. 16
40.12: 272–73, 275–77
40.13: 276
40.15: 56 n. 24
40.18: 273 n. 13, 274–78
41.40: 61
41.44–57: 270
45.28: 58 n. 29
47.19: 62
48.22: 418
49.1: 277
49.11–12: 448
49.19: 444 n. 3
49.24: 30

### Exodus

386, 444 n. 3

1.14: 274
1.19: 34–35
2.10: 444 n. 3
3.22: 444 n. 3
6.7: 192
6.22: 47
7.1: 321 n. 40
9.33: 54, 444 n. 3
12.29: 325 n. 50
12.42: 394 n. 8
13.16: 444 n. 3
13.17–15.26: 386, 396
13.21: 55
14.13: 390, 399

14.13–14: 387, 393–97, 399–400
14.14: 386, 390, 392, 395, 399–400
14.30–15.18: 12, 396, 400
15.2: 65
15.3: **385–404**
15.18: 394 n. 8
19.1–20.26: 386
21: 458 n. 25
21.6: 446 n. 5
21.12: 191 n. 7
21.13: 444 n. 3
24.10: 423
25.29: 276
28.22: 444 n. 3
33.13: 190
37.16: 276

Leviticus

444 n. 3
1.6: 447 n. 7
1.15: 445 n. 3
6.4: 447 n. 7
10.4: 47
14.4: 35
16.23: 447 n. 7
19.19: 444 n. 3
21.5: 117
23.40: 305
25.10: 446 n. 5
26.21: 444 n. 3
26.37: 54 n. 20

Numbers

444 n. 3
2.8: 445 n. 3
3.30: 47
4.7: 276
7.13, 19, 25, 31, 37, 43, 49, 55, 61, 67, 73, 79, 84–85: 276
6.1: 406 n. 2
6.24: 57 n. 27
6.24–26: 217
6.25: 59
9.67: 118
10.36: 445 n. 3
11.26: 273 n. 13
14.31: 48
16.19: 431
24.22: 273 n. 13

Deuteronomy

8, 188–89, 193 n. 9, 198–99, 202–3, 205–7, 445 n. 3
1.33: 55 n. 21
1.41: 189
2.37: 63 n. 38
4.1: 188–89, 199, 202
4.5: 189
4.6: 61 n. 35
4.10, 14: 189
4.25–27: 203
4.6–9: 217
4.31: 60
5.4: 316 n. 30, 321
5.5: 316, 320–21
5.31: 188
6.18: 110 n. 11
7.13: 445 n. 3
8.5: 61 n. 36
8.10: 110 n. 11
9.16: 189
11.17: 110 n. 11
11.19: 189
12.14: 61
12.28: 61
20.18: 188
21.12: 48
22.5: 406 n. 2
23.5: 61
24.13: 61
28.29: 270
31.6: 59
31.8: 59 n. 32
32.1: 273 n. 13
32.8: 414
32.10: 65 n. 41
32.26: 445 n. 3
32.33: 276
32.34: 276
33.11: 28

## Joshua

46

1.5: 59 n. 32
19.30: 47

## Judges

1.31: 47
5.25: 276
9.8: 64
9.44: 447 n. 7
9.54: 66 n. 45
14.17: 66 n. 45
20.42: 66 n. 45

## 1 Samuel

266

1.6: 65 n. 43
1.22: 48 n. 9
1.24: 66 n. 44
2.4: 53 n. 18
14.50: 47
16.14: 66
18.28: 66 n. 45
23.17: 59

## 2 Samuel

266

6.1: 125 n. 19
11.1: 121
13.20: 47
17.20: 445 n. 4
25.15: 110 n. 11

## 1 Kings

266

7.6: 108, 109 n. 9, 111–12
7.43: 111–12
10.7: 55

## 2 Kings

266

2: 46
5.10: 32
9.2: 48 n. 10
17.9: 445 n. 4
17.21: 324 n. 48
20.6: 55

## Isaiah

107, 139, 174, 175 n. 29, 192, 267, 268

3.1: 449 n. 12
4.5: 107
5.5: 21
5.19: 58 n. 28
7.14: 328 n. 54
7.17: 324 n. 48
8.14: 324 n. 48
8.18: 21, 107
9.7: 16 n. 1
13.20: 125 n. 19
13.21–22: 226 n. 23
16.11: 92 n. 14
19.8: 27
27.3: 276
28.13: 276
28.21: 107
34.7: 65 n. 43
34.14: 226 n. 23
35.9: 30
37.26: 48 n. 10
40.30: 51
42.4: 36
42.16: 21
43.28: 21
45.7: 170 n. 22
45.20–25: 192
46.10: 175
49.1: 107
49.7: 61
49.23: 192
49.26: 30
51.17, 22: 276
59.16: 66 n. 45
60.16: 30
62: 168

## Jeremiah

136, 140, 192–93, 206, 267

9.4: 193
12.16: 192
16.10–11: 203
16.13, 18: 202
16.19–21: 193

16.21: 192–93, 198–99
18.18: 58 n. 29
22.24: 65
23.17: 19
23.22: 33
25.9: 48 n. 9
25.13: 48
25.15: 276
31.31–34: 193, 198
31.34: 193
35.7: 19
42.18: 54
49.12: 276
49.24: 65 n. 43
50.29: 49 n. 11
50.43: 66 n. 45
51.7: 276

Ezekiel

5–6, **103–31**, 192, 198 n. 15

14.15: 65 n. 43
14.22: 49 n. 11
15.5: 66 n. 46
16.2: 198 n. 15
17.8: 110 n. 11
18.18: 110 n. 11
19.5, 12: 66 n. 45
20.25: 110 n. 11
20.42: 192
21.20: 445 n. 4
23.31–33: 276
23.33: 276
24.4: 110 n. 11
24.7: 66 nn. 45–46
24.15–24: 121
24.16–17: 121
24.17: 122–24
24.22–23: 122
24.23: 122–24
25.4: 453 n. 17
27.27: 113
30.19–39: 128
31.4: 66 n. 45
34.14: 110 n. 11
34.18: 110 n. 11
34.21: 20
36.23: 192, 198
36.31: 110 n. 11
38.23: 192
39.7: 192
40.3: 120
40.7, 21: 109
40.21: 110, 120 n. 17
40.32: 120
41.1: 108
41.16: 108 n. 8
41.21: 120
41.25: 108, 110 n. 11
41.26: 108
42.5: 125 n. 19
42.11: 119, 120, 126
43.3: 120
43.10: 125
43.21: 107 n. 6
43.26: 112–13
43.34: 120
44.1, 5, 7, 8, 9, 11, 15, 16: 107 n. 6
44.17–31: 118
44.18: 118, 123
44.20: 118, 123
44.22: 117
44.25: 118
44.30: 118
45.4, 18: 107 n. 6
45.20: 110 n. 11
47.12: 107 n. 6
47.14: 124
47.22: 124
48.8: 107 n. 6
48.10: 107 n. 6

Hosea

5.5: 52
13.5: 445 n. 4

Joel

107 n. 7

2.7: 445 n. 4

Amos

6.6: 276

Obadiah

1.16: 276

## Micah

1.10: 445 n. 4

## Nahum

2.4: 276
3.4: 25

## Habakkuk

1.12: 37
3.4: 26

## Zephaniah

1.4: 34
3.2: 63

## Zechariah

3.2: 229, 247
5.4: 66
11.7: 324 n. 48
12.8: 53 n. 18

## Psalms

8, 76, 136, 140, 189, 205–6, 217, 456

6.3: 27
11.6: 276
16.5: 277
25.1: 190
25.4–5: 189, 190
25.7: 190
25.8–9: 190, 199 n. 16
25.10: 190, 199 n. 16
26.2: 64
40.16: 62
51.1: 191
51.15: 192, 206
72.15: 65
74.21: 92 n. 14
75.9: 276
81.8: 61
83.1–4: 81
94.6: 20
94.10: 191
102.21: 30
104.29: 125 n. 19
105.19: 66 n. 45
105.21–22: 203
119.12: 199
132.2, 5: 30
139.8: 61
139.12: 49 n. 12

## Proverbs

52 n. 17, 140

1.28: 59 n. 31
4.6: 59
7.15: 61
7.21: 66 n. 44
16.1: 143
24.17: 24, 52, 54
25.11: 452
26.17: 31
31.1: 66 n. 44
31.12: 66 n. 46

## Job

58, 136, 139, 334, 362

4.12: 65
5.1: 61 n. 36
18.10: 419
20.9: 66 n. 44
20.14: 92 n. 14
21.18: 66 n. 44
27.20: 66 n. 44
28.7: 66 n. 44
33.20: 66 n. 44
33.32: 61 n. 35

## Song of Songs

298

## Ruth

2.16: 119
3.6: 65 n. 43
4.15: 66 n. 44

## Lamentations

298

1.20: 92 n. 14
2.11: 92 n. 14
4.21: 276

Ecclesiastes

298
6.3: 19
9.1: 36

Esther

302, 312 n. 21

Daniel

23–24, 51–52, 53 n. 18

Ezra

9.3: 117 n. 15

Nehemiah

3.34: 27
8.1–8: 15

2 Chronicles

46 n. 5, 47, 55, 266, 268
4.8, 11: 276
9.6: 55
13.9: 34
15.3: 324 n. 48
22.11: 66

## Second Temple Sources

### New Testament

Matthew

2.1: 115
11.12: 115
23.30: 115
24:37: 115

Luke

1.5, 18, 73: 115
4.25: 115
17.26, 28: 115

### Dead Sea Scrolls

Community Rule (1QS)

135 n. 2, 171, 205, 221 n. 11, 267–68

Damascus Document

4QD: 25

Genesis Apocryphon

323 n. 45

*Hodayot* (Thanksgiving Hymns, 1QH)

6–7, **133–53**, 174 n. 27, 196, 221 n. 11

1QH[a]: 137, 142, 144–49, 171, 174, 195–97, 199–200, 202–7

Hymns of the Maskil (Songs of the Sage)

8–9, **213–52**

4Q510: 216 n. 5, 219, 226, 232, 240 n. 47
4Q510–511: 9, 214, 219 n. 9, 247
4Q511: 216 n. 5, 219, 225 n. 22, 226, 232 n. 32, 240–44

Pesherim

37, 254

1QpHab: 37, 52, 276
4QpNah: 25

Songs of the Sabbath Sacrifice

7, **155–82**, 217 n. 7, 224, 247

4Q400: 155 n. 1
4Q401: 155 n. 1
4Q402: 161–66, 176
4Q403: 155 n. 1, 224 n. 20
4Q404: 155 n. 1
4Q405: 155 n. 1, 158 n. 6, 162
4Q406: 155 n. 1, 161, 165
11Q17: 155 n. 1

Temple Scroll

11Q19: 167

War Scroll (1QM)

123, 267, 324 n. 47

Biblical Scrolls

1QIsa: 48 n. 10
1QIsa$^a$: 21, 51
4QDeut$^a$: 116
4QJer: 58 n. 29
4QJer$^a$: 58
4QJob$^a$: 116
4QSam$^b$: 116
11QPs: 83 n. 6, 228 n. 26
11QPs$^a$: 83, 194–95, 199, 202–3, 205–7

Other Scrolls

2Q18: 83–84
4Q371–373: 207
4Q372 1: 8, **183–212**
4Q414: 54
4Q424: 54
4Q512: 54
4Q516: 217
4Q560: 215 n. 4
8Q5: 215 n. 4, 217
11Q11: 215 n. 4, 216, 217 nn. 6–8, 228 n. 26

## Other Second Temple Texts

Ben Sira

5, **73–102**, 266, 300

0.1–2: 300
3.28: 96 n. 20
4.3–4: 89
4.3–6: 89
4.17: 96 n. 20
5.1: 95 n. 18
11.25: 96 n. 20
12.11, 14: 96 n. 20
13.2, 17: 96 n. 20

14.11, 14: 96 n. 20
14.11–14: 92
15.14: 96 n. 20
15.20: 86
16.15: 96 n. 20
31.16: 86
31.22: 86
31.31: 86
32.1: 86
32.4: 86
37.1: 85
37.1–2: 84–85
37.2: 86

39.27: 84
42.23–43.1: 87–88
42.24: 83–84, 88
44.11–12: 86
44.17: 86
45.26: 86

1 Enoch

12.5: 239
13.1: 239
16.4: 239

## Rabbinic Sources

### Mishnah

Shabbat

32.4: 25

Megillah

1.8: 300, 302, 321
2.1: 302
4.1: 319 n. 35
4.1–2: 351
4.4: 350, 358–59
4.6: 311 n. 19, 312 nn. 21–22, 350
4.10: 313 n. 25, 350

Sotah

2.2: 276
7.1–2: 313 n. 25

Avot

4.19: 52 n. 17

Negaim

14.1: 276

Yadayim

4.5: 302, 349

## Tosefta

### Shabbat
13.1–2: 349
13.1–3: 334 n. 58
13.2: 317

### Sukkah
2.10: 312 nn. 23–24, 319 n. 35

### Megillah
2.5: 312 n. 22
3.12: 351
3.13: 306
3.20: 311 n. 18, 350
3.21: 311 n. 18, 321 n. 40
4(3).21: 311 n. 20
4(3).31–38: 313 n. 25

## Jerusalem Talmud

### Bikkurim
3.8[5]: 356

### Shabbat
6.4: 304
16.1: 318 n. 34

### Taanit
5.2: 386

### Megillah
3.7: 77 n. 4
4.1: 311 n. 18, 315, 351, 368

### Sotah
7.2: 332 n. 57

## Babylonian Talmud

### Berakhot
8a–b: 363 n. 19
45a: 313 n. 26
51b: 277

### Shabbat
63a: 448 n. 10, 450 n. 13

### Eruvin
23b: 449 n. 11
54a: 95

### Pesahim
119a: 431

Rosh Hashanah

27a: 311 n. 18, 351–2

Megillah

3a: 352 n. 5
8b: 302
14a: 319 n. 36
16b: 77 n. 4
18a: 302
21b: 311 n. 18, 352
23b: 356

Yevamot

11b: 448 n. 10, 450 n. 13
24a: 448 n. 10, 450 n. 13

Ketubot

111b: 448, 449 n. 11

Nedarim

32b: 326 n. 52

Qiddushin

49a: 350 n. 3, 354
80b: 449 n. 11

Bava Qama

67a: 108

Bava Batra

15a: 319 n. 36

Sanhedrin

110a: 431

Shevuot

15b: 217 n. 8

Hullin

6a: 449 n. 11
133b: 449 n. 11

Arakhin

8b: 449 n. 11
32a: 449 n. 11

# GENERAL INDEX

Abraham, 273–74, 325, 418, 425, 428
Adam, 411–12, 418, 420, 428, 430
amulets, 9, 214, 217 n. 8, 221–26, 231, 234, 237, 245–46, 304
angels, 158, 164, 166, 168, 173–76, 214, 221, 226–28, 229 n. 27, 232, 237 n. 44, 239–41, 242 n. 53, 244–45, 247, 413–15, 420–24
anti-Samaritan, 186, 206
Aquila, 34, 298, 303–5, 322, 334
Aramaic, 1–2, 10, 13–14, 22, 28, 35, 51 n. 14, 67 n. 48, 110, 119, 134, 150, 203, 224–25, 227 n. 24, 228–29, 276, **291–345**, 347–49, 352, 354, 359, 368–72, 386, 399 n. 10, 406, 441, 446, 447 n. 6, 448, 449 n. 11
Arba Kittin, *see* four groups
artefact, 1–2, 8, 183, 185, 205, 260–61, 278, 280
Babel, Tower of, 413–14
Babylonian, 17–20, 29–30, 32–34, 38, 52, 64 n. 40, 225, 298, 316, 325 n. 49, 350, 355, 359 n. 13

Babylonian Talmud, *see* Talmud
bilingual, 10, 295–96, 306, 309, 311, 317, 329, 331–34, 348 n. 2
Cain and Abel, 411–13, 428–29
Cairo Genizah, 25, 44, 225 n. 21, 233 n. 34, 269, 271, 304, 385, 393 n. 6, 407 n. 4
Cerquiglini, Bernard, 259–61
character of translation, 293, 297, 305, 308–9, 311, 313, 322, 327, 459
children, 35, 147, 189, 311, 423
code-switching, 292, 295–97, 310, 332
codex, 15, 19 n. 2, 46 n. 6, 49 n. 11, 89 n. 10, 104, 105 nn. 2–3, 121, 325, 361
composition, 2, 13, 52, 74, 80, 86, 88, 98, 135, 137, 140–41, 149, 155, 166, 171 n. 25, 172–73, 175 n. 30, 213–14, 218–20, 223–25, 227–28, 231, 234 n. 39, 235, 237 n. 44, 238, 242 n. 52, 245 n. 57, 254, 265–66, 271, 371, 445, 449, 451
configuration, 175, 184, 187–88, 193, 198, 202, 205–6, 245

conflation, 76, 94–97, 226 n. 23, 388 n. 3
continuous, 5, 83, 98, 260, 269–73, 279, 292 n. 2, 305, 364
cyclic permutation, 80, 82, 86, 97–98
*dagesh*, 30–34, 38, 59–61
David, 190–91, 206, 228–29
Dead Sea Scrolls, 6, 8, 44, 48, 53–54, 64, 76–77, 113, 119, 126, 134, 140, 157 n. 4, 162–63, 171, 184, 199, 205. *See also* Qumran
demons, 9, 214, 216, 217 n. 6, 221 n. 14, 226, 231–34, 236 n. 41, 239, 243, 247, 277
distich, 82, 89, 95–96
divine judgement, 114, 188, 194, 245
doublet, 39, 76, 89, 93, 95, 429
editors, editorial activity, 43 n. 1, 75, 253, 256, 262–63, 266, 274, 278, 298, 315, 320, 322, 370 n. 25
energic *nun*, 4, 57–60, 65
eschatology, 242 n. 52, 243–45
ethical reading, 150
Exodus Rabbah, 35
exorcism, 9, **213–52**
festival, 12, 145, 159, 167, 357–58, 361–62, 365–69, 369 n. 24, 370–72, 385–86, 393–94

Flood, 411, 427–28
*Fortschreibung*, 267
four groups, 12, 385–88, 391
Genesis Rabbah, 22, 263, 268, 276, 451
Greek, 6, 11, 20, 22, 33, 85–86, 89–90, 92–93, 95–96, **103–31**, 134, 150, 159 n. 8, 172 n. 25, 191, 228, 259, **291–345**, 454
Gröber, Gustav, 256–59
guttural, 6, 19–21, 38, 117, 119, 121, 123, 127–28
Hai Gaon, R., 354 n. 7, 355, 370 n. 25
HaNagid, R. Shmuel, 356–58
Hebrew, **1–14**, 22–23, 25–26, 29, 34, 37, 44, 46, 50, 51 n. 15, 53, 56–57, 66–67, 73–74, 77, 81–84, 89–90, 92, 96, 98, **103–31**, 134, 150, 171, 184, 187, 194, 199, 205, 214 n. 2, 222 n. 15, 224–25, 227 n. 24, 228–29, 230 n. 29, 270, 276–77, **291–345**, 347 n. 1, 350, 353, 358–59, 361 n. 17, 362–64, 369, 371, 373, 386–87, 408, 414, 417, 441, 444, 447–48, 451–53, 462
Biblical Hebrew, 23–25, 33, 35, 37, 49, 53 n. 18, 166 n. 17, 296 n. 5, 297, 325, 444, 447

Qumran Hebrew, 110 n. 11, 120, 126, 166
Rabbinic Hebrew, 13, 29, 35, 48–49, 52, 296, 309, 330, 446, 447 n. 6, 453 n. 17
Samaritan Hebrew, 120–21
Second Temple Hebrew, 120, 126–27
Hebrew Bible, 2–4, 8, 15–16, 19 n. 2, 20, 39, 43, 46 n. 7, 51, 58 n. 30, 106, 111, 134, 136, 140, 150, 156, 187–88, 198–99, 206, 276, 328–29, 347–50, 352, 453 n. 17
Hekhalot, 157 n. 3, 225 n. 21, 263–64, 266, 268
Hellenistic, 119, 134, 136 n. 3, 159 n. 8
hermeneutics, 133, 140, 309, 459
historical readership, 184, 187, 201–4, 206
hypercorrection, 123, 126–27
identification, 199 n. 16, 206–7, 235, 426
Jacob, 25, 30, 202, 273–74, 418, 420
Joseph, 8, 185–86, 200–7, 275, 277–78, 431–32
Jubilees, 221 n. 11, 265–66
Karaite, 19, 442, 454
Klein, Michael, 12, 112, 269–70, 275, 392–95
Lachmann, Karl, 256, 260

layout, 5, **73–102**, 157, 362–67, 373
Leviticus Rabbah, 263
liturgy, 7–8, 11, 135–37, 151, 155–57, 159–61, 171, 176, 214, 220–21, 223, 225, 247, 270, 292, 297, 299–300, 302, 306, 308, 314, 317, 322, **348–84**, 387, 393–96
magic, 8, 213–18, 221, 222 n. 15, 228, 237, 246
magic bowls, 9, 214, 217, 221, 223–24, 226, 227 n. 24, 230, 235–37, 245, 362 n. 18
*mahzorim*, 12, 361, 367, 385–87, 390, 393 n. 6, 394–97, 399, 400
Mahzor Vitry, 358 n. 12, 369, 386
manuscripts, 2, 5, 10–12, 15–16, 19 n. 2, 20, 24, 26, 29, 46 n. 6, 48, 49 n. 11, 52, 61 n. 34, **73–102**, 104–5, 116, 123, 125, 155, 157–58, 161, 254, 257, 261, 269–72, 304, 314, 318, 319 n. 36, 325, 328, 348–49, 351 n. 4, 352 n. 5, 361–68, 373, 385–87, 390, 393–96, 399–400, **405–39**, 444 n. 2, 452, 454 n. 18
Masoretic Text (MT), 3, 5–6, 15–16, 21, 25, 28, 33, 35, 37, 46, 48, 56 n. 24, 60, 64–

65, 67, 78–79, 81–82, **103–31**, 191, 265, 274, 320, 323, 325
mediator, 196, 199
Menahem ibn Saruk, 444–46
medieval, Middle Ages, 4, 10–13, 15–16, 19, 22, 46 n. 6, 48, 73, 75 n. 2, 83, 156, 225 n. 21, 255–56, 259–62, 271, 278–79, 302, 313–14, 331, 347–49, 357, 360–62, 363 n. 19, 367–69, 371–72, 385–86, 394, 396, 400, 441, 446–51, 459
midrash, 261–62, 266, 276, 305, 308, 325, 386, 405, 427–28 n. 6, 444, 447 n. 8, 449–52, 453 n. 17, 461
misreading, 105, 107, 125–26, 128–29
Moses, 188–89, 198–99, 202–3, 206, 314 n. 26, 318, 320–21, 387, 389–93, 397–99, 405, 431
multilingualism, 294, 331
Natronai b. Hilai Gaon, R., 352–54
*nif'al*-isation, 51 n. 14, 54
Nimrod, 418, 420, 425–27
Noah, 326, 411, 427–29
non-stichography, 74, 88–89, 92, 96
oral translation, 318
orthoepy, 18, 20

paleography, 104, 129
parallelism, 77, 80, 82, 91, 192, 201, 445 n. 4
*parallelism membrorum*, 80
synonymous parallelism, 81–82, 92
Paris, Gaston, 255–58, 260, 269, 387
participle, 24, 27–28, 36, 45 n. 4, 53, 56, 61, 63, 109, 110 n. 11, 111–12, 122, 191, 235
Peletith (daughter of Lot), 416
Pentateuch, 47, 54, 55 n. 21, 118–19, 269–70, 273 n. 13, 299, 354, 361–62, 364–65
perfection, 8, 135
performance, 1, 4, 7–9, 15–16, 133, 137, 141, 149, 151, 155–58, 159 n. 8, 160–61, 168, 171, 175–76, 214, 218, 220, 223, 229, 231–32, 238, 240 n. 46, 246–47, 253–54, 265, 310–12, 314, 318, 332, 351, 355, 368, 372
performative, 2, 7, 63, 136, 155–58, 160–61, 176, 213, 218, 231
Pesach, 12, 358, 364–65, 370, 386, 396, 400
*peshat*, 13, **441–65**
Peshitta, 108, 298 n. 8

philology, 2–3, 9–10, 14, 44, 137, 140–41, 157 n. 3, 217, 222, 246, **253–90**, 445

phonetics, 5–6, 18, 103, 117, 127, 227 n. 24

*Pirqe de-Rabbi Eliezer*, 12, **405–39**

*piyyut*, 37, 396

*piʿel*-isation, 51 n. 14

pluriformity, 16

poetic processes, 139–40

poetry, 3, 5, 7–8, 37–38, 49 n. 12, 65 n. 41, 74–75, 77, 80–82, 84, 89, 91, 97–98, 135, 139, 141, 148, **155–82**, 185, 370

praise, 7, 9, 143, 145–48, 158 n. 5, 168, 175 n. 30, 200, **213–52**, 389, 391, 398, 400, 420, 422

prayer, 12, 134–35, 139–40, 144–46, 158–59, 185, 192, 194, 200, 204–5, 216, 217 n. 8, 218, 223, 301, 361, 366, 370

  apotropaic prayer, 214–18, 220, 222, 224–25, 228 n. 26, 238, 247

  petitionary prayer, 218–19

predestination, 171

pronunciation, 4, 19, 22–23, 32, 44–45, 47, 61 n. 34, 66, 119–21

prophecy, 8, 107, 150, 168, 186, 192, 198–99, 201, 205–6, 299 n. 10, 369, 445 n. 4

punctuation, 78, 80–84, 92, 97–98

Qumran, 8–9, 15, 20, 24, 37, 51–52, 64, 67, 123, 125, 139, 171 n. 24, 186, 199, 207, 214–20, 224, 225 n. 21, 231, 237, 242 n. 52, 246, 292, 306. *See also* Dead Sea Scrolls

rabbi, 5, 12, 217 n. 8, 227, 291, 294, 303, 305–8, 310, 319, 321, 330, 332, 334–35, 353–54, 356, 405–6, 433, 442–43, 448–51, 459

rabbinic, 4, 9–10, 13–14, 25 n. 5, 27, 35, 43, 77 n. 4, 108, 214 n. 2, 261–62, **291–345**, 349, 351, 386, **441–65**

Rashbam, 458 nn. 24–25, 460

Rashi, 13–14, 352 n. 5, 441–46, 451–53, 460–61

reconfiguration, *see* configuration

responsa, 35 n. 7, 360, 370

Samaritan, 17, 24 n. 4, 27–28, 32, 35, 46, 48–49, 54, 55 n. 21, 56 n. 24, 119–20, 186, 206

scope of translation, 297, 300, 310

scribes, scribal activity, 2, 5–6, 9–10, 19, 45 n. 5, 67, **73–102**, 134, 150, 157, 161, 164, 166, 204, 213, 214 n. 2, 222–23, **253–90**, 304, 315 n. 28, 363–65, 366 n. 21, 367–68, 387, 388 n. 3, 396–97, 399–400, 417, 427, 456 n. 21

script, 6, 106, 116, 222 n. 15

scriptural vitality, 150

scripturalisation, 136

Second Temple, 3, 8–9, 15–20, 23, 32, 38, 109, 127, 141, 150, 156, 167–68, 184, 293, 296, 298

Secunda, 60

Seder Olam, 263

Sefer HaItim, 354, 356–57

Sefer HaItur, 359

*sensus litteralis*, 13, 443, 453, 461

Septuagint (LXX), 5–6, 16 n. 1, 32, **103–31**, 150, 190 n. 6, 191, 199 n. 16, 203, 291 n. 1, 298–99, 306, 322, 328 n. 54, 334

sinner, **183–212**

*sof passuq*, 89, 92, 96

stemma, *stemma codicum*, 75, 83, 86 n. 8, 256–57, 259, 434

stich, stichography, 5, **73–102**

supernatural audiences, 8, 213–14, 218, 220, 231–32, 238

synagogue, 12, 156, 300, 310, 315–17, 322, 361, 395

Talmud, 217 n. 8, 263 n. 8, 277, 296 n. 6, 301, 303, 310, 330, 333, 347–49, 351–54, 356, 363 n. 19, 367–68, 371, 386, 431–32, 447–50, 452

Targum, 10–12, 108, 150, 261, 270–71, 276, 279–80, **291–345**, **347–84**, 385–86, 393–95, 400, **405–39**

Fragment Targums (FragTgs), 269–70, 272, 274, 279, 385–86, 392, 393 n. 6, 394, 418

Haftarah Targum, 348–49, 356, 358–60, 361 n. 16, 362–64, 367–68, 370–73

Liturgical Targum, 310 n. 17, 386, 394, 396

Palestinian Targum (PalTg), 9–12, **253–90**, 308–9, 385–87, 390, 392, 396, 399–400, 405, 418

Targum Neofiti (TgNeof), 269–70, 272–78, 321, 326–27, 385, 392, 394, 418

Targum Onqelos (TgOnk), 10–11, 35, 271–72, 274, 276, 279, 291 n. 1, 297, 298 n. 8, 308–10, 321–23, 325–30, 354, 361 n. 15, 362 n. 18, 394, 396–400

Targum Pseudo-Jonathan (TgPsJ), 12–13, 35, 269, 271–72, 274–79, 385, 392, 394, **405–39**

Tosefta Targums, 270

teacher, 139, 145, **183–212**, 319, 444

Tetragrammaton, 105, 107–8, 170, 329–30, 388 n. 4

Tiberian, 3–4, **15–42**, 44–45, 54, 64, 66–67, 227 n. 24

Torah, 15, 135, 190 n. 6, 291 n. 1, 294, 297, 299, 301, 303, 312–13, 318–19, 321 n. 42, 322, 329, 333, 350–51, 355–57, 359–60, 361 n. 16, 363, 366 n. 21, 369–71, 435, 444, 452

Tosafot, 352 n. 5, 356, 358–61, 367–69, 371

Tosefta, 313, 317–18, 351

transgression, 144, 187–88, 192, 201

translation technique, 10–11, 110, 127

tristich, 5, 80, 82, 86, 92, 94–95, 97

*vav*, 22, 32, 92

*vayyiqtol*, 31–33

written translations, 301, 306, 312, 321

Yehudah b. Barzilai of Barcelona, R., 354–356

Yitzhak b. Abba Mari, R., 359

# About the Team

Alessandra Tosi and Geoffrey Khan were the managing editors for this book and provided quality control.

Tamar Karni and Anne Burberry performed the copyediting of the book in Word.

The fonts used in this volume are Charis SIL, Scheherazade New, SBL Hebrew and SBL Greek.

Annie Hine created all of the editions — paperback, hardback, and PDF. Conversion was performed with open source software freely available on our GitHub page at https://github.com/OpenBookPublishers.

Jeevanjot Kaur Nagpal designed the cover of this book. The cover was produced in InDesign using Fontin and Calibri fonts.

www.ingramcontent.com/pod-product-compliance
Lightning Source LLC
Chambersburg PA
CBHW062024290426
44108CB00025B/2774